SHAKESPEARE
Modern Essays in Criticism

SHAKESPEARE
Modern Essays in Criticism

REVISED EDITION

EDITED BY

LEONARD F. DEAN

NEW YORK UNIVERSITY

OXFORD UNIVERSITY PRESS

LONDON   OXFORD   NEW YORK

OXFORD UNIVERSITY PRESS

Oxford   London   New York
Glasgow   Toronto   Melbourne   Wellington
Cape Town   Salisbury   Ibadan   Nairobi   Lusaka   Addis Ababa
Bombay   Calcutta   Madras   Karachi   Lahore   Dacca
Kuala Lumpur   Hong Kong   Tokyo

Copyright © 1957, 1967 by Oxford University Press, Inc.
Library of Congress Catalogue Card Number: 67-10853
First published by Oxford University Press, New York, 1957
First published as an Oxford University Press paperback, 1957
Revised edition, 1967
This reprint, 1970
Printed in the United States of America

PREFACE

THE PURPOSE of this volume is to bring together some of the good modern essays on Shakespeare, as many as could be reprinted in a single volume at a reasonable price. I looked for essays offering a fresh and thoughtful interpretation of the plays; and I had in mind the general reader as well as the student, teacher, and critic. The plan was to include a few general essays, at least one on each of the major plays, and as far as possible several essays on a play or group of plays in order to represent contrasting or complementary critical views.

It turned out that almost all of the essays finally selected and available for reprinting had been written rather recently. It is likely, therefore, that this volume has some value as a sampling of contemporary Shakespearian criticism, even though no effort has been made to represent systematically whatever schools of criticism may exist. Good literary criticism is to some extent a creative act, a lucky thing which cannot quite be explained by circumstances; but luck takes different forms at different times and places, and perhaps it is not surprising or altogether accidental that many of the essays in this volume reflect contemporary interest in poetic language, the aesthetics of drama, the Elizabethan theater, and Renaissance modes of thought. Furthermore, critics are sensible people who find it dull to do over again what has already been well done, and this fact, too, helps to account for recent emphasis on patterns of imagery, the structure of ironic drama, and other topics somewhat neglected by earlier critics.

I am indebted to students and colleagues with whom I have

discussed Shakespearian criticism. They have helped to test my
judgment and have put me on the track of good things which I
might otherwise have missed. I am chiefly indebted, of course,
to the authors and publishers of the essays reprinted here; without their co-operation the book could not have been made. I re-
gret that it was impossible for various reasons to include many
fine essays. Shakespearian criticism has flourished in our time,
and a single volume cannot do justice to it all.

LEONARD F. DEAN

Storrs, Connecticut
January 1957

NOTE TO THE REVISED EDITION

TWENTY-ONE of the twenty-eight essays in the first edition have been retained and nine new ones have been added. Most of the new essays have appeared since 1957, and three were published during the past year. The chief aim, in short, has been to increase the usefulness of the book by adding essays from Shakespearian criticism of the last decade.

LEONARD F. DEAN

CONTENTS

SHAKESPEARE
Modern Essays in Criticism

Alfred Harbage

SHAKESPEARE'S AUDIENCE:
MODERN APPRAISALS

. . . . SHAKESPEARE like Falstaff is the cause that wit is in other men, and the most brilliant criticism in English has been provoked by Shakespeare's plays. But the least brilliant of this criticism is, I believe, that which relates the plays to their audience. It is usually incidental; and it is often careless, cynical, or marked by an incredible condescension. The Elizabethan stratum of humanity is divested of mystery, its common sense assessed at the rate of some early treatise on physiology, its perceptive range simplified to "two levels of intelligence," while whole battalions of our former fellow mortals are dismissed with placid allusions to "groundlings" or "a motley crew." At the safe remove of three centuries the nature of a generation collectively has even been deduced from a heap of nutshells. Sometimes distance lends courage also to the idealist, and the Globe is filled with mute inglorious Shakespeares, but normally we hear the voice of derision and disdain. Not all of the critical attitudes toward the audience are uncongenial, but none of them need be taken on faith.

We are familiar with the tendency in others (and ourselves) to apply colors recklessly to any part of a canvas depicting the lusty age of Elizabeth. Enthusiastic brushwork transforms human beings into Elizabethans. A brief description of Shakespeare's audience by Brander Matthews contains the following phrases: "suberabundant energy," "soaring imagination," "puffed with pride," "reckless daredevil," "sensuous and sensual," "furi-

From *Shakespeare's Audience*, 1941, pp. 138-57. Copyright 1941 by Columbia University Press. Reprinted by permission of the publisher.

ous in hate and love," "avid of swift sensation," "primitive savagery of manners," "violently passionate," "frankly brutal." [1] The portrait is exhilarating but conducive at last to sober reflection. Were Shakespeare's contemporaries truly such galvanic creatures? Imagine, if you will, some London carter plodding beside his oxen on the road to Hackney, some London housewife sewing a fine seam, some London mason patiently, skillfully pointing the stones of Bridge Gate at 1s. 4d. a long, long day. Imagine entering some Bread Street shop in 1601, fixing the proprietor with your eye, and saying: "You are puffed with pride, a reckless daredevil, furious in hate and love, violently passionate, and frankly brutal." Would he not reply with pardonable dismay: "Who? Me!" Nothing we can discover from examining their daily routine, their frugal expense accounts, and their quiet and sensible letters suggests that Elizabethans, individually or collectively, were vastly different from us. Their nature cannot be deduced from the defeat of the Armada or the public hangings in Tyburn. We ourselves live in a spectacular age, without being individually spectacular.

The kinship we feel with the old playgoers, those of us who love their drama, must not be confined to the upper classes, no matter what our own social allegiances or aspirations may be. I have previously quoted the statement that while Heywood wrote for apprentices and shopkeepers, Shakespeare "kept in his mind's eye the approval of the lordly patrons of Blackfriars." The writer, I suspect, would indignantly repudiate the implications of the statement if put in bald terms—the fine things in Elizabethan drama were written for the fine people, for lords. So prevalent is the notion that one is apt to countenance it through sheer inadvertence; the cloven hoof flashes out in half the Shakespearean criticism being written. Inadvertence can scarcely be the explanation for the following: "The movie seems to be quite as capable of proceeding on two levels as the Elizabethan tragedy: poetry and psychology for the gentlemen's galleries, action and blood for the pit." [2] The writer is a careful investigator in a modern field, repeating something evidently conceived to be a critical truism. But if we are to confuse social with spiritual distinction, we may as well subscribe at once to the belief that Shakespeare's plays were written by the Earl of

Oxford, or Southampton, or Rutland, or whoever the current candidate may be.

Misconceptions are prevalent concerning the intellectual and artistic attainments of the Elizabethan nobleman. One suspects that he is often patterned in the image of Sir Philip Sidney and the Earl of Southampton, the latter generously endowed with the qualities found in the literary works dedicated to him. It is true that the English Renaissance brought forth lords, knights, and gentlemen with literary gifts, in greater number, perhaps, than any comparable span of years, but it was a great age and the law of averages was operating. It is doubtful if the proportion of the genteel classes displaying such gifts, creative or appreciative, was higher than that of the literate ungenteel. That the nobility could produce a Sidney is the less remarkable in view of the ability of the middle classes to produce a Spenser and a Milton. Marlowe and Shakespeare illustrate the remarkable efficaciousness of extraction from workers in leather. Many men of high birth still looked with disdain upon anything so clerkly as literature, while many others, including nominal patrons of now famous dramatic companies, displayed simply a depressing indifference. The Elizabethan great world from the queen down, let the truth be told, was mean to its poets and dramatists.

As we read Sir Edmund Chambers's fine volumes on the Elizabethan stage, we come first to the queen, then to the royal household, then to the Revels Office, until by this magnificent route we arrive at the theatres and the acting companies. All is relevant and all is revealing, but, unless we are wary, we may gather the impression that the drama of the age was an appendage of the court. An equally valid approach to the stage would be a chronicle of London taverns and of enterprisers before James Burbage. Sir Edmund writes:

> It will be manifest, in the course of the present treatise, that the palace was the point of vantage from which the stage won its way, against the linked opposition of an alienated pulpit and an alienated municipality, to an ultimate entrenchment of economic independence.[3]

Let us not forget the spadesmen who dug that entrenchment, the anonymous thousands who dropped their pennies in the gatherer's box: these were the true patrons of Elizabethan drama. The queen, the Privy Council, and the (bribed) officials of the Revels Office sponsored a working arrangement whereby one minor means of her majesty's "solace" could be maintained at the public expense. It was quite unconsciously that the court performed its great service to art: poetry like Protestantism entered the palace through a postern gate.

Sir Edmund continues:

> On the literary side, the milieu of the Court had its profound effect in helping to determine the character of the Elizabethan play as a psychological hybrid, in which the romance and erudition, dear to the bower and the library, interact at every turn with the robust popular elements of farce and melodrama.

But the specifications of the habitué of bower and library had to be modified by something other than farce and melodrama before great drama could result. The appearance of its qualities of greatness awaited that "ultimate entrenchment in economic independence" provided by the populace of London. The names of great lords had been associated with acting companies for generations before plays show signs of poetic or other artistic worth. The drama was as popular at court before the eighties as after, and, for all we know otherwise, *Herpetulus the Blue Knight and Perobia* was as cordially received there in 1574 as *King Lear* in 1606. No great Elizabethan play was written by a sojourner in the great world, and, so far as we know, such plays appealed no more to that world than to the public at large. In fact, the highborn as a class showed a preference for pageantry and pedantry, for pastoral and mask, and the body of drama they ultimately created for themselves was, above all else, fantastic. The bane upon Renaissance drama in Italy was its failure to escape from the palace and the library. Elizabeth and James permitted Shakespeare to write, but there was another kind of permission not within the royal gift—permission to write as he did.

In one sense Elizabethan drama was lordly indeed, or kingly: a throne was the one indispensable piece of theatrical property. Thoughts flew upward, and the multitude had to be treated to displays of majesty. Playwrights shared this taste for grandeur, and the fine people in their audience must have been stimulating. Noble auditors, like command performances, would have given a cachet to dramatic activity. The lordly ones were still lordly; their functions were not all deputized: they were lawgivers and leaders in battle. They were personally imposing, so clad and attended as to give visible token of their power and affluence. They were distinguishable and on view—we may owe them something for that. Playwrights would have been conscious of their presence, and ambition and vanity are great releasers of energy.

It is even conceivable that some playwrights then, like some critics now, assumed the minds of lordly patrons to be as elegantly furnished as their bodies and for them, especially, hung out their "richest words as polisht jewels." But it is hard to believe that we owe the poetry and psychology of the drama to the accident of the writers' having been dazzled. Shakespeare knew an Osric when he saw one, and he knew that Osrics were more plentiful than Sidneys. *Hamlet* itself would not have been written for such courtiers as it portrays. Assuming among the writers a willingness to let the "candied tongue lick absurd pomp," would poetry and psychology have resulted? or satire, "wantonness," pomposity itself? We do not know as we read what sad jest may have been designed to tickle the Earl of Rutland, or what lovely song to charm the groundlings. "Why should the poor be flattered?" to ask Hamlet's question. Because in Shakespeare's theatre there were so many of them.

This is not to imply that poetry and psychology were wasted upon the "gentlemen's galleries." The patrician was as capable of rising above his class as the plebeian. It is only to insist, with weariness, that mentality should not be measured in terms of caste. If we substitute the word "taste" for "mentality," we must reckon with what has been deduced as to the essential "unity of taste" among all castes, and among playwrights and playgoers together, in Elizabethan times.[4] To assume that action and bloodshed (or farce and wordplay) were intended exclusively for the pit is simply not feasible. The disparate elements in the drama— the bloodshed and sweeping action on the one hand and poetry and psychology on the other—are explainable on a sounder principle than that of dual appeal to social levels in the audience.

The disparity may result from nothing more than a theatrical heightening of the actual contrast in life—between the constantly observable crudity of human action and refinement of human thought. Elizabethan drama is not the only great literature where the contrast is glaringly reflected. The soul stirrings of Achilles, kin of the gods, were necessarily infinite, but what he actually did was sulk in his tent or slay Trojans. The balance between the tendency to action and the tendency to reflection is more apt to be disturbed in favor of reflection among modern critical readers of Shakespeare than among Elizabethan playgoers (or human beings generally), so that the action of the plays is apt to seem intrusive. Naturally we wish to think of the nobility as sharing our tastes: we invite only the best people to join our club.

Sometimes Shakespeare's spectators are graded not according to a social hierarchy in his day but an intellectual hierarchy in ours. The "judicious" spectator is newly invoked, and he is endowed with the ability to discern in the play esoteric meanings not intended for the audience as a whole; in default of either his or the playwright's having left a commentary, the modern critic supplies it. Spectacular results can be achieved by this method, and, strangely enough, the most spectacular of all has been achieved by one of the most meticulous of scholars. W. W. Greg distinguishes between the "bulk" or "generality" of Shakespeare's audience and the "humaner minds" and argues that the playwright wrote two meanings into *Hamlet*: the "humaner minds" perceived that Claudius was no murderer and the Ghost's accusations were "a mere figment of Hamlet's brain." Greg presents this theory with earnestness and skill; then later he defends it, although he has "never discovered" whether he believes in it himself.[5] These are baffling tactics. If one were to describe a newly found quarto of the play with a title page bearing an unknown printer's device, stipulating that what appeared to be the device might be after all only the stain of a crushed roach, Greg's indignation can be imagined.

Evidently it is only with the "unknowable," with the meaning of the book rather than with the book as a physical fact, that we may take liberties. Whether Greg believes in his theory is immaterial; he certainly believes in the two levels of intelligence and in the "judicious" spectator. Yet his theory has demonstrated once and for all the slippery nature of this person: we never know when we have him in hand. Originally, he was the occult friend of the playwright; he now serves the critic in a like capacity. So far as the meaning of *Hamlet* is concerned, Adams, Schücking, Granville-Barker, W. W. Lawrence,[6] and presumably most others are content to stand with the "bulk" of the audience. But even if Greg had only a single opponent, J. Dover Wilson let us say, we should have to recognize that among the "humaner minds" in the audience, some were more human than others, and we should have to postulate not two levels of intelligence but three at least —Greg's, Wilson's, and the "generality's."

W. W. Lawrence has said that Shakespeare "provided for the more intellectual spectators something which the groundlings, with their imperfect mentality and defective education, could not perceive, but this was an extension of the simple meaning of his play, and not at variance with it." [7] With the main bearing of this statement, one must certainly agree. It is unfortunate, however, that perfection of mentality and adequacy of education seem still to be measured in ratio to distance from the ground. Are we not too facile in our generalizations about the education and mentality of the penny playgoers? It seems probable that the rank and file were more literate in the sixteenth century than in the eighteenth. In view of the profusion of schools,[8] of the tendency of the trade guilds to make literacy a qualification even for entrance into apprenticeship,[9] and of the manifest interest in self-instruction, we must revise any impressions we may ever have had that London workmen were "nine-tenths illiterate." In a period of eight months during the single year 1585, the publishers disposed of ten thousand copies of their reading primer, *The A B C and Little Catechism*.[10] Using this book, women at their wheels and men at their looms taught, for a pittance, the children of other workers how to read. In the opinion of the one who has most carefully investigated the subject, the people of London constituted "by no means an illiterate society." [11] It would be impossible to prove that more than a fraction even of the groundlings in Shakespeare's audience had no passport to books.

The groundlings, nevertheless, like the audience in general, did not read much: books, candles, and daylight leisure were all hard to come by. The great majority of men and women were "ignorant." But we must ask whether ignorance was so crippling in the time of Shakespeare as it is today. There were, without doubt, more unlighted chambers in the mind of the average spectator than in our own, and creatures of darkness found a dwelling there, but we are likely to overestimate the degree of this benightedness. Miss Doran, in her excellent attempt to discover the Elizabethan attitude toward the ghost in *Hamlet,* has mentioned the "lack of relevance between fact and theory" [12] in Renaissance science. Cannot one say, without casuistry, that when theory is fallacious, the ignorant benefit by their enforced reliance upon observable fact? The burned child who shuns the fire has been an inductive philosopher for ages. It was the learned ones who needed Bacon's recommendations. Edward Topsell was more "learned" about beasts than other Englishmen in 1607. But observe his earnest belief in the existence of the unicorn and his contempt for ignorant unbelievers:

> the vulgar sort of infidell people which scarcely beleeue any hearbe but such as they see in their owne Gardens, or any beast but such as in their own flocks, or any knowledge but such as in their own braines, or any birds which are not hatched in their own Nests.[13]

We must score one for the "vulgar." Topsell was relying upon authority, the rank and file upon experience. We must not decide upon the attitudes and beliefs held by the rank and file of Elizabethans through reading their authorities. We must not assume that credulity, concerning unicorns, satyrs, or even ghosts and demons, was then the especial mark of the uncultivated as it is now.

J. Dover Wilson is quite assured in his pronouncements on what Shakespeare's audience believed about various things.[14] It would be folly to ignore the erudition and analysis of so talented a writer. Inquiry into contemporary point of view is the current fashion in Shakespearean criticism, and a wholesome one, but we must look twice at all the conclusions. The difficulty is that we cannot consult the spectators at the Globe and make sure they had read the right books. If a critic quotes selected passages from selected works to prove what the audience thought upon selected topics, we are likely to witness only a sinister alliance between the pedantry of two ages. The following passage, I believe, does not aid in demonstrating that Hamlet was a man of action and would be so regarded by Shakespeare's audience:

> Perhaps most significant is the statement by the illustrious French physician Laurentius, whose works were read throughout Western Europe: "The melancholike are accounted as most fit to undertake matters of weightie charge and high attempt. Aristotle in his Problemes sayeth that the melancholike are most wittie and ingenious. . . ." If then ability to transact important business was one result assigned to the melancholy temperament, this temperament could hardly have been looked upon as causing morbid inaction. Why then did Shakespeare make Hamlet melancholy? [15]

There is always the possibility that both Shakespeare and his audience had formed an opinion about melancholy otherwise than by reading Laurentius.

An amusing revelation of the practical responses of the audience is offered by the fate of *The Faithful Shepherdess*. Fletcher complained that the audience, noting that the characters were shepherds, but "missing whitsun ales, creame, wasiel & morris-dances, began to be angry." [16] In a word, they wanted the shepherds to behave like shepherds. To them it meant nothing that the play obeyed, in Chapman's words of praise, "the holy lawes of homely pastorall." Unlike Chapman, they were ignorant of such laws. We see the force in operation again in *The Knight of the Burning Pestle*. When Merrythought in the play says, "Never trust a Tailor that does not sing at his work; his mind is of nothing but filching," the Grocer's wife in the audience comments, "Mark this George, 'tis worth noting: Godfrey my Tailor, you know never sings, and he had fourteen yards to make this gown; and I'll be sworn, Mistress Peniston the Draper's Wife had one made with twelve." [17] Here is dramatic criticism in its purest form.

The most invidious modern charge against Shakespeare's audience is that it was primitive, brutal, in some way spiritually debased. It is not infrequently made. In mild form the charge appears in the following passage forming part of an otherwise closely reasoned treatise on the acting time of Elizabethan plays:

Would this audience, composed largely of illiterate Londoners, be able without excess of mental and physical fatigue, to concentrate its undivided attention for three hours without a break upon such an enthralling melodrama as *Richard III* or such a soul-stirring tragedy as *Othello*? Could such primitive beings pay out the nervous energy needed to endure three hours of imaginative exaltation? The very rapidity of the actors' utterance must have imposed a tiresome strain upon untrained minds, toiling in vain to keep pace with speeches not half understood.[18]

The atmosphere created is suggestive of the Old Stone Age; evolutionary processes seem to have been marvelously accelerated since Shakespeare's day. We may be dealing here only with indiscretion of speech. Such cannot be said of the following, included in the most recent study of Shakespeare's audience, and inspired by the putting out of Gloucester's eyes and by other "horrors" in the plays:

What these horrors enable us to do is accurately to measure the sensibility of the audience and to gauge their imaginative reaction. On that evidence we have no choice but to rate both low. This deduction is, of course, amply borne out by our knowledge of the time. A strong vein of brutality and an insensitiveness to physical suffering were part and parcel of the mentality of the Elizabethan audience.

Miss Byrne's summing up presents the "psychological picture" of "an audience primitive and undeveloped imaginatively." [19]

The most furious assault upon the audience on the grounds of spiritual and moral depravity was made by Robert Bridges:

Shakespeare should not be put into the hands of the young without the warning that the foolish things in his plays are for the foolish, the filthy for the filthy, and the brutal for the brutal; and that, if out of veneration for his genius we are led to admire or even tolerate such things, we may be thereby not conforming ourselves to him, but only degrading ourselves to the level of his audience, and learning contamination from those wretched beings who can never be forgiven their share in preventing the greatest poet and dramatist of the world from being the best artist.[20]

A. C. Bradley, the poet laureate's good and even deferential friend, could not let these words pass wholly unrebuked, although in the traditional manner of scholars, he placed the disagreeable matter in a footnote and almost in Latin.[21] Bridges's essay as a whole scarcely invites refutation. The details considered "filthy," "foolish," and "brutal" are of a type to be found also in nondramatic works such as few members of the popular audiences could have afforded to buy. The words themselves are too harsh. To share Bridges's attitude toward the audience, we must share his view that Falstaff was at last bidden a "triumphant farewell" by a creator recoiling in moral disgust; we must be willing to exchange Falstaff as he is for Falstaff as Bridges would have him. There is an obvious risk in endorsing a conception of the audience based upon such details of the plays as "most offend the simple taste" of a particular critic, no matter how eminent he may be; fortunately, scolding the audience is an alternative to excising the plays.

That our "knowledge of the time," as Miss Byrne maintains, establishes the presumption of "a strong vein of brutality and an insensitiveness to physical suffering" is a courageous assertion, placing a tremendous burden upon our knowledge of the time. Miss Byrne is identifying Elizabethans with certain of their institutions. We must consent, presumably, to be identified with certain of ours. The children once harnessed to coal carts in the tunnels of English mines should send us seeking brutality in the poetry of Coleridge and Wordsworth. If we do not find it, perhaps we should wonder how these poets could have been so brutally aloof. It is easy to cast stones. Children are harnessed no more, but evils still are permitted to exist. It would be an indiscretion of taste to mention some of these evils, since we have become so sensitive, so ingenious in evading the spectacle of suffering, so convinced of the ethical superiority of looking the other way.

Each age has its own brutalities. The Elizabethans were forced to live more intimately with theirs, and they acceded to the conditions of their existence. Shakespeare's auditors look at Talbot spattered with stage blood; but as they look, they weep. Throngs gather to see the felons hanged at Tyburn, but "the criminals' friends come and draw them down by their feet, that they may die all the sooner." [22] Is this brutality or tenderness? Animals are baited and whipped in the pits, but voices are raised in protest and the sport is declining.[23] Beneath its "callouses" human nature must have been the same in Shakespeare's day as in ours. The range of feeling must have been the same. People are still compounded of heaven and earth: kind fathers are harsh creditors, decent folk exchange ribaldries, and ruffians rescue puppies. We need to know more about human impulses in all ages before we grow rash about the Elizabethans. We need to distinguish between what is fundamental in human nature and what is superficial adjustment to environment. Perhaps the whole range of impulses was more operative in the less comfortable age of Shakespeare and more apt to impress itself upon art. It is more accurate to say that the audience expected and accepted brutality than that they demanded and enjoyed it. There is a manifest injustice in charging Shakespeare's audience with brutality because of the putting out of Gloucester's eyes, unless we credit it with an exquisite tenderness because of Lear's words over the body of Cordelia.

Among the hosts of books about Shakespeare's plays, some are ignorant and foolish; one can always make a Roman holiday by quoting such books. I have avoided doing so, at the cost of comic relief. The only alternative has involved a certain injustice; one never represents fairly the views of responsible writers by quoting a few vulnerable statements. I have not pretended to evaluate in their entirety the essays I have quoted, but to illustrate from them some of the commoner attitudes toward Shakespeare's audience. That these attitudes may be mistaken is illustrated by opposing counsel. The treatment by Thorndike, although deficient in proof and perhaps mistaken in details, strikes me as essentially true.[24] Bradley, although almost in wonder, affirmed that "the audience had not only imagination and the power to sink its soul in the essence of drama. It had something else of scarcely less import for Shakespeare, the love of poetry." [25] Elmer E. Stoll, in his most recent utterance, rejects the judicious few:

by ear the audience through lifelong attendance responded to the niceties of the different art in the Forum and the Athenian and London theatres. The technique as such they did not understand; but the ideas, sentiments, and morals, the language and situations, were not above their heads, and to what they heard they were accustomed, attuned.[26]

Felix E. Schelling holds no brief for lordly patrons:

> The drama of Shakespeare and his immediate fellows spoke to men by right of their manhood, not by virtue of their gentility. It stirred in its appeal the depths of a large and generous humanity.[27]

And Charles J. Sisson points out that most of those qualities with which Beaumont mockingly endowed his citizen-grocer—patriotism, personal pride, love of romance, and the rest—can, in the "spectateur représentatif," scarcely be considered undesirable.[28]

The "representative spectator" may be as much an abstraction as the "typical man," but conveniences must sometimes be used. We may say in the present case, quite apart from Beaumont's satirical use of them as the spectators in *The Knight of the Burning Pestle*, that a grocer, his wife, and their young apprentice form as acceptable an epitome of Shakespeare's audience as any the facts will warrant us to choose. If Shakespeare did not write to please such a little cockney family as this, he did not write to please his audience. But if he did so write, then there must be some correspondence in quality between the plays and our sample three—the grocer, his wife, and their young apprentice.

Reflection may reduce our amazement. That the potentialities of the human mind are unaffected by time, place, and social position is sound biology, and we may safely presume that our little group possessed human minds. We may even presume that they possessed the right kind of minds. We find them in the theatre separated from many of their neighbors—the stolid, the material, the bigoted, the folk of predominately animal appetite. That they had read few books is no stigma upon them. The modern correspondence between the reading habit and active mentality is a product of new folkways. Even complete illiteracy, when not the product of incapacity or indifference, but of mere conformity, may be consonant with the highest intelligence, sometimes even with heightened powers of memory and observation.

The minds of our spectators have been sharpened by urban life. The cockney as a type has seldom been accused of stupidity. In 1601 London is growing rapidly, teeming with life and variegated activity. As like as not our little group are first generation Londoners, as stimulated and knowledgeable as modern New Yorkers lately transplanted from their prairie homes. In any case, in the crowded London of 1601 alertness is a condition of survival.

They are easy in the company of the audible arts. Music, preaching, speechmaking, storytelling, disputation—these have been available even when food and warmth have not. There is lacking the tremendous range of diversions and distractions to be devised by later centuries, but there is always the spectacle of humanity, the balm of melody, the marvel of words. The theatres have been standing a lifetime, offering an education in literature and history. Wide vistas have been opened to the mind and have furnished it with powers of association. The unlearned have been taught "the knowledge of many famous histories" and few playgoers are "of that weake capacity that cannot discourse of any notable things." [29]

The factor above all else that we must reckon with in assessing the quality of our sample spectators is the almost incalculable effect of interest upon understanding. We have all been amazed at the proficiency of small boys in analyzing batting averages and of certain of their elders, dense in every other way, in moving easily through technical labyrinths concerning their business. Let us assume that our three spectators are intensely interested in plays. Of course, our instincts may still instruct us that no one out of a London shop could possibly have appreciated *Hamlet*— just as no one out of a Stratford shop could possibly have written it.

NOTES

1. In *Shakspere as a Playwright*, pp. 294-312.
2. Thorp, *America at the Movies*, p. 23.
3. *Elizabethan Stage*, I, 3.

4. See Bradley, "Shakespeare's Theatre and Audience," *Oxford Lectures on Poetry;* and, especially, Sisson, *Le Goût public et le théâtre élisabéthain,* Chapter III (Unité du goût public).

5. "Hamlet's Hallucination," *Modern Language Review,* XII (1917), 393-421; "Re-Enter Ghost: A Reply to Mr. J. Dover Wilson, ibid., XIV (1919), 353-69; "What Happens in 'Hamlet,' " ibid., XXXI (1936), 145-54.

6. For a review of the controversy and a restatement of his own sound position, see Lawrence, "Hamlet and the Mouse-Trap," *PMLA,* LIV (1939), 709-35.

7. *Shakespeare's Problem Comedies,* p. 15.

8. Knights, "Education and the Drama in the Age of Shakespeare," *Criterion,* XI (1931-32), 599-625. Most of the spectators at the Globe "were likely to have received an education of the Grammar school type" (p. 607), i.e., such as Shakespeare himself had received.

9. Dunlop, *English Apprenticeship and Child Labour,* pp. 45, 136.

10. Plant, *English Book Trade,* p. 40.

11. Adamson, "The Extent of Literacy in England in the Fifteenth and Sixteenth Centuries: Notes and Conjectures," *Library,* Ser. IV, x (1929), 163-93.

12. "On Elizabethan Credulity," *Journal of the History of Ideas,* I (1940), 166.

13. *The Historie of Foure-Footed Beastes* (1607), quoted in ibid., p. 166.

14. *What Happens in Hamlet, passim.*

15. Draper, *The Hamlet of Shakespeare's Audience,* pp. 177-8. I question the premise of the concluding statement in the book: "Shakespeare's audience was an audience of men, and Shakespeare's Hamlet was a man's Hamlet."

16. To the Reader.

17. Act II, scene i.

18. Hart, "The Time Allotted for Representation of Elizabethan and Jacobean Plays," *Review of English Studies,* VIII (1932), 412.

19. Byrne, "Shakespeare's Audience," in Shakespeare Association, *A Series of Papers on Shakespeare and the Theatre,* pp. 200, 215.

20. "On the Influence of the Audience," *The Works of William Shakespeare* (Shakespeare Head Press ed.), x, 334.

21. *Oxford Lectures on Poetry.* He is "not always repelled" by the things condemned in Mr. Bridges's "very interesting and original contribution" and suggests "reasons for at least diminishing the proportion of defect attributable to a conscious sacrifice of art to the tastes of the audience" (p. 367, note 4).

22. *Thomas Platter's Travels in England,* 1599, p. 174.

23. Bearbaiting and bullbaiting were cruel, but they were enjoyed not as cruelty but as sport. There were a conflict of forces and sharing of risks. The activity was more lethal to the dogs than to the bulls, and even the men who whipped the bears took serious risks. Baiting was sometimes for "her Majesty's disport," and interest in it was not a matter of class distinction. Not the "brutal" element but the "sporting" element was attracted. The attitude toward animals, shared by Shakespeare himself, was still strictly utilitarian.

24. *Shakespeare's Theater,* pp. 404-31.

25. *Oxford Lectures on Poetry,* p. 392.

26. "Poetry and the Passions: An Aftermath," *PMLA,* LV (1940), 982-3.

27. *Elizabethan Drama,* I, xxxviii.

28. *Le Goût public et le théâtre élisabéthain,* pp. 52-65.

29. Heywood, *Apology for Actors* (1612), Shakespeare Society Publications, No. III, pp. 52-3.

Alan S. Downer

THE LIFE OF OUR DESIGN:
THE FUNCTION OF
IMAGERY IN THE POETIC DRAMA

Why, there you touch'd the life of our design.
(Troilus and Cressida, II, ii, 194.)

IN DISCUSSING poetic drama one has to begin with a number of
negative generalizations: there is no such thing; there once was
such a thing; it is a lost art, though not necessarily a dead one.
Perhaps it is dormant because it has been defined as if it were a
joining of two elements, poetry and drama, when actually it is
only one: poetic drama. That is, it will not be resurrected by a
poet, like Byron or Stephen Phillips, writing a play, or by a playwright, like Sheridan Knowles or Maxwell Anderson, trying to
write a poem. Poetic drama must be written by dramatic poets.
If the truism is chiastic, truth yet lies in the figure.

But if the definition of poetic drama is schismatic, so too is its
criticism and analysis. In Miss Bradby's fascinating and infuriat-
ing little anthology of *Shakespeare Criticism*, 1919-1935, the
critical lines are drawn: on the one side is the Shakespeare-as-a-
dramatist brigade commanded by Granville-Barker and J. Isaacs;
on the other, Shakespeare-as-a-poet, better equipped and manned,
and officered by Spurgeon and Murry and G. Wilson Knight. The
strange thing about this general confrontation of critical armies
is that although the roll is taken on each side, and all are present

From *The Hudson Review*, II, 2 (Summer 1949), 242-60. Copyright 1949 by The Hudson Review, Inc. Reprinted by permission of
the publisher and author.

and as fully armed as possible, no attempt seems to be made to join battle. Mr. Barker will occasionally take issue in a footnote with Professor Bradley, and a junior officer like Eric Bentley speak a few ill-mannered words about the enemy, but nothing conclusive ever happens. Not a shot is fired, not an attempt is made to storm the barricades, or on the other hand to sign a treaty of friendship and mutual aid. It is as if each side felt that something too precious to risk might be involved in either engagement or compromise. As a consequence, both sides are impoverished, and the neutrals uneasily trade with both at once in a state of utter uncertainty. Yet Union is possible with Honor and without Compromise; and it could stem from a recognition of the true nature of poetic drama.

The drama is a unique form of expression in that it employs living actors to tell its story; its other aspects—setting, characters, dialogue, action and theme—it shares with other forms of communication. But the fact that the dramatist is not dealing with characters merely, but with three-dimensional persons is paralleled by the fact that he is not dealing with a setting verbally described but three-dimensionally realized, with action that actually occurs in time and space, with dialogue which is spoken by human voices for the human ear: so many tools, so many tribulations. One of the very real problems of the dramatist is just this, that he, unlike the poet, must deal with the thingness of things; to him a mossy stone must be a mossy stone and a ship tossed on an ocean a ship tossed on an ocean, not a synonym for *peace* or *turmoil*. But the point is, surely, that for the poetic dramatist the stone is more than a stone without ever losing its stoniness, and the tempest may be a highly symbolic one without losing its reality. So, although the drama in general makes considerable use of physical objects—"props"—to tell its story, the higher drama transmutes the physical prop into a symbol, gaining richer meaning without expansion. The poetic drama relates the dramatic symbol to the poetic image, intensifying the unity of the work, and gaining still greater richness without greater bulk, compression being the ever-present necessity of the form.

It is my present purpose to examine the function of imagery in poetic drama, the language of poetry, and its relation to the essentially dramatic devices which might be similarly named the language of props, the language of setting, and the language of action. In the interests of communication I have chosen most of my illustrations from Shakespeare.

The more perceptive of the poetic critics have recognized the existence of this dramatic language, if they have refused to see its true relation to the verbal. Coleridge, for example: "Shakespeare as a poet was providing in images a substitute for that visual language which in his dramatic works he got from his actors." The definition of action as visual language is so illuminating that one wonders why Coleridge did not see by its flash the limitation of the earlier portion of his statement.

In the same chapter of the *Biographia Literaria* he gives the cue to most of his successors: the poetic power, he declares, consists in part of "reducing multitude into unity of effect, and modifying a series of thoughts by some one predominant thought or feeling." In particular this inspired Caroline Spurgeon in her counting and analysis of Shakespeare's images to determine, where possible, the "iterative images" of the plays. Using *image* broadly to cover every kind of simile and metaphor, she produced a documented and be-graphed volume which is the happy hunting ground of the anti-theatrical critics. Miss Spurgeon, however, felt that the results of her study could be used as a more general tonic. In her estimation the iterative image is a revelation of the writer's personality, temperament and quality of mind, and it throws fresh light on individual plays by serving as Background and Undertone, raising and sustaining emotion, providing atmosphere, and emphasizing a theme. It reminds one of the old patent medicines which cured everything from sterility to toothache. From her analysis, for instance, Miss Spurgeon concludes that Shakespeare was more sensitive to the horror of bad odors than to the allure of fragrant ones, and to the loathsomeness of bad cooking than to appreciation of delicate and good, presumably because he had "more opportunity of experiencing the one than the other." There is no other evidence that Miss Spurgeon had a sense of humor.

On the other hand, her extended discussion of the martlet image in *Macbeth* very nearly penetrates to the heart of Shakespeare's dramatic technique. The martlet is a foolish bird and Banquo notices him on Macbeth's castle:

> no jutty, frieze,
> Buttress, nor coign of vantage, but this bird
> Hath made his bed and procreant cradle.

Martlet was a slang word for dupe, like the word gull; that is, a metaphor. But in the *Macbeth* scene the bird is imagined to be present as part of the "setting," and therefore becomes, not a poetic image, but a dramatic symbol, of the "guest who is to be 'fooled.'" Into dramatic symbolism, even when it is so intimately linked with the poetic imagery of the play, Miss Spurgeon will not go. She is, for instance, rather annoyed at the gardener's scene in *Richard II* because "no human gardeners ever discoursed like these," though she recognizes its importance in, as she says, "gathering up, focussing and pictorially presenting," the leading theme of the play.

The other school of modern interpretation of Shakespeare is perhaps best represented by Granville-Barker's essay on *King Lear*, in which he restores the play to the stage and demonstrates that it is essentially theatrical. "The whole scheme and method of its writing is a contrivance for its effective acting. The contrast and reconciliation of grandeur and simplicity, this setting of vision in terms of actuality, this inarticulate passion which breaks now and again into memorable phrases—does not even the seeming failure of expression give us a sense of the helplessness of humanity pitted against higher powers? All the magnificent art of this is directed to one end; the play's acting in a theater." The reactions to this kind of statement are violent and equally dogmatic—mere theatricalism, declared one reviewer.

It is surely too late to go around saying that *King Lear* is not adapted to theatrical representation. Is it not also too late to declare that poetic drama cannot reveal its meaning and depth and implications on the stage as fully as any other work of art in its own medium?

In seeing Shakespeare on the modern stage, we take immediate pleasure in the story and a secondary pleasure in the characterization. But certain critical writers have suggested that there is a third and more important pleasure—the meaning as interpreted by the interplay of images. Since we are reasonably deaf to spoken poetry, it would seem that this is a pleasure reserved, as the critics suggest, for the study. Aside from the fact that this makes Shakespeare look a little foolish, like a composer who writes a quartet to be performed by a one-armed violinist, is it true? I believe that it is not; that Shakespeare, if he began as two characters, the Poet and the Playwright, managed to unite them somehow as the Poetic Dramatist; if he began by using the language of action *and* the language of poetry he soon learned to use the language of *imagery in action* which is the major characteristic of poetic drama.

Perhaps the theatricalist and the reader of poetry can find common ground in a consideration of dramatic symbolism. At any rate, in this subject there is less excuse for the automatic or reflex sneer at the other's expense, since symbolism is as basic to drama as imagery is to poetry.

Symbolism grows naturally out of the materials of the drama. The successful unravelling of the plot dilemma in a Greek tragedy or a Roman comedy frequently depended upon the manipulation of some physical object, some prop, a piece of cloth, a footprint, a birthmark, a chest. In the more intricate popular drama of the last century, a cache of gold, a missent letter, a list of conspirators might be the mainspring of the action. In such plays, however, one tires very quickly of the mere ingenuity by which the eventual discovery of the gold, or arrival of the letter is held off.

It was a considerable step up the ladder of dramatic interest and intensity in the nineteenth century when Ibsen discovered that the game of "pistol-pistol-who's-got-the-pistol" could not only make a fascinating plot but could suggest the relation of the action to some aspect of the experience of the audience. When Hedda Gabler produces a case of pistols at the beginning of her play, it is basic dramatic economy that she should give one to Lövborg to commit suicide with, and use the other to put an end to her own wretched life. Further, it is nicely ironic. But when the point is carefully made that these pistols are her sole material heritage from General Gabler, a parallel avenue of suggestion is opened. She has inherited her personal characteristics from the old general, and the pistols are symbols, not only of the spiritual heritage but of the order which shaped it—the empty, decadent life of the military caste. At the end of the play it is clear that Hedda's environment and heredity shaped all her actions, drove her to urge Lövborg's suicide and finally caused her own death. The pistols are not merely the means of the action, but the meaning of the action.

Lest it be objected that such an interpretation of a dramatic symbol stems from the study rather than the stage, a current example may be added. One of the earliest and sturdiest of the successes of the 1947-48 season on Broadway was William Wister Haines's *Command Decision*. There is no pretense about this play: it is a tightly constructed, efficient product, intended for the open market. Yet despite its employment of stereotypes, conventions, and elements of melodrama, the audience is caught up in the movement of the play: we who have usually been asked to worry only about the problems of the doughboy and GI Joe, are suddenly emotionally involved in the problems of majors and brigadier-generals, hitherto satirized or portrayed as villains.

The action takes place in a Nissen hut, headquarters of an airforce command in England. The setting is narrow: the back wall, only a few feet from the footlights, is papered with a huge geodetic survey map of Western Europe. Throughout most of the performance, this map is covered, the curtains being withdrawn only when it is necessary to explain current operations. At such times the audience sees the major target cities to be destroyed and the pitifully short arc of fighter cover. The decision, which the title reflects, is whether the destruction of the targets warrants the certain loss of American soldiers.

These soldiers, whose lives are at stake, and who would be the main concern of the conventional war play or film, we never see. We see only the men whose responsibility it is to send them out and who are popularly supposed to die in bed. Yet humanity is never remote. The whole world of the action is brought into the Nissen hut; each revelation of the map creates increasing tension. At its first showing, it is merely expository: this is where we must operate. At its second, it begins to become symbolic: this is the awful dilemma which presses upon the leading character. Finally, it symbolizes the underlying meaning of the play; the desperate nature of any decision for any man under competing pressures. The map as symbol enables the audience to participate in the emotional tension of the play, serves as a unifying force, and reveals the deeper significance of what might all too easily have been a routine piece of theatrical journalism. It is, further, the best kind of dramatic symbol in that it is never obtrusive, being equally germane to the action and the theme.

It may very well be that Mr. Haines stumbled upon this dramatic symbol quite unconsciously. There is nothing in his work as a novelist to indicate that he is particularly concerned with form in that medium. His experience in Hollywood working with a medium which deals largely and conventionally in visual symbols may have led him unawares to the device. The point is that the device is there for the use of the most prosaic dramatist and it serves to enrich his work by requiring the mechanical aspects of the play to do double duty.

This "language of props" is equivalent to the simpler uses of imagery in poetry, but it can become highly complex in the poetic drama. For the sake of familiarity, if for no other reason, one turns to Shakespeare for illustration. Since it is, however, somewhat unfair to the authors of both works to juxtapose *Richard II* and *Command Decision,* a contemporary of Shakespeare's may be used as bridge and buffer. The simpler uses of dramatic symbolism in the poetic drama are clearly exhibited in the first part of Marlowe's *Tamburlaine.* The Scythian tyrant is obsessed with the idea of power as symbolized in the "sweet fruition of an earthly crown." It is not surprising that the crown—a commonplace symbol, wholly apart from its use in the drama—figures largely in the action.

In the first scene, Cosroe is crowned emperor. In the second act, foolish Mycetes rushes on stage seeking to hide his crown in a simple hole. Tamburlaine overtakes him:

Tam. Is this your crown? (*Taking it*)
Myc. Ay, didst thou ever see a fairer? (*Relinquishing it*)
Tam. (*Ironically*) You will not sell it, will you?
Myc. Such another word and I will have thee executed.
    Come, give it me!
Tam. No, I took it prisoner.
Myc. You lie; I gave it you.
Tam. Then, 'tis mine.
Myc. No, I mean I let you keep it.

> *Tam.* Well, I mean you shall have it again.
> Here, take it for a while: I lend it thee,
> Till I may see thee hemmed with armed men;
> Then shalt thou see me pull it from thy head:
> Thou art no match for mighty Tamburlaine.

Later, as Cosroe dies, Tamburlaine puts on his crown; a banquet of crowns is introduced; and the play ends with the triumphant crowning of Zenocrate. Throughout all this action, the symbol remains as simple as possible—verbalized, the crown stands for "perfect bliss" and "sole felicity," its

> virtues carry with it life and death;
> To ask and have, command and be obeyed.

The crown is the symbol of the king's rank, the ruler's god-like power.

The crown which is handled so dramatically in the deposition scene of *Richard II* is, to be sure, the symbol of the king's rank. But it is not simply the sole felicity in which Tamburlaine displayed such interest. It is the symbol of the condition of England, as in the words of Gaunt:

> A thousand flatterers sit within thy crown
> Whose compass is no bigger than thy head;
> And yet, incaged in so small a verge,
> The waste is no whit lesser than thy land.

And Northumberland proposes to "redeem from broking pawn the blemish'd crown." Further, it is the symbol of Richard as actor:

> within the hollow crown
> That rounds the mortal temples of a king
> Keeps death his court; and there the antic sits,
> Scoffing his state and grinning at his pomp;
> Allowing him a breath, a little scene,
> To monarchize. . . .

It is a symbol of that "divinity doth hedge a king":

> For every man that Bolingbroke hath press'd
> To lift shrewd steel against our golden crown

> God for his Richard hath in heavenly pay
> A glorious angel. . . .

The divinity which the crown symbolizes is strengthened by
a second image, the king as the sun:

> knowst thou not
> That when the searching eye of heaven is hid
> Behind the globe, that lights the lower world,
> Then thieves and robbers range abroad unseen. . . .
> But when from under this terrestrial ball
> He fires the proud tops of the Eastern pines. . . .
> Then murthers, treasons and detested sins,
> The cloak of night being pluck'd from off their backs,
> Stand bare and naked, trembling at themselves?
> So when this thief, this traitor Bolingbroke,
> Who all this while hath revell'd in the night
> Whilst we were wand'ring in th'Antipodes,
> Shall see us rising in our throne, the East,
> His treasons will sit blushing in his face,
> Not able to endure the sight of day,
> But self-affrighted tremble at his sin.

The image is extended and explicit. Even the dullest in the audience must have been impressed by it. At any rate, Bolingbroke
is not slow to seize upon it:

> See, see, King Richard doth himself appear,
> As doth the blushing discontented sun
> From out the fiery portal of the east. . . .

At this moment (iii, 3) Richard is standing upon the walls of
Flint Castle, which is to say the upper stage, and Bolingbroke is
on the ground. At the end of the scene in response to his opponent's demands, Richard descends to the main stage, with still
another reference to the sun image:

> Down, down I come like glist'ring Phaeton,
> Wanting the manage of unruly jades. . . .

He sees himself no longer as king, but an unsuccessful pretender
to the title.

The climax of the action of the play, in which the complexity of the image is finally revealed, is the deposition of Richard. In the drama, the whole Parliament is assembled, with the lords and bishops of England providing not only a larger audience for the display of Richard's theatrical talents, but a more impressive background for the action. When the great moment comes, Richard makes the most of it, in a scene which should be compared with Tamburlaine's taking and returning of Mycetes' crown.

> Give me the crown. Here, cousin, seize the crown.
> (*As Bolingbroke hesitates*) Here, cousin,
> (*A pause; Bolingbroke steps to him, and Richard holds
> the crown between them*)
>   on this side my hand, and on that side yours.
> Now is this golden crown like a deep well
> That owes two empty buckets,

and so on. How carefully Shakespeare has pointed the action here; not simply a passing of the crown from one hand to the other, but a tableau, and an extended simile to illustrate it. So the visual symbolic exchange of the crown, to quote Miss Spurgeon's words on another matter, "gathers up, focusses and pictorially presents" the downfall of a man whose nature was ill-suited to kingship, and who has to some extent come to realize the fact.

There are striking uses of this "language of props," the realization of the verbal image in dramatic terms, in later Shakespearean tragedy. For example, in *Macbeth* Miss Spurgeon found repeated iteration in the dialogue of the idea of ill-fitting clothes. Mr. Cleanth Brooks has related the image somewhat more closely to the play by seeing it as an interpretation of Macbeth's position as usurper: he is uncomfortable in garments not his own. Actually, the image suggests disguise. Macbeth is an unhappy hypocrite who declares before the murder of Duncan, "False face must hide what the false heart doth know," and before the murder of Banquo, "We must . . . make our faces vizards to our hearts, disguising what they are."

But the image is more than a mere verbal one. It is *realized*, made visual in the action of the play.

The first four scenes are various moments during and after a battle. In them, Macbeth will naturally be wearing his warrior's costume, his armor, as much a symbol of his nature and achievements as is Duncan's crown. When he defeats Norway, for instance, he is "lapped in proof," but when Ross and Angus greet him as Thane of Cawdor, he protests, "Why do you dress me in borrowed robes?" The image continues, verbally, as Banquo observes, half-jesting,

> New honors come upon him
> Like our strange garments, cleave not to their mold
> But with the aid of use.

Under pressure from his wife, however, he resolves to seize the kingship, to cover his warrior's garments and the golden opinions that went with them with the clothing that was properly Duncan's. The murder is committed with constant reference in the dialogue to the clothing image (skilfully interpreted by Mr. Brooks) and the scene as marked in the Folio ends with the flight of Macbeth and his Lady from the crime as she urges him to

> Get on thy nightgown, lest occasion call us
> And show us to be watchers.

When next Macbeth enters he is wearing his dressing gown, and if the actor is wise it will be such a gown as calls attention to itself, for at this point the change in costume, the disguising of the armor, dramatizes both the change in Macbeth's nature and the iterated poetic image. From now until nearly the end of the play, Macbeth is cowardly, melancholic, suspicious, and unhappy; the reverse of all the qualities that had made him the admired warrior of the early scenes. He cannot buckle his distempered cause within the belt of rule; and Macduff's fear is prophetic, "Adieu, lest our old robes sit easier than our new," prophetic not only for the unhappy Scots, but for Macbeth himself.

One of the achievements of this highly skilful play is the maintaining of interest in, if not sympathy for, the central figure; assassin, evil governor, usurper, and murderer. Shakespeare maintains this interest not merely by portraying Macbeth as a man in the control of wyrd, or too susceptible to uxorial suggestion, but,

I think, by making us constantly aware of the armor—the honest warrior's nature—under the loosely hanging robes of a regicide. Until Act II, scene 3, Macbeth is quite possibly dressed as a warrior. From that point, until Act v, scene 3, he is dressed in his borrowed robes. But in the latter scene, with his wife eliminated as a motivating force, and with the English army moving against him, he begins to resume some of his former virtues: his courage returns, his forthrightness, his manliness. "Give me my armor," he cries, and in a lively passage with the Doctor, he makes grim jests about the power of medicine as Seyton helps him into his warrior's dress. He is all impatience to be back at the business he understands as he does not understand government:

> Macbeth.
>> Give me my armour.
>
> Seyton.
>> 'Tis not needed yet.
>
> Macbeth.
>> Give me my armour.
>> Send out moe horses, skirr the country round;
>> Hang those that talk of fear. Give me mine
>>> armour. . . .
>> Throw physic to the dogs, I'll none of it!—
>> Come put mine armour on. Give me my staff.—
>> Seyton, send out.—Doctor, the thanes fly from
>>> me.—
>> Come, sir, despatch.—If thou couldst, doctor,
>>> cast
>> The water of my land, find her disease,
>> And purge it to a sound and pristine health,
>> I would applaud thee to the very echo,
>> That should applaud again.—Pull't off, I say.—

The tragic fall of this good man is dramatically underlined in his attempts to resume his old way of life. His infirmity of purpose cannot be more strongly presented than in his donning and doffing of the armor, and his bragging exit, with the equally revealing order:

> Bring it after me!

This is not an isolated, but only a more complex use of costume as symbol in poetic drama. For subtlety it might be contrasted with the costume changes of Tamburlaine, who, appearing first in his shepherd's weeds, casts them off contemptuously at his first triumph:

> Lie here ye weeds that I disdain to wear!
> This complete armour and this curtle axe
> Are adjuncts more beseeming Tamburlaine;

and who later wears in sequence white, scarlet, and black armor to indicate the stiffening of his attitude towards his victims. This is a simple dramatic device. In *Macbeth* the costume change is related to the iterated image to make concrete Macbeth's state of mind, and related also to the larger problem, the power of evil to corrupt absolutely, with which the play is concerned.

Without insisting too strongly on this kind of relation of image and symbol to clothe the idea of the play in reality, a few familiar instances may make the process clearer. *Hamlet,* for example, establishes in its opening scene, with the ghost, and the references to decay and unwholesomeness, what Mr. Knight calls "the embassy of death." The hand of death is upon the play from the very start and references to it are constantly reiterated. However, it is death of a particular sort, not just Hamlet's musings upon the possibilities of suicide. Hamlet speaks of the sun breeding "maggots in a dead dog," the king compares his nephew to a foul disease, and describes his subjects as "muddied, Thick and unwholesome in their thoughts and whispers." The idea is repeated over and over in the play which has been made explicit at the very start, "Something is rotten in the state of Denmark."

But if we have missed it through insensitivity, Shakespeare presents his symbol of the state of Denmark dramatically, in terms of the theater, before our eyes: *Enter two clowns,* who discourse learnedly of death and suicide and toss skulls and bones about the stage remarking on the pocky corpses they now must deal with; "Faith, if 'a be not rotten before 'a die," catches up the very word Marcellus had used earlier to describe the condition of the state.

It is this same kind of symbolism that Miss Spurgeon noticed with some surprise in the Gardener's scene of *Richard II,* in which the "leading theme . . . (is) gathered up, focussed, and pictorially presented." As she points out, this could hardly be missed by any careful reader. The lines of the play are larded with images of nature gone awry, the ugly clouds flying in the fair and crystal sky, the flourishing branch cracked and hacked down, and the summer leaves faded; there is a fearful tempest, a flood tide;

> The bay trees in our country all are withered,
> And meteors fright the fixed stars of heaven;
> The pale-faced moon looks bloody on the earth. . . . ;

an unseasonable stormy day causes rivers to flood. But where the other characters of the play refer to the disordered political conditions in England in terms of unkempt nature, the Gardener reverses them by comparing the task of ordering his garden to the task of the governor of a commonwealth.

> O what pity it is
> That he had not so trimm'd and dress'd his land
> As we this garden!

Miss Spurgeon declares the scene to have been "deliberately inserted at the cost of any likeness to nature, for no human gardeners ever discoursed like these." To demand verisimilitude in what is obviously a poetic device is to apply to Shakespeare the standards of David Belasco. Probably even the most theatrical of theatricalists would be willing to grant the rightness and the effectiveness of the device, for it does realize dramatically and visually in terms of character and action the theme of the play. On reconsideration it may seem over-deliberate, super-imposed, introducing as it does two totally new characters for the sole purpose of the device, but Shakespeare had not yet learned dramatic economy. In *Hamlet,* the gravediggers belong to the plot as well as to the imagery.

The repeated pictures of natural conditions in *Richard II* introduce a second important function of the image in Elizabethan poetic drama. We are all convinced, I suppose, that the dramatist was forced to work without the benefit or encumbrance

of representational scenery, and that the formal nature of the
background of the Globe is the excuse for so many of those

> Barkloughly Castle call they this at hand

speeches, and such more extended and always (on the modern
stage) intrusive passages in which we are informed,

> The grey-eyed morn smiles on the frowning night,
> Check'ring the Eastern clouds with streaks of light,

together with other meteorological data. But perhaps the Elizabethan playwright was more fortunate than his cabined, cribbed
and confined successor. Not only could he shift his scene at will,
or indeed not bother with a "scene" at all, but he could in his
images create a world for his action more complete than any producer could provide, and uniquely adapted to the needs of both
his play and his theme.

In *Richard*, for example, the action transpires not before
painted seacoasts and cardboard castles, but in an envelope
which is at once scenic and emotional. The cumulative effect of
the nature images is not merely to suggest the political condition
of England, but the kind of world in which such a conflict as
that between Bolingbroke and Richard could take place. The
device is not very skillfully used, perhaps, for *Richard* is close to
being an apprentice play. In the later works, the setting as an
emotional envelope is more artfully handled.

Lear is a case in point and a particularly striking contrast to
Richard. Instead of giving magnitude to his action (as in the
other tragedies) by relating the struggles of the protagonist to
affairs of state, in England, Rome, or Denmark, Shakespeare
creates a world of his own, a special world of King Lear, and
he creates it by means of imagery.

It is the worst of all possible worlds. The animals which inhabit it are dragons, curs, rats, geese, kites, wolves, vultures,
tigers. It is a world of disease, of plagues, carbuncles, boils.
Whatever happens in this world happens in the most violent
manner, wrenched, beaten, pierced, stung, scourged, flayed,
gashed, scalded, tortured, broken on the rack. All this has been
noted before by Miss Spurgeon and others. The world of Lear
is a world of torment, a world unfriendly to man. In such a world

the events of the play are entirely natural, possible, logical. The imagery, better than any possible stage setting, provides a background for the action, enriching the language of the play and serving to unify its execution.

For what, strangely enough, does not seem to have been commented on is the realization of this metaphorical world in the action of the play, in the tempest which runs through its center and in the torturing and blinding of Gloucester. Both scenes have come in for critical attack as incapable of presentation or too horrible for effective use. But it is clear that both are as essential to the play's action as to its theme, and that the blinding of Gloucester—detailed as it is—is made as horrible as possible for a purpose. If we experience an emotion of disgust, or terror, it is because both elements are present, not simply in the action, but in the world of the play. It is the dramatization of the image which makes the meaning of the play evident. If Richard's crown is the "language of props," Lear's tempest is the "language of setting."

The most difficult of the dramatist's devices to appreciate in the study is his primary device, the "language of action." Our modern playwrights are at some pains to render the action clear in extended stage directions, separated from the dialogue by italics and parentheses. Now Shakespeare resorts to a stage direction only rarely, most of the movement in his plays being implicit in the poetry. The significance of this lies less in the freedom of interpretation permitted the actor than in the indication of a further unity between the devices of poetry and the theater in the poetic drama.

For a simple and clear instance of this we may again turn to *Richard II*. The plot of this play, the conflict between Richard and Bolingbroke, might be diagrammed by tracing the letter X and letting the downward stroke stand for the king, the upward for the usurper, and the point of crossing the deposition scene. It is curious to note how the dominance of first the king and then the usurper is symbolized in their positions on the stage as well as in the imagery and the plot line. For three acts, Richard is in the ascendant. Whatever Bolingbroke's activities, Richard maintains his position as king. This is indeed symbolized by his appearance "on the walls" of Flint Castle, while Bolingbroke

and his followers remain below. His descent to Bolingbroke's
level is accompanied by a punning speech:

> Base court, where kings grow base,
> To come at traitors' calls and do them grace;

but his recognition of the true state of affairs is indicated as
Bolingbroke kneels and Richard raises him up. In the deposition
scene the shift in positions is completed, and verbalized by
Richard in a final allusion to the sun image:

> O that I were a mockery king of snow,
> Standing before the sun of Bolingbroke
> To melt myself away in water drops.

It is a sign of the maturing artist that as his skill increases in
each of the dramatic forms he elects to try, Shakespeare relies
more and more upon the essentially dramatic materials available
to him, the actors, their movements and physical relationships. In
the most perfect of the histories, for instance, *1 Henry IV*, he has
involved himself in a highly complex plot, the handling of which
is a constant source of wonder and admiration. Ostensibly, Shakespeare is relating the events of a portion of the reign of Henry IV,
a revolt engineered by the Percy family, and the waywardness of
the Prince of Wales. But the two problems confronting the king
are brought into significant relationship to one another, and the
facts of history are made to serve the purposes of art. The subject of the play is not English history, but the general education
of princes. Events have been so modified that the play actually
confronts two ways of life—Hotspur's and Falstaff's—and presents
the dilemma of Hal in choosing between them. Although a good
deal of ink has been spilled over the character of Falstaff, and a
number of romantic female tears over Percy, Shakespeare's intention is clear from his manipulation of the characters in a
crucial scene. In Act v, scene 4, Douglas enters, challenges
Henry IV, they fight and, "the King being in danger, enter
Prince of Wales." One must perhaps visualize the scene in the
Elizabethan theater—a broad platform projecting into the audience with entrance doors on each side at the rear. Douglas and
the Prince fight, and "Douglas flieth" through one of the doors. As

the King goes to join his troops, enter, through the opposite door, Hotspur. The two youths exchange challenges; "They fight."

> *Enter Falstaff.*
> *Falstaff.* Well said, Hal! to it, Hal! Nay you shall find no boy's play here, I can tell you.
> *Enter Douglas. He fighteth with Falstaff, who falls down as if he were dead. (Exit Douglas.) The Prince killeth Percy.*

Percy dies, still prating romantically of his honor and his proud titles which now accrue to Hal; Hal speaks his eulogy and turns from the body to go to the nearest door. But on his way, "He spieth Falstaff on the ground." As in *Richard II* the positions of the characters in the scene are symbolic. Hal has, seemingly, been presented with a choice between the way of life represented by Hotspur and the way of life represented by Falstaff. And here they are, two (apparent) corpses on the ground, one on either side of him. The choice is to make, and he chooses—neither. Having bid farewell to Percy, he now bids farewell to Jack, confirming the promise of his first soliloquy and anticipating the rejection of Falstaff at the end of Part II.

Significant illustrations of this "language of action" could be chosen from nearly any of the plays. Indeed, nearly all the most familiar, most memorable scenes involve some kind of symbolic action. Not merely in tragedy, with Lear buffeted by the tempest, or Hamlet leaping into the grave of Ophelia, but in comedy, with Titania fondly caressing the hairy snout of ass-headed Bottom, or Feste torturing Malvolio into a realization of his humanity. The very essence of the tragic idea of *Hamlet* and *Lear* and the comic idea of *A Midsummer Night's Dream* and *Twelfth Night* is contained in those moments of action. This is not to say that the poetry is superfluous. These are further instances of the complete welding of the elements of poetry and the elements of theater which constitute successful poetic drama.

Harley Granville-Barker

THE MERCHANT OF VENICE

The Merchant of Venice is a fairy tale. There is no more reality in Shylock's bond and the Lord of Belmont's will than in Jack and the Beanstalk.

Shakespeare, it is true, did not leave the fables as he found them. This would not have done; things that pass muster on the printed page may become quite incredible when acted by human beings, and the unlikelier the story, the likelier must the mechanism of its acting be made. Besides, when his own creative impulse was quickened, he could not help giving life to a character; he could no more help it than the sun can help shining. So Shylock is real, while his story remains fabulous; and Portia and Bassanio become human, though, truly, they never quite emerge from the enchanted thicket of fancy into the common light of day. Aesthetic logic may demand that a story and its characters should move consistently upon one plane or another, be it fantastic or real. But Shakespeare's practical business, once he had chosen these two stories for his play, was simply so to charge them with humanity that they did not betray belief in the human beings presenting them, yet not so uncompromisingly that the stories themselves became ridiculous.

What the producer of the play must first set himself to ascertain is the way in which he did this, the nice course that—by reason or instinct—he steered. Find it and follow it, and there need be no running on the rocks. But logic may land us anywhere. It can turn Bassanio into a heartless adventurer. Test the

From *Prefaces to Shakespeare*, by H. Granville-Barker, Vol. II, 1947. Copyright 1947 by Princeton University Press. Reprinted by permission of Princeton University Press and B. T. Batsford Ltd.

clock of the action by Greenwich time, it will either be going too fast or too slow. And as to Portia's disguise and Bellario's law, would the village policeman be taken in by either? But the actor will find that he simply cannot play Bassanio as a humbug, for Shakespeare does not mean him to. Portias and Nerissas have been eclipsed by wigs and spectacles. This is senseless tomfoolery; but how make a wiseacre producer see that if he does not already know? And if, while Shylock stands with his knife ready and Antonio with his bared breast, the wise young judge lifting a magical finger between them, we sit questioning Bellario's law —why, no one concerned, actors or audience, is for this fairyland, that is clear.

The Merchant of Venice is the simplest of plays, so long as we do not bedevil it with sophistries. Further, it is—for what it is!— as smoothly and completely successful, its means being as well fitted to its end, as anything Shakespeare wrote. He was happy in his choice of the Portia story; his verse, which has lost glitter to gain a mellower beauty and an easier flow, is now well attuned to such romance. The story of Shylock's bond is good contrast and complement both; and he can now project character upon the stage, uncompromising and complete. Yet this Shylock does not overwhelm the play, as at a later birth he might well have done—it is a near thing, though! Lastly, Shakespeare is now enough of the skilled playwright to be able to adjust and blend the two themes with fruitful economy.

THE CONSTRUCTION OF THE PLAY
THE PROBLEM OF "DOUBLE-TIME"

This blending of the themes would, to a modern playwright, have been the main difficulty. The two stories do not naturally march together. The forfeiture of the bond must be a matter of months; with time not only of the essence of the contract, but of the dramatic effect. But the tale of the caskets cannot be enlarged, its substance is too fragile; and a very moderate charge of emotion would explode its pretty hollowness altogether. Critics have credited Shakespeare with nice calculation and amazing subtlety in his compassing of the time-difficulty. Daniel gives us one analysis, Halpin another, Eccles a third, and Furness finds the

play as good a peg for the famous Double Time theory as Wilson,
its inventor, found Othello. All very ingenious; but is the ingenuity Shakespeare's or their own? [1] For him dramatic time was
a naturally elastic affair. (It still is, though less so, for the modern
playwright, whose half-hour act may commonly suggest the passing of an hour or two; this also is Double Time.) Shakespeare
seems to think of it quite simply in terms of effect, as he thought
of dramatic space, moving his characters hither and thither without considering the compassing of yards or miles. The one freedom will imply and enhance the other. The dramatist working
for the "realistic" stage must settle definitely where his characters
are to be and keep them there till he chooses to change the
scenery. Shakespeare need not; and, in fact, he never insists upon
place at all, unless it suits him to; and then only to the extent that
it suits him. [2] In this play, for instance, where we find Shylock and
Antonio will be Venice, but whereabouts in Venice is usually no
matter; when it is—at Shylock's door or in court before the Duke
—it will be made clear enough to us. And where Portia is, is Belmont. He treats time—and the more easily—with a like freedom,
and a like aim. Three months suits for the bond; but once he has
pouched the money Bassanio must be off to Belmont, and his
calendar, attuned to his mood, at once starts to run by hours
only. The wind serves, and he sails that very night, and there is
no delay at Belmont. Portia would detain him some month or
two before he ventures; and what could be more convenient for
a Shakespeare bent on synchronizing the two stories? For that
matter, he could have placed Belmont a few hundred miles off,
and let the coming and going eke out the time. Did the problem
as a whole ever even occur to him? If it did, he dismissed it as of
no consequence. What he does is to set each story going according to its nature; then he punctuates them, so to speak, for effect.
By the clock they are not even consistent in themselves, far less
with each other. But we should pay just the sort of attention to
these months, days or hours that we do, in another connection, to
the commas and semicolons elucidating a sentence. They give us,
and are meant to, simply a *sense* of time and its exactions. It is
the more easily done because our own sense of time in daily life
is far from consistent. Time flies when we are happy, and drags
in anxiety, as poets never tire of reminding us. Shakespeare's own

reflections on the phenomenon run to half a column of the con-
cordance, and he turns it quite naturally to dramatic account.

THE TRUE PROBLEM

How to blend two such disparate themes into a dramatically
organic whole; that was his real problem. The stories, linked in
the first scene, will, of themselves, soon part company. Shakespeare has to run them neck and neck till he is ready to join
them again in the scene of the trial. But the difficulty is less that
they will not match each other by the clock than that their whole
gait so differs, their very nature. How is the flimsy theme of the
caskets to be kept in countenance beside its grimly powerful
rival? You cannot, as we said, elaborate the story, or charge it
with emotion; that would invite disaster. Imagine a Portia seriously alarmed by the prospect of an Aragon or a Morocco for
husband. What sort of barrier, on the other hand, would the
caskets be to a flesh-and-blood hero and heroine fallen in love?
Would a Romeo or Rosalind give a snap of the finger for them?
As it is, the very sight of Bassanio prompts Portia to rebellion;
and Shakespeare can only allow his lovers a few lines of talk
together, and that in company, dare only color the fairy tale
with a rhetorically passionate phrase or so before the choice is
made and the caskets can be forgotten—as they are!—altogether.
Nor does anything in the play show the artist's supreme tact in
knowing what *not* to do better than this?

But you cannot neglect the Portia story either, or our interest
in her may cool. Besides, this antiphony of high romance and
rasping hate enhances the effect of both. A contrasting of subjects, scene by scene, is a trick (in no depreciatory sense) of
Shakespeare's earliest stagecraft, and he never lost his liking for
it.[3] Then if the casket-theme cannot be neglected, but cannot be
elaborated, it must somehow be drawn out, its peculiar character
sustained, its interest husbanded while its consummation is
delayed.

Shakespeare goes straightforwardly enough to work. He puts
just as little as may be into Portia's first scene; but for the one
sounding of Bassanio's name there would be only the inevitable
tale of the caskets told in tripping prose and the conventional

joking upon the suitors. Portia and Nerissa, however, seen for the first time in the flesh, give it sufficient life, and that "Bassanio" one vivid spark more. Later, in due course, come Morocco's choice of the gold casket and Aragon's of the silver. We remark that Morocco is allotted two scenes instead of one. The reason is, probably, that Shakespeare has now enriched himself with the Lorenzo-Jessica story (not to mention the episode of the Gobbos, father and son), and, with this extra weight in the Venetian scale of the action, is put to it to maintain the balance. He could, of course, finish with both Morocco and Aragon earlier and give Bassanio two scenes instead of one.[4] And if a romantic hero could not well wait till after dinner to make his choice, as Morocco does, Solanio's arrival with the ill news of Antonio could easily have been kept for the later scene. But this will not do either— most characteristically will not do for Shakespeare. He has held his lovers apart, since the air of the Belmont of the caskets is too rarefied for flesh and blood to breathe. And Portia herself has been spellbound; we have only had jaunty little Nerissa to prophesy that love (by the pious prevision of the late lord) would somehow find out the way.[5] But once he brings them to-gether Bassanio must break the spell. It is the story of the sleeping beauty and the prince in another kind; a legitimate and traditional outcome. And once Shakespeare himself has broken free of the fairy tale and brought these two to life (for Bassanio as well has been till now a little bloodless) it is not in him to let them lapse from the scene unproved, and to the full. The long restraint has left him impatient, and he must, here and now, have his dramatic fling. We need not credit—or discredit him, if you like—with much calculation of the problem. It was common prudence both to keep Belmont as constantly in our view as Venice, and the emancipating Bassanio clear of it for as long as possible. And he is now in the middle of his play, rather past it, ready to link his two stories together again. He worked forthrightly; that is written plain over most of his work. Though he might now find that he had here material for two scenes, he would not return in his tracks, telescope Aragon and Morocco— and take, in fact, all the sort of trouble we, who are his critics, must take to explain what a much more compact job he could have made of it! Besides, here is his chance to uplift the two as hero and heroine, and he will not dissipate its effectiveness.

For Bassanio, as we said, has been till now only little less bound than Portia in the fetters of a fairy tale; and later, Shylock and the bond will condemn him to protesting helplessness, and the affair of the rings to be merrily befooled.[6] The wonder indeed is, considering the rather poor figure—painfully poor by the gospel according to Samuel Smiles—the coercion of the story makes him cut, that throughout he measures up so well to the stature of sympathetic hero. Shakespeare contrives it in two ways. He endows him with very noble verse; and, whenever he can, throws into strong relief the Bassanio of his own uncovenanted imagination. He does this here. The fantasy of the caskets brought to its due crisis, charged with an emotion which blows it for a finish into thin air, he shows us Bassanio, his heart's desire won, agonized with grief and remorse at the news of Antonio's danger. Such moments do test a man and show him for what he is; and this one, set in bright light and made the scene's turning point, counts for more in the effect the character makes on us than all the gentlemanly graces of his conventional equipment. Unless the actor is much at fault, we shall hear the keynote to the true Bassanio struck in the quiet simplicity—such contrast to his rhetoric over the caskets, even though this was less mere rhetoric than Morocco's and Aragon's—of the speech which begins

> O sweet Portia,
> Here are a few of the unpleasant'st words
> That ever blotted paper! . . .
> Rating myself at nothing, you shall see
> How much I was a braggart. When I told you
> My state was nothing, I should then have told you
> That I was worse than nothing; for indeed
> I have engaged myself to a dear friend,
> Engaged my friend to his mere enemy,
> To feed my means. . . .

Here speaks Shakespeare's Bassanio; and it is by this, and all that will belong to it, that he is meant to live in our minds.

Producer and actors must look carefully into the way by which in this scene the method that has served for the casket story is resolved into something better fitted to the theme of the bond (dominant from the beginning of the play, and now to absorb and transform the dedicated Portia and her fortunes). It is a change—though we must not insist on the contrast more than Shakespeare does—from dramatic convention to dramatic life. From the beginning the pulse of the scene beats more strongly; and Portia's

> I pray you, tarry: pause a day or two
> Before you hazard; for in choosing wrong,
> I lose your company; therefore forbear awhile. . . .

is not only deeper in feeling (there has been little or nothing to rouse her till now; she has had to be the picture of a Portia, hardly more, with a spice of wit to help her through), but how much simpler in expression! When Bassanio turns to those obsessing caskets she must lapse again for a space into fancies of his swan-like end, her eye the watery deathbed for him, into talk about Hercules and Alcides (borrowed, one fears, from Morocco), about Dardanian wives and the like—even as he will be conventionally sententious over his choice. But note how, within the convention, preparing an escape from it, emotion is roused and sustained. With the rhetoric of Portia's

> Go, Hercules!
> Live thou, I live: with much, much more dismay
> I view the fight, than thou that mak'st the fray.

for a springboard, the song and its music are to stir us,

> *whilst Bassanio comments on the caskets to himself.*

So (let the actor remember) when he does at last speak, the emotional ascent will have been half climbed for him already. And while he pays his tribute of trope and maxim, Portia, Nerissa and the rest watch him in silence, at full strain of attention, and help to keep us, too, intent. The speech itself sweeps unhindered to its height, and the pause while the casket is unlocked is filled and enriched by the intensity of Portia's

> How all the other passions fleet to air . . .

most cunningly contrived in meaning and melody, with its emphasis on "despair" and "ecstasy" and "excess," to hold us upwrought. The fairy tale is finally incarnate in the fantastic word-painting of the portrait and the reading of the scroll. Then, with a most delicate declension to reality, Bassanio comes to face her as in a more actual world, and the curtains can be drawn upon the caskets for the last time. Observe that not for a moment has Shakespeare played his fabulous story false. He takes his theater too seriously to go spoiling an illusion he has created. He consummates it, and turns the figures of it to fresh purpose, and they seem to suffer no change.

Throughout the scene—throughout the play, and the larger part of all Elizabethan drama for that matter—effects must be valued very much in terms of music. And, with the far adventuring of his playwriting hardly begun, Shakespeare's verse is already fairly flawless, and its maneuvering from mood to mood masterly, if still simple. We have the royal humility of the speech in which Portia yields herself (Bassanio slips back to his metaphors for a moment after this); then, for contrast, the little interlude of Gratiano and Nerissa, with the tripping monosyllables of Gratiano's

> I wish you all the joy that you can wish;
> For I am sure you can wish none from me. . . .

to mark the pace and the tone of it. Then follows the arrival of Antonio's messenger with Lorenzo and Jessica; done in plain, easy-moving verse that will not discount the distressed silence in which he reads the letter, nor the quiet candor of his confession to Portia. Now comes another crescendo—two voices added to strengthen it—leading up to her generous, wide-eyed

> What sum owes he the Jew?

Bassanio.

> For me, three thousand ducats.

Portia.

> What, no more!
> Pay him six thousand, and deface the bond;
> Double six thousand, and then treble that. . . .

which itself drops to the gentleness of

Since you are dear bought I will love you dear.

Then, to strengthen the scene's ending, we have the austere prose of Antonio's letter, chilling us to misgiving. And since—in stage practice, and with the prevailing key of the play's writing to consider—this will not do for an actual finish, there is a last modulation into the brisk coda of

> Since I have your good leave to go away,
> I will make haste: but till I come again,
> No bed shall e'er be guilty of my stay,
> Nor rest be interposer 'twixt us twain.

Lorenzo and Jessica make another link (though their relation to Belmont is pretty arbitrary) between the two stories. This, however, is but the secondary use of them. There must be a sense of time passing in Venice while the bond matures, yet we must have continuous action there, too, while the ritual at Belmont goes its measured way; so, as there can be little for Shylock and Antonio to do but wait, this third, minor theme is interposed. It brings fresh impetus to the action as well as new matter; and it shows us—very usefully—another and more human side of Shylock. Shakespeare does not scheme it out overcarefully. The masking and the elopement and the coming and going they involve are rather inconveniently crowded together (the pleasant episode of the Gobbos may have stolen a little necessary space); and one chapter of the story—for were we perhaps to have seen Shylock at supper with Bassanio, Lorenzo and the rest while the disguised Jessica waited on them?—was possibly crowded out altogether.

Once the fugitives, with some disregard of likelihood, have been brought to Belmont, Gobbo in attendance, Shakespeare turns them to account quite shamelessly. They play a mighty poor scene to give Portia and Nerissa time to disguise themselves as doctor and clerk.[7] They will have to play another while doctor and clerk change to Portia and Nerissa again; but for that, as if in compensation, they are to be dowered with the loveliest lines in the play.[8] With the junction of the themes in the trial-scene the constructive problem is, of course, solved. Shylock disappearing, the rest is simple.

SHAKESPEARE'S VENICE

If Lorenzo and Jessica and a little poetry and the consort of music, which no well-regulated great household of his time would be without, are Shakespeare's resources (he had no other; and what better should we ask?) for the painting of the star-lit garden of Belmont at the play's end, for its beginning he must show us Venice. He troubles with no verbal scene-painting here; throughout the first scene the very word is but spoken twice, and quite casually. We might be anywhere in the city, or out of it, even. Thereafter we hear of the Rialto, of a gondola, of the common ferry and suchlike incidentals; but of the picturesque environment to which modern staging has accustomed us there is no suggestion at all. Yet he does present a Venice that lived in the Elizabethan mind, and it is the Venice of his dramatic needs; a city of royal merchants trading to the gorgeous East, of Jews in their gaberdines (as rare a sight, remember, as to us a Chinese mandarin is, walking the London streets today), and of splendid gentlemen rustling in silks. To the lucky young Englishman who could hope to travel there Venice stood for culture and manners and the luxury of civilization; and this—without one word of description—is how Shakespeare pictures it.

We are used nowadays to see the play begun by the entry of a depressed, sober-suited, middle-aged man and two skipping youths, who make their way with a sort of desperate merriment through such lines as the producer's blue pencil has left them, vanish shamefacedly, reappear at intervals to speak the remnant of another speech or two, and slip at last unregarded into oblivion. These are Solanio and Salarino, cursed by actors as the two worst bores in the whole Shakespearean canon; not excepting, even, those other twin brethren in nonentity, Rosencrantz and Guildenstern.[9] As characters, Shakespeare has certainly not been at much pains wtih them; they could exchange speeches and no one would be the wiser, and they move about at everybody's convenience but their own. But they have their use, and it is an important one; realize it, and there may be some credit in fulfilling it. They are there to paint Venice for us, the Venice of the magnificent young man. Bassanio embodies it also; but there are other calls on him, and he will be off to Belmont soon. So do Gratiano and Lorenzo; but they will be gone too. Solanio and Salarino will not fail us; they hoist this flag at the play's beginning and keep it bravely flying for as long as need be. When Salarino, for a beginning, addresses Antonio with

> There, where your argosies with portly sail,
> Like signiors and rich burghers on the flood,
> Or, as it were, the pageants of the sea,
> Do overpeer the petty traffickers,
> That curt'sy to them, do them reverence
> As they fly by them with their woven wings.

—there should be no skipping merriment in this.

They are argosies themselves, these magnificent young men, of high-flowing speech; pageants to overpeer the callow English ruffians, to whom they are here displayed. The talk passes from spices and silks into fine classical phrases; and with what elaborate, dignified dandyism it ends!

Enter Bassanio, Lorenzo and Gratiano.

Solanio.

Here comes Bassanio, your most noble kinsman,
Gratiano, and Lorenzo. Fare you well;
We leave you now with better company

Salarino.

I would have stayed till I had made you merry,
If worthier friends had not prevented me.

Antonio.

Your worth is very dear in my regard.
I take it, your own business calls on you,
And you embrace the occasion to depart.

Salarino.

Good-morrow, my good lords.

Bassanio.

Good signiors both, when shall we laugh? Say, when?
You grow exceeding strange: Must it be so?

Salarino.

We'll make our leisures to attend on yours.

No apologetic gabbling here: but such a polish, polish as might have satisfied Mr. Turveydrop. Solanio—if one could distinguish between them—might cut the finer figure of the two. When the Masque is in question:

'Tis vile [he says], unless it may be quaintly ordered,
And better, in my mind, not undertook.

Salarino has a cultured young gentleman's turn for classical allusion. He ranges happily from two-headed Janus and Nestor to Venus' pigeons.

But it is, as we said, when Bassanio and Gratiano and Lorenzo with his Jessica have departed, that the use these two are to the play becomes plainest. They give us the first news of Antonio's losses, and hearsay, filtering through them, keeps the disaster conveniently vague. If we saw the blow fall on Antonio, the far more dramatic scene in which Shylock is thrown from depth to heights and from heights to depth as ill news and this good news strike upon him would be left at a discount. In this scene they are most useful (if they are not made mere targets for a star actor to shoot at). For here again is Venice, in the contrast between sordid Shylock and Tubal and our magnificent young gentlemen, superfine still of speech and manner, but not above a little Jew-baiting. They sustain that theme—and it must be sustained—till it can be fully and finally orchestrated in the trial-scene. It is a simple stagecraft which thus employs them, and their vacuity as characters inclines us to forget this, their very real utility. Forgetting it, Shakespeare's histrionic Venice is too often forgotten also.

THE CHARACTERS, AND THE CRISIS OF THE ACTION

None of the minor characters does much more than illustrate the story; at best, they illuminate with a little lively detail their own passage through it. Not the Duke, nor Morocco, Aragon, Tubal, Lorenzo, Jessica, nor the Gobbos, nor Nerissa, had much being in Shakespeare's mind, we feel, apart from the scenes they played, and the use they were to him. It is as futile, that is to say, to discuss Jessica's excuses for gilding herself with ducats

when she elopes as it is to work out her itinerary via Genoa to
Belmont; we might as well start writing the life-story of Mistress
Margery Gobbo.

PORTIA

Shakespeare can do little enough with Portia while she is still
the slave of the caskets; incidentally, the actress must resist the
temptation to try and do more. She has this picture of an enchanted princess to present, verse and prose to speak perfectly,
and she had better be content with that. But we feel, nevertheless (and in this, very discreetly, she may at once encourage us),
that here, pent up and primed for escape, is one of that eminent
succession of candid and fearless souls: Rosaline, Helena, Beatrice, Rosalind—they embodied an ideal lodged for long in Shakespeare's imagination; he gave it expression whenever he could.
Once he can set his Portia free to be herself, he quickly makes
up for lost time. He has need to; for from the moment of that
revealing

> You see me, Lord Bassanio, where I stand. . . .

not half the play's life is left her, and during a good part of this
she must pose as the young doctor of Rome whose name is
Balthasar. He does not very deliberately develop her character;
he seems by now to know too much about her to need to do that.
He reveals it to us mainly in little things, and lets us feel its
whole happy virtue in the melody of her speech. This it is that
casts its spell upon the strict court of Venice. The

> Shed thou no blood. . . .

is an effective trick. But

> The quality of mercy is not strained;
> It droppeth as the gentle rain from heaven
> Upon the place beneath. . . .

with its continuing beauty, gives the true Portia. To the very
end she expands in her fine freedom, growing in authority and
dignity, fresh touches of humor enlightening her, new traits of
graciousness showing. She is a great lady in her perfect sim-

plicity, in her ready tact (see how she keeps her guest Antonio free from the mock quarrel about the rings), and in her quite unconscious self-sufficiency (she jokes without embarrassment about taking the mythical Balthasar to her bed, but she snubs Gratiano the next minute for talking of cuckoldry, even as she snubbed Nerissa for a very mild indelicacy—she is fond of Nerissa, but no forward waiting-women for her!). Yet she is no more than a girl.

Here is an effect that we are always apt to miss in the acting of Shakespeare today. It is not the actress's fault that she cannot be what her predecessor, the boy-Portia, was; and she brings us compensation for losses which should leave us—if she will mitigate the losses as far as she can—gainers on the whole. But the constant play made in the Comedies upon the contrast between womanly passion or wisdom and its very virginal enshrining gives a delicacy and humor to these figures of romance which the limited resources of the boy left vivid, which the ampler endowment of the woman too often obscures. This is no paradox, but the obvious result of a practical artistry making the most of its materials. Portia does not abide in this dichotomy as fully as, for instance, Rosalind and Viola do; but Shakespeare turns it to account with her in half a hundred little ways, and to blur the effect of them is to rob her of much distinction.

The very first line she speaks, the

> By my troth, Nerissa, my little body is aweary of this
>   great world.

is likely to come from the mature actress robbed of half its point. This will not matter so much. But couple that "little body" with her self-surrender to Bassanio as

>   an unlessoned girl, unschooled, unpractised;
>   Happy in this, she is not yet so old
>   But she may learn . . .

and with the mischief that hides behind the formal courtesies of the welcome to Aragon and Morocco, with the innocence of the amazed

>   What no more!
>   Pay him six thousand and deface the bond . . .

with the pretty sententiousness of her talk of herself, her

> I never did repent of doing good,
> Nor shall not now . . .

followed by the artless

> This comes too near the praising of myself . . .

and the figure built up for us of the heiress and great lady of
Belmont is seen to be a mere child, too, who lives remote in her
enchanted world. Set beside this the Portia of resource and command, who sends Bassanio posthaste to his friend, and beside
that the schoolgirl laughing with Nerissa over the trick they are
to play their new lords and masters. Know them all for one
Portia, a wise and gallant spirit so virginally enshrined; and we
see to what profit Shakespeare turned his disabilities. There is,
in this play, a twofold artistry in the achievement. Unlikelihood
of plot is redeemed by veracity of character; while the artifice of
the medium, the verse and its convention, and the stylized acting of boy as woman, re-reconciles us to the fantasy of the plot.

But a boy-Portia's advantage was chiefly manifest, of course, in
the scene of the trial; and here in particular the actress of today
must see that she lessens it no more than she need. The curious
process of what we may call the "double negative," by which an
Elizabethan audience first admitted a boy as a girl and then
enjoyed the pretense that the girl was a boy, is obsolete for us;
make-believe being the game, there was probably some pleasure
just in this complication of it. This beside, there was the direct
dramatic effect, which the boy made supremely well in his own
person, of the wise young judge, the Daniel come to judgment.
Shylock (and Shakespeare) plucks the allusion from the popular
story of Susanna; but there may be some happy confusion, perhaps, with that other Daniel who was among ". . . the children
of Israel, of the king's seede and of the Prince's: Springaldes
without any blemish, but well-favoured, studious in all wisdome,
skillful for knowledge, able to utter knowledge, and such as have
livelinesse in them, that they might stand in the king's palace. . . ." For this is the very figure we should see. Here is the
strict court of Venice, like enough to any law court, from East
to West, from Shakespeare's time to now, in that it will seem

to the stranger there very dry and discouraging, airless, lifeless. Age and incredulity preside; and if passion and life do enter, they must play upon muted strings. The fiercely passionate Shylock is anomaly enough in such surroundings. Then comes this youth, as brisk and businesslike as you please, and stands before the judges' bench, alert, athletic, modest, confident. He is life incarnate and destined to victory; and such a victory is the fitting climax to a fairy tale. So the Portia that will—as most Portias do —lapse into feminine softness and pitch the whole scene in the key of the speech on mercy, and that in a key of sentiment, damns the scene and herself and the speech, all three. This amazing youth has the ear of the court at once; but he'll only hold it by strict attention to business. Then, suddenly, out of this, comes the famous appeal, and catches us and the court unaware, catches us by the throat, enkindles us. In this lies the effect. Prepare for it, or make the beauty of it overbeautiful (all the more now, because it is famous and hackneyed) and it becomes a dose of soothing syrup.

This, be it further remembered, is not the scene's top note; conflict and crisis are to come. They are brought about simply and directly; the mechanical trick of the "No jot of blood" that is to resolve them asks nothing else. Shakespeare keeps the medium of the verse as simple; it flows on with hardly a broken line. The conflict is between Portia and Shylock. Bassanio's agony, Antonio's stoic resignation cannot be given great play; the artifice of the story will not even now sustain crosscurrents of human passion. But the constraint of the business of a court accounts well enough for their quiescence (the actors need do nothing to discount it) and the few notes that are struck from them suffice. The action must sweep ahead and no chance be given us to question its likelihood. Even when all is over the Duke departs with not much more comment upon this amazing case than an invitation to the learned young doctor to come to dinner, and Antonio and his friends are as casual about it and almost as calm. There is tactful skill in this. Shylock has gone, that fairy tale is done with; the less we look back upon it, the sooner we come to fresh comedy again the better.

Throughout the scene a Portia must, of course, by no smallest sign betray to us—as well betray it to Bassanio—that she is other than she now seems. No difficulty here, as we said, for Shakespeare's Portia, or his audience either. There was no wondering as he faced the judges why they never saw this was a woman (since very obviously he now wasn't) nor why Bassanio did not know his wife a yard off. The liquid sentences of the Mercy speech were no betrayal, nor did the brusque aside of a young lawyer, intent upon his brief—

> Your wife would give you little thanks for that,
> If she were by to hear you make the offer.

—lose its quite casual humor. All this straightforwardness the modern actress must, as far as she can, restore.

ANTONIO, GRATIANO AND OTHERS

In these early plays character does not as a rule outrun the requirements of the plot. Shakespeare is content enough with the decorative, the sententious, the rhetorical, in his casual Venetians, in Aragon and Morocco; with the conventional in Launcelot, who is the stage clown—the juggler with words, neat, agile, resourceful and occasionally familiar with the audience, as a clown and a juggler should be—under a thin disguise of character; with old Gobbo for a minute or two's incidental fun; with the pure utility of Tubal.

Antonio is flesh and blood. He is the passive figure of the story's demand; but Shakespeare refines this in the selflessness that can send Bassanio to Belmont and be happy in a friend's happiness, in the indifference to life that lets him oppose patience to his enemy's fury; and he makes him more convincingly this sort of man by making him just a little self-conscious too.

> In sooth, I know not why I am so sad. . . .

If he does not, it is not for want of thinking about it. He takes a sad pleasure in saying that he is

> a tainted wether of the flock,
> Meetest for death . . .

But there is a redeeming ironic humor in

> You cannot better be employed, Bassanio,
> Then to live still and write mine epitaph.

He is sufficiently set forth, and there is conveyed in him a better dignity than mere words give. [10]

Nerissa is echoing merriment; not much more.

Shakespeare may have had half a mind to make something a little out of the way of Gratiano. He starts him with a temperament and a witty speech; but by the play's end we have not had much more from him than the "infinite deal of nothing" of Bassanio's gibe, rattling stuff, bouncing the play along, but revealing no latent Gratiano. It all makes a good enough pattern of this sort of man, who will be a useful foil to Bassanio, and can be paired off for symmetry with Portia's foil, Nerissa; and the play needed no more. But there is enough of him, and enough talk about him, for one to feel that he missed by only a little the touch of magic that would have made something more of him and added him to the list of those that survive the lowering of the lights and the theater's emptying. There is a moment while he waits to take his share in Jessica's abduction, and sits reflecting:

> All things that are,
> Are with more spirit chased than enjoyed.
> How like a yonker or a prodigal,
> The scarfed bark puts from her native bay,
> Hugg'd and embraced by the strumpet wind!
> How like a prodigal doth she return;
> With over-weather'd ribs, and ragged sails,
> Torn, rent and beggared by the strumpet wind!

Harsh enough similes for such an occasion! Is this another side to the agreeable rattle? Does the man who exclaims

> Let me play the fool!
> With mirth and laughter let old wrinkles come. . . .

find life in fact rather bitter to his taste? But one must beware of reading subtleties into Shakespeare. If such a Gratiano was ever shadowed in his mind, he made no solid substance of him.

Bassanio we have spoken of; play the part straightforwardly and it will come right.

There remains Shylock. He steps into the play, actual and individual from his first word on, and well might in his strength (we come to feel) have broken the pinchbeck of his origin to bits, had a later Shakespeare had the handling of him. As it is, his actuality is not weakened by the fantasy of the bond, as is Portia's by her caskets. For one thing, our credulity is not strained till the time comes for its maturing, and by then—if ever—the play and its acting will have captured us. For another, the law and its ways are normally so uncanny to a layman that the strict court of an exotic Venice might give even stranger judgments than this and only confirm us in our belief that once litigation begins almost anything may happen. Despite the borrowed story, this Shylock is essentially Shakespeare's own. But if he is not a puppet, neither is he a stalking-horse; he is no more a mere means to exemplifying the Semitic problem than is Othello to the raising of the color question. "I am a Jew." "Haply, for I am black. . . ." Here we have—and in Shylock's case far more acutely and completely—the *circumstances* of the dramatic conflict; but at the heart of it are men; and we may surmise, indeed, that from a maturer Shakespeare we should have had, as with Othello, much more of the man, and so rather less of the alien and his griefs. However that may be, he steps now into the play, individual and imaginatively full-grown, and the scene of his talk with Bassanio and Antonio is masterly exposition.

The dry taciturnity of his

Three thousand ducats; well?

(the lure of that thrice-echoed "Well"!) and the cold dissecting of the business in hand are made colder, drier yet by contrast with the happy sound of Portia's laughter dying in our ears as he begins to speak. And for what a helpless innocent Bassanio shows beside him; overanxious, touchy, overcivil! Shylock takes his time; and suddenly we see him peering, myopic, beneath his brows. Who can the newcomer be? And the quick brain answers beneath the question's cover: They must need the money badly if Antonio himself comes seeking me. Off goes Bassanio to greet his friend; and Shylock in a long aside can discharge his obligations to the plot.[11] These eleven lines are worth comment. In them is all the motive power for drama that the story, as Shakespeare found it, provides; and he throws this, with careless opulence, into a single aside. Then he returns to the upbuilding of *his* Shylock.

Note the next turn the scene takes. From the snuffling depreciation of his present store, for his own wonted fawning on these Christian clients, Shylock unexpectedly rises to the dignities of

> When Jacob grazed his uncle Laban's sheep . . .

And with this the larger issue opens out between Gentile and Jew, united and divided by the scripture they revere, and held from their business by this tale from it—of flocks and herds and the ancient East. Here is another Shylock; and Antonio may well stare, and answer back with some respect—though he recovers contempt for the alien creature quickly enough. But with what added force the accusation comes:

> Signior Antonio, many a time and oft
> In the Rialto you have rated me. . . .
> You called me misbeliever, cut-throat dog,
> And spit upon my Jewish gaberdine. . . .

The two Venetians see the Ghetto denizen again, and only hear the bondman's whine. But to us there is now all Jewry couched and threatening there, an ageless force behind it. They may make light of the money bond, but we shall not.

Shakespeare keeps character within the bounds of story with great tact; but such a character as this that has surged in his imagination asks more than such a story to feed on. Hence, partly at least, the new theme of Jessica and her flight, which will give Shylock another and more instant grudge to satisfy. It is developed with strict economy. Twenty-one lines are allowed to Jessica and Launcelot, another twenty or so to her lover and their plans; then, in a scene not sixty long, Shylock and his household are enshrined. As an example of dramatic thrift alone this is worth remark. The parting with Launcelot: he has a niggard liking for the fellow, is even hurt a little by his leaving, touched in pride, too, and shows it childishly.

> Thou shalt not gormandize
> As thou hast done with me. . . .

But he can at least pretend that he parts with him willingly and makes some profit by it. The parting with Jessica, which we of the audience know to be a parting indeed; that constant calling her by name, which tells us of the lonely man! He has looked to her for everything, has tasked her hard, no doubt; he is her jailer, yet he trusts her, and loves her in his extortionate way. Uneasy stranger that he is within these Venetian gates; the puritan, who, in a wastrel world, will abide by law and prophets! So full a picture of the man does the short scene give that it seems hardly possible we see no more of him than this between the making of the bond and the climacteric outbreak of passion upon Jessica's loss and the news of Antonio's ruin.[12]

References to him abound; Shylock can never be long out of our minds. But how deliberate is the thrift of opportunity we may judge by our being shown the first effect of the loss on him only through the ever-useful eyes of Salarino and Solanio. This is politic, however, from other points of view. Look where the scene in question falls, between Morocco's choice of his casket and Aragon's. Here or hereabouts some such scene must come, for the progress of the Antonio and Shylock story cannot be neglected. But conceive the effect of such a tragic outcry as Shylock's own,

> So strange, outrageous, and so variable . . .

—of such strong dramatic meat sandwiched between pleasant conventional rhetoric. How much of the credibility of the casket story would survive the association, with how much patience should we return to it? But Salarino and Solanio tone down tragedy to a good piece of gossip, as it becomes young men of the world to do. We avoid an emotional danger zone; and, for the moment at least, that other danger of an inconvenient sympathy with "the dog Jew." When Shylock's outbreak of anguish does come, the play is nearer to its climax, Bassanio's choice is about to free Portia's story from its unreality, and his savage certainty of revenge upon Antonio will now depress the sympathetic balance against him.

But, considering the story's bounds, what a full-statured figure we already have! Compare the conventional aside, the statement of the theme, in the earlier scene, the bald

> I hate him for he is a Christian. . . .

with the deluge of molten passion which descends upon the devoted Solanio and Salarino, obliterating their tart humor; compare the theme, that is to say, with its development, mere story with character, and measure in the comparison Shakespeare's growing dramatic power.

In tone and temper and method as well this scene breaks away from all that has gone before. The very start in prose, the brisk

> Now, what news on the Rialto?

even, perhaps, Solanio's apology for former

> slips of prolixity or crossing the plain highway of talk . . .

seem to tell us that Shakespeare is now asserting the rights of his own imagination, means, at any rate, to let this chief creature of it, his Shylock, off the leash. And verily he does.

The scene's method repays study. No whirling storm of fury is asked for; this is not the play's crisis, but preparation for it still. Shylock is wrapped in resentful sorrow, telling over his wrong for the thousandth time. Note the repetition of thought and phrase. And how much more sinister this sight of him with the wound festering than if we had seen the blow's instant fall! His mind turns to Antonio, and the thrice told

> let him look to his bond.

is a rope of salvation for him; it knots up the speech in a dreadful strength. Then, on a sudden, upon the good young Salarino's reasonable supposition that what a moneylender wants is his money back; who on earth would take flesh instead?—

> What's that good for?

—there flashes out the savagery stripped naked of

To bait fish withal: if it will feed nothing else, it will feed
my revenge.

Now we have it; and one salutes such purity of hatred. There
follows the famous speech—no need to quote it—mounting in
passionate logic, from its

He hath disgraced me . . . and what's his reason?
I am a Jew.

to the height of

If a Jew wrong a Christian, what is his humility? Revenge. If a Christian wrong a Jew, what should his suffer-
ence be by Christian example? Why, revenge. The villainy
you teach me I will execute, and it shall go hard but I will
better the instruction.

This is a Shylock born of the old story, but transformed, and
here a theme of high tragedy, of the one seemingly never-ending
tragedy of the world. It is the theme for a greater play than
Shakespeare was yet to write. But if this one cannot be sustained on such a height, he has at least for the moment raised
it there.

Solanio and Salarino are quite oblivious to the great moral
issue opened out to them; though they depart a little sobered—
this Jew seems a dangerous fellow. There follows the remarkable
passage with Tubal; of gruesome comedy, the apocalyptic Shylock shrunk already to the man telling his ill-luck against his
enemy's, weighing each in scales (love for his daughter, a memory of his dead wife thrown in!) as he is used to weigh the coin
which is all these Christians have left him for his pride. It is
technically a notable passage, in that it is without conflict or contrast, things generally necessary to dramatic dialogue; but the
breaking of a rule will be an improvement, now and then, upon
obedience to it. So Shakespeare, for a finish, lowers the scene
from its crisis, from that confronting of Christian and Jew, of
hate with hate, to this raucous assonance of these two of a kind
and mind, standing cheek to cheek in common cause, the excellent Tubal fueling up revenge.

Such a finish, ousting all nobility, both shows us another facet of Shylock himself (solid figure enough now to be turned any way his maker will) and is, as we saw, a shadow against which the high romance of Bassanio's wooing will in a moment shine the more brightly. Sharp upon the heels of this, he comes again; but once more apocalyptic, law incarnate now.

> *Shylock.* Gaoler, look to him; tell me not of mercy;
>   This is the fool that lent out money gratis:
>   Gaoler, look to him.
> *Antonio.*   Hear me yet, good Shylock.
> *Shylock.* I'll have my bond; speak not against my bond:
>   I have sworn an oath that I will have my bond.

Verse and its dignity are needed for this scene; and note the recurring knell of the phrases:

> I'll have my bond; I will not hear thee speak:
> I'll have my bond, and therefore speak no more.
> I'll not be made a soft and dull-eyed fool,
> To shake the head, relent, and sigh, and yield
> To Christian intercessors. Follow not;
> I'll have no speaking: I will have my bond.

Here is a Shylock primed for the play's great scene; and Shakespeare's Shylock wrought ready for a catastrophe, which is a deeper one by far than that the story yields. For not in the missing of his vengeance on Antonio will be this Shylock's tragedy, but in the betrayal of the faith on which he builds.

> I've sworn an oath that I will have my bond. . . .

How many times has the synagogue not heard it sworn?

> An oath, an oath. I have an oath in Heaven. . . .

He has made his covenant with an unshakable God:

> What judgment shall I dread, doing no wrong?

—and he is to find himself betrayed.

It is the apocalyptic Shylock that comes slowly into court, solitary and silent, to face and to outface the Duke and all the moral power of Venice.[13] When he does speak he answers the Duke

as an equal, setting a sterner sanction against easy magnanimity
—at other people's expense! One could complain that this first appeal for mercy discounts Portia's. To some extent it does; but
the more famous speech escapes comparison by coming when
the spell of the young doctor is freshly cast on us, and by its
finer content and larger scope. Structurally, the Duke's speech
is the more important, for it sets the lists, defines the issue and
provokes that

> I have possessed your grace of what I purpose;
> And by our holy Sabbath have I sworn
> To have the due and forfeit of my bond. . . .

So confident is he that he is tempted to shift ground a little
and let yet another Shylock peep—the least likable of all. He
goes on

> You'll ask me, why I rather choose to have
> A weight of carrion flesh, than to receive
> Three thousand ducats: I'll not answer that,
> But say it is my humour. . . .

Legality gives license to the hard heart. Mark the progression.
While the sufferer cried

> The villainy you teach me I will execute, and it shall
> go hard but I will better the instruction.

with the law on his side it is

> What judgment shall I dread, doing no wrong?

from which he passes, by an easy turn, to the mere moral anarchy of

> The pound of flesh, which I demand of him,
> Is dearly bought; 'tis mine, and I will have it. . . .

and in satanic heroism stands defiant:

> If you deny me, fie upon your law!
> There is no force in the decrees of Venice.
> I stand for judgment. Answer: shall I have it?

There is a dreadful silence. For who, dwelling unquestioningly under covenant of law, shall gainsay him?

It says much for the mental hypnosis which the make-believe of the theater can induce that this scene of the trial holds us so spellbound. Its poetry adds to the enchantment—let anyone try rewriting it in prose—and the exotic atmosphere helps. But how much more is due to the embroidering of character upon story so richly that the quality of the fabric comes to matter little! Shakespeare, at any rate, has us now upon the elemental heights of drama. He cannot keep us there. Portia must perform her conjuring trick; perhaps this is why he gives Shylock full scope before she arrives. But he brings us down with great skill, maneuvering character to the needs of the story, and turning story to character's account.

The coming of the young judge's clerk does not impress Shylock. How should it. Little Nerissa! He has won, what doubt of it? He can indulge then—why not?—the lodged hate and loathing he bears Antonio. The Duke is busy with Bellario's letter and the eyes of the court are off him. From avenger he degenerates to butcher. To be caught, lickerish-lipped, by Bassanio; and Gratiano's rough tongue serves him as but another whetstone for savagery! He turns surly at first sight of the wise young judge—what need of such a fine fellow and more fine talk—and surlier still when it is talk of mercy. He stands there, he tells them yet again, asking no favors, giving none.

> My deeds upon my head! I crave the law,
> The penalty and forfeit of my bond.

Why does Shakespeare now delay the catastrophe by a hundred lines, and let Portia play cat-and-mouse with her victim? From the story's standpoint, of course, to keep up the excitement a while longer. We guess there is a way out. We wonder what it can be; and yet, with that knife shining, Antonio's doom seems to come nearer and nearer. This is dramatic child's play, and excellent of its sort. But into it much finer stuff is woven. We are to have more than a trick brought off; there must be a better victory; this faith in which Shylock abides must be broken. So first she leads him on. Infatuate, finding her all on his side, he finally and formally refuses the money—walks into the trap. Next she plays upon his fanatical trust in his bond, sets him searching in mean mockery for a charitable comma in it—had one escaped his cold eye—even as the Pharisees searched their code to convict Christ. Fold by fold, the prophetic dignity falls from him. While Antonio takes his selfless farewell of his friend, Shylock must stand clutching his bond and his knife, only contemptible in his triumph. She leads him on to a last slaveringly exultant cry: then the blow falls.

Note that the tables are very precisely turned on him.

> if thou tak'st more,
> Or less, than just a pound, be it so much
> As makes it light or heavy in the substance,
> Or the division of the twentieth part
> Of one poor scruple, nay, if the scale do turn
> But in the estimation of a hair . . .

is exact retaliation for Shylock's insistence upon the letter of his bond. Gratiano is there to mock him with his own words, and to sound, besides, a harsher note of retribution than Portia can; for the pendulum of sympathy now swings back a little—more than a little, we are apt to feel. But the true catastrophe is clear. Shylock stood for law and the letter of the law; and it seemed, in its kind, a noble thing to stand for, ennobling him. It betrays him, and in the man himself there is no virtue left.

> Is *that* the law?

he gasps helplessly. It is his only thought. The pride and power in which legality had wrapped him, by which he had outfaced them all, and held Venice herself to ransom, are gone. He stands stripped, once more the sordid Jew that they may spit upon, greedy for money, and hurriedly keen to profit by his shame.

> I take this offer then; pay the bond thrice,
> And let the Christian go.

Here is Shakespeare's Shylock's fall, and not in the trick the law plays him.

He is given just a chance—would the story let him take it!—

to regain tragic dignity. What is passing in his mind that prompts Portia's

> Why doth the Jew pause? Take thy forfeiture. [14]

No, nothing, it would seem, but the thought that he will be well out of the mess with his three thousand ducats safe.

Shakespeare has still to bring his theme full circle. He does it with doubled regard to character and story.

> Why, then the devil give him good of it!
> I'll stay no longer question.

If he were not made to stay, by every canon of theatrical justice Shylock would be let off too lightly; wherefore we find that the law has another hold on him. It is but a logical extending of retribution, which Gratiano is quick to reduce to its brutal absurdity. Here is Shylock with no more right to a cord with which to hang himself than had Antonio to a bandage for his wound. These quibbling ironies are for the layman among the few delights of law. Something of the villainy the Jew taught them the Christians will now execute; and Shylock, as helpless as Antonio was, takes on a victim's dignity in turn. He stays silent while his fate, and the varieties of official and unofficial mercy to be shown him, are canvassed. [15] He is allowed no comment upon his impoverishing for the benefit of "his son Lorenzo" or upon his forced apostasy. But could eloquence serve better than such a silence?

> *Portia.*   Art thou contented, Jew? What dost thou say?
> *Shylock.*   I am content.

With the three words of submission the swung pendulum of the drama comes to rest. And for the last of him we have only

> I pray you give me leave to go from hence;
> I am not well. Send the deed after me,
> And I will sign it.

Here is the unapproachable Shakespeare. "I am not well." It nears banality and achieves perfection in its simplicity. And what a completing of the picture of Shylock! His deep offense has been against human kindness; he had scorned compassion and prayed God himself in aid of his vengeance. So Shakespeare dismisses him upon an all but ridiculous appeal to our pity, such as an ailing child might make that had been naughty; and we should put the naughtiness aside. He passes out silently, leaving the gibing Gratiano the last word, and the play's action sweeps on without pause. There can be no greater error than to gerrymander Shylock a strenuously "effective exit"—and most Shylocks commit it. From the character's point of view the significant simplicity of that

> I am not well.

is spoiled; and from the point of view of the play the technical skill with which Shakespeare abstracts from his comedy this tragic and dominating figure and avoids anticlimax after is nullified.

THE RETURN TO COMEDY

The tragic interest is posted to oblivion cavalierly indeed. Seven lines suffice, and the Duke's processional departure. The business of the rings is then briskly dispatched, and made the brisker by the businesslike matter of the signing of the deed being tacked to it. Thence to Belmont; and while Lorenzo and Jessica paint its moonlit beauty for us, Balthasar and his clerk have time to change costume and tire their heads again for Portia and Nerissa. They have evidently, as we saw, none too much time; for Launcelot is allowed a last—and an incongruously superflous—piece of clowning. But the musicians can play ahead for an extra minute or two if hooks and eyes refuse to fasten, and no one will notice the delay. The last stretch of dialogue is lively; a comic quartet coming after the consort of viols, and it asks for a like virtuosity. The play ends, pleasantly and with formality, as a fairy tale should. One may wonder that the last speech is left (against tradition) to Gratiano; but one practical reason is plain. Portia and Bassanio, Antonio, Lorenzo and Jessica must pace off the stage in their stately Venetian way, while Gratiano's harmless ribaldry is tossed to the audience as an epilogue. Then he and Nerissa, now with less dignity than ever to lose, skip quickly after.

ACT-DIVISION AND STAGING

However well the First Folio's five-act rule may fit other plays, and whatever, in Elizabethan stage practice, division into five acts implied, there is ample evidence that *The Merchant of Venice* was meant to be played without an effective break. The scenes, and the padding in them, that give time for Portia and Nerissa to change clothes, are one sign of it. The first of these is padding unalloyed, and very poor padding at that. For the second, Shakespeare finds better and pleasanter excuse; but in part, at least, we owe that charming duet between Lorenzo and Jessica to this practical need.[16]

A case of a sort can be made out for the division in the Folio. Granted five acts, this fourth and fifth are manifest; the beginnings and finishings of the first three make useful milestones in the story, but others every bit as useful could be set up. It is worth noting that this act-division does nothing to elucidate the complex time-scheme of our anxious editors; but the Folio's expert play-divider would be no more bothered by that problem than Shakespeare had been. Nor was he concerned to end his acts memorably; the second leaves Aragon in our minds and the third ends with Jessica and Lorenzo's and the play's worst scene.[17] There might, however, be good enough reason in the Elizabethan theater for making an act's first scene arresting and for letting its last tail away; for they had, of course, no curtain to lower upon a climax, and after an interval interest would need quick rekindling. No producer today, one hopes, will want to lower a picture-stage curtain at such points. Nor, if he is wise, while his stories are working to their joint crisis will he give us pause to think by what strange leaps in time and space they travel.

But surely there are many signs that—however, for convenience sake, it is to be acted, with or without pause—Shakespeare has conceived and constructed the play indivisibly. There is the alternating between Venice and Belmont, and the spinning-out of the Portia story to fit with the other; neither device gains by or countenances act-division. There is the unhesitating sweep of the action up to the trial-scene, and indeed beyond it. One can parcel it up in various ways—the Folio's and half a dozen others—and on various pleas; but will any one of them make the story clearer; will it not, on the contrary, do something to disclose its confusions? Prose and blank verse, rhymed couplets and a quatrain are used indifferently for tags; so these form no consistent punctuation. There is no scene, not even the trial-scene, that ends with a full close, until the play ends. There is, in fact, no inherent, no dramatic pause in the action at all; nor can any be made which will not be rather hindrance than help to a performance.

Well-paced acting will take the play straight through in the traditional, vague two hours. But if, for the weakness of the flesh, there must be pauses, division into three parts will be a little less awkward than into two. If you do not stop before the trial-scene you cannot, of course, stop at all; the play will be virtually over. You may reasonably pause at the end of the Folio's Act III. This alone, though, will make very unequal division. For an earlier pause, the moment of Bassanio's departure from Venice will serve.[18] This splits the first three acts of the Folio all but exactly in two. Delay the pause another scene and we shall have done with Morocco. The second part would then begin with the tale of how Shylock took his loss and our first news of Antonio's losses, and would develop this interest till the eve of the trial. Incidentally it would hold all the inordinate time-telescoping; a helpful quickening, this, to its pulse. But these divisions and the choice of them have no other validity than convenience; the play must be thought of as an integral whole.

Needless to say that the confusion of scene-divisions in most modern editions (a very riot of it when Jessica is eloping) is not Shakespeare's; nor is the expert of the Folio responsible, nor even Rowe, who contents himself with marking the moves from Venice to Belmont and back. [19] For a century editors disputed as to when *Venice, a street,* shifted to *A room in Shylock's house,* or to *Another street,* or to *Before Shylock's house,* and chopped up the action and checked its impetus, when one glance at Shakespeare's stage, its doors and balcony and traverses, shows with what swift unity the play and its playing flow on. And whatever picturing of Venice and Belmont a producer may design, this swift-flowing unity he must on no account obstruct. Let that be clear.

But there is little difficulty in the play's production, once its form is recognized, its temper felt, the tune of its verse and the rhythm of its prose rightly caught. The text is very free from errors, there are no puzzles in the actual stagecraft. The music may come from Elizabethan stock, and the costuming is obvious. Nothing is needed but perception and good taste, and from the actors, acting.

NOTES

1. If the effect is one and the same, one might think the question unimportant. But Daniel, making out his three months, is generous of "intervals," not only between acts, but between scenes; and even Furness, on his subtler scent, can say, "One is always conscious that between the acts of a play a certain space of time elapses. To convey this impression is one of the purposes for which a drama is divided into acts." Therefore an important and a much-disputed question is involved—and begged. And, in practice, the pernicious hanging-up of performances by these pauses is encouraged, to which scenery and its shifting is already a sufficient temptation.

2. See also Preface to *Antony and Cleopatra*.

3. It is, one may say, a commonplace of stagecraft, Elizabethan or other; but none the less worthy for that.

4. And such interest as there is in Aragon's scene is now lessened, perhaps, by our knowledge that Bassanio is on his way; even more, by the talk in the scene before of Antonio's misfortune. But Shakespeare, as his wont is, plucks some little advantage from the poverty of the business by capping Aragon's vapidity with the excitement of the news of Bassanio's arrival.

5. Though there are commentators who maintain that Nerissa—even Portia, perhaps—gives Bassanio the hint to choose lead, or has it sung to him:

> Tell me, where is fancy *bred*,
> In the heart, or in the *head*?
> How begot, how *nourished*?

And if he'll only listen carefully he will note that they all rhyme with *lead*.

Shakespeare was surely of a simpler mind than this—his audiences too. And he had some slight sense of the fitness of things. Would he—how *could* he?—wind up this innocent fairy tale with such a slim trick? Besides, how was it to be worked; how is an audience to be let into the secret? Are they likely to tag extra rhymes to the words of a song as they listen to it? Or is Nerissa —not Portia, surely!—at some point to tip Bassanio "the wink" while he smiles knowingly back to assure her that he has "cottoned on"? Where, oh, where indeed, are such dramatic fancies bred? Not in any head that will think out the effect of their realization.

6. Little to be found in him, upon analysis, to refute the frigid verdict lately passed upon him by that distinguished and enlightened—but in this instance, surely, most mistakenly whimsical—critic, Sir Arthur Quiller-Couch, of fortune-hunter, hypocrite and worse. Is anything more certain than that Shakespeare did not *mean* to present us with such a hero? If Sir Arthur were producing the play, one pities the actor asked to give effect to his verdict.

7. Possible extra time was needed for the shifting of the caskets and their furniture and the setting of the chairs of state for the Duke and the Magnificoes. But in that case these last must have been very elaborate.

8. For the bearing of this upon the question of act-division, see p. 66.

9. But Rosencrantz and Guildenstern, as Shakespeare wrote them, are not the mere puppets that the usual mangling of the text leaves them.

10. It is worth remarking that the word "sad," as Shakespeare uses it, may mean rather solemn and serious than definitely miserable.

11. This is one of the ever-recurring small strokes of stagecraft that are hardly appreciable apart from an Elizabethan stage. Shylock and Bassanio are to the front of the platform. Antonio, near the door, is by convention any convenient distance off; by impression, too, with no realistic scenery to destroy

the impression. Shylock is left isolated, so isolated that the long aside has all the importance and the force of a soliloquy.

12. And so strange has this seemed to many a producer of the play and actor of Shylock, that we have been given scenes of pantomime in which Shylock comes back from Bassanio's supper to find Jessica flown. The solitary figure with a lantern, the unanswered rapping at the door, has become all but traditional. Irving did it, Coghlan had already done something of the sort, and—I fancy—Booth. An ingenious variation upon a theme by Shakespeare, that yet merely enfeebles the theme. The lengthier elaboration of a Shylock seen distracted at the discovery of his loss is, of course, even more inadmissible, since Shakespeare has deliberately avoided the situation.

13. Upon the modern stage he usually has Tubal for a companion; one has even seen him seconded by a small crowd of sympathetic Jews. How any producer can bring himself so to discount the poignant sight of that drab, heroic figure, lonely amid the magnificence around, passes understanding!

14. See Furness for an elaborate, illuminating and witty comment upon the situation.

15. It is hard to see why Antonio's taking the money to pass on to "the gentleman that lately stole his daughter" and providing that, for his half-pardon "he presently become a Christian," should be so reprobated by some critics. If we have less confidence today than had Antonio in the efficacy of baptism, have we none left in the rightfulness of reparation? Not much in its efficacy, perhaps. Antonio, one must insist, does not mean to keep any of the money for himself. One hopes he never lapsed into self-righteousness in recalling this. Nothing is said, however, about the original three thousand ducats!

16. The two scenes are, to a line, of the same length. Add to the one the opening of the trial-scene, and to the other, for safety's sake, twenty bars or so of music, and we have the time allotted for the change of costume.

17. Furness sees dramatic point in the second act ending with Bassanio on the doorstep. I suggest that Nerissa's tag is meant to keep Belmont a little in our minds during the strenuous scene between Shylock and Tubal which follows; but that, if anything, it tells against an act-pause falling here, rather than for it.

18. There is, as we have seen, a possible contracting of the action here that gives a summariness to the last few lines and suggests (to the modern ear, truly) a "curtain."

19. Lord Lansdowne's Jew held the stage in Rowe's time; and for this reason, it may just possibly be, he does not trouble to bring the play into closer relation with his own theater.

Caroline F E. Spurgeon

THE IMAGERY OF *ROMEO AND JULIET*

IT HAS NOT, so far as I know, ever yet been noticed that recurrent images play a part in raising, developing, sustaining, and repeating emotion in the tragedies, which is somewhat analogous to the action of a recurrent theme or "motif" in a musical fugue or sonata, or in one of Wagner's operas.

Perhaps, however, a more exact analogy to the function of Shakespeare's images in this respect is the unique work of another great artist, of the peculiar quality of which they constantly remind one, that is, Blake's illustrations to his prophetic books. These are not, for the most part, illustrations in the ordinary sense of the term, the translation by the artist of some incident in the narrative into a visual picture; they are rather a running accompaniment to the words in another medium, sometimes symbolically emphasizing or interpreting certain aspects of the thought, sometimes supplying frankly only decoration or atmosphere, sometimes grotesque and even repellent, vivid, strange, arresting, sometimes drawn with an almost unearthly beauty of form and colour. Thus, as the leaping tongues of flame which illuminate the pages of *The Marriage of Heaven and Hell* show the visual form which Blake's thought evoked in his mind, and symbolize for us the purity, the beauty, and the two-edged quality of life and danger in his words, so the recurrent images in *Macbeth* or *Hamlet* reveal the dominant picture or sensation—and for Shakespeare the two are identical—in terms of which he sees and feels the main problem or theme

From *Leading Motives in the Imagery of Shakespeare's Tragedies*, paragraphs 1-17. The Shakespeare Association Lecture for 1930. Reprinted by permission of the Association and the Clarendon Press, Oxford.

of the play, thus giving us an unerring clue to the way he looked at it, as well as a direct glimpse into the working of his mind and imagination.

These dominating images are a characteristic of Shakespeare's work throughout, but whereas in the earlier plays they are often rather obvious and of set design, taken over in some cases with the story itself from a hint in the original narrative; in the later plays, and especially in the great tragedies, they are born of the emotions of the theme, and are, as in *Macbeth*, subtle, complex, varied, but intensely vivid and revealing; or as in *Lear*, so constant and all-pervading as to be reiterated, not only in the word-pictures, but also in the single words themselves.

Any reader, of course, must be aware of certain recurrent symbolic imagery in Shakespeare, such as that of a tree and its branches, and of planting, lopping, or rooting up, which runs through the English historical plays; they are conscious of the imaginative effect of the animal imagery in *Lear*, or of the flash of explosives in *Romeo and Juliet*, but it was not until the last few years, when in the course of an intensive study of Shakespeare's imagery I had listed and classified and card-indexed and counted every image in every play thrice over, that the actual facts as to these dominating pictures stared me in the face.

I found that there is a certain range of images, and roughly a certain proportion of these, to be expected in every play, and that certain familiar categories, of nature, animals, and what one may call "everyday" or "domestic," easily come first. But in addition to this normal grouping, I have found, especially in the tragedies, certain groups of images which, as it were, stick out in each particular play and immediately attract attention because they are peculiar either in subject or quantity, or both.

These seem to form the floating image or images in Shakespeare's mind called forth by that particular play, and I propose now, as briefly as possible, just to look at the tragedies from the point of view of these groups of images only.

In *Romeo and Juliet* the beauty and ardour of young love is seen by Shakespeare as the irradiating glory of sunlight and starlight in a dark world. The dominating image is *light*, every form and manifestation of it; the sun, moon, stars, fire, lightning, the flash of gunpowder, and the reflected light of beauty and of love; while by contrast we have night, darkness, clouds, rain, mist, and smoke.

Each of the lovers thinks of the other as light; Romeo's overpowering impression when he first catches sight of Juliet on the fateful evening at the Capulets' ball is seen in his exclamation,

> O, she doth teach the torches to burn bright!

To Juliet, Romeo, is "day in night"; to Romeo, Juliet is the sun rising from the east, and when they soar to love's ecstasy, each alike pictures the other as stars in heaven, shedding such brightness as puts to shame the heavenly bodies themselves.

The intensity of feeling in both lovers purges even the most highly affected and euphuistic conceits of their artificiality, and transforms them into the exquisite and passionate expression of love's rhapsody.

Thus Romeo plays with the old conceit that two of the fairest stars in heaven, having some business on earth, have entreated Juliet's eyes to take their place till they return, and he conjectures,

> What if her eyes were there, they in her head?

If so,

> The brightness of her cheek would shame those stars,
> As day-light doth a lamp:

and then comes the rush of feeling, the overpowering realization and immortal expression of the transforming glory of love,

>   her eyes in heaven
> Would through the airy region stream so bright
> That birds would sing and think it were not night.

And Juliet, in her invocation to night, using an even more extravagant conceit such as Cowley or Cleveland at his wildest never exceeded, transmutes it into the perfect and natural expression of a girl whose lover to her not only radiates light but is, indeed, very light itself:

> Give me my Romeo; and, when he shall die,
> Take him and cut him out in little stars,

> And he will make the face of heaven so fine,
> That all the world will be in love with night,
> And pay no worship to the garish sun.

Love is described by Romeo, before he knows what it really is, as

> a smoke raised with the fume of sighs;
> Being purged, a fire sparkling in lovers' eyes;

and the messengers of love are seen by Juliet, when she is chafing under the nurse's delay, as one of the most exquisite effects in nature, especially on the English hills in spring, of the swift, magical, transforming power of light; "love's heralds," she cries, "should be thoughts,

> Which ten times faster glide than the sun's beams,
> Driving back shadows over louring hills."

The irradiating quality of the beauty of love is noticed by both lovers; by Juliet in her first ecstasy, when she declares that lovers' "own beauties" are sufficient light for them to see by, and at the end by Romeo, when, thinking her dead, he gazes on her and cries

> her beauty makes
> This vault a feasting presence full of light.

There can be no question, I think, that Shakespeare saw the story, in its swift and tragic beauty, as an almost blinding flash of light, suddenly ignited and as swiftly quenched. He quite deliberately compresses the action from over nine months to the almost incredibly short period of five days; so that the lovers meet on Sunday, are wedded on Monday, part at dawn on Tuesday, and are reunited in death on the night of Thursday. The sensation of swiftness and brilliance, accompanied by danger and destruction, is accentuated again and again; by Juliet when she avows their bethrothal

> is too rash, too unadvised, too sudden,
> Too like the lightning, which doth cease to be
> Ere one can say 'It lightens';

and by Romeo and the Friar, who instinctively make repeated
use of the image of the quick destructive flash of gunpowder
(III. iii. 103, 132; v. i. 63). Indeed the Friar, in his well-known
answer to Romeo's prayer for instant marriage, succinctly, in the
last nine words, sums up the whole movement of the play,

> These violent delights have violent ends,
> And in their triumph die; like fire and powder
> Which as they kiss consume.

Even old Capulet, whom one does not think of as a poetical person, though he uses many images—some of great beauty—carries
on the idea of light to represent love and youth and beauty, and
of the clouding of the sun for grief and sorrow. He promises
Paris that on the evening of the ball he shall see at his house

> Earth-treading stars that make dark heaven light,

and when he encounters Juliet weeping, as he thinks for her
cousin Tybalt's death, he clothes his comment in similar nature-
imagery of light quenched in darkness,

> When the sun sets, the air doth drizzle dew;
> But for the sunset of my brother's son
> It rains downright.

In addition to this more definite symbolic imagery we find that
radiant light, sunshine, starlight, moonbeams, sunrise and sunset, the sparkle of fire, a meteor, candles, torches, quick-coming
darkness, clouds, mist, rain, and night, form a pictorial background or running accompaniment to the play, which augments
unconsciously in us this same sensation.

We meet it at once in the Prince's description of the attitude
of the rival houses

> That quench the fire of your pernicious rage
> With purple fountains issuing from your veins;

and later, in the talk of Benvolio and Montagu about the rising
sun, the dew, and clouds (I. i. 117-18, 130-36), followed by
Romeo's definition of love (I. i. 189-90), Capulet's words just
quoted, Benvolio's riming proverb about fire (I. ii. 46), the talk
of Romeo and Mercutio about torches, candles, lights, and lamps

(I. iv. 35-45), the flashing lights and torches of the ball, four times accentuated (I. v. 28, 45, 88, 126), Romeo's conception of Juliet as a "bright angel," "as glorious to this night"

> As is a winged messenger of heaven;

the moonlight in the orchard, the sunrise Friar Lawrence watches from his cell, the sun clearing from heaven Romeo's sighs (II. iii. 73), the exquisite light and shadow swiftly chasing over Juliet's words in the orchard (II. v. 4-11), the "black fate" of the day on which Mercutio was killed, the "fire-eyed fury" which leads Romeo to challenge Tybalt, their fight, to which they go "like lightning," the sunset which Juliet so ardently desires to be swift "and bring in cloudy night immediately," the exquisite play of quivering light from darkness through dawn, till

> jocund day
> Stands tip-toe on the misty mountain tops,

which forms the theme of the lovers' parting song; and at the last, Romeo's anguished reply to Juliet, pointing the contrast between the coming day and their own great sorrow,

> More light and light: more dark and dark our woes!

And then at the end we see the darkness of the churchyard, lit by the glittering torch of Paris, quickly quenched; Romeo's arrival with his torch, the swift fight and death, the dark vault, which is not a grave but a lantern irradiated by Juliet's beauty, Romeo's grim jest on the "lightning before death," followed immediately by the self-slaughter of the "star-crossed" lovers, the gathering together of the stricken mourners as the day breaks, and the "glooming" peace of the overcast morning when

> The sun for sorrow will not show his head.

Shakespeare's extraordinary susceptibility to suggestion and readiness to borrow is well exemplified in this running imagery. He took the idea from the last place we should expect, from the wooden doggerel of Arthur Brooke, and the germ of it is in the sing-song line in which Brooke describes the attitude of the lovers,

> For each of them to other is as to the world the sun.

Their mutual feeling and the feud of the families is constantly referred to by Brooke as "fire" or "flame"; in the beginning, he speaks of the feud as a "mighty fire"; the families "bathe in blood of smarting wounds," and the Prince hopes he may "quench the sparks that burned within their breast." These three images are combined and unified by Shakespeare in the two lines already quoted (ɪ. i. 83-4).

Other suggestions also come from Brooke, such as the emphasis on the bright light of the torches at the ball; and Romeo's first sight of Juliet, which is a "sudden kindled fire"; her first impression of him when he

> in her sight did seem to pass the rest as far
> As Phoebus' shining beams do pass the brightness of a star;

and his description in his first talk to her, of the

> quick sparks and glowing furious glead
> . . . from your beauty's pleasant eyne, Love caused to
> proceed
> Which have so set on fire each feeling part of mine
> That lo, my mind doth melt away, my outward parts do
> pine,

which is transmuted to the delightful image of the stars which have changed places with her eyes (ɪɪ. ii. 15-22).

But although Shakespeare took the idea from his original it scarcely needs saying that, in taking it, he has transformed a few conventional and obvious similes of little poetic worth into a continuous and consistent running image of exquisite beauty, building up a definite picture and atmosphere of brilliance swiftly quenched, which powerfully affects the imagination of the reader.

Northrop Frye

THE ARGUMENT OF COMEDY

THE GREEKS produced two kinds of comedy, Old Comedy, represented by the eleven extant plays of Aristophanes, and New Comedy, of which the best known exponent is Menander. About two dozen New Comedies survive in the work of Plautus and Terence. Old Comedy, however, was out of date before Aristophanes himself was dead; and today, when we speak of comedy, we normally think of something that derives from the Menandrine tradition.

New Comedy unfolds from what may be described as a comic Oedipus situation. Its main theme is the successful effort of a young man to outwit an opponent and possess the girl of his choice. The opponent is usually the father (*senex*), and the psychological descent of the heroine from the mother is also sometimes hinted at. The father frequently wants the same girl, and is cheated out of her by the son, the mother thus becoming the son's ally. The girl is usually a slave or courtesan, and the plot turns on a *cognitio* or discovery of birth which makes her marriageable. Thus it turns out that she is not under an insuperable taboo after all but is an accessible object of desire, so that the plot follows the regular wish-fulfillment pattern. Often the central Oedipus situation is thinly concealed by surrogates or doubles of the main characters, as when the heroine is discovered to be the hero's sister, and has to be married off to his best friend. In Congreve's *Love for Love*, to take a modern instance well within the Menandrine tradition, there are two Oedipus themes in

From *English Institute Essays, 1948,* 1949, pp. 58-73. Copyright 1949 by Columbia University Press. Reprinted by permission of the publisher.

counterpoint: the hero cheats his father out of the heroine, and his best friend violates the wife of an impotent old man who is the heroine's guardian. Whether this analysis is sound or not, New Comedy is certainly concerned with the maneuvering of a young man toward a young woman, and marriage is the tonic chord on which it ends. The normal comic resolution is the surrender of the *senex* to the hero, never the reverse. Shakespeare tried to reverse the pattern in *All's Well That Ends Well,* where the king of France forces Bertram to marry Helena, and the critics have not yet stopped making faces over it.

New Comedy has the blessing of Aristotle, who greatly preferred it to its predecessor, and it exhibits the general pattern of Aristotelian causation. It has a material cause in the young man's sexual desire, and a formal cause in the social order represented by the *senex,* with which the hero comes to terms when he gratifies his desire. It has an efficient cause in the character who brings about the final situation. In classical times this character is a tricky slave; Renaissance dramatists often use some adaptation of the medieval "vice"; modern writers generally like to pretend that nature, or at least the natural course of events, is the efficient cause. The final cause is the audience, which is expected by its applause to take part in the comic resolution. All this takes place on a single order of existence. The action of New Comedy tends to become probable rather than fantastic, and it moves toward realism and away from myth and romance. The one romantic (originally mythical) feature in it, the fact that the hero or heroine turns out to be freeborn or someone's heir, is precisely the feature that trained New Comedy audiences tire of most quickly.

The conventions of New Comedy are the conventions of Jonson and Molière, and a fortiori of the English Restoration and the French rococo. When Ibsen started giving ironic twists to the same formulas, his startled hearers took them for portents of a social revolution. Even the old chestnut about the heroine's being really the hero's sister turns up in *Ghosts* and *Little Eyolf.* The average movie of today is a rigidly conventionalized New Comedy proceeding toward an act which, like death in Greek tragedy, takes place offstage, and is symbolized by the final embrace.

In all good New Comedy there is a social as well as an individual theme which must be sought in the general atmosphere of reconciliation that makes the final marriage possible. As the hero gets closer to the heroine and opposition is overcome, all the right-thinking people come over to his side. Thus a new social unit is formed on the stage, and the moment that this social unit crystallizes is the moment of the comic resolution. In the last scene, when the dramatist usually tries to get all his characters on the stage at once, the audience witnesses the birth of a renewed sense of social integration. In comedy as in life the regular expression of this is a festival, whether a marriage, a dance, or a feast. Old Comedy has, besides a marriage, a *komos,* the processional dance from which comedy derives its name; and the masque, which is a by-form of comedy, also ends in a dance.

This new social integration may be called, first, a kind of moral norm and, second, the pattern of a free society. We can see this more clearly if we look at the sort of characters who impede the progress of the comedy toward the hero's victory. These are always people who are in some kind of mental bondage, who are helplessly driven by ruling passions, neurotic compulsions, social rituals, and selfishness. The miser, the hypochondriac, the hypocrite, the pedant, the snob: these are humors, people who do not fully know what they are doing, who are slaves to a predictable self-imposed pattern of behavior. What we call the moral norm is, then, not morality but deliverance from moral bondage. Comedy is designed not to condemn evil, but to ridicule a lack of self-knowledge. It finds the virtues of Malvolio and Angelo as comic as the vices of Shylock.

The essential comic resolution, therefore, is an individual release which is also a social reconciliation. The normal individual is freed from the bonds of a humorous society, and a normal society is freed from the bonds imposed on it by humorous individuals. The Oedipus pattern we noted in New Comedy belongs to the individual side of this, and the sense of the ridiculousness of the humor to the social side. But all real comedy is based on the principle that these two forms of release are ultimately the same: this principle may be seen at its most concentrated in *The Tempest.* The rule holds whether the resolution is expressed in social terms, as in *The Merchant of Venice*, or in individual terms, as in Ibsen's *An Enemy of the People*.

The freer the society, the greater the variety of individuals it can tolerate, and the natural tendency of comedy is to include as many as possible in its final festival. The motto of comedy is Terence's "Nothing human is alien to me." This may be one reason for the traditional comic importance of the parasite, who has no business to be at the festival but is nevertheless there. The spirit of reconciliation which pervades the comedies of Shakespeare is not to be ascribed to a personal attitude of his own, about which we know nothing whatever, but to his impersonal concentration on the laws of comic form.

Hence the moral quality of the society presented is not the point of the comic resolution. In Jonson's *Volpone* the final assertion of the moral norm takes the form of a social revenge on Volpone, and the play ends with a great bustle of sentences to penal servitude and the galleys. One feels perhaps that the audience's sense of the moral norm does not need so much hard labor. In *The Alchemist*, when Lovewit returns to his house, the virtuous characters have proved so weak and the rascals so ingenious that the action dissolves in laughter. Whichever is morally the better ending, that of *The Alchemist* is more concentrated comedy. *Volpone* is starting to move toward tragedy, toward the vision of a greatness which develops *hybris* and catastrophe.

The same principle is even clearer in Aristophanes. Aristophanes is the most personal of writers: his opinions on every subject are written all over his plays, and we have no doubt of his moral attitude. We know that he wanted peace with Sparta and that he hated Cleon, and when his comedy depicts the attaining of peace and the defeat of Cleon we know that he approved and wanted his audience to approve. But in *Ecclesiazusae* a band of women in disguise railroad a communistic scheme through the Assembly, which is a horrid parody of Plato's *Republic*, and proceed to inaugurate Plato's sexual communism with some astonishing improvements. Presumably Aristophanes did not applaud this, yet the comedy follows the same pattern and the same resolution. In *The Birds* the Peisthetairos who defies Zeus and blocks out Olympus with his Cloud-Cuckoo-

Land is accorded the same triumph that is given to the Trygaeus of the *Peace* who flies to heaven and brings a golden age back to Athens.

Comedy, then, may show virtue her own feature and scorn her own image—for Hamlet's famous definition of drama was originally a definition of comedy. It may emphasize the birth of an ideal society as you like it, or the tawdriness of the sham society which is the way of the world. There is an important parallel here with tragedy. Tragedy, we are told, is expected to raise but not ultimately to accept the emotions of pity and terror. These I take to be the sense of moral good and evil, respectively, which we attach to the tragic hero. He may be as good as Caesar, and so appeal to our pity, or as bad as Macbeth, and so appeal to terror, but the particular thing called tragedy that happens to him does not depend on his moral status. The tragic catharsis passes beyond moral judgment, and while it is quite possible to construct a moral tragedy, what tragedy gains in morality it loses in cathartic power. The same is true of the comic catharsis, which raises sympathy and ridicule on a moral basis, but passes beyond both.

Many things are involved in the tragic catharsis, but one of them is a mental or imaginative form of the sacrificial ritual out of which tragedy arose. This is the ritual of the struggle, death, and rebirth of a God-Man, which is linked to the yearly triumph of spring over winter. The tragic hero is not really killed, and the audience no longer eats his body and drinks his blood, but the corresponding thing in art still takes place. The audience enters into communion with the body of the hero, becoming thereby a single body itself. Comedy grows out of the same ritual, for in the ritual the tragic story has a comic sequel. Divine men do not die: they die and rise again. The ritual pattern behind the catharsis of comedy is the resurrection that follows the death, the epiphany or manifestation of the risen hero. This is clear enough in Aristophanes, where the hero is treated as a risen God-Man, led in triumph with the divine honors of the Olympic victor, rejuvenated, or hailed as a new Zeus. In New Comedy the new human body is, as we have seen, both a hero and a social group. Aristophanes is not only closer to the ritual pattern, but contemporary with Plato; and his comedy, unlike Menander's, is

Platonic and dialectic: it seeks not the entelechy of the soul but the Form of the Good, and finds it in the resurrection of the soul from the world of the cave to the sunlight. The audience gains a vision of that resurrection whether the conclusion is joyful or ironic, just as in tragedy it gains a vision of a heroic death whether the hero is morally innocent or guilty.

Two things follow from this: first, that tragedy is really implicit or uncompleted comedy; second, that comedy contains a potential tragedy within itself. With regard to the latter, Aristophanes is full of traces of the original death of the hero which preceded his resurrection in the ritual. Even in New Comedy the dramatist usually tries to bring his action as close to a tragic overthrow of the hero as he can get it, and reverses this movement as suddenly as possible. In Plautus the tricky slave is often forgiven or even freed after having been threatened with all the brutalities that a very brutal dramatist can think of, including crucifixion. Thus the resolution of New Comedy seems to be a realistic foreshortening of a death-and-resurrection pattern, in which the struggle and rebirth of a divine hero has shrunk into a marriage, the freeing of a slave, and the triumph of a young man over an older one.

As for the conception of tragedy as implicit comedy, we may notice how often tragedy closes on the major chord of comedy: the Aeschylean trilogy, for instance, proceeds to what is really a comic resolution, and so do many tragedies of Euripides. From the point of view of Christianity, too, tragedy is an episode in that larger scheme of redemption and resurrection to which Dante gave the name of *commedia*. This conception of *commedia* enters drama with the miracle-play cycles, where such tragedies as the Fall and the Crucifixion are episodes of a dramatic scheme in which the divine comedy has the last word. The sense of tragedy as a prelude to comedy is hardly separable from anything explicitly Christian. The serenity of the final double chorus in the St. Matthew Passion would hardly be attainable if composer and audience did not know that there was more to the story. Nor would the death of Samson lead to "calm of mind all passion spent" if Samson were not a prototype of the rising Christ.

New Comedy is thus contained, so to speak, within the symbolic structure of Old Comedy, which in its turn is contained within the Christian conception of *commedia*. This sounds like a logically exhaustive classification, but we have still not caught Shakespeare in it.

It is only in Jonson and the Restoration writers that English comedy can be called a form of New Comedy. The earlier tradition established by Peele and developed by Lyly, Greene, and the masque writers, which uses themes from romance and folklore and avoids the comedy of manners, is the one followed by Shakespeare. These themes are largely medieval in origin, and derive, not from the mysteries or the moralities or the interludes, but from a fourth dramatic tradition. This is the drama of folk ritual, of the St. George play and the mummers' play, of the feast of the ass and the Boy Bishop, and of all the dramatic activity that punctuated the Christian calendar with the rituals of an immemorial paganism. We may call this the drama of the green world, and its theme is once again the triumph of life over the waste land, the death and revival of the year impersonated by figures still human, and once divine as well.

When Shakespeare began to study Plautus and Terence, his dramatic instinct, stimulated by his predecessors, divined that there was a profounder pattern in the argument of comedy than appears in either of them. At once—for the process is beginning in *The Comedy of Errors*—he started groping toward that profounder pattern, the ritual of death and revival that also underlies Aristophanes, of which an exact equivalent lay ready to hand in the drama of the green world. This parallelism largely accounts for the resemblances to Greek ritual which Colin Still has pointed out in *The Tempest*.

The Two Gentlemen of Verona is an orthodox New Comedy except for one thing. The hero Valentine becomes captain of a band of outlaws in a forest, and all the other characters are gathered into this forest and become converted. Thus the action of the comedy begins in a world represented as a normal world, moves into the green world, goes into a metamorphosis there in which the comic resolution is achieved, and returns to the normal world. The forest in this play is the embryonic form of the fairy world of *A Midsummer Night's Dream*, the Forest of Arden in *As You Like It*, Windsor Forest in *The Merry Wives of Windsor*, and the pastoral world of the mythical sea-coasted Bohemia in *The Winter's Tale*. In all these comedies there is the same rhythmic movement from normal world to green world and back again. Nor is this second world confined to the forest comedies. In *The Merchant of Venice* the two worlds are a little harder to see, yet Venice is clearly not the same world as that of Portia's mysterious house in Belmont, where there are caskets teaching that gold and silver are corruptible goods, and from whence proceed the wonderful cosmological harmonies of the fifth act. In *The Tempest* the entire action takes place in the second world, and the same may be said of *Twelfth Night*, which, as its title implies, presents a carnival society, not so much a green world as an evergreen one. The second world is absent from the so-called problem comedies, which is one of the things that makes them problem comedies.

The green world charges the comedies with a symbolism in which the comic resolution contains a suggestion of the old ritual pattern of the victory of summer over winter. This is explicit in *Love's Labour's Lost*. In this very masque-like play, the comic contest takes the form of the medieval debate of winter and spring. In *The Merry Wives of Windsor* there is an elaborate ritual of the defeat of winter, known to folklorists as "carrying out Death," of which Falstaff is the victim; and Falstaff must have felt that, after being thrown into the water, dressed up as a witch and beaten out of a house with curses, and finally supplied with a beast's head and singed with candles while he said, "Divide me like a brib'd buck, each a haunch," he had done about all that could reasonably be asked of any fertility spirit.

The association of this symbolism with the death and revival of human beings is more elusive, but still perceptible. The fact that the heroine often brings about the comic resolution by disguising herself as a boy is familiar enough. In the Hero of *Much Ado About Nothing* and the Helena of *All's Well That Ends Well*, this theme of the withdrawal and return of the heroine comes as close to a death and revival as Elizabethan conventions will allow. The Thaisa of *Pericles* and the Fidele of *Cymbeline* are beginning to crack the conventions, and with the disappearance and revival of Hermione in *The Winter's Tale*, who actually returns once as a ghost in a dream, the original nature-myth of

Demeter and Proserpine is openly established. The fact that the dying and reviving character is usually female strengthens the feeling that there is something maternal about the green world, in which the new order of the comic resolution is nourished and brought to birth. However, a similar theme which is very like the rejuvenation of the *senex* so frequent in Aristophanes occurs in the folklore motif of the healing of the impotent king on which *All's Well That Ends Well* is based, and this theme is probably involved in the symbolism of Prospero.

The conception of a second world bursts the boundaries of Menandrine comedy, yet it is clear that the world of Puck is no world of eternal forms or divine revelation. Shakespeare's comedy is not Aristotelian and realistic like Menander's, nor Platonic and dialectic like Aristophanes', nor Thomist and sacramental like Dante's, but a fourth kind. It is an Elizabethan kind, and is not confined either to Shakespeare or to the drama. Spenser's epic is a wonderful contrapuntal intermingling of two orders of existence, one the red and white world of English history, the other the green world of the Faerie Queene. The latter is a world of crusading virtues proceeding from the Faerie Queene's court and designed to return to that court when the destiny of the other world is fulfilled. The fact that the Faerie Queene's knights are sent out during the twelve days of the Christmas festival suggests our next point.

Shakespeare too has his green world of comedy and his red and white world of history. The story of the latter is at one point interrupted by an invasion from the comic world, when Falstaff *senex et parasitus* throws his gigantic shadow over Prince Henry, assuming on one occasion the role of his father. Clearly, if the Prince is ever to conquer France he must reassert the moral norm. The moral norm is duly reasserted, but the rejection of Falstaff is not a comic resolution. In comedy the moral norm is not morality but deliverance, and we certainly do not feel delivered from Falstaff as we feel delivered from Shylock with his absurd and vicious bond. The moral norm does not carry with it the vision of a free society: Falstaff will always keep a bit of that in his tavern.

Falstaff is a mock king, a lord of misrule, and his tavern is a Saturnalia. Yet we are reminded of the original meaning of the

Saturnalia, as a rite intended to recall the golden age of Saturn. Falstaff's world is not a golden world, but as long as we remember it we cannot forget that the world of *Henry V* is an iron one. We are reminded too of another traditional denizen of the green world, Robin Hood, the outlaw who manages to suggest a better kind of society than those who make him an outlaw can produce. The outlaws in *The Two Gentlemen of Verona* compare themselves, in spite of the Italian setting, to Robin Hood, and in *As You Like It* Charles the wrestler says of Duke Senior's followers: "There they live like the old Robin Hood of England: they say many young gentlemen flock to him every day, and fleet the time carelessly, as they did in the golden world."

In the histories, therefore, the comic Saturnalia is a temporary reversal of normal standards, comic "relief" as it is called, which subsides and allows the history to continue. In the comedies, the green world suggests an original golden age which the normal world has usurped and which makes us wonder if it is not the normal world that is the real Saturnalia. In *Cymbeline* the green world finally triumphs over a historical theme, the reason being perhaps that in that play the incarnation of Christ, which is contemporary with Cymbeline, takes place offstage, and accounts for the halcyon peace with which the play concludes. From then on in Shakespeare's plays, the green world has it all its own way, and both in *Cymbeline* and in *Henry VIII* there may be suggestions that Shakespeare, like Spenser, is moving toward a synthesis of the two worlds, a wedding of Prince Arthur and the Faerie Queene.

This world of fairies, dreams, disembodied souls, and pastoral lovers may not be a "real" world, but, if not, there is something equally illusory in the stumbling and blinded follies of the "normal" world, of Theseus' Athens with its idiotic marriage law, of Duke Frederick and his melancholy tyranny, of Leontes and his mad jealousy, of the Court Party with their plots and intrigues. The famous speech of Prospero about the dream nature of reality applies equally to Milan and the enchanted island. We spend our lives partly in a waking world we call normal and partly in a dream world which we create out of our own desires. Shakespeare endows both worlds with equal imaginative power, brings them opposite one another, and makes each world seem

unreal when seen by the light of the other. He uses freely both
the heroic triumph of New Comedy and the ritual resurrection of
its predecessor, but his distinctive comic resolution is different
from either: it is a detachment of the spirit born of this reciprocal
reflecton of two illusory realities. We need not ask whether this
brings us into a higher order of existence or not, for the question
of existence is not relevant to poetry.

We have spoken of New Comedy as Aristotelian, Old Comedy
as Platonic and Dante's *commedia* as Thomist, but it is difficult
to suggest a philosophical spokesman for the form of Shakespeare's comedy. For Shakespeare, the subject matter of poetry
is not life, or nature, or reality, or revelation, or anything else
that the philosopher builds on, but poetry itself, a verbal universe. That is one reason why he is both the most elusive and the
most substantial of poets.

G. K. Hunter

A MIDSUMMER-NIGHT'S DREAM

EACH OF Shakespeare's plays is a unique organism, as unique as
an individual human being; but a number of them share common elements, and it is a convenience of exposition to dispose
of the common elements before discussing the individual variations. This is an especial convenience in a work as short as this
present; but with the four plays before us it involves certain dis-
advantages, and I should mention these. The plays in the present
pamphlet do not hang together as inseparables: three of them—
Much Ado About Nothing, As You Like It, and *Twelfth Night*—
are normally placed in contiguous years of composition (1598-
1600), and are often taken together by criticism to represent the
peak of Shakespeare's achievement as a comic dramatist; but the
perspective drawn by this very tenable view of these plays is
unfair to the fourth play on our list—*A Midsummer-Night's
Dream,* which is also a great comic drama, but of a very different kind, and of a distinct date (1594/5).

If we wish to define the particular kind of excellence that
reaches definitive form in *Much Ado, As You Like It,* and
Twelfth Night, and then passes away, then we have to speak of
these plays as comedies of love. The common element in the different achievements is the power to realize love as a force making for proper happiness and reconciliation over a wide area of
human experience, and as a spectrum which shows sanity and
eccentricity in their social setting. In these comedies, to an extent beyond that of any other comic tradition in Europe (Aristophanes, Plautus, Ben Jonson, Molière, Wilde, Shaw), we *share*

From *Shakespeare: The Later Comedies,* Writers and Their
Works, No. 143, Longmans, Green & Co. Ltd., 1962, pp. 7-20. Copyright © 1962 by G. K. Hunter. Reprinted by permission.

a sense of the absurdity of love with characters who know their own absurdity, and whose success we desire. The ideal of social balance and reconciliation (which all comedies share) is realized here in the power to live with one's own absurdity, with ease and with confidence.

Shakespeare's concern for this mode of comic vision could be shown by a detailed comparison of his plays and their source material, but there is not space for this. One must state, however, that the "comedy of love" as manifested in these three plays is an individual creation; even in Shakespeare's own earlier comedies, love is only one of several modes of reconciling the major characters. In *The Comedy of Errors* the relationship of the individual to the family group is far more important than sexual love. In *The Taming of the Shrew*, wifely obedience (not quite the same thing as love) provides the focus; even in *Two Gentlemen of Verona* the reconciliation of friends is at least as important as the fulfilment of love in marriage. *A Midsummer-Night's Dream* is probably best grouped with these plays, and with *Love's Labour's Lost*; it holds together with unique delicacy of balance the variety of experience which they contain—love, clownishness, obedience to husband or to parent, friendship, woodland romance, sophistication in the court, and royalty of nature—and it is like them (and unlike the later comedies) in seeking to reconcile, without judging, the comparative merits of the different worlds that are shown. *A Midsummer-Night's Dream* is best seen, in fact, as a lyric divertissement, or a suite of dances—gay, sober, stately, absurd. Shakespeare has lavished his art on the separate excellencies of the different parts, but has not sought to show them growing out of one another in a process analogous to that of symphonic "development." The play is centred on Love, but it moves by exposing the varieties of love, rather than by working them against one another in a process of argument. This is probably another way of saying that the plan contains no personalities, no figures like Beatrice, Rosalind or Olivia, who, being self-aware, are also self-correcting; on the whole, the characters remain fixed in their attitudes; those who change, like Demetrius, Lysander and Titania, are lifted bodily, without conflict of character, and without volition, from one attitude to another. In the case of Titania, the induced passion for Bottom im-

prisons her but does not infringe her dignity; she can change back
without loss of face; in the case of the lovers, the change must be
preserved, to complete the pattern, and is accepted in those terms;
it is this pattern, not the individuals who compose it, that is the
play's concern:

> When they next wake, all this derision
> Shall seem a dream and fruitless vision;
> And back to Athens shall the lovers wend,
> With league whose date till death shall never end.[1]
>
> (III. ii. 370-73)

Shakespeare has, of course, made some rudimentary distinctions between the lovers, and these are sometimes seized upon
as important clues to his conception of their "characters": Helena
is taller and Hermia more shrewish; but these are, in fact, only
"odorous" comparisons to be thrown around in argument, not
important traits, with consequences in action. Puck is told,
"Thou shalt know the man By the Athenian garments he hath
on" (II. i. 263-4); this is a fair enough description of either lover;
we should beware of adding to it. As far as the play is concerned,
the lovers are like dancers who change partners in the middle of
a figure; the point at which partners are exchanged is determined
by the dance, the pattern, and not by the psychological state of
the dancers:

> But, my good lord, I wot not by what power—
> But by some power it is—my love to Hermia,
> Melted as the snow, seems to me now
> As the remembrance of an idle gaud
> Which in my childhood I did dote upon;
> And all the faith, the virtue of my heart,
> The object and the pleasure of mine eye,
> Is only Helena.
>
> (IV. i. 161-8)

The pattern of the dance is what matters, and the pattern is
one which works through an alternation of errors, trying out all
possible combinations of persons: Helena in love with Demetrius,
Demetrius in love with Hermia, Hermia in love with Lysander,
and then (change partners) Hermia in love with Lysander, Ly-

sander in love with Helena, Helena in love with Demetrius,
Demetrius in love with Hermia—but this is worse, so change
again: Hermia in love with Lysander, Lysander in love with
Helena, Helena in love with Demetrius, but completely at a loss
when Demetrius seems to be pretending to return her love;
finally we settle on the only stable arrangement, where no-one is
left out:

> That every man should take his own
> In your waking shall be shown:
> > Jack shall have Jill;
> > Nought shall go ill;
> The man shall have his mare again, and all shall be well.
> > > > (III. ii. 459-63)

The naivety of these "country proverb" lines sums up the kind of
world which Shakespeare has tried to create for his Athenian
lovers: a world in which the country superstitions of May Day
or Midsummer Eve (when maidens are supposed to dream of
the man they will marry), together with the traditional figure of
Robin Goodfellow, the Puck, are used to give body and background to the adolescent and unserious (but socially accepted
and necessary) process of "pairing off."

The dance is a dance of emotions, but the emotions are not
subjected to anything like a psychological analysis; Shakespeare
limits our response by showing us the lovers as the mere puppets
of the fairies. They act on their emotions, but what is action to
them is only "an act" to those who (invisible themselves) watch,
manipulate and comment:

> > Shall we their fond pageant see?
> > Lord, what fools these mortals be!
> > > (III. ii. 114-15)

The verse itself helps to "distance" the scenes of the lovers'
cross-purposes. Many critics have objected to verse like the following:

> *Helena.* . . . But who is here? Lysander! on the ground!
> Dead? or asleep? I see no blood, no wound.
> Lysander, if you live, good sir, awake.

Lys. And run through fire I will for thy sweet sake.
Transparent Helena! Nature shows art,
That through thy bosom makes me see thy heart.
Where is Demetrius? O, how fit a word
Is that vile name to perish on my sword!
   Hel. Do not say so, Lysander; say not so.
What though he love your Hermia? Lord, what though?
Yet Hermia still loves you; then be content.
   Lys. Content with Hermia! No; I do not repent
The tedious minutes I with her have spent.
Not Hermia but Helena I love:
Who will not change a raven for a dove?

(II. ii. 100-114)

This is certainly not an exchange one would wish to anthologize
in "Great Moments with the Bard," but it does perfectly what the
play requires it to do. It reduces the passions to a comic level
where we do not feel called upon to share them; but it remains
poetic and charming, and there is no difficulty in distinguishing
the comedy of this scene from the farce of the Pyramus and
Thisbe play.

Seen against the fairies, the lovers are absurd; set against the
rational love of Theseus and Hippolyta, the mature and royal
lovers who frame and explain the occasion of the play, it is the
irrationality of their emotion which is emphasized. This receives
its magisterial definition in Theseus' famous speech about "The
lunatic, the lover and the poet." But even if Theseus had not
spoken, or even if we were disposed not to allow the objectivity
of what he says, there is plenty of evidence from the lovers' own
lips to convict their love of irrationality:

Things base and vile, holding no quantity,
Love can transpose to form and dignity:
Love looks not with the eyes, but with the mind;
And therefore is wing'd Cupid painted blind:
Nor hath Love's mind of any judgement taste;
Wings, and no eyes, figure unheedy haste:
And therefore is Love said to be a child,
Because in choice he is so oft beguil'd.

> As waggish boys in game themselves forswear,
> So the boy Love is perjur'd everywhere.
>
> (I. i. 232-41)

This description of love, which Helena puts forward to justify her betrayal of friendship and abandonment of reason, is picked up in the next act in a more obviously fallacious form. In Act II, scene ii, when Lysander awakes to find himself in love with Helena (I have quoted the passage above) he justifies his change of heart in the following terms:

> The will of man is by his reason sway'd
> And reason says you are the worthier maid.
> Things growing are not ripe until their season:
> So I, being young, till now ripe not to reason;
> And touching now the point of human skill,
> Reason becomes the marshal to my will,
> And leads me to your eyes; where I o'erlook
> Love's stories, written in love's richest book.
>
> (II. ii. 115-22)

Helena remarks on the capacity of love to work without knowing the evidence of the senses (the eyes); in Lysander's case *reason* is only a means of returning to the *eyes* of his mistress, and reading irrational love stories. But the clearest comment on this infatuation comes not in the adventures of the lovers at all, but in the parallel situation of Titania and Bottom. Titania awakes and finds herself in love with Bottom, ass's head and all. Like the other lovers, her first care is to justify the *wisdom* of her choice:

> *Titania.* . . . So is mine eye enthralled to thy shape;
> And thy fair virtue's force perforce doth move me
> On the first view to say, to swear, I love thee.
> *Bottom.* Methinks, mistress, you should have little
> reason for that: and yet, to say the truth, reason and
> love keep little company together now-a-days; the
> more the pity that some honest neighbours will not
> make them friends.
>
> (III. i. 127-33)

Just as Bottom is the only mortal to see the fairies, so here he is the only one in the moonlit wood to see the daylight truth about love. But in both cases the knowledge is useless to him, since he supposes that "man is but an ass, if he go about to expound this." The advantage he has over the lovers is illusory, for he cannot make use of it.

Seen against the fairies or the royal pair, the lovers—who cannot fight back against either of these—cut rather poor figures. But the play does not leave them in this posture; there is a fourth term which helps to restore their dignity. The play of Pyramus and Thisbe, rehearsed by the mechanicals or handicraftsmen of Athens, shows a similar situation to that of Hermia and Lysander: lovers obstructed by parental opposition agree to run away from home and meet unobserved, at night. But the mechanicals' monumental unawareness of what is happening in their scene of "very tragical mirth" makes the Athenian lovers seem, by contrast, to be in control of their destinies. The innocence of the lovers reduces them in a comparison with the mature gravity of Theseus or with the omniscience of Oberon, but innocence is a virtue still, and an effective one when set against the *ignorance* of the mechanicals. Indeed there is one moment in the play where the innocence of the lovers is celebrated on its own account; it is, significantly enough, the moment at which the moonlight world of their illusions is passing into the daylight world of their responsibilities:

> *Demetrius.* These things seem small and undistinguishable,
> Like far-off mountains turned into clouds.
> *Hermia.* Methinks I see these things with parted eye,
> When every thing seems double.
> *Helena.*   So methinks;
> And I have found Demetrius like a jewel,
> Mine own and not mine own.
> *Demetrius.*   Are you sure
> That we are awake? It seems to me
> That yet we sleep, we dream. Do not you think
> The Duke was here, and bid us follow him?
>
> (IV. i. 184-92)

The humility, the sense of wonder, the hushed note of gratitude here are not available to anyone else in the play.

The contrast between the lovers and the mechanicals is not one which works exclusively by compensating the former at the expense of the latter. In the final scene the lovers make great fun of the ineptitudes in the play being performed; I think we are intended to see the irony of this. Those who were the unwitting performers in a love-play stage-managed and witnessed by the fairies are now, very self-consciously, the superior spectators of another play. We can laugh with them at the mechanicals, but we also laugh at them. Similarly, the aplomb with which Bottom accepts the advances of the fairy queen contrasts in a double-edged way with the frenetic activity of the lovers; immovable ignorance is set against the levity which reacts to every puff of wind, in a fashion which does not redound to the credit of either.

The play is thus a pattern of attitudes, none of which is central and all of which cast light on the others. Shakespeare has obviously laboured (and not in vain) to create complementary visions, and has sought to make each a complete world in itself. In some cases this latter need not have been difficult: the lovers and the mechanicals live inside fairly standard comic conventions. But in the case of the fairies Shakespeare is to be credited with the creation, single-handed, of an entirely new world. What the play required was a world which was both benevolent and mysterious, romantically beautiful enough to suggest a life not inferior to that of royalty, and one whose blessing on the royal bed would be appropriate; but at the same time it had to be an inhuman world, which would not compete with the dignity of Theseus. One can see that this problem would be especially pressing for Shakespeare if, as most critics suppose, the play was written to celebrate the wedding of a noble patron, whose greatness Theseus in some way mirrored. At any rate, some felt inappropriateness in the rustic spirits of fertility prompted Shakespeare to invent a new world of miniscule fairy spirits which has become so standard in English literary mythology that we tend to forget the originality that is involved. The power to create and sustain this world is largely a poetic power; the natural beauties of the moonlit wood are sumptuously described in order to evoke the spirits who dwell among them:

> I know a bank where the wild thyme blows,
> Where oxlips and the nodding violet grows,
> Quite over-canopied with luscious woodbine,
> With sweet musk-roses and with eglantine:
> There sleeps Titania sometime of the night,
> Lull'd in these flowers with dances and delight;
> And there the snake throws her enamell'd skin,
> Weed wide enough to wrap a fairy in.
>
> (II. i. 249-56)

Shakespeare's fairies are not only different in size from those who were part of folk-lore; their rulers are concerned not with mischief, as traditionally, but with *order* in a quasi-human fashion, and this of course makes it easier to fit their action into that of the play. The quarrel of Oberon and Titania has caused natural havoc, which may serve throughout the play as an image of discord in matrimony, and therefore as a warning to all the intending couples:

> The seasons alter: hoary-headed frosts
> Fall in the fresh lap of the crimson rose;
> And on old Hiems' thin and icy crown
> An odorous chaplet of sweet summer buds
> Is, as in mockery, set . . .
> And this same progeny of evil comes
> From our debate, from our dissension.
>
> (II. i. 107-16)

Shakespeare has indicated the difference between his fairies and the traditional spirits by having one of the latter as a member of his fairy court—I mean Puck or Robin Goodfellow, whose traditional role is described in a full-scale exposition:

> *Fairy.* Either I mistake your shape and making quite,
> Or else you are that shrewd and knavish sprite
> Call'd Robin Goodfellow. Are not you he
> That frights the maidens of the villagery,
> Skim milk, and sometimes labour in the quern,
> And bootless make the breathless housewife churn,

> And sometime make the drink to bear no barm,
> Mislead night-wanderers, laughing at their harm?
> Those that Hobgoblin call you, and sweet Puck,
> You do their work, and they shall have good luck.
> Are not you he?
>   *Puck.*   Thou speakest aright:
> I am that merry wanderer of the night.
> I jest to Oberon and make him smile
> When I a fat and bean-fed horse beguile
> Neighing in likeness of a filly foal.
>
>   (II. i. 32-46)

Puck supplies the element of mischief and even malice which is lacking in Shakespeare's other fairies. As jester to Oberon, he shares some features with Shakespeare's later jesters, Touchstone and Feste—detachment from the problems of those around him and attachment to his own off-beat conception of wit:

> Then will two at once woo one.
> That must needs be sport alone;
> And those things do best please me
> That befall prepost'rously.
>
>   (III. ii. 118-21)

As Oberon's agent in the affair of the lovers he also serves to keep the lovers apart from the fairy world proper, so that neither the benevolence of Oberon nor the slow development of the plot is infringed.

Another world of the play which Shakespeare has been at some pains to define effectively is the antique heroic world of Theseus and Hippolyta. It is obviously in an effort to create an image of antique chivalry that he gives them their resonant hunting speeches in Act IV:

> *Hippolyta.* I was with Hercules and Cadmus once
> When in a wood of Crete they bay'd the bear
> With hounds of Sparta; never did I hear
> Such gallant chiding; for, besides the groves,
> The skies, the fountains, every region near,
> Seem'd all one mutual cry: I never heard
> So musical a discord, such sweet thunder.

Theseus. My hounds are bred out of the Spartan kind . . .
Slow in pursuit, but match'd in mouth like bells,
Each under each. A cry more tuneable
Was never holla'd to, nor cheer'd with horn
In Crete, in Sparta, nor in Thessaly.

(IV. i. 109-23)

Shakespeare is obviously concerned to fix this image of harmonious control over brute impulse, for this idea of achieved
self-possession which Theseus, I take it, represents, cannot be
projected through external action, and the psychological dimension of inner debate is not one that this play employs. All Shakespeare can do is to show Theseus and Hippolyta, set in graceful
posture of power at rest, like antique statuary, larger than life
size. Larger than any other characters, they foreknow the nature
of the play between the opening speech and their marriage—the
focal point towards which all the action of the play tends:

Hippolyta. Four days will quickly steep themselves in night;
Four nights will quickly dream away the time;
And then the moon, like to a silver bow
New-bent in heaven, shall behold the night
Of our solemnities.
Theseus.   Go, Philostrate,
Stir up the Athenian youth to merriments;
Awake the pert and nimble spirit of mirth;
Turn melancholy forth to funerals;
The pale companion is not for our pomp.
Hippolyta, I woo'd thee with my sword,
And won thy love doing thee injuries;
But I will wed thee in another key,
With pomp, with triumph and with revelling.

(I. i. 7-19)

The combination of romance and merriment here nicely catches
the prevailing tone of the play, and suggests a settled and rational
state of loving that has lived through the violent half-knowledge
of passion; the concluding lines with their image of violence
transposed into revelry (a Feast of the Lapithae in reverse) sug-

gested a Theseus who has also lived in the moonlit wood, and who, led by Titania

> through the glimmering night
> From Perigouna, whom he ravished
> [Did] with fair Ægles break his faith,
> With Adriadne and Antiopa;
>
> (II. i. 77-80)

but who has learned (as Titania does) to

> Think no more of this night's accidents
> But as the fierce vexation of a dream.
>
> (IV. i. 65-6)

The image of Theseus and Hippolyta is a magnetic one, built up with a marvellous economy of means. But it seems a mistake to see the whole play from their point of view. Theseus is no Rosalind: he does not control what happens in the wood—that is Oberon's province; and he does not have to deal with the assaults and temptations of other kinds of love—no-one in the play is involved in that kind of interaction. The play is constructed by contrast rather than interaction, and the difference between it and later comedies may be expressed as the difference between a two-dimensional art (like that of Matisse) which sets clear colours against one another, and an art (like that of Rembrandt) which asks us to peer into the luminous depths where colour lies behind colour. The relationship between Rosalind's love and Touchstone's is one which helps to define Rosalind's own nature, for she has to absorb Touchstone's parody (of Orlando's poems, for example) before she can declare her own position. The relationship between Theseus and Bottom is, formally, of a similar kind: the poise and self-confidence of one, in the courtly world of Athens, is met by an equal poise, among

> Hard-handed men that work in Athens here.

Self-knowledge and self-ignorance face one another across the play; but they do not interact; neither learns from the other. The meanings that they establish only meet in the total meaningful pattern of the play.

The problem posed between moonlight or dream, on the one hand, and daylight or "reality" on the other, is one that the play does not solve, but rather *uses;* and it is one whose usefulness is disrupted by too rigorous an attempt to *judge* the different levels. Was the adventure of the lovers true or false, real or imaginary? The play would seem to answer, "both true and false." For Theseus it is false, for Theseus lives in a rational daylight world where, as for any good ruler, things have to be defined before they can be accepted. But the lovers can live in the result of their "dream" without worrying about the status of its truth. For them, as for most men, unconscious adjustments are acceptable if they work, and are not made more effective by being understood. It is often asked if the lovers develop in the course of the play, and the assumption that their love is immature while Theseus' is mature, may suggest that they grow to be more like him. But this is an unwarranted assumption; there is nothing in the play to support it. The virtues of a ruler are not required of the lovers, and there is no ground for judging them sub-standard, though they never possess these heroic virtues, nor even seek to acquire them.

Something of the same kind can be said of the mechanicals in this play, and it may be useful to make a general point here about Shakespeare's clowns, citizens and rustics. They are unfit for the court and make fools of themselves when they try to appear there, but our laughter is not entirely scornful. There is an absurd truth in Bottom's dignity, as in Dogberry's, which touches an awareness of the genuine limitations on *anyone's* understanding, and catches our involvement even if it does not control our sympathy. Here among the muddled roots of humanity it is dangerous to laugh too loud, for Shakespeare makes it clear that it is *ourselves* we are laughing at.

NOTES

1. Shakespeare is quoted here in the text of the *Complete Works* edited by Peter Alexander (1951), and it is to this edition that the lineation refers.

M. C. Bradbrook

MUCH ADO ABOUT NOTHING

IF *Romeo and Juliet* was a tragedy with its full complement of comedy, and *The Merchant of Venice* a comedy with an infusion of tragic pity and fear, *Much Ado About Nothing* is a comedy of Masks where the deeper issues are overlaid with mirth, and appear only at the climax of the play, the church scene. It is for this reason that so very mechanical a villain as Don John becomes a necessity of the plot. A true villain, like Shylock or Edmund or Richard III, would destroy the comedy: those who protest at the insufficiency of Don John should consider what would happen to the total composition if he were other than he is.[1] The old worn device of a maid dressing up in her mistress's clothes—one of the commonplaces of European fiction for centuries—is also used for a special purpose. It is not perhaps so incredible as modern readers tend to think it: the story of Gratiano and Nerissa should have served as reminder that gentlewomen really might ape their mistresses,[2] and talking with a man out at a window had happened in Shakespeare before without incurring moral disapprobation, even of the strictest; it was only as it happened on her wedding eve to the betrothed Hero that it took on the colouring of perfidy as well as lightness. Nevertheless the convention is used in a frankly conventional way; Margaret does not intervene when Claudio lodges his accusation, and Claudio does not fall upon the interloper and run him through like the hero of *A Blot in the Scutcheon*, both of which are obvious, natural, and probable, but inappropriate things for them to do.

From *Shakespeare and Elizabethan Poetry*, 1951, pp. 179-88. Reprinted by permission of Chatto and Windus Ltd. and Oxford University Press, Inc.

In *Much Ado,* as Masefield pointed out,[3] the two plots are linked by the common theme of credulity and self-deception. Claudio believes first that Don Pedro, then that Hero plays him false: Benedick and Beatrice believe the stories of their friends, thereby building a truth upon a fabulous basis. Dogberry and Verges need no one to lay them a trap; they are perpetually deceiving themselves, and invent a wonderful fabrication from the conversation of Borachio and Conrad. Yet it is they who unmask the villainy, thus robbing it of a good deal of its sinister value.

Credulity and foolish mistakings are the natural effects of love: we have already seen Valentine unable to fathom Silvia's meaning in asking him to write a love-letter, and the courtly ladies of *Love's Labour's Lost* are unable to distinguish between jest and earnest—though here perhaps the fault lies rather with their lovers, who are so unpracticed at expressing their feelings. Love's power to trip the heels, baffle the wits, and transform the person is a staple of Shakespearean comedy. Within the frame of a formal narrative, with its set situations—their staginess underlined rather than disguised—Shakespeare develops the personal and natural feelings of his lovers, working by implication and by strong use of contrast.

It does not need a critic to observe that Benedick and Beatrice are flirting from the beginning. The technique of a "merry war" is not unknown to clowns, and if Shakespeare had not happened to have met it in real life, he could have found it plentifully enough in literature.

Nevertheless discussions as to whether Benedick and Beatrice are "really" in love will lead precisely nowhere. That in a sense is the point of their wit-combat; what they think they are, what their friends think they are, what they really might be, are left as a series of alluring possibilities. "I confess nothing nor I deny nothing" says Beatrice at the climax of the church scene; it was a situation to which the practice of courtship must have given precedents enough. The dancing spray of the dialogue could not, at all events, rise from mutual boredom.

As in *Love's Labour's Lost,* but not in *Two Gentlemen of Verona* and *Twelfth Night,* the jesting is extremely broad. If Beatrice is translated into modern English some of her language

would not be heard far west of Leicester Square. Yet she is hit,
as Phoebe and Olivia were to be hit, by a good scolding from
another woman. It seems to have been Shakespeare's grand
strategy for subduing the female sex. Benedick on the other hand
is caught with an appeal to his pity. The means are nicely varied;
so are the responses. His long, natural and entertaining soliloquy,
"Love me? why it must be requited," is based on the soliloquies
of Berowne (*Love's Labour's Lost*, III, i, 184-215: IV, iii, 1-21),
in its use of the debating form, with questions and answers, and
the picture of the reluctant lover haled into love, against his will
but not unwillingly. Benedick like Berowne takes to sonnetting,
though more unsuccessfully: but his physical transformation is
not of the old fashion, to let himself appear distraught and
ungartered; on the contrary, like Orlando, he goes point-devise
and shaves himself, which may be a proof merely that he is
ignorant of the rules. His wooing—and his sparring—is all conducted in russet yeas and honest kersey noes: the language of
the play is in revolt against courtly decorum throughout.

Yet Beatrice's reaction to the news is given in ten rhymed lines
of extreme formality:

> What fire is in mine eares? can this be true?
> Stand I condemned for pride and scorn so much?
> Contempt farewell, and maiden pride adew,
> No glory liues behind the back of such.
> And *Benedick*, loue on, I will requite thee,
> Taming my wild heart to thy louing hand:
> If thou dost loue, my kindenesse shall incite thee
> To binde our loues up in a holy band.
> For others say thou dost deserue, and I
> Believe it better than reportingly.
>
> (III, i, 107-16)

This cannot be carelessness, remains of an old play, or laziness:
it is a most important moment in the story. Yet here is the verbal
equivalent of the dummy villain. Beatrice is to be shown still
preserving some of her defences until the climax of the church
scene, her next encounter with Benedick, and therefore nothing
personal enters into her confession because her feeling must be
held back for the critical release. He, being given the wooer's

role, can be allowed to speak his mind after the eavesdropping.

Both Benedick and Beatrice are comic without being ridiculous, and they provide the audience with the same kind of mirth that they are supposed to provide their friends. Their transparent attempts at disguising their feelings under the form of a toothache and a cold in the head, their slight peevishness and their extreme gullibility, Benedick's halting sonnet and February face, and Beatrice's extraordinary taciturnity, allow their friends to tease them, and the audience to indulge that particularly pleasing kind of superiority which arises when one's own predicaments are recognizably displayed in larger forms than life. If the two were not so admirable in all their more important actions—if Benedick were not so honest and soldierly, Beatrice so constant and loyal—there would be a good deal less pleasure in this identification. But to see characters in all other respects heroic reduced to such complete helplessness by Nature's ruthless device for ensuring that "the world must be peopled" is exhilarating in the extreme. It was a form of entertainment which was to be exploited much more coarsely by Fletcher with his conquering heroes reduced to absolute imbecility, like Arbaces, and his heroines of a wide-eyed innocence verging on impropriety, like Ordella.[4] To an age brought up on the Platonic politenesses, such a display of Nature must have been doubly engaging. The frank bawdiness and the human inconsistencies of Benedick and Beatrice must be seen against the proprieties of Valentine and Silvia, the stately splendour of Belmont, to win their full value.

To make the human relationship between two lovers display itself through the wit-combat of courtly love, by the simple process of extending the role of "unwilling" lover to the lady as well as the gentleman [5] was a stroke of genius which once achieved, takes on the appearance of the obvious. To quarrel was the stock recipe for comedy. Beatrice may indeed have owed something to the earlier Kate of *The Taming of the Shrew,* for her wit was certainly more forcible as well as more nimble than stage tradition would allow the court. Rosaline of *Love's Labour's Lost* is, like Beatrice, tilting against a professed enemy to her sex and is therefore justified of her tartness; Rosalind of *As You Like It* is speaking in the role of a pert page. Beatrice is called on for a moment of clarity which all the merry wars, the evasions and dissemblings serve to throw into high relief—the moment when she is confronted and in her turn confronts Benedick with a choice. Like the choice of the caskets, it is perilous: Benedick hesitates. For he has "to give and hazard" something which he weighs with the whole world.

> *Beatrice.* I love you with so much of my heart, that none is left to protest.
> *Benedick.* Come, bid me doe anything for thee.
> *Beatrice.* Kill *Claudio.*
> *Benedick.* Ha, not for the wide world.
> *Beatrice.* You kill me to denie it, farewell.
>
> (IV, i, 291ff)

Beatrice's passion is no assertion of principle: it is blind, savage and generous, offering Benedick simply the testimony of character, the testimony of her unshakable faith in her cousin's innocence. This is weighed against the sworn ocular proof of his two closest friends.[6] His acceptance of the challenge is prosaic in manner as well as in form.

> Enough, I am engaged, I will challenge him, I will kiss your hand and so leave you: by this hand Claudio shall render me a deere account: as you heare of me so thinke of me: goe comfort your cousin, I must say she is dead, and so farewell.
>
> (IV, i, 339ff)

These are the sort of old ends that were flouted by Claudio and Don Pedro; they are part of Benedick's soldierly plainness, and it is this quality—his readiness to act on his belief without hesitation and without requiring more conviction than Beatrice's oath and his own intuition—which gives him an easy lead among Shakespeare's heroes of comedy.

Claudio has on the other hand been the object of a good deal of critical venom. He has much larger stretches of flat dialogue to sustain but his part is developed from a courtly to a natural one in the course of his wooing. In contrast to Benedick and Beatrice, Claudio and Hero are silent lovers. Hero chatters to Beatrice and her women or under the protection of a mask (II, i, 90-104): Claudio, "Lord Lack beard," is similarly at ease with

Benedick and the Prince, but he can only introduce Hero's name in his conversation by asking the Prince a question whose answer is already known to him (I, i, 304-306). He and Hero have seen each other in public; but virtually all he knows of her is her looks. He has fallen in love with a pretty face and a modest manner. It is quite natural to him to think that the Prince must want Hero too. Fancy is not bred altogether in his eyes, nor, though it has an interest, in his liver.

In the betrothal scene both the lovers are prompted by Beatrice:

> *Leonato.* . . . his grace hath made the match, and all grace say, Amen to it.
> *Beatrice.* Speake Count, tis your Qu.
> *Claudio.* Silence is the perfectest Herrault of Ioy, I were but little happy if I could say, how much? Lady, as you are mine, I am yours, I giue away myself for you and dote upon the exchange.
> *Beatrice.* Speake cosin . . .
>
> (II, i, 316ff)

Like Bassanio Claudio is bereft of words; but when Pedro asks him to name the marriage day, his precipitate "To-morrow, my lord" is as telling as the fact that he has not exchanged one word more with Hero nor she with him—except in his ear, to be interpreted by Beatrice to the company.

So the shock of the ocular proof which Don John offers has little but Hero's appearance to contradict it; and hence the agony of Claudio's dilemma. Claudio's idealization of Hero is shown by his first comment, "Is it not a modest young lady?" He is horribly mocked, as he takes it, by the "seeming" which she maintains under his accusations.

> Behold how like a maid she blushes here! . . .
> Would you not sweare
> All you that see her, that she were a maide,
> By these exterior shewes?
>
> (IV, i, 34-40)

When he speaks of his own behavior, "like a brother to a sister," Hero asks:

> And seem'd I ever otherwise to you?

The word is match to tinder.

> Out on thee seeming, I will write against it,
> You seeme to me as Dian in her orb.

That is, she *still* "seems" so. The speech looks back to Bassanio's comment on the caskets and the false seeming of gold; it looks forward to Hamlet's "Seems, madam! nay, it is, I know not seemes." The lament which follows, lovely in its rhythm—

> O *Hero*! what a *Hero* hadst thou beene
> If halfe thy outward graces had been placed
> About thy thoughts and counsels of thy heart?
> But fair thee well, most foul, most faire, farewell
> Thou pure impiety and impious purity—

has not the agonized force of his question to Leonato:

> Is this face *Hero's*? are our eyes our own?

So Troilus, looking at Cressid, was to exclaim, "This is and is not Cressid" while Thersites commented, "Wil he swagger himself out on's eyes?"

And Borachio, confessing his villainy to the Prince, says, "I haue deceiued euen your verie eies." It is the "image of *Hero*" that then reappears to Claudio "in the rare semblance that I lou'd it first."

Hero has indeed nothing but her image, her appearance with which to defend herself. Like Desdemona, Hermione or Imogen she is too shocked at first even for a verbal denial. She is left with nothing but a bare protest when the Friar puts his gentle question to her (but be it noted, the question contains a trap). The Friar can read faces: he takes as sure testimony what to Claudio had been hideous "seeming," [7] and what he proposes is that Claudio should be left with the memory of Hero's image which will in time work its conviction upon him also.

> The Idea of her life shall sweetly creep
> Into his study of imagination.
> And every lovely Organ of her life,
> Shall come apparel'd in more precious habite,

More mouing delicate and full of life
Into the eye and prospect of his soule
Than when she liv'd indeed.
(IV, i, 226-32)

The relation of the men and women of the play depends upon such an attraction and such an imperfect knowledge: but they each know their own sex extremely well. Hero knows the surest way to catch Beatrice and sometimes explains her meaning to others.[8] Beatrice champions her cousin sooner than the girl's own father dares to do. Claudio, the Prince and Benedick are a sufficiently good set of messmates (princely aloofness a little slackened in the field) for Benedick's challenge to Claudio to extend as far as an indirect giving of the lie to Don Pedro as well:

> My lord, for your manie courtesies I thank you, I must discontinue your companie . . . you haue among you kill'd a sweet and innocent Ladie.
>
> (v, i, 195ff)

Claudio's flippancy about the pitiful insults of Leonato and Antonio (though he behaved admirably in their presence) and his readiness to take a second bride in reparation for the first create difficulties for the modern reader where they are not likely to have existed for an Elizabethan. Leonato's challenge in the presence of the Prince was a social outrage which would have landed the greatest nobleman in prison (Benedick draws Claudio aside to make his defiance). As for the marriage, it may rank with other fictions; by this time the audience and everyone but Claudio can see the happy conclusion, and to treat Claudio as an independent character at this point, and upbraid him for his failure to lodge an objection—like Bassanio when he was asked for the ring—is to abandon all sense of theatrical propriety and comic decorum for the sake of a psychological consistency which would defeat its own ends. Claudio cannot now be made into a tragic character or allowed more than a pretty lyric by way of remorse. In the church scene he had spoken out, and spoken the words which his earlier character warranted. There is no further role for him, or for Hero, save to make a pair in the final dance.

They each sink back into the kind of formality which the plot allowed, and the conclusion belongs to Benedick and Beatrice. The full story was not to be told till Shakespeare wrote *Cymbeline*, and depicted remorse in Posthumus, with constancy in Imogen.

In both *Much Ado* and *The Merchant of Venice* the clowns are ingeniously but loosely attached to the main plot by a few lines of intrigue—Gobbo acts as go-between for Jessica, Dogberry serves to keep Borachio in safe custody till Act v. Their real function is to act as parody or, in musical analogy, as undersong; Lancelot's debate with the fiend about his leaving his master, "who (God blesse the marke) is a kind of deuill," is a very pretty speech for the clown and reflects in a charmingly direct manner upon the brisk decision of Jessica, to leave her Hell. Dogberry and Verges are clearly reincarnations of Gobbo and his father, and their role of comic policeman was one of the oldest and most assured cards in popular comedy. But their parts are confined to scenes immediately preceding and following the church scene, where the relief of their broad comedy is most tellingly juxtaposed with the straightforward drama of the main plot. As interludes between the wit combats of Benedick and Beatrice they would have been unnecessary. The clowns of the later comedies were more closely woven into the main structure of the play, and indeed Feste is the central figure of *Twelfth Night;* but here the low comedy serves rather by contrast to strengthen the range and complexity of "interchangeable variety."

This variety, which, if it did not extend to hornpipes and funerals, extended to wedding festivity and mock-funerals, is marked by a strict control. Nothing could be further than the masterly shaping of Shakespeare's art from the wild incongruities of the Elizabethan hacks or the baroque eclecticism of the Jacobeans. The nearest analogue to the bold contrasts of these middle comedies is probably to be found in Chaucer, where the Canterbury Pilgrims tell their tales and conduct their debates in such a way as to bring out the individuality of each, whilst subordinating it to the whole pattern. Shakespeare, like Chaucer, drew largely from life, though both his heroic and his low characters were also recognized literary types. Shakespeare, like Chaucer, defined his characters largely in terms of their idiom, their own private speech. Both are given to raising moral issues, but not to pronouncing on them, except by implication. Both present a picture of the world which is above all wise and humane.

NOTES

1. It is clear that Don John has been fighting his brother and that this has been the subject of the recent wars: Don John hates Claudio because he won glory in the wars by Don John's overthrow (I, iii, 67-71): Don John is virtually a released prisoner of war. This might have been made plain in the staging. His bastardy, which explains his malignity, is not revealed till Act v, but it should be clear from the way he is treated that he is not really the heir of Arragon.

2. Borachio says that they shall hear him call Margaret Hero and hear Margaret term him Claudio (II, ii, 44-5). It would not help the plot to hear Margaret call him Claudio: but it suggests that she will wear her mistress's clothes and use her name in the kind of court game that is familiar from courtesy books and other plays (e.g. *Cynthia's Revels*), i.e. she will assume a character as a kind of masquerade (that of the bride of to-morrow) in order to be courted with a more highflown set of compliments by her sweetheart. If this is the explanation, Leonato seems to be right in dropping his first view that Margaret was an accomplice (v, i, 309-12) and accepting that she was in fault against her will (v, iv, 4-6). But the whole point is left extremely vague.

3. In his book on Shakespeare in the Home University Library series.

4. Arbaces is the hero of *A King and No King*, Ordella the heroine of *Thierry and Theodoret*.

5. The unwilling lover had been studied already in Berowne.

6. At first "attired in wonder," Benedick is apparently convinced by the Friar, as the first words of his colloquy with Beatrice show, that Hero is innocent: it follows, as Beatrice convinces him, that Claudio must have wronged her.

7. Claudio like Posthumus is to be converted simply by the beauty of Hero as it survives in his memory, and his conversion will depend on the strength of his first impressions conquering

his "knowledge." Compare Othello as he looks at the sleeping Desdemona:

> Be thus when thou art dead, and I will kill thee
> And loue thee after.

8. E.g. I, i, 35-6. It is Hero who convicts Beatrice in the end by producing the poem stolen from her pocket, containing her affection unto Benedick.

Harold Jenkins

AS YOU LIKE IT [1]

A MASTERPIECE is not to be explained, and to attempt to explain
it is apt to seem ridiculous. I must say at once that I propose
nothing so ambitious. I merely hope, by looking at one play,
even in what must necessarily be a very fragmentary way and
with my own imperfect sight, to illustrate something of what
Shakespeare's method in comedy may be. And I have chosen
As You Like It because it seems to me to exhibit, most clearly
of all the comedies, Shakespeare's characteristic excellences in
this kind. This is not to say that *As You Like It* is exactly a
representative specimen. Indeed I am going to suggest that it is
not. In this play, what I take to be Shakespeare's distinctive
virtues as a writer of comedy have their fullest scope; but in
order that they may have it, certain of the usual ingredients of
Shakespeare's comedy, or indeed of any comedy, have to be—not
of course eliminated, but very much circumscribed. In *As You
Like It,* I suggest, Shakespeare took his comedy in one direction
nearly as far as it could go. And then, as occasionally happens
in Shakespeare's career, when he has developed his art far in
one direction, in the comedy which succeeds he seems to readjust
his course.

If our chronology is right, after *As You Like It* comes, among
the comedies, *Twelfth Night.* And while we may accept that
Twelfth Night is, as Sir Edmund Chambers says, very much akin
to *As You Like It* "in style and temper," in some important respects it returns to the method and structure of the previous
comedy of *Much Ado About Nothing.* Sandwiched between these

From *Shakespeare Survey,* Vol. 8, 1955, pp. 40-51. Reprinted by
permission of the editor and Cambridge University Press.

two, *As You Like It* is conspicuously lacking in comedy's more robust and boisterous elements—the pomps of Dogberry and the romps of Sir Toby. More significantly, it has nothing which corresponds to the splendid theatricalism of the church scene in *Much Ado,* nothing which answers to those crucial bits of trickery by which Benedick and Beatrice in turn are hoodwinked into love. Even if, as may be objected, they are not hoodwinked but merely tricked into removing their hoods, still those stratagems in Leonato's orchard are necessary if the happy ending proper to the comedy is to be brought about. These ambushes, if I may call them so—they are really inverted ambushes—are paralleled, or should one say parodied, in *Twelfth Night* in the scene where Malvolio is persuaded that he too is beloved. And this ambush too is necessary if, as the comedy demands, Malvolio is to have his sanity called in question and his authority undermined. The slandering of Hero in *Much Ado* also is to have its counterpart in *Twelfth Night.* For the slandering of Hero, with its culmination in the church scene, forces one pair of lovers violently apart while bringing another pair together. And in *Twelfth Night* the confusion of identities holds one pair of lovers—Orsino and Viola —temporarily apart, yet forces another pair—Olivia and Sebastian—with some violence together. A satisfactory outcome in *Much Ado* and *Twelfth Night* depends on such embroilments; and the same is even more true in an earlier comedy like *A Midsummer Night's Dream.* In *As You Like It* I can hardly say that such embroilments do not occur, but they are not structural to anything like the same degree. Without the heroine's masculine disguise Phebe would not have married Silvius any more than in *Twelfth Night* Olivia would have married Sebastian; but the confusions of identity in *As You Like It* have no influence whatever upon the ultimate destiny of Rosalind and Orlando, or of the kingdom of Duke Senior, or of the estate of Sir Rowland de Boys. Yet these are the destinies with which the action of the play is concerned. It is in the defectiveness of its action that *As You Like It* differs from the rest of the major comedies—in its dearth not only of big theatrical scenes but of events linked together by the logical intricacies of cause and effect. Of comedy, as of tragedy, action is the first essential; but *As You Like It* suggests that action is not, if I may adapt a phrase of Marston's, "the life of these things." It may be merely the foundation on which they are built. And *As You Like It* further shows that on a very flimsy foundation, if only you are skilful enough, a very elaborate structure may be poised. But the method has its dangers, and though Shakespeare's skill conceals these dangers from us, *Twelfth Night,* as I said, returns to a more orthodox scheme.

The story which provides the action for *As You Like It* belongs to the world of fairy-tale or folk-lore. This is a world which supplied the plots of a number of Shakespeare's plays, including the greatest, notably *King Lear.* And fairy-tales have many advantages for the dramatist, among which is their total disregard of practical probabilities. In fairy-tales, for example, evil is always absolute, clearly recognized, and finally overthrown; all of which may have something to do with the Aristotelian theory that while history records what has happened, poetry shows what should happen. Relaxing the more prosaic demands of verisimilitude, the fairy-tale invites the imagination. It can certainly provide a convenient road into the Forest of Arden. And this is not less true for Shakespeare because the road had already been built for him by Lodge.

A man has died and left three sons. Three is the inevitable number, and though Shakespeare, like Lodge, forgets to do much with the middle one, he is not therefore unimportant. The eldest brother is wicked, the youngest virtuous—and does fabulous feats of strength, notably destroying a giant in the shape of Charles the wrestler, who has torn other hopeful youths to pieces. Orlando therefore wins the princess, herself the victim of a wicked uncle, who has usurped her father's throne. This is the *story* of *As You Like It.* And Shakespeare, making the journey of the imagination far more quickly than Lodge, gets most of it over in the first act. That is what is remarkable. By the time we reach the second act Rosalind has already come safe to the Forest of Arden, by the aid of her man's disguise. From this disguise, as everybody knows, springs the principal comic situation of the play. But such is the inconsequential nature of the action that this comic situation develops only when the practical need for the disguise is past. The course of true love has not run smooth. But most of its obstacles have really disappeared before the main comedy begins. It only remains for the wicked to be converted, as they duly are at the end, all in comedy's good but arbitrary time, when the wicked eldest brother makes a suitable husband for the second princess. Or a most *un*suitable husband, as all the critics have complained. But this, I think, is to misunderstand. Instead of lamenting that Celia should be thrown away on Oliver, he having been much too wicked to deserve her, we should rather see that Oliver's getting this reward is a seal set on his conversion, and a sign of how good he has now become.

The first act of *As You Like It* has to supply the necessary minimum of event. But, Quiller-Couch notwithstanding, this first act is something more than mechanical.[2] It is for one thing a feat of compression, rapid, lucid and, incidentally, theatrical. In fifty lines we know all about the three brothers and the youngest is at the eldest's throat. In three hundred more we know all about the banished Duke and where and how he lives, and the giant has been destroyed before our eyes. But there is more to the first act than this. Before we enter Arden, to "fleet the time carelessly, as they did in the golden world," we must be able to contrast its simple life with the brittle refinement of the court. This surely is the point of some of what "Q" called the "rather pointless choplogic"; and also of the courtier figure of Le Beau, a little sketch for Osric, with his foppery of diction and his expert knowledge of sport. Le Beau's notion of sport provokes Touchstone's pointed comment on the courtier's values: "Thus men may grow wiser every day: it is the first time that ever I heard breaking of ribs was sport for ladies." This *is* the callousness one learns at a court ruled by a tyrannous Duke, whose malevolent rage against Rosalind and Orlando not only drives them both to Arden but completes the picture of the world they leave behind.

This first act, then, shows some instinct for dramatic preparation, though we may grant that Shakespeare's haste to get ahead makes him curiously perfunctory. He is in two minds about when Duke Senior was banished; and about which Duke is to be called Frederick; and whether Rosalind or Celia is the taller. He has not quite decided about the character of Touchstone. I do not think these are signs of revision. They simply show Shakespeare plunging into his play with some of its details still but half-shaped in his mind. The strangest of these details is the mysterious middle brother, called Fernan-

dyne by Lodge but merely "Second Brother" in *As You Like It,*
when at length he makes his appearance at the end. Yet in
the fifth line of the play he was already christened Jaques. And
Shakespeare of course afterwards gave this name to someone
else. It seems clear enough that these two men with the same
name were originally meant to be one. As things turned out
Jaques could claim to have acquired his famous melancholy
from travel and experience; but I suspect that it really began
in the schoolbooks which were studied with such profit by
Jaques de Boys. Though he grew into something very different,
Jaques surely had his beginnings in the family of De Boys and
in such an academy as that in Navarre where four young men
turned their backs on love and life in the belief that they could
supply the want of experience by study and contemplation.

Interesting as it might be to develop this idea, the important point of comparison between *As You Like It* and *Love's
Labour's Lost* is of another kind. And to this I should like
briefly to refer before I come to discuss the main part of *As
You Like It.* *Love's Labour's Lost* is the one play before *As
You Like It* in which Shakespeare sought to write a comedy
with the minimum of action. Four young men make a vow to
have nothing to do with a woman; each breaks his oath and
ends vowing to serve a woman. That is the story; far slighter
than in *As You Like It.* Yet, in contrast with *As You Like It,* the
careful and conspicuous organization of *Love's Labour's Lost*
distributes its thin action evenly through the play. And the
characters always act in concert. In the first act the men, all
together, make their vow; in the second the ladies, all together,
arrive and the temptation begins. The climax duly comes,
where you would expect it, in a big scene in Act IV, when each
in turn breaks his vow and all together are found out. *Love's
Labour's Lost* is the most formally constructed of all the comedies. When the ladies and gentlemen temporarily exchange
partners, this is done symmetrically and to order. Indeed the
movement of the whole play is like a well-ordered dance in
which each of the participants repeats the steps of the others.
But this is exactly what does *not* happen in *As You Like It,*
where the characters do *not* keep in step. When they *seem* to
be doing the same thing they are really doing something dif-

ferent, and if they ever echo one another they mean quite
different things by what they say—as could easily be illustrated
from the little quartet of lovers in the fifth act ("And so am I
for Phebe.—And I for Ganymede.—And I for Rosalind.—And I
for no woman"), where the similarity of the tune they sing
conceals their different situations. The pattern of *As You Like It*
comes not from a mere repetition of steps, but from constant
little shifts and changes. The formal parallelisms of *Love's
Labour's Lost* are replaced by a more complex design, one
loose enough to hold all sorts of asymmetries within it.

But of course the effect of variations upon a theme instead
of simple repetitions is not new in *As You Like It*. It is the tendency of Shakespeare's comedy from the start. In *Love's Labour's
Lost* itself the courtly gestures of the four young men are bur-
lesqued by those of a fantastic knight, and while the four young
men are vowing not to see a woman, Costard the clown is
"taken with a wench." Moreover, one of the four, though he
goes through the movements with the others, has some trouble
to keep in step, and is always threatening to break out of the
ring. Even when he makes his vow with the others, he knows
that necessity will make him break it. As he joins in their purposes he knows them to be foolish and he mocks at ideals
which he at the same time pursues. Human activity offers itself to the dramatist in a large variety of forms and the same
individual can play contradictory parts. The drunken tinker in
The Taming of the Shrew does not know whether he may not
really be a noble lord. Although Shakespeare did not invent
this situation, it was just the thing to appeal to him. For he
knew that a man is very easily "translated." In the middle of
his fairy play he put a man with an ass's head. In perhaps
the most remarkable encounter in Shakespeare the daintiest
fairy queen caresses a man turned brute, who, with a fairy
kingdom around him, can think only of scratching his itch.
When the animal appears in a man it may terrify his fellows;
it may also attract to it his finest dreams and fancies, corrupting them, or being uplifted by them to a vision of new wonder.
Shakespeare of course does nothing as crude as *say* this. He
knows as well as the Duke in Arden that sermons may be found
in stones, but much better than the Duke that it is tedious to

preach them, a thing, incidentally, he does not permit the Duke to do. What Shakespeare characteristically does in his comedy is to set together the contrasting elements in human nature and leave them by their juxtaposition or interaction to comment on one another.

In *As You Like It* the art of comic juxtaposition is at its subtlest. It is to give it fullest scope that the action can be pushed up into a corner, and the usual entanglements of plotting, though not dispensed with altogether, can be loosened. Freedom, of course, is in the hospitable air of Arden, where convenient caves stand ready to receive outlaws, alfresco meals are abundantly provided, with a concert of birds and running brooks, and there is no worse hardship than a salubrious winter wind. This is "the golden world" to which, with the beginning of his second act, Shakespeare at once transports us, such a world as has been the dream of poets since at least the time of Virgil when, wearied with the toilings and wranglings of society, they yearn for the simplicity and innocence of what they choose to think man's natural state.[3] It is of course a very literary tradition that Shakespeare is here using, but the long vogue of the pastoral suggests that it is connected with a universal impulse of the human mind, to which Shakespeare in *As You Like It* gives permanent expression. But this aspect of the play is merely the one which confronts us most conspicuously. There are many others. *As You Like It* has been too often praised for its idyllic quality alone, as though it were some mere May-morning frolic prolonged into a lotos-eating afternoon. A contrast with the ideal state was necessitated by the literary tradition itself, since the poet seeking an escape into the simple life was expected to hint at the ills of the society he was escaping from. That meant especially the courts of princes, where life—it was axiomatic—was at its most artificial. And the vivid sketching in of the courtly half of the antithesis is, as I have shown, an important function of *As You Like It's* maligned first act. With the first speech of the banished Duke at the opening of the second act, the complete contrast is before us; for, while introducing us to Arden, this speech brings into sharp focus that first act which has just culminated in the usurper's murderous malice. "Are not these woods more free from peril than the

envious court?" Though the contrast is traditional, it comes
upon us here, like so many things in Shakespeare, with the vitality of fresh experience. The Forest of Arden comes to life in
numerous little touches of the country-side, and the heartless
self-seeking of the outer world is concentrated into phrases
which have the force of permanent truth. The line that "Q"
admired—"And unregarded age in corners thrown"—might have
come from one of the sonnets, and when Orlando observes how
"none will sweat but for promotion" we recognize the fashion
of our times as well as his. As the play proceeds, it is easy
enough for Shakespeare to keep us ever aware of the forest,
what with Amiens to sing for us, the procession home after
the killing of the deer, an empty cottage standing ready for
Rosalind and Celia, surrounded by olive-trees beyond a willow
stream, and a good supply of oaks for Orlando or Oliver to
lie under. It cannot have been quite so easy to keep us in touch
with the court life we have now abandoned; but nothing is
neater in the construction of the play than those well-placed
little scenes which, by despatching first Orlando and then Oliver
to the forest, do what is still required by the story and give
the illusion that an action is still going briskly forward, while
at the same time they renew our acquaintance with the wicked
world. After the first scene in the ideal world of Arden and a
sentimental discourse on the deer, there is Frederick again in
one of his rages, sending for Oliver, who, an act later, when
we are well acclimatized to the forest, duly turns up at court.
Then occurs a scene of eighteen lines, in which Shakespeare
gives as vivid a sketch of the unjust tyrant as one could hope
to find. The tyrant prides himself upon his mercy, punishes one
man for his brother's sins, and finds in his victim's excuses further cause of offence. Oliver's plaint that he had never loved
his brother brings the instant retort, "More villain thou. Well,
push him out of doors." As this eruption dies down, there appears in the Forest of Arden the cause of all the trouble
quietly hanging his verses on a tree.

The contrast between court and country is thus presented
and our preference is very plain. Yet as a counterpoise to all
this, there is one man in the country-side who actually prefers
the court. Finding himself in Arden, Touchstone decides: "When

I was at home, I was in a better place." It is no doubt important that he is a fool, whose values may well be topsy-turvy. But in one word he reminds us that there are such things as domestic comforts. And presently we find that the old man whom society throws into the corner is likely in the "uncouth forest" to die of hunger and exposure to the "bleak air." There is clearly something to be said on the other side; the fool may anatomize the wise man's folly. And there is also Jaques to point out that the natural life in Arden, where men usurp the forest from the deer and kill them in their "native dwelling-place," while deer, like men, are in distress abandoned by their friends, is as cruel and unnatural as the other. When Amiens sings under the greenwood tree and turns "his merry note unto the sweet bird's throat," inviting us to shun ambition and be pleased with what we get, Jaques adds a further stanza to the song which suggests that to leave your "wealth and ease" is the act of an ass or a fool. Most of us, I suppose, have moods in which we would certainly agree with him, and it is a mark of Shakespeare's mature comedy that he permits this criticism of his ideal world in the very centre of it. The triumphal procession after the killing of the deer, a symbolic ritual of the forester's prowess, is accompanied by a mocking song, while the slayer of the deer is given its horns to wear as a somewhat ambiguous trophy.

It is Jaques, mostly, with the touch of the medieval buffoon in him, who contributes this grotesque element to the songs and rituals of Arden. Like Touchstone he is not impressed by Arden, but unlike Touchstone he does not prefer the court. Indeed, as we have seen, he is able to show that they are very much alike, infected by the same diseases. No doubt his is a jaundiced view of life, and it is strange that some earlier critics should have thought it might be Shakespeare's. Shakespeare's contemporaries would hardly have had difficulty in recognizing in Jaques a variant of the Elizabethan melancholy man—the epithet is applied to him often enough—though I remain a little sceptical when I am told by O. J. Campbell that from the first moment they heard Jaques described, the Elizabethans would have perceived "the unnatural melancholy produced by the adustion of phlegm." [4] Whatever its physiological kind, the important thing about his melancholy is that it is not the fatigue of spirits of the man who has found the world too much for him, but an active principle manifesting itself in tireless and exuberant antics. Far from being a morose man, whether he is weeping with the stag or jeering at the huntsman, he throws himself into these things with something akin to passion. His misanthropy is a form of self-indulgence, as is plain enough in his very first words:

> *Jaques.* More, more, I prithee, more.
> *Amiens.* It will make you melancholy, Monsier Jaques.
> *Jaques.* I thank it. More, I prithee, more. I can
>   suck melancholy out of a song.

His own comparison with a weasel sucking eggs suggests what a ferocious and life-destroying thing this passion is. Shakespeare's final dismissal of Jaques is profound. Far from making Celia a better husband than Oliver, as George Sand apparently thought, he is the one person in the play who could not be allowed to marry anyone, since he can have nothing to do with either love or generation. His attempt to forward the nuptials of Touchstone and Audrey serves only to postpone them. He is of course the one consistent character in the play in that he declines to go back with the others to the court that they have scorned. Yet how *can* he go back when the court has been converted? Jaques's occupation's gone. And he will not easily thrive away from the social life on which he feeds. It is notable that the place he really covets, or affects to, is that of the motley fool, licensed to mock at society, indulged by society but not of it. Yet, seeking for a fool, he has only to look in the brook to find one; and it is the romantic hero who will tell him so.

Shakespeare, then, builds up his ideal world and lets his idealists scorn the real one. But into their midst he introduces people who mock their ideals and others who mock *them*. One must not say that Shakespeare never judges, but one judgement is always being modified by another. Opposite views may contradict one another, but of course they do not cancel out. Instead they add up to an all-embracing view far larger and more satisfying than any one of them in itself.

Now when Orlando tells Jaques that he may see a fool by

looking in the brook, this is not the first time that Jaques and Orlando meet; and the relations between the two of them are worth a moment's glance. Their first encounter occurs in public when the Duke and his retinue are met for one of their forest repasts. Jaques has just been eloquent about the vices of mankind and is justifying the satirist who scourges them, when he is confronted with the romantic hero in his most heroic attitude, rushing into the middle of the scene with drawn sword,[5] crying, "Forbear, and eat no more." But Jaques is not the man to be discomposed, even when a sudden interruption throws him off his hobby-horse. When he has inquired, "Of what kind should this cock come of?," the heroic attitude begins to look extravagant. The hero stands his ground: "Forbear, I say: He dies that touches any of this fruit"; at which Jaques nonchalantly helps himself to a grape, saying, "An you will not be answered with reason (raisin), I must die." Heroism now appears thoroughly deflated, or would do if Jaques were attended to by the company at large. The hero is in fact saved by the Duke's "civility"; and their talk of "gentleness" and "nurture" even throws back into perspective Jaques's recent attack upon society. The situation as a whole retains its equilibrium. And yet as a result of this little incident we are bound to feel that the romantic hero is very vulnerable to the ridicule of the satirist, until their duel of wit in the following act readjusts our view by allowing Orlando his retort.

There is a formal point to notice here, easy to miss but full of meaning. The wit-combat between Jaques and the hero is matched an act or so later—there is no strict regularity about these things—by a similar wit-combat between Jaques and the heroine. On each occasion Jaques is worsted and departs, leaving Rosalind and Orlando to come together. In fact the discomfiture of Monsieur Melancholy by one or other of the lovers is the prelude to each of the two big love-scenes of the play. And this arrangement makes a point more prettily than any action-plot involving Jaques could do. The mocking words of Jaques's farewell are in each case illuminating: "Farewell, good Signior Love"; and "Nay, then, God be wi' you, an you talk in blank verse." The gibe at blank verse is not an incidental or decorative jest. It makes it clear that, however we judge of

them, the melancholy spirit of Jaques and the romantic emotion
of Rosalind and Orlando cannot mingle. Shakespeare dismisses
the melancholy man before he gives the lovers their scope. And
in this I follow his example.

So far I have dealt only with the immigrants to Arden. There
is of course a native population. The natural world of the poet's
dreams has always been inhabited by shepherds, who from the
time of Theocritus have piped their songs of love. And Rosalind and Celia have been in the forest for only twenty lines
when two shepherds appear pat before them. In an earlier
comedy perhaps these might have been a similar pair singing
comparable love-ditties. But in *As You Like It*—Shakespeare
making the most of what is offered him by Lodge—they are a
contrasting pair. One is young and one is old, one is in love
and one is not. The lover is the standard type. But the notion
of love has undergone a change since classical times and the
shepherds of Renaissance pastorals have all been bred in the
schools of courtly love. So young Silvius is the faithful abject
lover who finds disdain in his fair shepherdess's eye and sighs
"upon a midnight pillow"—Shakespeare always fixes on a detail
in which a whole situation is epitomized. There are of course
many other lovers in the play, but the story of Silvius and Phebe
is of the pure pastoral world, the familiar literary norm against
which all the others may be measured. First against Silvius and
Phebe are set Rosalind and Orlando, and the immediate result
of this is that Rosalind and Orlando, though they clearly belong to the pastoral world, seem much closer to the ordinary
one. Indeed, since Silvius and Phebe relieve them of the necessity of displaying the lovers' more extravagant postures, Rosalind
and Orlando are freer to act like human beings. Rosalind need
only play at taunting her adorer while allowing her real woman's
heart to be in love with him in earnest. In an earlier comedy
like *The Two Gentlemen of Verona* the heroes themselves had
to undergo those "bitter fasts, with penitential groans, With
nightly tears and daily heart-sore sighs," and these are what, as
H. B. Charlton says, may make Valentine look a fool. But with
Silvius to take this burden from him, Orlando can really be
a hero, performing the traditional hero's fabulous feats, and
upon occasion may even be a common man like ourselves. He

has, for example, the very human trait of unpunctuality; he is twice late for an appointment. And although on one occasion he has the perfect excuse of a bloody accident, on the other he has nothing to say, beyond "My fair Rosalind, I come within an hour of my promise." Such engaging casualness is of course outside Silvius's range. And although Orlando has his due share of lovers' sighs and is indeed the "unfortunate he" who hangs the verses on the trees, in so human a creature these love-gestures appear not as his *raison d'être* but as an aberration. A delightful aberration, no doubt—"I would not be cured, youth," he says—but still an aberration that can be the legitimate subject of our mockery. Lying contemplating his love under an oak, ne seems to Celia "like a dropped acorn," and both the ladies smile at his youthful lack of beard. But Orlando is robust enough to stand their mockery and ours, and Shakespeare's superb dramatic tact arranges that Orlando shall draw our laughter towards him so that he may protect the fragile Silvius from the ridicule which would destroy *him*. Rosalind alone is privileged to make fun of Silvius; and that because searching his wounds, she finds her own. The encounters which do not occur have their significance as well as those which do: Touchstone is only once, and Jaques never, allowed a sight of Silvius before the final scene of the play. Silvius has not to be destroyed or the play will lack something near its centre.

If in a pastoral play the ideal shepherd is satirized it must be indirectly. But that he is, through his complete unreality, a likely target for satire has been commonly recognized by the poets, who have therefore had a habit of providing him with a burlesque counterpart to redress the balance and show that they did know what rustics were like in real life. As Gay was to put it in his proem to *The Shepherd's Week*, the shepherd "sleepeth not under myrtle shades, but under a hedge"; and so when Gay's shepherd makes love it is in a sly kiss behind a haycock to the accompaniment of the lady's yells of laughter. This may have been the method of Shakespeare's William, for, far from inditing verses to his mistress, William is singularly tongue-tied; though he is "five and twenty" and thinks he has "a pretty wit," the biggest of his eleven speeches is only seven words long. And his partner is just as much a contrast to the shepherdess of pastoral legend. She thanks the gods she is not beautiful, does not even know the meaning of "poetical," and her sheep, alas, are goats.

Shakespeare, then, presents the conventional pastoral, and duly burlesques it. But with a surer knowledge of life than many poets have had, he seems to suspect that the burlesque as well as the convention may also miss the truth. Do shepherds really sleep under hedges? In order to be unsophisticated, must they be stupid too? So among his varied array of shepherds, Silvius and Ganymede and William, Shakespeare introduces yet another shepherd, the only one who knows anything of sheep, whose hands even get greasy with handling them. It does not matter that Shakespeare got the hint for Corin from Corydon in Lodge. For Lodge found Corydon in literature and for Corin Shakespeare went to life. Lodge's Corydon, though he may make the king smile with his clownish salutation, has evidently been bred at court himself. Would he ever else accost a lady in distress in strains like these

If I should not, fair damosel, occasion offence, or renew your griefs by rubbing the scar, I would fain crave so much favour as to know the cause of your misfortunes.

Shakespeare's Corin speaks at once of grazing and shearing and an unkind master; and when he talks about the shepherd's life he shows that he knows the value of money and that fat sheep need good pasture. His greatest pride is to see his ewes graze and his lambs suck. This is the note of his philosophy, and if it has its limitations, it is far from despicable and is splendidly anchored to fact. His attitude to love is that of the fully sane man undisturbed by illusions. Being a man, he has been in love and can still guess what it is like; but it is so long ago he has forgotten all the details. How little he belongs to Arcadia may be discovered from Sidney, whose shepherd-boy went on piping "as though he should never be old." In *As You Like It* perpetual youth is the happiness of Silvius, and his fate. *That* much of the difference between Silvius and Corin is apparent from the short dialogue of twenty lines which first introduces them together to us.

In Corin Shakespeare provides us with a touchstone with which to test the pastoral. Corin's dialogue with the Touchstone of the court, dropped into the middle of the play, adds to the conventional antithesis between courtier and countryman a glimpse of the real thing. Our picture of the court as a place of tyranny, ambition and corruption is no doubt true enough. But its colours are modified somewhat when Touchstone gives us the court's plain routine. For him, as he lets us know on another occasion, the court is the place where he has trod a measure, flattered a lady, been smooth with his enemy and undone three tailors. Though Touchstone seeks to entangle Corin in the fantastications of his wit, his arguments to show that the court is better than the sheepfarm have a way of recoiling on himself. What emerges from the encounter of these two realists is that ewe and ram, like man and woman, are put together and that though the courtier perfumes his body it sweats like any other creature's. In city or country, *all* ways of life are at bottom the same, and we recognize a conclusion that Jaques, by a different route, has helped us to reach before.

The melancholy moralizings of Jaques and the Robin Hood raptures of the Duke, though in contrast, are equally the product of man's spirit. There has to be someone in Arden to remind us of the indispensable flesh. It was a shrewd irony of Shakespeare's to give this office to the jester. Whether he is wiser or more foolish than other men it is never possible to decide, but Touchstone is, as well as the most artificial wit, the most natural man of them all; and the most conscious of his corporal needs. After the journey to the forest Rosalind complains of a weariness of spirits, to which Touchstone retorts "I care not for my spirits, if my legs were not weary." And when he displays his wit at the expense of Orlando's bad verses, saying "I'll rhyme you so eight years together," he remembers to add "dinners and suppers and sleeping-hours excepted." A "material fool," as Jaques notes. This preoccupation with the physical makes Touchstone the obvious choice for the sensual lover who will burlesque the romantic dream. So Touchstone not only deprives the yokel William of his mistress, but steals his part in the play, making it in the process of infinitely greater significance. However, Shakespeare from the beginning cast

Touchstone for this burlesque role, though he may not have
seen at first what form the burlesque would take. When Silvius
first exhibits his love to us, and reminds Rosalind of hers, Touchstone completes the trio on his discordant note:

> I remember, when I was in love I broke my sword upon
> a stone and bid him take that for coming a-night to Jane
> Smile; and I remember the kissing of . . . the cow's dugs
> that her pretty chopt hands had milked.

This sort of extravagance—in the burlesque-chivalrous vein—is
not, I think, developed; but an indecent jest about a peascod
does point forward to the animal lust which propels him towards
Audrey, and his amour with her forms the perfect contrast to
the three idealized courtships of the play. If we need a formal
juxtaposition of the two kinds of love to point the matter further, I note that it is just when Rosalind has met Orlando in the
forest and Orlando has promised to woo her "by the faith of
[his] love" and "with all [his] heart" that we see Touchstone
courting the goat-girl regretting that fair women should be
honest and talking of sexual desire.

The fool is not only a material touchstone; he is also the
time-keeper of the play. At least, in the forest, where "there's no
clock," he carries a time-piece with him; and it provokes the
reflection: "It is ten o'clock . . . 'Tis but an hour ago since it
was nine, And after one hour more 'twill be eleven." The people
of Arcadia will do well to take note of this, but if all you can
do with your hours is to count them, this undeniable truth may
seem a trifle futile. Touchstone, to do him justice, goes on:
"And so, from hour to hour, we ripe and ripe, And then, from
hour to hour, we rot and rot." He dares to speak in Arcadia,
where one can never grow old, of Time's inevitable processes of
maturity and decay. By this the ideal life of the banished Duke
is mocked, and since Touchstone's words are repeated by
Jaques with delighted and uproarious laughter, the mockery is
double. Yet, in accordance with the play's principle of counter-
ing one view with another, there are two things that may be
noted: first, that in a later scene Touchstone, who sums up life
as riping and rotting, is compared by Rosalind to a medlar,
which is rotten before it is ripe; and second, that it is at this

very point, when the ideal life is doubly mocked, that the Duke administers to the mocker Jaques a direct and fierce rebuke, charging the mocker of the world's vices with having lived a vicious life himself.

The satirist, of course, is far from silenced; it is now that he ridicules the romantic hero, and presently he delivers his famous speech on the seven ages of man, brilliantly summing up the course of human life, but omitting to notice anything in it that is noble or even pleasant. However, as has often been observed, though the seven ages speech ends with a description of man's final decrepitude— "sans teeth, sans eyes, sans taste, sans everything"—it has not yet left the speaker's tongue when an aged man appears who is at once addressed as "venerable." There is always this readjustment of the point of view. Senility and venerableness—are they different things or different ways of looking at the same? Certainly the entry of the venerable Adam does not disproves what Jaques says; Shakespeare seeks no cheap antithesis. "Sans teeth"—Adam himself has admitted to being toothless, Orlando has called him "a rotten tree," and his helplessness is only too visible when he is *carried* on to the stage. Yet he *is* carried, tenderly, by the master whom he has followed "to the last gasp, with truth and loyalty." Here is the glimpse of human virtue that the seven ages speech omitted. And then it is upon this moving spectacle of mutual affection and devotion that Amiens sings his song, "Blow, blow, thou winter wind, Thou art not so unkind As man's ingratitude." Placed here, this lovely lyric, blend of joy and pathos, has a special poignancy.

The arrangement of the play depends upon many such piquant but seemingly casual juxtapositions. *As You Like It* contemplates life within and without Arden, with numerous shifts of angle, alternating valuations, and variations of mood. As for action, incident—life in the Forest of Arden does not easily lend itself to those. I have suggested that Shakespeare does something to supply this want by a glance or two back at what is happening at court. And departures from the court are matched by arrivals in the forest. For events, of course, even in Arden do sometimes occur. Orlando arrives dramatically, even melodramatically. Presently Rosalind learns that he is about. A little later on they meet. Later still Oliver arrives and is rescued

from a lioness. Shakespeare still keeps up a sense of things going on. But the manner of the play, when once it settles down in
the forest, is to let two people drift together, talk a little, and
part, to be followed by two more. Sometimes a pair will be
watched by others, who will sometimes comment on what they
see. Sometimes of course there is a larger group, once or twice
even a crowded stage; but most often two at a time. When they
part they may arrange to meet again, or they may not. Through
the three middle acts of the play, though there are two instances of love at first sight (one of them only reported), it is
rare that anything happens in any particular encounter between
these people of the sort that changes the course of their lives,
anything, that is to say, that goes to make what is usually called
a plot. Yet the meetings may properly be called "encounters,"
because of the impact the contrasting characters make on one
another and the sparkle of wit they kindle in one another. What
is important in each meeting is our impression of those who
meet and of their different attitudes to one another or to one
another's views of life, an impression which is deepened or
modified each time they reappear with the same or different
partners. As I describe it, this may all sound rather static, but
such is the ease and rapidity with which pairs and groups
break up, re-form, and succeed one another on the stage that
there is a sense of fluid movement. All is done with the utmost
lightness and gaiety, but as the lovers move through the forest,
part and meet again, or mingle with the other characters in
their constantly changing pairs and groups, every view of life
that is presented seems, sooner or later, to find its opposite.
Life is "but a flower in spring time, the only pretty ring time,"
but for the unromantic Touchstone there is "no great matter in
the ditty" and he counts it but time lost—his eye no doubt still
on his timepiece—"to hear such a foolish song." A quartet of
lovers avowing their love is broken up when one of them says

> Pray you, no more of this; 'tis like the howling of Irish
> wolves against the moon.

And the one who says this is she who cannot tell "how many
fathom deep" she is in love. Dominating the centre of the play,
playing both the man's and woman's parts, counsellor in love

and yet its victim, Rosalind gathers up into herself many of its roles and many of its meanings. Around her in the forest, where the banished Duke presides, is the perfect happiness of the simple life, an illusion, much mocked at, but still cherished. She herself, beloved of the hero, has all the sanity to recognize that "love is merely a madness" and that lovers should be whipped as madmen are, but admits that "the whippers are in love too." Heroine of numerous masquerades, she is none the less always constant and never more true than when insisting that she is counterfeiting. For she is an expert in those dark riddles which mean exactly what they say. Though things are rarely what they seem, they may sometimes be so in a deeper sense. What is wisdom and what is folly is of course never decided—you may have it "as you like it." Or, as Touchstone rejoined to Rosalind, after her gibe about the medlar, "You have said; but whether wisely or no, let the forest judge."

It may be possible to suggest that the forest gives its verdict. For if *As You Like It* proclaims no final truth, its ultimate effect is not negative. Longing to escape to our enchanted world, we are constantly brought up against reality; sanity, practical wisdom sees through our illusions. Yet in *As You Like It* ideals, though always on the point of dissolving, are for ever recreating themselves. They do not delude the eye of reason, yet faith in them is not extinguished in spite of all that reason can do. "I would not be cured, youth."

NOTES

1. A lecture delivered to the Shakespeare Conference at Stratford-upon-Avon, 18 August 1953.

2. Quiller-Couch, *Shakespeare's Workmanship* (1918), p. 130. In spite of some radical disagreement, I have got a number of hints from "Q"'s essay.

3. This is not to imply that Shakespeare's "golden world" is at all the same as the primitive life of the mythical golden age, in which, by contrast with the Forest of Arden, there was no winter wind, sheep went unshorn, and man, at peace with all creatures, neither killed the deer nor was threatened by the snake and lion. Virgil associated the simplicity of pastoral life

with the golden age, and the two ideals were frequently combined, not to say confused, by later pastoralists (cf. Roy Walker, *The Golden Feast,* 1952, p. 133).

4. *Huntington Library Bulletin,* VIII (1935), 85.

5. *"Enter Orlando"* says the Folio simply, but the dialogue justifies Theobald's *"with Sword drawn."*

Joseph H. Summers

THE MASKS OF *TWELFTH NIGHT*

LOVE and its fulfillment are primary in Shakespeare's comedies.
Its conflicts are often presented in terms of the battle of the
generations. At the beginning of the plays the bliss of the
young lovers is usually barred by an older generation of parents
and rulers, a group which has supposedly experienced its own
fulfillment in the past and which is now concerned with preserving old forms or fulfilling new ambitions. The comedies usually
end with the triumph of young love, a triumph in which the
lovers make peace with their elders and themselves assume
adulthood and often power. The revolutionary force of love becomes an added element of vitality in a re-established society.

Twelfth Night does not follow the customary pattern. In this
play the responsible older generation has been abolished, and
there are no parents at all. In the first act we are rapidly introduced into a world in which the ruler is a love-sick Duke—in
which young ladies, fatherless and motherless, embark on disguised actions, or rule, after a fashion, their own households, and
in which the only individuals possibly over thirty are drunkards,
jokesters, and gulls, totally without authority. All the external
barriers to fulfillment have been eliminated in what becomes
almost a parody of the state desired by the ordinary young
lovers, the Hermias and Lysanders—or even the Rosalinds and
Orlandos. According to the strictly romantic formula, the happy
ending should be already achieved at the beginning of the
play: we should abandon the theater for the rites of love. But
the slightly stunned inhabitants of Illyria discover that they are

From *The University Review*, XXII (Autumn 1955), 25-32. Copyright 1955 by the University of Missouri at Kansas City. Reprinted by
permission of the editor and the author.

anything but free. Their own actions provide the barriers, for most of them know neither themselves, nor others, nor their social world.

For his festival entertainment, Shakespeare freshly organized all the usual material of the romances—the twins, the exile, the impersonations—to provide significant movement for a dance of maskers. Every character has his mask, for the assumption of the play is that no one is without a mask in the serio-comic business of the pursuit of happiness. The character without disguises who is not ridiculous is outside the realm of comedy. Within comedy, the character who thinks it is possible to live without assuming a mask is merely too naive to recognize the mask he has already assumed. He is the chief object of laughter. As a general rule, we laugh with the characters who know the role they are playing and we laugh at those who do not; we can crudely divide the cast of *Twelfth Night* into those two categories.

But matters are more complicated than this, and roles have a way of shifting. All the butts except perhaps Sir Andrew Aguecheek have moments in which they are the masters of our laughter; yet all the masters have moments in which they appear as fools. In our proper confusion, we must remember the alternative title of the play, "What You Will." It may indicate that everyone is free to invent his own title for the proceedings. It also tells the author's intention to fulfill our desires: we wish to share in the triumphs of love and we wish to laugh; we wish our fools occasionally to be wise, and we are insistent that our wisest dramatic figures experience our common fallibility. Most significantly, the title may hint that what "we" collectively "will" creates all the comic masks—that society determines the forms of comedy more directly than it determines those of any other literary genre.

At the opening of the play Orsino and Olivia accept the aristocratic (and literary) ideas of the romantic lover and the grief-stricken lady as realities rather than as ideas. They are comic characters exactly because of that confusion. Orsino glories in the proper moodiness and fickleness of the literary lover; only our own romanticism can blind us to the absurdities in his opening speech. Orsino first wishes the music to continue so that the appetite of love may "surfeit"; immediately, however, he demands that the musicians stop the music they are playing to repeat an isolated phrase—an awkward procedure and a comic bit of stage business which is rarely utilized in productions. Four lines later the music must stop entirely because the repeated "strain" no longer *is* sweet, and the appetite is truly about to "surfeit." He then exclaims that the spirit of love is so "quick and fresh" that like the sea (hardly a model of freshness)

> naught enters there,
> Of what validity and pitch soe'er,
> But falls into abatement and low price,
> Even in a minute!

Orsino is a victim of a type of madness to which the most admirable characters are sometimes subject. Its usual causes are boredom, lack of physical love, and excessive imagination, and the victim is unaware that he is in love with love rather than with a person.

In the same scene, before we ever see the lady, Olivia's state is as nicely defined. Valentine, Orsino's messenger, has acquired something of his master's extraordinary language, and his report on his love mission manages both to please the Duke and to convey his own incredulity at the excess of Olivia's vow for her brother. In his speech the fresh and the salt are again confused. It is impossible to keep fresh something so ephemeral as grief; Olivia can make it last and "season" it, however, by the process of pickling—the natural effect of "eye-offending brine." Orsino feels unbounded admiration for the depth of soul indicated by Olivia's vow and at the same time he assumes that the vow can easily be broken by a lover. He departs for "sweet *beds* ot flow'rs" which are somehow to provide a *canopy* for "love-thoughts."

Both Orsino and Olivia have adopted currently fashionable literary postures; yet neither of them is a fool. We are glad to be reassured by the Captain that Orsino is "A noble duke, in nature as in name," and that his present infatuation is only a month old. Sir Toby's later remark "What a plague means my niece, to take the death of her brother thus?" indicates that

Olivia too had seemed an unlikely candidate for affectation. She is also an unconvincing practitioner. Although at our first glimpse of her she is properly the grief-stricken lady ("Take the fool away"), her propriety collapses under Feste's famous catechism. We discover that Olivia is already bored and that she really desires to love. Outraged nature has its full and comic revenge when Olivia falls passionately in love with a male exterior and acts with an aggressiveness which makes Orsino seem almost feminine. Still properly an actor in comedy, Olivia quickly changes from the character who has confused herself with a socially attractive mask to one who fails to perceive the mask which society has imposed on another.

Viola's situation allows time for neither love- nor grief-in-idleness. A virgin, shipwrecked in a strange land, possessing only wit and intelligence and the Captain's friendship, she must act immediately if she is to preserve herself. She, like Olivia, has "lost" a brother, but the luxury of conventional mourning is quickly exchanged for a *willed* hope that, as she was saved, "so perchance may he be." With Viola's wish for time to know what her "estate is," before she is "delivered to the world," we are reminded that society often requires a mask, neither for the relief of boredom nor the enjoyment of acting, but merely for self-preservation. While Antonio, "friend to Sebastian," almost loses his life because of his failure to assume a disguise, Viola suffers from no failure of discretion or imagination. She must assume a disguise as a boy and she must have help in preparing it.

Although she knows the ways of the world, Viola takes the necessary chance and wills to trust the Captain:

> There is a fair behavior in thee, Captain.
> And though that Nature with a beauteous wall
> Doth oft close in pollution, yet of thee
> I will believe thou hast a mind that suits
> With this thy fair and outward character.

We have in this second scene not only the beginning of one strand of the complicated intrigue, but also the creation of the one character active in the intrigue who provides a measure for the comic excesses of all the others. (Feste's role as observer is analogous to Viola's role as "actor.") Although Viola chooses to impersonate Cesario from necessity, she later plays her part with undisguised enjoyment. She misses none of the opportunities for parody, for confession, and for *double entendre* which the mask affords, and she never forgets or lets us forget the biological distance between Viola and Cesario. Except in the fencing match with Sir Andrew Aguecheek, she anticipates and directs our perception of the ludicrous in her own role as well as in the roles of Orsino and Olivia.

Sebastian is the reality of which Cesario is the artful imitation. Viola's twin assumes no disguises; Viola and the inhabitants of Illyria have assumed it for him. He is, to the eye, identical with Viola, and his early scenes with Antonio serve to remind us firmly of his existence as well as to introduce an initial exhilarating confusion at the entrance of either of the twins. When he truly enters the action of the play in Act IV he is certainly the object of our laughter, not because he has confused himself with an ideal or improper mask, but because he so righteously and ineffectually insists on his own identity in the face of unanimous public opposition. Our attitude quickly changes, however, to a mixture of amused patronization and identification: we do, after all, *know* so much more than does Sebastian; yet, within the context of the play, we can hardly keep from identifying with the gentleman who, practically if not idealistically, decides not to reject the reality of a passionate Olivia just because he has never seen her before:

> Or I am mad, or else this is a dream.
> Let fancy still my sense in Lethe steep.
> If it be thus to dream, still let me sleep!

The other characters in the play do not truly belong to an aristocracy of taste and leisure. For some of them, that is the chief problem. Malvolio and Sir Andrew Aguecheek are ruled by their mistaken notions of the proper role of an upper-class gentleman, and they fail to perceive the comic gaps between themselves and their ideal roles, and between those ideals and the social reality. Sick with self-love as he is, Malvolio is also sick with his desire to rise in society: "an affectioned ass, that cons state without book and utters it by great swaths: the best persuaded of himself, so crammed, as he thinks, with excellencies, that it is his grounds of faith that all that look on him love him." Although he knows it without, he has learned his "state" by book —but such a pupil inevitably distorts the text. He dreams of ruling a thrifty and solemn household while he plays with "some rich jewel," a dream characteristically attractive to the *arriviste* and absolutely impossible to the *arrive*. We, like Maria, "can hardly forbear hurling things at him." His is as absurd as the reverse image which possesses Sir Andrew, a carpet-knight rightly described by Sir Toby as "an ass-head and a coxcomb and a knave, a thin-faced knave, a gull!" In the gallery of false images Sir Andrew's roaring boy hangs opposite Malvolio's burgher. Although in a low moment Sir Andrew may think that he has "no more wit than a Christian or an ordinary man has," he never has such grave self-doubt for long. Like a true gull, he tries to assume the particular role which, of all others, he is most poorly equipped to play: drinker, fighter, wencher.

Sir Andrew, however, would hardly exist without Sir Toby Belch: the gull must have his guller. Sir Toby may fulfill Sir Andrew's idea of what a gentleman should be, but Sir Toby himself has no such odd idea of gentility. (Sir Andrew may be "a dear manikin to you, Sir Toby," but Sir Toby has a superlatively good reason for allowing him to be: "I have been dear to him, lad, some two thousand strong, or so.") Even at his most drunken, we are delightfully unsure whether we laugh at or with Sir Toby, whether he is or is not fully conscious of the effects as well as the causes of his "mistakes," his verbal confusions, and even his belches. Like another drunken knight, and like Viola, Toby possesses a range of dramatic talents and he enjoys using them. He is equally effective as the fearless man of action, as the practitioner of noble "gentleness" with the "mad" Malvolio, and as the experienced alcoholic guide to Sir Andrew. His joy is in the jest as well as in the bottle, and he can bring himself to abandon the latter long enough to marry Maria simply in admiration for her ability as an intriguer. But like other knowing players, Sir Toby is vulnerable to deception. He is object rather than master of our laughter from the time when he mistakes Sebastian for Cesario and attempts to assert his masculine ability as a swordsman.

In the business of masking, Feste is the one professional among a crowd of amateurs; he does it for a living. He never makes the amateur's mistake of confusing his personality with his mask—he wears not motley in his brain. Viola recognizes his wisdom and some kinship in the fact that each "must observe their mood on whom he jests." But though Feste may have deliberately chosen his role, society determines its conditions. Now that he is growing old, the conditions become difficult: "Go to, you're a dry fool, I'll no more of you. Besides, you grow dishonest." While all the other characters are concerned with gaining something they do not have, Feste's struggle is to retain his mask and to make it again ingratiating. He is able to penetrate all the masks of the others, and he succeeds in retaining his own.

However fanciful its dreams of desire, the play moves within a context of an almost real world, from one disguise and half-understood intrigue to another, until all its elements are whirled into a complexly related and moving figure. With the constant contrasts and parallels and reversals in character, situation, and intrigue, we find ourselves at last, along with Malvolio and Olivia and Viola and the rest, in a state of real delirium. Until the concluding scene, however, we can largely agree with Sebastian: if we dream, we do not wish to wake; if this is madness, it is still comic madness, and we do not envy the sane. The attempts at false and inflexible authority are being defeated, the pretentious are being deflated, and the very sentimentality of the likable sentimentalists has led them close to biological reality. We are particularly delighted with Viola. Young, intelligent, zestful, she is a realist. She cuts through the subterfuges and disguises of the others with absolute clarity, and she provides us with a center for the movement, a standard of normality which is never dull. In her rejection of the artificial myths of love, moreover, Viola never becomes the advocate of a far more terrifying myth, the myth of absolute rationality. In a completely rational world, Shakespeare never tires of pointing out, what we know as love could not exist. We have never desired such a world.

From the time of her first aside to the audience after she has seen Orsino ("Yet a barful strife!/Whoe'er I woo, myself would be his wife"), Viola directly admits her irrational love. She differs, then, from Orsino and Olivia not in any invulnerability to

blindness and passion, but in the clarity and simplicity with
which she recognizes and accepts her state. Reason is not abandoned: she rationally admits her irrationality and her inability
to cope with the situation:

> O Time, thou must untangle this, not I!
> It is too hard a knot for me to untie!

Viola needs a miracle. Although she may imagine herself as
"Patience on a monument, smiling at grief," she remains as close
as possible to her loved one and waits for the miracle to happen.
Since we have seen Sebastian, we know that the miracle will
occur; yet through our identification with Viola we come to know
the comic burden, the masker's increasing weariness of the mask
which implies that love is still pursued rather than possessed.

The burden becomes comically unbearable only in the final
scene, when it is cast off. Here Shakespeare underscores all those
possibilities of violence and death which are usually submerged
in comedy. Antonio is arrested and in danger of his life. Orsino,
finally recognizing the hopelessness of his suit to Olivia, shows
the vicious side of sentimentality. After considering the possibility
of killing Olivia "like to the Egyptian thief," he determines to do
violence to "Cesario":

> Come, boy, with me. My thoughts are ripe in mischief.
> I'll sacrifice the lamb that I do love,
> To spite a raven's heart within a dove.

Olivia is hysterical at what seems to be the baseness of Cesario.
Sir Toby has a broken pate to show for his one major failure to
penetrate a mask. The dance must stop. The miracle must occur.

The entrance of Sebastian is "what we will." It is the most
dramatic moment of the play. The confrontation of Sebastian and
Cesario-Viola, those identical images, concludes the formal plot
and provides the means for the discarding of all the lovers' masks.
The moment must be savored and fully realized. As Viola and
Sebastian chant their traditional formulas of proof, both the audience and the other characters on the stage undistractedly view
the physical image of the duality which has made the confusion
and the play. The masks and the play are to be abandoned for a
vision of delight beyond delight, in which lovers have neither to

wear nor to penetrate disguises since they are at last invulnerable
to error and laughter.

Yet the play does not resolve into a magic blessing of the
world's fertility as does *A Midsummer Night's Dream*. We have
been promised a happy ending, and we receive it. We are grate-
ful that the proper Jacks and Jills have found each other, but
the miracle is a limited miracle, available only to the young
and the lucky. Not every Jack has his Jill even in Illyria, and after
the general unmasking, those without love may seem even
lonelier. Malvolio, of course, is justly punished. He has earned
his mad scene, and with the aid of Feste he has made it comic.
As a result of his humiliation he has also earned some sort of
redress. Yet he is ridiculous in his arrogance to the end, and his
threatened revenge, now that he is powerless to effect it, sustains
the comedy and the characterization and prevents the obtrusion
of destructive pathos.

It is Feste rather than Malvolio who finally reminds us of the
limitations and the costs of the romantic vision of happiness with
which we have been seduced. However burdensome, masking is
his career, and romantic love provides no end for it. Alone on
the stage at the end of the play, he sings a song of unfulfilled love
which shows the other side of the coin. For Feste, as for his audience, the mask can never be finally discarded: the rain it raineth
every day. His song has those overtones, I believe, but they are
only overtones. The music, here and elsewhere in the play, provides an element in which oppositions may be resolved. And the
song itself, like the movement which must accompany it, is crude
and witty as well as graceful and nostalgic. However far it may
have missed the conventionally happy ending, Feste's saga of
misfortunes in love is comic, even from his own point of view.
The exaggeration so often operative in the refrains of Elizabethan
lyrics emphasizes that the watery as well as the sunny vision can
become funny: it doesn't rain every day by a long shot.

The song, which begins as the wittiest observer's comment on
the denouement of the play, ends as a dissolution of the dramatic
fiction:

> A great while ago the world begun,
>   With hey, ho, the wind and the rain,

> But that's all one, our play is done,
> And we'll strive to please you every day.

The audience has been a participant in the festivity. As the fictional lovers have unmasked to reveal or realize their "true" identities, it is only proper that the clown, the only character who might move freely in the environs of Bankside, as well as in the realm of Illyria, should unmask the whole proceeding for the imitation of a desired world which it has been. The audience must be returned from "What You Will" to its own less patterned world where the sea rarely disgorges siblings given up for lost, where mistaken marriages rarely turn out well, where Violas rarely catch Dukes, and where Malvolios too often rule households with disturbing propriety. The lovers have met, and Feste announces that present laughter has come to an end. But the actors, those true and untiring maskers, will continue to "strive to please" us. They will find few occasions in the future in which their efforts will be more sure of success.

Twelfth Night is the climax of Shakespeare's early achievement in comedy. The effects and values of the earlier comedies are here subtly embodied in the most complex structure which Shakespeare had yet created. But the play also looks forward: the pressure to dissolve the comedy, to realize and finally abandon the burden of laughter, is an intrinsic part of its "perfection." Viola's clear-eyed and affirmative vision ot her own and the world's irrationality is a triumph and we desire it; yet we realize its vulnerability, and we come to realize that virtue in disguise is only totally triumphant when evil is not in disguise—is not truly present at all. Having solved magnificently the problems of this particular form of comedy, Shakespeare was evidently not tempted to repeat his triumph. After *Twelfth Night* the so-called comedies require for their happy resolutions more radical characters and devices—omniscient and omnipresent Dukes, magic, and resurrection. More obvious miracles are needed for comedy to exist in a world in which evil also exists, not merely incipiently but with power.

C. L. Barber

FROM RITUAL TO COMEDY:
AN EXAMINATION OF *HENRY IV*

MY GENERAL CONCERN is with the relation of comedy to analogous forms of symbolic action in folk rituals: not only the likenesses of comedy to ritual, but the differences, the features of comic form which make it comedy and not ritual. I want to point out what seem to me striking analogies between the comedy in the two parts of *Henry IV* and the customary misrule of traditional saturnalian holidays.[1] These analogies, I think, prove to be useful critical tools: they lead us to see structure in the play. And they also raise fascinating historical and theoretical questions about the relation of drama to other products of culture. One way in which our time has been seeing the universal in literature has been to find in complex literary works patterns which are analogous to myths and rituals and which can be regarded as archetypes, in some sense primitive or fundamental. I find this approach very exciting indeed. But at the same time, such analysis can be misleading if it leads to equating the literary form with primitive analogues. When we deal with so developed an art as Shakespeare's, in so complex an epoch as the Renaissance, primitive patterns may be seen in literature mainly because literary imagination, exploiting the heritage of literary form, disengages them from the suggestions of a complex culture. And the primitive levels are articulated in the course of reunderstanding their nature—in-

From *English Stage Comedy: English Institute Essays, 1954,* 1955, pp. 22-51. Copyright 1955 by Columbia University Press. Reprinted by permission of the publisher and the author.

deed, the primitive can be fully expressed only on condition that the artist can deal with it in a most civilized way. Shakespeare presents patterns analogous to magic and ritual in the process of redefining magic as imagination, ritual as social action.

Shakespeare was neither primitive nor primitivistic, for in his culture what we search out and call primitive was in the blood and bone as a matter of course. The problem was to deal with it, to master it. The Renaissance was a moment when educated men were modifying a ceremonial conception of human life to create a historical conception. The ceremonial view, which assumed that names and meanings are fixed and final, expressed experience as pageant and ritual—pageant where the right names could march in proper order, or ritual where names could be changed in the right, the proper way. The historical view expresses life as drama. People in drama are not identical with their names, for they gain and lose their names, their status, and meaning—and not by settled ritual: the gaining and losing of names, of meaning, is beyond the control of any set ritual sequence. Shakespeare's plays are full of pageantry and of action patterned in a ritualistic way. But the pageants are regularly interrupted; the rituals are abortive or perverted; or if they succeed, they succeed against odds or in an unexpected fashion. The people in the plays try to organize their lives by pageant and ritual, but the plays are dramatic precisely because the effort fails. This failure drama presents as history and personality; in the largest perspective, as destiny. At the heart of the plays there is, I think, a fascination with the individualistic use or abuse of ritual—with magic.

There is an intoxication with the possibility of an omnipotence of mind by which words might become things, by which a man might "gain a deity," might achieve, by making his own ritual, an unlimited power to incarnate meaning. This fascination is expressed in the poetry by which Shakespeare's people envisage their ideal selves. But his drama also expresses an equal and complementary awareness that magic is delusory, that words can become things or lead to deeds only within a social group, by virtue of a historical and psychological situation beyond the mind and discourse of any one man. This awareness of limitations is expressed by the ironies, whether comic or tragic, which Shakespeare embodies in the dramatic situations of his speakers, the ironies which bring down the selves or meanings which fly high in winged words.

We can explore one instance of this dramatic tension by looking in *Henry IV* at the relation of Shakespeare's festive comedy to ritual prototypes. As I see it, the gay comedy in Shakespeare is fundamentally saturnalian rather than satiric. A saturnalian pattern for organizing experience came to Shakespeare from many sources, in both social and artistic tradition. In the theatrical institution of clowning, the clown or Vice, when Shakespeare started to write, was a recognized anarchist who made aberration obvious by carrying release to absurd extremes. The cult of fools and folly, half social and half literary, embodied a similar polarization of experience. In social life, folly was customarily cultivated on traditional holidays such as Shrove Tuesday, Hocktide, May Day, Whitsuntide, Midsummer Eve, Harvest Home, and the twelve days of Christmas ending with Twelfth Night. The festival occasion provides a paradigm for the organization of impulse and awareness not only in those comedies where Shakespeare drew largely and directly on holiday motifs, like *Love's Labour's Lost, A Midsummer Night's Dream,* and *Twelfth Night,* but also in plays where there is relatively little direct use of holiday, notably *As You Like It* and *Henry IV.* The language that described festive occasions, or was used in them, provides a vocabulary for making explicit the "form of mirth" in the plays about pleasure. The attitudes adopted on holiday were archetypes in English Renaissance culture for the attitudes adopted about pleasure whenever people set out to have a good time. So Shakespeare's gay comedy dramatizes pleasure as release from normal limitations, and the judgments implicit in its humor primarily concern the relation between man and the nature celebrated by holiday, not relations between social classes or types. The plays give form to feeling and knowledge by a movement which can be summarized in the formula: *through release to clarification.*

I cannot even survey Shakespeare's development in relation to this holiday tradition here. My view, briefly, is that, although he began writing comedy with literary models (Plautus,

Italian comedy, and narrative romances), he found a satisfactory form for the whole play only when, in *Love's Labour's Lost* and *A Midsummer Night's Dream,* he shaped the whole action so as to express the release of a revel and so provide occasion for comic clarification of the relation between man's vital energies and the rest of his experience.

My thesis is that, in creating the Falstaff comedy, Shakespeare fused two main saturnalian traditions: the clowning customary on the stage, and the folly customary on holiday. Northrop Frye has effectively summarized the holiday aspect of Falstaff in saying that he is "a mock king, a lord of misrule, and his tavern is a saturnalia." [2] To see Falstaff in this role is not to suppose that Shakespeare arbitrarily imitates festivities at the Inns of Court or elsewhere, though such experience obviously is used. Rather, it seems to me Shakespeare arrives at such a figure by developing the saturnalian implications of the clown's role in the directions suggested by the saturnalian customs and sensibility of his time and in response to the need for such a role within the imaginative economy of the whole complex historical drama which he was working out.

The tradition of clowning had been from long before Shakespeare integrally related to the use of double plots. William Empson has made some fine observations here, to which I am indebted.[3] It was of course a practice, going back at least as far as the *Second Shepherd's Play,* for the clowns to present a burlesque version of actions performed seriously by their betters. Wagner's conjuring in *Dr. Faustus* is an obvious example. In the drama just before Shakespeare began writing, there are a great many parallels of this sort between the low comedy and the main action. One suspects that they often resulted from the initiative of the clown performer—he was, as Sidney said, thrust in "by head and shoulders to play a part in majestical matters"—and the handiest part to play was a low take-off of what the high people were doing. Though Sidney objected that the procedure was "without decency or decorum," such burlesque, when properly controlled, had an artistic logic which Shakespeare was quick to develop.

At the simplest level the clowns were foils, as one of the aristocrats remarks in *Love's Labour's Lost:*

'Tis some policy
To have one show worse than the king's and his company.

But burlesque could also have a positive effect, as a vehicle
for expressing aberrant impulse and thought. When the aberration was made relevant to the main action, clowning could
provide both release for impulses which run counter to decorum and the clarification about limits which comes from
going beyond the limit. Shakespeare used this movement from
release to clarification with masterful control in clown episodes
as early as *Henry VI, Part II*. The scenes of the Jack Cade rebellion in that history are an astonishingly consistent expression
of anarchy by clowning: the popular rising is presented throughout as a saturnalia, ignorantly undertaken in earnest; Cade's
motto is "then are we in order when we are most out of order."

The implications of a saturnalian attitude are more drastically
and complexly expressed in *Henry IV* than anywhere else, because here saturnalia is presented along with other kinds of
experience, in an environment, so that Shakespeare dramatizes
not only holiday but also the need for holiday and the need to
limit holiday. Misrule is more drastic and meaningful here than
in, say, *Twelfth Night*, because misrule is presented along
with rule and along with the tensions that challenge rule. In
the idyllic plays there is a humor of perspective which recognizes the limitations of the reigning festive moment by looking
outward, from it, to the work-a-day world beyond. But in the
two parts of *Henry IV*, holiday is balanced against everyday
and doomsday within the play. The comedy expresses impulses
and awareness excluded by the urgency and decorum of political
life, so that the comic and serious strains are contrapuntal, each
conveying ironies limiting the other.

The issue, so far as it concerns Prince Hal, can be summarized quite adequately in our key terms. As the nonhistorical
material came to Shakespeare in *The Famous Victories of
Henry the Fifth*, the prince was cast in the traditional role of
the prodigal son while his disreputable companions functioned
as tempters in the same general fashion as the Vice of the
morality plays. At one level Shakespeare keeps this pattern, but
he shifts the emphasis away from simple moral terms. The issue,

in his hands, is not whether Hal will be good or bad but whether he will be noble or degenerate, whether his holiday will become his everyday. The interregnum of a Lord of Misrule, delightful in its moment, might develop into the anarchic reign of a favorite dominating a dissolute king. Hal's secret, which he confides early to the audience, is that for him Falstaff is merely a pastime, to be dismissed in due course:

> If all the year were playing holidays,
> To sport would be as tedious as to work.

The prince's sports, accordingly, express not dissoluteness but a fine excess of vitality—"as full of spirit as the month of May"—together with a capacity for occasionally looking at the world as though it were upside down. His energy is controlled by an inclusive awareness of the rhythm in which he is living: despite appearances, he will not make the mistake which undid Richard II, who played at saturnalia until it caught up with him in earnest. During the battle of Shrewsbury (when, in Hotspur's phrase, "Doomsday is near"), Hal dismisses Falstaff with "What! is't a time to jest and dally now?" This sense of timing, of the relation of holiday to everyday, contributes to establishing the prince as an inclusive, sovereign nature. At the close of battle, in the moment of stillness when Hal stands poised above the prostrate bodies of Hotspur and Falstaff, his position on the stage and his lines about the two heroes express a nature which includes within a larger order the now subordinated parts of life which are represented in those two: in Hotspur, honor, the social obligation to courage and self-sacrifice, a value which has been isolated in this magnificently anarchical feudal lord to become almost the whole of life; and in Falstaff, the complementary *joie de vivre* which rejects all social obligations because "I like not such grinning honour as Sir Walter hath." At this point, Shakespeare was in a wonderful position to end *Henry IV;* he could have left Falstaff really dead, since he is effectually dead for the Prince. Instead the dramatist brought him back to life, jumping up like Bottom after Pyramus in a triumph which reminds one of the comic resurrections in the St. George plays.

When Falstaff jumps up, his apology for counterfeiting cuts deeply indeed, because it does not apply merely to himself; we can relate it, as Empson has shown, to the counterfeiting of the king. Bolingbroke knows when it is time to counterfeit, both in this battle, where he survives because he has many marching in his coats, and throughout the political career where, as he acknowledges to Hal, he manipulates the symbols of majesty with a calculating concern for ulterior results. L. C. Knights, noticing this relation and the burlesque, elsewhere in Falstaff's part, of the attitudes of chivalry, concluded with nineteenth-century critics like Ulrici and Victor Hugo that the comedy should be taken as a devastating satire on war and government.[4] But this is obviously an impossible, anachronistic view, based on the assumption of the age of individualism that politics and war are unnatural activities that can be done without. Knights would have it that the audience should feel a jeering response when Henry sonorously declares, after Shrewsbury: "Thus ever did rebellion find rebuke." This interpretation makes a shambles of the heroic moments of the play—makes them clearly impossible to act. My own view, as my introductory remarks will have made clear, is that the dynamic relation of comedy and serious action is saturnalian rather than satiric, that the misrule works, through the whole dramatic rhythm, to consolidate rule. But it is also true, as Empson remarks, that "the double plot is carrying a fearful strain here."[5] Shakespeare is putting an enormous pressure on the comedy to resolve the challenge posed by the ironic perceptions presented in his serious action.

This can be made clearer, I hope, by reference now to the scapegoat aspect of saturnalian ritual. We do not need to assume that Shakespeare had any such ritual patterns consciously in mind; whatever his conscious intention, it seems to me that these analogues illuminate patterns which his poetic drama presents concretely and dramatically. After such figures as the Mardi Gras or Carnival have presided over a revel, they are frequently turned on by their followers, tried in some sort of court, convicted of sins notorious in the village during the last year, and burned or buried in effigy to signify a new start. In other ceremonies described in The Golden Bough, mockery kings appear as recognizable substitutes for real kings, stand trial in their stead, and carry away the evils of their realms into exile or death. One such scapegoat figure, as remote as could be from Shakespeare, is the Tibetan King of the Years, who enjoyed, until very recently at least, ten days' misrule during the annual holiday of Buddhist monks at Lhasa. At the climax of his ceremony, after doing what he liked while collecting bad luck by shaking a black yak's tail over the people, he mounted the temple steps and ridiculed the representative of the Grand Lama, proclaiming heresies like "What we perceive through the five senses is no illusion. All you teach is untrue." A few minutes later, discredited by a cast of loaded dice, he was chased off to exile and possible death in the mountains.[6] One cannot help thinking of Falstaff's catechism on honor, spoken just before another valuation of honor is expressed in the elevated blank verse of a hero confronting death: "Can honour . . . take away the grief of a wound? No. . . . What is honour? a word. What is that word, honour? Air." And Hal's final expulsion of Falstaff appears in the light of these analogies to carry out an impersonal pattern, not merely political but ritual in character. After the guilty reign of Bolingbroke, the prince is making a fresh start as the new king. At a level beneath the moral notions of a personal reform, we can see a nonlogical process of purification by sacrifice —the sacrifice of Falstaff. The career of the old king, a successful usurper whose conduct of affairs has been skeptical and opportunistic, has cast doubt on the validity of the whole conception of a divinely ordained and chivalrous kingship to which Shakespeare and his society were committed. And before Bolingbroke, Richard II had given occasion for doubts about the rituals of kingship in an opposite way, by trying to use them magically. Shakespeare had shown Richard assuming that the symbols of majesty should be absolutes, that the names of legitimate power should be transcendently effective regardless of social forces. Now both these attitudes have been projected also in Falstaff; he carries to comically delightful and degraded extremes both a magical use of moral sanctions and the complementary opportunistic manipulation and skepticism. So the ritual analogy suggests that by turning on Falstaff as a scapegoat, as the villagers turned on their Mardi Gras, the prince can free himself from the sins, the "bad luck," of Richard's reign and of his father's reign, to become a king in whom chivalry and a sense of divine ordination are restored.

Now this process of carrying off bad luck, if it is to be made *dramatically* cogent, as a symbolic action accomplished in and by dramatic form, cannot take place magically in Shakespeare's play: the magical analogy can be only a useful way of organizing our awareness of a complex symbolic action. The expulsion of evil works as dramatic form only in so far as it is realized in a movement from participation to rejection which happens, moment by moment, in our response to Falstaff's clowning misrule. We watch Falstaff adopt one posture after another, in the effort to give himself meaning at no cost; and moment by moment we see that the meaning is specious. So our participation is repeatedly diverted to laughter. The laughter signalizes our mastery by understanding of the tendency which has been misapplied or carried to an extreme; this mastery leaves us free to laugh off energy originally mobilized to respond to a valid meaning.

Consider, for example, the use of magical notions of royal power in the most famous of all Falstaff's burlesques:

By the Lord, I knew ye as well as he that made ye . . . . was it for me to kill the heir-apparent? Should I turn upon the true prince? Why, thou knowest I am as valiant as Hercules; but beware instinct; the lion will not touch the true prince. Instinct is a great matter, I was a coward on instinct. I shall think the better of myself and thee during my life; I for a valiant lion, and thou for a true prince. But, by the Lord, lads, I am glad you have the money. Hostess, clap to the doors: watch to-night, pray to-morrow.

Here Falstaff has recourse to the brave conception that legitimate kingship has a magical potency. This is the sort of absolutist appeal to sanctions which Richard II keeps falling back on in his desperate "conjuration" by hyperbole:

So when this thief, this traitor, Bolingbroke

. . . . .

Shall see us rising in our throne, the east,
His treasons will sit blushing in his face,
Not able to endure the sight of day. . . .

> The breath of worldly men cannot depose
> The deputy elected by the Lord.
> For every man that Bolingbroke hath press'd
> To lift shrewd steel against our golden crown,
> God for his Richard hath in heavenly pay
> A glorious angel.

In Richard's case, a tragic irony enforces the fact that heavenly angels are of no avail if one's coffers are empty and the Welsh army have dispersed. In Falstaff's case, the irony is comically obvious, the "lies are like the father that begets them; gross as a mountain, open, palpable." Hal stands for the judgment side of our response, while Falstaff embodies the enthusiastic, irrepressible conviction of fantasy's omnipotence. The Prince keeps returning to Falstaff's bogus "instinct": "Now, sirs . . . you are lions too, you ran away upon instinct, you will not touch the true prince; no, fie!" After enjoying the experience of seeing through such notions of magical majesty, he is never apt to make the mistake of assuming that, just because he is king, lions like Northumberland will not touch him. King Richard's bad luck came precisely from such an assumption—unexamined, of course, as fatal assumptions always are. Freud's account of bad luck, in *The Psychopathology of Everyday Life,* sees it as the expression of unconscious motives which resist the conscious goals of the personality. This view helps to explain how the acting out of disruptive motives in saturnalia or in comedy can serve to master potential aberration by revaluing it in relation to the whole of experience. So Falstaff, in acting out this absolutist aberration, is taking away what might have been Hal's bad luck, taking it away in a real, though not magical way: the comedy is a civilized equivalent of the primitive rite. I hope it will be clear by analogy that a similar mastery of potential aberration is promoted by the experience of seeing through Falstaff's burlesque of the sort of headlong chivalry presented seriously in Hotspur.

In order to put the symbolic action of the comedy in larger perspective, it will be worth while to consider further, for a moment, the relation of language to stage action and dramatic situation in *Richard II.* That play is a pioneering exploration of the semantics of royalty, shot through with talk about the potency and impotence of language. In the first part, we see a Richard who is possessor of an apparently magical omnipotence: for example, when he commutes Bolingbroke's banishment from ten to six years, Bolingbroke exclaims:

> How long a time lies in one little word!
> Four lagging winters and four wanton springs
> End in a word: such is the breath of kings.

Richard assumes he has such magic breath inevitably, regardless of the breath of worldly men. When he shouts things like "Is not the king's name twenty thousand names? Arm, arm, my name!" he carries the absolutist assumption to the giddiest verge of absurdity. When we analyze the magical substitution of words for things in such lines, looking at them from outside the rhythm of feeling in which they occur, it seems scarcely plausible that a drama should be built around the impulse to adopt such an assumption. It seems especially implausible in our own age, when we are so conscious, on an abstract level, of the dependence of verbal efficacy on the social group. The analytical situation involves a misleading perspective, however; for, whatever your assumptions about semantics, when you have to act, to be somebody or become somebody, there is a moment when you have to have faith that the unknown world beyond will respond to the names you commit yourself to as right names.[7] The Elizabethan mind, moreover, generally assumed that one played one's part in a divinely ordained pageant where each man *was* his name and the role his name implied. The expression of this faith, and of the outrage of it, is particularly drastic in the Elizabethan drama, which can be regarded, from this vantage, as an art form developed to express the shock and exhilaration of the discovery that life is not pageantry. As Professor Tillyard has pointed out, *Richard II* is the most ceremonial of all Shakespeare's plays, and the ceremony all comes to nothing.[8] In Richard's deposition scene, one way in which anguish at his fall is expressed is by a focus on his loss of names: he responds to Northumberland's "My Lord—" by flinging out

> No Lord of thine, thou haught insulting man,
> Nor no man's lord; I have no name, no title,

> No, not that name was given me at the font,
> But 'tis usurp'd: alack the heavy day!
> That I have worn so many winters out,
> And know not now what name to call myself.
> O! that I were a mockery king of snow,
> Standing before the sun of Bolingbroke,
> To melt myself away in water-drops.

His next move is to call for the looking glass in which he stares at his face to look for the meaning the face has lost. To lose one's meaning, one's social role, is to be reduced to mere body.

Here again the tragedy can be used to illuminate the comedy. Since the Elizabethan drama was a double medium of words and of physical gestures, it frequently expressed the pathos of the loss of meaning by emphasizing moments when word and gesture, name and body, no longer go together, just as it presented the excitement of a gain of meaning by showing a body seizing on names when a hero creates his identity. In the deposition scene, Richard says "mark me how I will undo myself." Then he gives away by physical gestures the symbolic meanings which have constituted that self. When at last he has no name, the anguish is that the face, the body, remain when the meaning is gone. Of course there is also a narcissism in Richard's lines which, beneath the surface of his self-pity, relishes such reduction to his body, a self-love which looks towards fulfillment in that final reduction of all to the body which is death. This narcissistic need for the physical is the other side of the attitude that the magic of the crown should altogether transcend the physical—and the human:

> Cover your heads, and mock not flesh and blood
> With solemn reverence: throw away respect,
> Tradition, form, and ceremonious duty,
> For you have but mistook me all this while:
> I live with bread like you, feel want,
> Taste grief, need friends: subjected thus,
> How can you say to me I am a king?

In expressing the disappointment of Richard's magical expectations, as well as their sweeping magnificence, the lines make manifest the aberration which is mastered in the play by tragic form.

The same sort of impulse is expressed and mastered by comic form in the *Henry IV* comedy. When Richard wishes he were a mockery king of snow, to melt before the sun of Bolingbroke, the image expresses on one side the wish to escape from the body with which he is left when his meaning has gone—to weep himself away in water drops. But the lines also look wistfully towards games of mock royalty where, since the whole thing is based on snow, the collapse of meaning need not hurt. Falstaff is such a mockery king. To be sure, he is flesh and blood, of a kind: he is tallow, anyway. He "sweats to death And lards the lean earth as he walks along." (The image is strikingly reminiscent of Richard's melting snowman.) Of course he is not just a mockery, not just his role, not just bombast. Shakespeare, as always, makes the symbolic role the product of a life which includes contradictions of it, such as the morning-after regrets when Falstaff thinks of the inside of a church and notices that his skin hangs about him like an old lady's loose gown. Falstaff is human enough so that "Were't not for laughing, . . . [we] should pity him." But we do laugh, because when Falstaff's meanings collapse, almost nothing but make-believe has been lost

> *Prince:* Do thou stand for my father, and examine me upon the particulars of my life.
> *Falstaff:* Shall I? content: this chair shall be my state, this dagger my sceptre, and this cushion my crown.
> *Prince:* Thy state is taken for a joint-stool, thy golden sceptre for a leaden dagger, and thy precious rich crown for a pitiful bald crown!

Falstaff's effort to make his body and furnishings mean sovereignty is doomed from the start; he must work with a leaden dagger, the equivalent of a Vice's dagger of lath. But Falstaff does have golden words, and an inexhaustible vitality in using them. He can name himself nobly, reordering the world verbally so as to do himself credit:

> No, good my lord; banish Peto, banish Bardolph, banish Poins; but for sweet Jack Falstaff, kind Jack Falstaff, true

Jack Falstaff, valiant Jack Falstaff, and therefore more
valiant being, as he is, old Jack Falstaff, banish not him thy
Harry's company: banish not him thy Harry's company:
Banish plump Jack, and banish all the world.

I quote such familiar lines to recall their effect of incantation:
they embody an effort at a kind of magical naming. Each repetition of "sweet Jack Falstaff, kind Jack Falstaff" aggrandizes an
identity which the serial clauses caress and cherish. At the very
end, in "plump Jack," the disreputable belly is glorified.

In valid heroic and majestic action, the bodies of the personages are constantly being elevated by becoming the vehicles of
social meanings; in the comedy, such elevation becomes burlesque, and by the repeated failures to achieve a fusion of body
and symbol, abstract meanings keep falling back into the physical. "A plague of sighing and grief! it blows a man up like a
bladder." The repetition of such joking about Falstaff's belly
makes it meaningful in a very special way, as a symbol of the
process of inflation and reduction. So it represents the power of
the individual life to continue despite the collapse of social roles.
This continuing on beyond definitions is after all what we call
"the body" in one main meaning of the term: Falstaff's belly is
thus the essence of body—an essence which can be defined only
dynamically, by failures of meaning. The effect of indestructible
vitality is reinforced by the association of Falstaff's figure with
the gay eating and drinking of Shrove Tuesday and Carnival.
Whereas, in the tragedy, the reduction is to a body which can
only die, here reduction is to a body which typifies our power
to eat and drink our way through a shambles of intellectual and
moral contradictions.

So we cannot resist sharing Falstaff's genial self-love when he
commends his vision of plump Jack to the Prince, just as we share
the ingenuous self-love of a little child. But the dramatist is ever
on the alert to enforce the ironies that dog the tendency of
fantasy to equate the self with "all the world." So a most monstrous watch comes beating at the doors which have been clapped
to against care; everyday breaks in on holiday.

Part I can be summarized, in terms of our analogy, as the
reign of Carnival; *Part II* as his trial. To put Carnival on trial, run

him out of town, and burn or bury him is in folk custom a way of limiting, by ritual, the attitudes and impulses set loose by ritual. Such a trial, though conducted no doubt with gay hoots and jeers, serves to swing the mind round to a new vantage, where it sees misrule no longer as a benign release for the individual, but as a source of destructive consequences for society. This sort of reckoning is what *Part II* brings to Falstaff.

But Falstaff proves extremely difficult to bring to book—more difficult than an ordinary mummery king—because his burlesque and mockery are developed to a point where the mood of a moment crystallizes as a settled attitude of skepticism. In a static, monolithic society, a Lord of Misrule can be put back in his place after the revel with relative ease. The festive burlesque of solemn sanctities does not seriously threaten social values in a monolithic culture, because the license depends utterly upon what it mocks: liberty is unable to envisage any alternative to the accepted order except the standing of it on its head. But Shakespeare's culture was not monolithic: though its moralists assumed a single order, skepticism was beginning to have ground to stand on and look about—especially in and around London. So a Lord of Misrule figure, brought up, so to speak, from the country to the city, or from the traditional past into the changing present, could become on the Bankside the mouthpiece not merely for the dependent holiday skepticism which is endemic in a traditional society, but also for a dangerously self-sufficient everyday skepticism. When such a figure is set in an environment of sober-blooded great men behaving as opportunistically as he, the effect is to raise radical questions about social sanctities. At the end of *Part II*, the expulsion of Falstaff is presented by the dramatist as getting rid of this threat; he has recourse to a primitive procedure to meet a modern challenge. We shall find reason to question whether this use of ritual succeeds.

But the main body of *Part II*, what I am seeing as the trial as against the execution, is of course wonderfully effective drama. The first step in trying Carnival, the first step in ceasing to be his subjects, would be to stop calling him "My Lord" and call him instead by his right name, Misrule. Now this is just the step which Falstaff himself takes for us at the outset of *Part II;* when we first see him, he is setting himself up as an institution, con-

gratulating himself on his powers *as* buffoon and wit. He glories
in his role with what Dover Wilson has aptly called "comic
hubris." [9] In the saturnalian scenes of *Part I*, where we first see
him, it is impossible to say just who he is, for he is constantly
renaming himself:

> . . . let not us that are squires of the night's body be
> called thieves of the day's beauty: let us be Diana's foresters,
> gentlemen of the shade, minions of the moon; and let men
> say, we be men of good government. . . .

Here Misrule is asking to be called Good Government, as it is his
nature to do—though of course he does so with a wink which
sets real good government at naught. But in *Part II*, Falstaff sets
himself up at the outset as Falstaff:

> I am not only witty in myself, but the cause that wit is in
> other men.
>
>   .   .   .   .   .   .
>
> A pox of this gout! or, a gout of this pox! for the one or the
> other plays the rogue with my great toe. 'Tis no matter if I
> do halt; I have the wars for my colour, and my pension shall
> seem the more reasonable. A good wit will make use of any-
> thing; I will turn diseases to commodity.

In the early portion of *Part I* he never spoke in asides, but now
he constantly confides his schemes and his sense of himself to the
audience. We do not have to see through him, but watch instead
from inside his façades as he imposes them on others. Instead of
warm amplifications centered on himself, his talk now consists
chiefly of bland impudence or dry, denigrating comments on the
way of the world. Much of the comedy is an almost Jonsonian
spectacle where we relish a witty knave gulling fools.

It is this self-conscious Falstaff, confident of setting up his
holiday license on an everyday basis, who at once encounters,
of all awkward people, the Lord Chief Justice. From there on,
during the first two acts, he is constantly put in the position of
answering his way of life; in effect he is repeatedly called to trial
and keeps eluding it only by a "more than impudent sauciness"
and the privilege of his official employment in the wars. Mistress

Quickly's attempt to arrest him is wonderfully ineffectual; but he notably fails to thrust the Lord Chief Justice from a level consideration. Hal and Poins then disguise themselves, not this time for the sake of the incomprehensible lies that Falstaff will tell, but in order to try him, to see him "bestow himself . . . in his true colours." So during the first two acts we are repeatedly put in the position of judging him, although we continue to laugh with him. A vantage is thus established from which we watch him in action in Gloucestershire, where the Justice he has to deal with is so shallow that Falstaff's progress is a triumph. The comedy is still delightful; Falstaff is still the greatest of wits; but we are constantly shown that fun involves fraud. Falstaff himself tells us so, with proud relish. Towards the end of the play, Hal's reconciliation with his father and then with the Lord Chief Justice reemphasizes the detached vantage of judgment. So no leading remarks are necessary to assure our noting and marking when we hear Falstaff shouting, "Let us take any man's horses; the laws of England are at my commandment. Happy are they which have been my friends, and woe unto my lord chief justice!" The next moment we watch Doll and the Hostess being hauled off by beadles because "the man is dead that you and Pistol beat among you."

Many of the basic structures in this action no doubt were shaped by morality-play encounters between Virtues and Vices, encounters which from our vantage today can be seen as part of the festive and scapegoat pattern. The trial of Falstaff is so effective *as drama* because no one conducts it—it happens. Falstaff, being a dramatic character, not a mummery, does not know when he has had his day. And he does not even recognize the authority who will finally sentence him: he mistakes Hal for a bastard son of the king's. The result of the trial is to make us see perfectly the necessity for the rejection of Falstaff as a man, as a favorite for a king, as the leader of an interest at court.

But, in justifying the rejection of Falstaff as a mode of awareness, I do not think that the dramatist is equally successful. The problem is not in justifying rejection morally but in making the process cogent *dramatically*, as in *Part I* we reject magical majesty or intransigent chivalry. The bad luck which in *Part II* Falstaff goes about collecting, by shaking the black yak's tail of his wit over people's heads, is the impulse to assume that nothing is sacred. In a play concerned with ruthless political maneuver, much of it conducted by impersonal state functionaries, Falstaff turns up as a functionary too, with his own version of maneuver and impersonality: "If the young dace be a bait for the old pike, I see no reason in the law of nature but I may snap at him." Now this attitude is a most appropriate response to the behavior of the high factions beneath whose struggles Falstaff plies his retail trade. In the Gaultree parleys, Lord John rebukes the Archbishop for his use of the counterfeited zeal of God—and then himself uses a counterfeited zeal of gentlemanly friendship to trick the rebels into disbanding their forces. The difference between his behavior and Falstaff's is of course that Lancaster has the sanction of the state on his side, a sanction supported, if not by legitimacy, at least by the desperate need for social order. This is a real difference, but a bare and harsh one. After all, Falstaff's little commonwealth of man has its pragmatic needs too: as he explains blandly to the Justice, he needs great infamy, because "he that buckles him in my belt cannot live in less."

The trouble with trying to get rid of this attitude merely by getting rid of Falstaff is that the attitude is too pervasive in the whole society of the play, whether public or private. It is too obviously *not* just a saturnalian mood, an extravagant aberration; it is presented instead as in grain, as the way of the world. Shakespeare might have let the play end with this attitude dominant, a harsh recognition that life is a nasty business where the big fishes eat the little fishes, with the single redeeming consideration that political order is better than anarchy, so that there is a pragmatic virtue in loyalty to the power of the state. But instead the dramatist undertakes, in the last part of the play, to expel this view of the world and to dramatize the creation of legitimacy and sanctified social power. Although the final scenes are fascinating, with all sorts of illuminations, it seems to me that at this level they partly fail.

We have seen that Shakespeare typically uses ritual patterns of behavior and thought precisely in the course of making clear, by tragic or comic irony, that rituals have no *magical* efficacy. The reason for his failure at the close of *Part II* is that at this point he uses ritual, not ironically transformed into drama, but magically. To do this involves a restriction instead of an extension of awareness. An extension of control and awareness is consummated in the epiphany of Hal's majesty while he is standing over Hotspur and Falstaff at the end of *Part I*. But *Part II* ends with a drastic restriction of awareness which goes with the embracing of magical modes of thought, not humorously but sentimentally.

It is true that the latter half of *Part II* very effectively builds up to this finale by recurrent expression of a laboring need to be rid of a growth or humor. King Henry talks of the body of his kingdom as foul with rank diseases, and recalls Richard's prophecy that "foul sin gathering head Shall break into corruption." There are a number of other images of expulsion, of which I can notice here only the very striking case where the rebels speak of the need to "purge the obstructions which begin to stop Our very veins of life." Henry himself, of course, is sick in the last half of the play, and there are repeated suggestions that his sickness is the consequence both of his sinful usurpation and of the struggle to defend it. Since his usurpation was almost a public duty, and his defense of order clearly for England's sake as well as his own advantage, he becomes in these last scenes almost a sacrificial figure, a king who sins for the sake of society, suffers for society in suffering for his sin, and carries his sin off into death. Hal speaks of the crown having "fed upon the body of my father." Henry, in his last long speech, summarizes this pattern in saying:

> God knows, my son,
> By what by-paths and indirect crook'd ways
> I met this crown; and I myself know well
> How troublesome it sat upon my head:
> To thee it shall descend with better quiet,
> Better opinion, better confirmation;
> For all the soil of the achievement goes
> With me into the earth.

The same image of burying sin occurs in some curious lines with which Hal reassures his brothers:

> My father is gone wild into his grave,
> For in his tomb lie my affections.

This conceit not only suggests an expulsion of evil, but hints at the patricidal motive which is referred to explicitly elsewhere in these final scenes and is the complement of the father-son atonement.

Now this sacrificial imagery, where used by and about the old king, is effectively dramatic, because it does not ask the audience to abandon any part of the awareness of the human, social situation which the play as a whole has expressed. But the case is altered when Hal turns on "that father ruffian" Falstaff. The new king's whip-lash lines stress Falstaff's age and glance at his death:

> I know thee not, old man: fall to thy prayers;
> How ill white hairs become a fool and jester!
> I have long dream'd of such a kind of man,
> So surfeit-swell'd, so old, and so profane;
> But being awak'd, I do despise my dream.
> Make less thy body hence, and more thy grace;
> Leave gormandising; know the grave doth gape
> For thee thrice wider than for other men.

The priggish tone, to which so many readers, including Bradley, have objected, can be explained at one level as appropriate to the solemn occasion of a coronation. But it goes with a drastic narrowing of awareness. There are of course occasions in life when people close off parts of their minds—a coronation is a case in point: Shakespeare, it can be argued, is simply putting such an occasion into his play. But even his genius could not get around the fact that to block off awareness of irony is contradictory to the very nature of drama, which has as one of its functions the extension of such awareness. Hal's lines, redefining his holiday with Falstaff as a dream, and then despising the dream, seek to invalidate that holiday pole of life, instead of including it, as his lines on his old acquaintance did at the end of *Part I*. Elsewhere in Shakespeare, to dismiss dreams categorically is foolhardy. And those lines about the thrice-wide grave: are they a threat or a joke? We cannot tell, because the sort of awareness that would confirm a joke is being damped out: "Reply not to me with a fool-born jest." If ironies about Hal were expressed by the context, we could take the scene as the representation of his becoming a prig. But there is simply a blur in the tone, a blur which results, I think, from a retreat into magic by the *dramatist,* as distinct from his characters. Magically, the line about burying the belly is exactly the appropriate threat. It goes with the other images of burying sin and wildness and conveys the idea that the grave can swallow what Falstaff's belly stands for. To assume that one can cope with a pervasive attitude of mind by dealing physically with its most prominent symbol—what is this but magic-mongering? It is the same sort of juggling which we get in Henry IV's sentimental lines taking literally the name of the Jerusalem chamber in the palace:

> Laud be to God! Even there my life must end.
> It hath been prophesied to me many years
> I should not die but in Jerusalem.

One can imagine making a mockery of Henry's pious ejaculation by catcalling a version of his final lines at the close of *Richard II:*

> Is this that voyage to the Holy Land
> To wash the blood from off your guilty hand?

An inhibition of irony goes here with Henry's making the symbol do for the thing, just as it does with Hal's expulsion of Falstaff. A return to an official view of the sanctity of state is achieved by sentimental use of magical relations.

Henry IV is only one instance, but we can now at least suggest a few tentative conclusions of a general sort about the relation of comedy to ritual. It appears from this example that comedy uses ritual in the process of redefining ritual as the expression of particular personalities in particular circumstances. The heritage of ritual gives universality and depth. The persons of the drama make the customary gestures developed in ritual observance, and, in doing so, they project in a wholehearted way attitudes which are not normally articulated at large. At the same time, the dramatization of such gestures involves being aware of their relation to the whole of experience in a way which is not necessary for the celebrants of a ritual proper. In the actual observance of customary misrule, the control of the disruptive motives which the festivity expresses is achieved by the group's recognition of the place of the whole business within the larger

rhythm of their continuing social life. No one need decide, therefore, whether the identifications involved in the ceremony are
magically valid or merely expressive. But in the drama, perspective and control depend on presenting, along with the ritual
gestures, an expression of a social situation out of which they
grow. So the drama controls magic by reunderstanding it as
imagination: dramatic irony constantly dogs the wish that the
mock king be real, that the self be all the world or set all the
world at naught. When, through a failure of irony, the dramatist
presents ritual as magically valid, the result is sentimental, since
drama lacks the kind of control which comes when the auditors
are participants. Sentimental "drama," that which succeeds in
being neither comedy nor tragedy, can be regarded from this
vantage as theater used as a substitute for ritual, without the
commitment to participation proper to ritual nor the commitment to the fullest understanding proper to comedy or tragedy.

Historically, Shakespeare's drama can be seen as part of the
process by which our culture has moved from absolutist modes
of thought towards a historical and psychological view of man
by which all the world is a stage. But though the Renaissance
moment made the tension between a magical and an empirical
view of man particularly acute, this pull is of course always
present: it is the tension between the heart and the world. By
incarnating ritual as plot and character, the dramatist finds an
embodiment for the heart's drastic gestures while recognizing
how the world keeps comically and tragically giving them the lie.

NOTES

1. This paper is a development of an interpretation of *Henry IV*
originally sketched in a more general article, "The Saturnalian
Pattern in Shakespeare's Comedy," *Sewanee Review*, LIX (Autumn 1951), 593-611. A number of sentences from the earlier
account are included here in the course of setting up the problem
of distinguishing comedy from ritual.
2. "The Argument of Comedy," *English Institute Essays, 1948,*
ed. by D. A. Robertson, Jr. (New York, 1949), p. 71. Mr. Frye's
essay brilliantly summarizes Shakespeare's relation to the whole
tradition of literary comedy. His account of the way comic form

expresses reconciliation is a more generalized description than mine here; it outlines an "argument" which fits the saturnalian pole of comic release as well as the idyllic and millennial.

3. Mr. Empson's discussion of the effects achieved by such double plots is in *English Pastoral Poetry* (New York, 1938), chap. II.

4. "A Note on Comedy," *Determinations,* ed. by F. R. Leavis (London, 1934).

5. Op. cit. p. 46.

6. See James G. Frazer, *The Scapegoat* (London, 1914), pp. 218-23.

7. I am indebted to my colleagues Professor Theodore Baird and Professor G. Armour Craig for this general conception of the relations of names to developing situations.

8. See *Shakespeare's History Plays* (New York, 1946), pp. 245ff.

9. *The Fortunes of Falstaff* (New York, 1944), chap. v, "Falstaff High on Fortune's Wheel."

E. M. W. Tillyard

RICHARD II

Richard II is imperfectly executed, and yet, that imperfection granted, perfectly planned as part of a great structure. It is sharply contrasted, in its extreme formality of shape and style, with the subtler and more fluid nature of *Henry IV;* but it is a necessary and deliberate contrast; resembling a stiff recitative composed to introduce a varied and flexible *aria*. Coming after *King John* the play would appear the strangest relapse into the official self which Shakespeare had been shedding; taken with *Henry IV* it shows that Shakespeare, while retaining and using this official self, could develop with brilliant success the new qualities of character and style manifested in the Bastard. *Richard II* therefore betokens no relapse but is an organic part of one of Shakespeare's major achievements.

But the imperfections are undoubted and must be faced. As a separate play *Richard II* lacks the sustained vitality of *Richard III*, being less interesting and less exacting in structure and containing a good deal of verse which by the best Shakespearean standards can only be called indifferent. Not that there is anything wrong with the structure, which is that of *2 Henry VI*, the rise of one great man at the expense of another; but it is simple, as befits an exordium and does not serve through the excitement of its complications to make the utmost demand on the powers of the author. For illustrating the indifferent verse I need not go beyond the frequent stretches of couplet-writing and the occasional quatrains that make such a contrast to the verse of

From *Shakespeare's History Plays*, by E. M. W. Tillyard, 1946, pp. 244-63. Copyright 1946 by The Macmillan Co. Reprinted by permission of Barnes and Noble, Inc., and Chatto and Windus Ltd.

Henry IV. It is not that these have not got their function, which will be dealt with later, but that as poetry they are indifferent stuff. They are as necessary as the stiff lines in *3 Henry VI* spoken by the Father who has killed his Son, and the Son who has killed his Father; but they are little better poetically. For present purposes it does not matter in the least whether they are relics of an old play, by Shakespeare or by someone else, or whether Shakespeare wrote them with the rest. They occur throughout the play and with the exception of perhaps two couplets are not conspicuously worse in the fifth act than anywhere else. There is no need for a theory that in this act, to save time, Shakespeare hurriedly began copying chunks from an old play. Until there is decisive proof of this, it is simplest to think that Shakespeare wrote his couplets along with the rest, intending a deliberate contrast. He had done the same thing with the Talbots' death in *1 Henry VI*, while, to account for the indifferent quality, one may remember that he was never very good at the couplet. The best couplets in *A Midsummer Night's Dream* are weak compared with the best blank verse in that play, while few of the final couplets of the sonnets are more than a competent close to far higher verse.

I turn now to a larger quality of the play, of which the couplets are one of several indications.

Of all Shakespeare's plays *Richard II* is the most formal and ceremonial. It is not only that Richard himself is a true king in appearance, in his command of the trappings of royalty, while being deficient in the solid virtues of the ruler; that is a commonplace: the ceremonial character of the play extends much wider than Richard's own nature or the exquisite patterns of his poetic speech.

First, the very actions tend to be symbolic rather than real. There is all the pomp of a tournament without the physical meeting of the two armed knights. There is a great army of Welshmen assembled to support Richard, but they never fight. Bolingbroke before Flint Castle speaks of the terrible clash there should be when he and Richard meet:

> Methinks King Richard and myself should meet
> With no less terror than the elements

> Of fire and water, when their thundering shock
> At meeting tears the cloudy cheeks of heaven.

But instead of a clash there is a highly ceremonious encounter
leading to the effortless submission of Richard. There are violent
challenges before Henry in Westminster Hall, but the issue is
postponed. The climax of the play is the ceremony of Richard's
deposition. And finally Richard, imprisoned at Pomfret, erects
his own lonely state and his own griefs into a gigantic ceremony.
He arranges his own thoughts into classes corresponding with
men's estates in real life; king and beggar, divine, soldier, and
middle man. His own sighs keep a ceremonial order like a clock:

> Now, sir, the sound that tells what hour it is
> Are clamorous groans, which strike upon my heart,
> Which is the bell: so sighs and tears and groans
> Show minutes, times, and hours.

Second, in places where emotion rises, where there is strong
mental action, Shakespeare evades direct or naturalistic presentation and resorts to convention and conceit. He had done the same
when Arthur pleaded with Hubert for his eyes in *King John,* but
that was exceptional to a play which contained the agonies of
Constance and the Bastard's perplexities over Arthur's body.
Emotionally Richard's parting from his queen could have been
a great thing in the play: actually it is an exchange of frigidly
ingenious couplets.

Rich.
> Go, count thy way with sighs; I mine with groans.

Qu.
> So longest way shall have the longest moans.

Rich.
> Twice for one step I'll groan, the way being short,
> And piece the way out with a heavy heart.

This is indeed the language of ceremony not of passion. Exactly
the same happens when the Duchess of York pleads with Henry
against her husband for her son Aumerle's life. Before the climax,
when York gives the news of his son's treachery, there had been
a show of feeling; but with the entry of the Duchess, when emo-

tion should culminate, all is changed to prettiness and formal antiphony. This is how the Duchess compares her own quality of pleading with her husband's:

> Pleads he in earnest? look upon his face;
> His eyes do drop no tears, his prayers are jest;
> His words come from his mouth, ours from our breast:
> He prays but faintly and would be denied;
> We pray with heart and soul and all beside:
> His weary joints would gladly rise, I know;
> Our knees shall kneel till to the ground they grow:
> His prayers are full of false hypocrisy;
> Ours of true zeal and deep integrity.

And to "frame" the scene, to make it unmistakably a piece of deliberate ceremonial, Bolingbroke falls into the normal language of drama when having forgiven Aumerle he vows to punish the other conspirators:

> But for our trusty brother-in-law and the abbot,
> And all the rest of that consorted crew,
> Destruction straight shall dog them at the heels.

The case of Gaunt is different but more complicated. When he has the state of England in mind and reproves Richard, though he can be rhetorical and play on words, he speaks the language of passion:

> Now He that made me knows I see thee ill.
> Thy death-bed is no lesser than thy land
> Wherein thou liest in reputation sick.
> And thou, too careless patient as thou art,
> Commit'st thy anointed body to the cure
> Of those physicians that first wounded thee.
> A thousand flatterers sit within thy crown,
> Whose compass is no bigger than thy head.

But in the scene of private feeling, when he parts from his banished son, both speakers, ceasing to be specifically themselves, exchange the most exquisitely formal commonplaces traditionally deemed appropriate to such a situation.

> Go, say I sent thee for to purchase honour
> And not the king exil'd thee; or suppose
> Devouring pestilence hangs in our air
> And thou art flying to a fresher clime.
> Look, what thy soul holds dear, imagine it
> To lie that way thou go'st, not whence thou com'st.
> Suppose the singing birds musicians,
> The grass whereon thou tread'st the presence strew'd,
> The flowers fair ladies, and thy steps no more
> Than a delightful measure or a dance;
> For gnarling sorrow hath less power to bite
> The man that mocks at it and sets it light.

Superficially this may be maturer verse than the couplets quoted, but it is just as formal, just as mindful of propriety and as unmindful of nature as Richard and his queen taking leave. Richard's sudden start into action when attacked by his murderers is exceptional, serving to set off by contrast the lack of action that has prevailed and to link the play with the next of the series. His groom, who appears in the same scene, is a realistic character alien to the rest of the play and serves the same function as Richard in action.

Thirdly, there is an elaboration and a formality in the cosmic references, scarcely to be matched in Shakespeare. These are usually brief and incidental, showing indeed how intimate a part they were of the things accepted and familiar in Shakespeare's mind. But in *Richard II* they are positively paraded. The great speech of Richard in Pomfret Castle is a tissue of them: first the peopling of his prison room with his thoughts, making its microcosm correspond with the orders of the body politic; then the doctrine of the universe as a musical harmony; then the fantasy of his own griefs arranged in a pattern like the working of a clock, symbol of regularity opposed to discord; and finally madness as the counterpart in man's mental kingdom of discord or chaos. Throughout the play the great commonplace of the king on earth duplicating the sun in heaven is exploited with a persistence unmatched anywhere else in Shakespeare. Finally (for I omit minor references to cosmic lore) there is the scene (III.4) of the gardeners, with the elaborate comparison of the

state to the botanical microcosm of the garden. But this is a
scene so typical of the whole trend of the play that I will speak
of it generally and not merely as another illustration of the traditional correspondences.

The scene begins with a few exquisitely musical lines of
dialogue between the queen and two ladies. She refines her grief
in a vein of high ceremony and sophistication. She begins by
asking what sport they can devise in this garden to drive away
care. But to every sport proposed there is a witty objection.

> *Lady.*
>> Madam, we'll tell tales.
>
> *Queen.*
>> Of sorrow or of joy?
>
> *Lady.*
>>> Of either, madam.
>
> *Queen.*
>> Of neither, girl:
>> For if of joy, being altogether wanting,
>> It doth remember me the more of sorrow;
>> Or if of grief, being altogether had,
>> It adds more sorrow to my want of joy.
>> For what I have I need not to repeat,
>> And what I want it boots not to complain.

Shakespeare uses language here like a very accomplished musi-
cian doing exercises over the whole compass of the violin. Then
there enter a gardener and two servants: clearly to balance the
queen and her ladies and through that balance to suggest that
the gardener within the walls of his little plot of land is a king.
Nothing could illustrate better the different expectations of a
modern and of an Elizabethan audience than the way they would
take the gardener's opening words:

> Go, bind thou up yon dangling apricocks,
> Which, like unruly children, make their sire
> Stoop with oppression of their prodigal weight.

The first thought of a modern audience is: what a ridiculous
way for a gardener to talk. The first thought of an Elizabethan
would have been: wnat is the symbolic meaning of those words,

spoken by this king of the garden, and how does it bear on the play? And it would very quickly conclude that the apricots had grown inflated and overweening in the sun of the royal favour; that oppression was used with a political as well as a physical meaning; and that the apricots threatened, unless restrained, to upset the proper relation between parent and offspring, to offend against the great principle of order. And the rest of the gardener's speech would bear out this interpretation.

> Go thou, and like an executioner
> Cut off the heads of too fast growing sprays,
> That look too lofty in our commonwealth.
> All must be even in our government.
> You thus employ'd, I will go root away
> The noisome weeds, which without profit suck
> The soil's fertility from wholesome flowers.

In fact the scene turns out to be an elaborate political allegory with the Earl of Wiltshire, Bushy, and Green standing for the noxious weeds which Richard, the bad gardener, allowed to flourish and which Henry, the new gardener, has rooted up. It ends with the queen coming forward and joining in the talk. She confirms the gardener's regal and moral function by calling him "old Adam's likeness," but curses him for his ill news about Richard and Bolingbroke. The intensively symbolic character of the scene is confirmed when the gardener at the end proposes to plant a bank with rue where the queen let fall her tears, as a memorial:

> Rue, even for ruth, here shortly shall be seen
> In the remembrance of a weeping queen.

In passing, for it is not my immediate concern, let me add that the gardener gives both the pattern and the moral of the play. The pattern is the weighing of the fortunes of Richard and Bolingbroke:

> Their fortunes both are weigh'd.
> In your lord's scale is nothing but himself
> And some few vanities that make him light;

But in the balance of great Bolingbroke
Besides himself are all the English peers,
And with that odds he weighs King Richard down.

For the moral, though he deplores Richard's inefficiency, the gardener calls the news of his fall "black tidings" and he sympathises with the queen's sorrow. And he is himself, in his microcosmic garden, what neither Richard nor Bolingbroke separately is, the authentic gardener-king, no usurper, and the just represser of vices, the man who makes "all even in our government."

The one close Shakespearean analogy with this gardener is Iden, the unambitious squire in his Kentish garden, who stands for "degree" in 2 Henry VI. But he comes in as an obvious foil to the realistic disorder just exhibited in Cade's rebellion. Why was it that in Richard II, when he was so much more mature, when his brilliant realism in King John showed him capable of making his gardeners as human and as amusing as the grave-diggers in Hamlet, Shakespeare chose to present them with a degree of formality unequalled in any play he wrote? It is, in a different form, the same question as that which was implied by my discussion of the other formal or ceremonial features of the play: namely, why did Shakespeare in Richard II make the ceremonial or ritual form of writing, found in differing quantities in the Henry VI plays and in Richard III, not merely one of the principal means of expression but the very essence of the play?

These are the first questions we must answer if we are to understand the true nature of Richard II. And here let me repeat that though Richard himself is a very important part of the play's ceremonial content, that content is larger and more important than Richard. With that caution, I will try to explain how the ritual or ceremonial element in Richard II differs from that in the earlier History Plays, and through such an explanation to conjecture a new interpretation of the play. There is no finer instance of ceremonial writing than the scene of the gnosts at the end of Richard III. But it is subservient to a piece of action, to the Battle of Bosworth with the overthrow of a tyrant and the triumph of a righteous prince. Its duty is to make that action a matter of high, mysterious, religious import. We are not invited to dwell on the ritual happenings as on a resting-place, to

deduce from them the ideas into which the mind settles when
the action of the play is over. But in *Richard II*, with all the
emphasis and the point taken out of the action, we are invited,
again and again, to dwell on the sheer ceremony of the various
situations. The main point of the tournament between Bolingbroke and Mowbray is the way it is conducted; the point of
Gaunt's parting with Bolingbroke is the sheer propriety of the
sentiments they utter; the portents, put so fittingly into the mouth
of a Welshman, are more exciting because they are appropriate
than because they precipitate an event; Richard is ever more
concerned with how he behaves, with the fitness of his conduct
to the occasion, than with what he actually does; the gardener
may foretell the deposition of Richard yet he is far more interesting as representing a static principle of order; when Richard is
deposed, it is the precise manner that comes before all—

> With mine own tears I wash away my balm,
> With mine own hands I give away my crown,
> With mine own tongue deny my sacred state,
> With mine own breath release all duty's rites.

We are in fact in a world where means matter more than ends,
where it is more important to keep strictly the rules of an elaborate game than either to win or to lose it.

Now though compared with ourselves the Elizabethans put a
high value on means as against ends they did not go to the extreme. It was in the Middle Ages that means were so elaborated,
that the rules of the game of life were so lavishly and so minutely
set forth. *Richard II* is Shakespeare's picture of that life.

Of course it would be absurd to suggest that Shakespeare pictured the age of Richard II after the fashion of a modern historian. But there are signs elsewhere in Shakespeare of at least
a feeling after historical verity; and there are special reasons
why the age of Richard II should have struck the imaginations
of the Elizabethans.

I noted above that at the end of *2 Henry VI* Clifford and York,
though enemies, do utter some of the chivalric sentiments proper
to medieval warfare. Such sentiments do not recur in *3 Henry VI*,
where we have instead the full barbarities of Wakefield and
Towton. Shakespeare is probably recording the historical fact

that the decencies of the knightly code went down under the stress of civil carnage. But the really convincing analogy with *Richard II* is the play of *Julius Caesar*. There, however slender Shakespeare's equipment as historian and however much of his own time he slips in, he does succeed in giving his picture of antique Rome, of the dignity of its government and of the stoic creed of its great men. T. S. Eliot has rightly noted how much essential history Shakespeare extracted from Plutarch. And if from Plutarch, why not from Froissart likewise?

Till recently Shakespeare's debt to Berner's translation of Froissart's Chronicle has been almost passed over, but now it is rightly agreed that it was considerable. To recognise the debt helps one to understand the play. For instance, one of the minor puzzles of the play is plain if we grant Shakespeare's acquaintance with Froissart. When York, horrified at Richard's confiscating Gaunt's property the moment he died, goes on to enumerate all Richard's crimes, he mentions "the prevention of poor Bolingbroke about his marriage." There is nothing more about this in the play, but there is a great deal about it in Froissart—Richard had brought charges against the exile Bolingbroke which induced the French king to break off Bolingbroke's engagement with the daughter of the Duke of Berry, the king's cousin. If Shakespeare had been full of Froissart when writing *Richard II* he could easily have slipped in this isolated reference. But quite apart from any tangible signs of imitation it is scarcely conceivable that Shakespeare should not have read so famous a book as Berners's Froissart, or that having read it he should not have been impressed by the bright pictures of chivalric life in those pages. Now among Shakespeare's History Plays *Richard II* is the only one that falls within the period of time covered by Froissart. All the more reason why on this unique occasion he should heed this great original. Now though Froissart is greatly interested in motives, he also writes with an eye unmatched among chroniclers for its eager observation of external things and with a mind similarly unmatched for the high value it placed on the proper disposition of those things. In fact he showed a lively belief in ceremony and in the proprieties of heraldry akin to Elizabethan belief yet altogether more firmly attached to the general scheme of ideas that prevailed at the time. Shakespeare's brilliant wit must have grasped this; and *Richard II* may be his intuitive rendering of Froissart's medievalism.

But there were other reasons why the reign of Richard II should be notable. A. B. Steel, his most recent historian, begins his study by noting that Richard was the last king of the old medieval order:

> the last king ruling by hereditary right, direct and undisputed, from the Conqueror. The kings of the next hundred and ten years . . . were essentially kings *de facto* not *de jure,* successful usurpers recognised after the event, upon conditions, by their fellow-magnates or by parliament.

Shakespeare, deeply interested in titles as he had showed himself to be in his early History Plays, must have known this very well; and Gaunt's famous speech on England cannot be fully understood without this knowledge. He calls England

> This nurse, this teeming womb of royal kings,
> Fear'd by their breed and famous by their birth,
> Renowned for their deeds as far from home,
> For Christian service and true chivalry,
> As is the sepulchre in stubborn Jewry
> Of the world's ransom, blessed Mary's son.

Richard was no crusader, but he was authentic heir of the crusading Plantagenets. Henry was different, a usurper; and it is with reference to this passage that we must read the lines in *Richard II* and *Henry IV* which recount his desire and his failure to go to Palestine. That honour was reserved for the authentic Plantagenet kings. Richard then had the full sanctity of medieval kingship and the strong pathos of being the last king to possess it. Shakespeare probably realised that however powerful the Tudors were and however undisputed their hold over their country's church, they had not the same sanctity as the medieval kings. He was therefore ready to draw from certain French treatises, anti-Lancastrian in tone, that made Richard a martyr and compared him to Christ and his accusers to so many Pilates giving him over to the wishes of the London mob. Shakespeare's Richard says at his deposition:

> Though some of you with Pilate wash your hands,
> Showing an outward pity; yet you Pilates
> Have here deliver'd me to my sour cross,
> And water cannot wash away your sin.

Holy and virtuous as the Earl of Richmond is in *Richard III*, he does not pretend to the same kingly sanctity as Richard II. Such sanctity belongs to a more antique, more exotically ritual world; and Shakespeare composed his play accordingly.

Not only did Richard in himself hold a position unique among English kings, he maintained a court of excessive splendour. Froissart writes as follows in the last pages of his chronicle:

> This King Richard reigned king of England twenty-two year in great prosperity, holding great estate and signory. There was never before any king of England that spent so much in his house as he did by a hundred thousand florins every year. For I, Sir John Froissart, canon and treasurer of Chinay, knew it well, for I was in his court more than a quarter of a year together and he made me good cheer. . . . And when I departed from him it was at Windsor; and at my departing the king sent me by a knight of his, Sir John Golofer, a goblet of silver and gilt weighing two mark of silver and within it a hundred nobles, by the which I am as yet the better and shall be as long as I live; wherefore I am bound to pray to God for his soul and with much sorrow I write of his death.

But Shakespeare need not have gone to Froissart for such information. In an age that was both passionately admiring of royal magnificence and far more retentive of tradition than our own the glories of Richard's court must have persisted as a legend. Anyhow that Shakespeare was aware of them is plain from Richard's address to his own likeness in the mirror:

> Was this face the face
> That every day under his household roof
> Did keep ten thousand men?

The legend must have persisted of this court's continental elegance, of the curiosities of its dress, of such a thing as Anne

of Bohemia introducing the custom of riding side-saddle, of
Richard's invention of the handkerchief for nasal use. Then there
were the poets. Shakespeare must have associated the beginnings
of English poetry with Chaucer and Gower; and they wrote
mainly in Richard's reign. There must have been much medieval
art, far more than now survives, visible in the great houses of
Elizabeth's day, illuminated books and tapestry; and it would
be generally associated with the most brilliant reign of the
Middle Ages. Finally in Richard's reign there was the glamour
of a still intact nobility: a very powerful glamour in an age still
devoted to heraldry and yet possessing an aristocracy who, compared with the great men of Richard's day, were upstarts.

   All these facts would have a strong, if unconscious, effect on
Shakespeare's mind and induce him to present the age of Richard
in a brilliant yet remote and unrealistic manner. He was already
master of a certain antique lore and of a certain kind of ceremonial writing: it was natural that he should use them, but with
a different turn, to do this particular work. Thus he makes more
solemn and elaborates the inherited notions of cosmic correspondences and chivalric procedure and he makes his ritual style
a central and not peripheral concern. Hence the portentous
solemnity of the moralising gardeners, the powerful emphasis on
the isolated symbol of the rue-tree, the elaborate circumstances
of the tournament between Bolingbroke and Mowbray, and the
unique artifice of Richard's great speeches: speeches which are
the true centre of the play but central with a far wider reference
than to the mere character of Richard.

   In speaking of medieval illuminated books and tapestry I do
not wish to imply anything too literal: that Shakespeare had
actual examples of such things in mind when he wrote *Richard II*.
But it is true that many passages in this play call them up and
that unconscious memory of them *might* have given Shakespeare
help. Take a passage from one of Richard's best known speeches.

> For God's sake, let us sit upon the ground
> And tell sad stories of the death of kings:
> How some have been depos'd, some slain in war,
> Some haunted by the ghosts they have depos'd,
> Some poison'd by their wives, some sleeping kill'd;

> All murder'd: for within the hollow crown
> That rounds the mortal temples of a king
> Keeps Death his court, and there the antic sits,
> Scoffing his state and grinning at his pomp,
> Allowing him a breath, a little scene,
> To monarchise, be fear'd, and kill with looks,
> Infusing him with self and vain conceit,
> As if this flesh which walls about our life
> Were brass impregnable, and, humour'd thus,
> Comes at the last and with a little pin
> Bores through his castle wall, and farewell king!

Critics have seen a reference here to the *Mirror for Magistrates,* but Chaucer's Monk's Tale would suit much better. Death, keeping his court, is a pure medieval motive. Still, these motives were inherited and need imply nothing unusual. But Death the skeleton watching and mocking the king in his trappings is a clear and concrete image that reminds one of the visual arts: and above all the exquisiteness, the very remoteness from what could have happened in an actual physical attempt, of someone boring through the castle wall with a little pin precisely recaptures the technique of medieval illumination. Before the tournament Bolingbroke prays God:

> And with thy blessings steel my lance's point
> That it may enter Mowbray's waxen coat.

That again is just like medieval illumination. When a wound is given in medieval art there is no fusion of thing striking with thing stricken; the blow simply rests in a pre-existing hole, while any blood that spouts out had pre-existed just as surely. This is the kind of picture called up by Mowbray's "waxen coat." Or take this comparison. If anywhere in *Henry IV* we might expect medievalism it is in the description of the Prince performing the most spectacular of chivalric actions: vaulting onto his horse in full armour.

> I saw young Harry, with his beaver on,
> His cuisses on his thighs, gallantly arm'd,
> Rise from the ground like feather'd Mercury,
> And vaulted with such ease into his seat,

> As if an angel dropp'd down from the clouds,
> To turn and wind a fiery Pegasus
> And witch the world with noble horsemanship.

There is nothing medieval here. It is a description recalling the
art of the high Renaissance with fused colours and subtle transi-
tions. Set beside it Gaunt's advice to Bolingbroke about to go into
exile:

> Suppose the singing birds musicians,
> The grass whereon thou tread'st the presence strew d,
> The flowers fair ladies, and thy steps no more
> Than a delightful measure or a dance.

Here each item is distinct, and the lines evoke the mincing figures of a medieval tapestry in a setting of birds and flowers.

The case for the essential medievalism of *Richard II* is even
stronger when it is seen that the conspirators, working as such,
do not share the ceremonial style used to represent Richard and
his court. Once again the usual explanation of such a contrast is
too narrow. It has been the habit to contrast the "poetry" of
Richard with the practical common sense of Bolingbroke. But
the "poetry" of Richard is all part of a world of gorgeous tourna-
ments, conventionally mournful queens, and impossibly sententious gardeners, while Bolingbroke's common sense extends to
his backers, in particular to that most important character,
Northumberland. We have in fact the contrast not only of two
characters but of two ways of life.

One example of the two different ways of life has occurred
already: in the contrast noted between the mannered pleading of
the Duchess of York for Aumerle's life and Henry's vigorous
resolve immediately after to punish the conspirators. The
Duchess and her family belong to the old order where the means,
the style, the embroidery matter more than what they further or
express. Henry belongs to a new order, where action is quick
and leads somewhere. But other examples are needed to back
up what to many readers will doubtless seem a dangerous and
forced theory of the play's significance. First, a new kind of
vigour, the vigour of strong and swift action, enters the verse
of the play at II. 1. 224, when, after Richard has seized Gaunt's

property and announced his coming journey to Ireland, Northumberland, Ross, and Willoughby remain behind and hatch their
conspiracy. Northumberland's last speech especially has a different vigour from any vigorous writing that has gone before:
from the vigour of the jousters' mutual defiance or York's moral
indignation at the king's excesses. After enumerating Bolingbroke's supporters in Brittany, he goes on:

> All these well furnish'd by the Duke of Brittain
> With eight tall ships, three thousand men of war,
> Are making hither with all due expedience
> And shortly mean to touch our northern shore:
> Perhaps they had ere this, but that they stay
> The first departing of the king for Ireland.
> If then we shall shake off our slavish yoke,
> Imp out our drooping country's broken wing,
> Redeem from broken pawn the blemish'd crown,
> Wipe off the dust that hides our sceptre's gift
> And make high majesty look like itself,
> Away with me in post to Ravenspurgh.

The four lines describing by different metaphors how the land is
to be restored are not in a ritual manner but in Shakespeare's
normal idiom of Elizabethan exuberance. It is not for nothing
that the next scene shows the Queen exchanging elegant conceits about her sorrow for Richard's absence with Bushy and
Green. But the largest contrast comes at the beginning of the
third act. It begins with a very fine speech of Bolingbroke recounting to Bushy and Green all their crimes, before they are
executed. It has the full accent of the world of action, where
people want to get things and are roused to passion in their
attempts:

> Bring forth these men.
> Bushy and Green, I will not vex your souls
> (Since presently your souls must part your bodies)
> With too much urging your pernicious lives,
> For 'twere no charity.

That is the beginning, and the speech goes on to things themselves not to the way they are done or are embroidered. And when

at the end Bolingbroke recounts his own injuries it is with plain
and understandable passion:

> Myself a prince by fortune of my birth,
> Near to the king in blood, and near in love
> Till you did make him misinterpret me,
> Have stoop'd my neck under your injuries
> And sigh'd my English breath in foreign clouds,
> Eating the bitter bread of banishment.

The scene is followed by Richard's landing in Wales, his pitiful
inability to act, and his wonderful self-dramatisation. As a display of externals, as an exaltation of means over ends (here carried to a frivolous excess), it is wonderful; yet it contains no
lines that for the weight of unaffected passion come near Bolingbroke's single line,

> Eating the bitter bread of banishment.

The world for which Bolingbroke stands, though it is a usurping
world, displays a greater sincerity of personal emotion.

Thus *Richard II*, although reputed so simple and homogeneous
a play, is built on a contrast. The world of medieval refinement
is indeed the main object of presentation but it is threatened and
in the end superseded by the more familiar world of the present.

In carrying out his object Shakespeare shows the greatest skill
in keeping the emphasis sufficiently on Richard, while hinting
that in Bolingbroke's world there is the probability of development. In other words he makes the world of Bolingbroke not so
much defective as embryonic. It is not allowed to compete with
Richard's but it is ready to grow to its proper fulness in the next
plays. This is especially true of the conspirators' characters.
Hotspur, for instance, is faintly drawn yet in one place he
speaks with a hearty abruptness that shows his creator had conceived the whole character already. It is when Hotspur first
meets Bolingbroke, near Berkeley Castle. Northumberland asks
him if he has forgotten the Duke of Hereford, and Hotspur
replies:

> No, my good lord, for that is not forgot
> Which ne'er I did remember: to my knowledge
> I never in my life did look on him.

At the beginning of the same scene Northumberland's elaborate
compliments to Bolingbroke show his politic nature: it is the same
man who at the beginning of 2 *Henry IV* lies "crafty-sick."
Bolingbroke too is consistent with his later self, though we are
shown only certain elements in his character. What marks out
the later Bolingbroke and makes him a rather pathetic figure is
his bewilderment. For all his political acumen he does not know
himself completely or his way about the world. And the reason
is that he has relied in large part on fortune. Dover Wilson remarked truly of him in *Richard II* that though he acts forcibly he
appears to be borne upward by a power beyond his volition. He
is made the first mover of trouble in the matter of the tournament and he wants to do something about Woodstock's murder.
But he has no steady policy and having once set events in motion
is the servant of fortune. As such, he is not in control of events,
though by his adroitness he may deal with the unpredictable as
it occurs. Now a man who, lacking a steady policy, begins a
course of action will be led into those "by-paths and indirect
crook'd ways" of which Henry speaks to his son in 2 *Henry IV*.
Shakespeare says nothing of them in *Richard II*, but they are yet
the inevitable result of Henry's character as shown in that play.
It is worth anticipating and saying that Prince Hal differs from
his father in having perfect knowledge both of himself and of
the world around him. Of all types of men he is the least subject
to the sway of fortune.

Another quality shown only in embryo is humour. It is nearly
absent but there is just a touch: sufficient to assure us that
Shakespeare has it there all the time in readiness. It occurs in
the scene where Aumerle describes to Richard his parting from
Bolingbroke.

Rich.

And say, what store of parting tears were shed?

Aum.

Faith, none for me: except the north-east wind
Which then blew bitterly against our faces,
Awak'd the sleeping rheum, and so by chance
Did grace our hollow parting with a tear.

Richard II thus at once possesses a dominant theme and contains within itself the elements of those different things that are to be the theme of its successors.

It must not be thought, because Shakespeare treated history, as described above, in a way new to him that he has lost interest in his old themes. On the contrary he is interested as much as ever in the theme of civil war, in the kingly type, and in the general fortunes of England. And I will say a little on each of these before trying to sum up the play's meaning in the tetralogy to which it belongs.

Richard II does its work in proclaiming the great theme of the whole cycle of Shakespeare's History Plays: the beginning in prosperity, the distortion of prosperity by a crime, civil war, and ultimate renewal of prosperity. The last stage falls outside the play's scope, but the second scene with the Duchess of Gloucester's enumeration of Edward III's seven sons, her account of Gloucester's death, and her call for vengeance is a worthy exordium of the whole cycle. The speeches of the Bishop of Carlisle and of Richard to Northumberland, parts of which were quoted near the beginning of this chapter, are worthy statements of the disorder that follows the deposition of the rightful king. In doctrine the play is entirely orthodox. Shakespeare knows that Richard's crimes never amounted to tyranny and hence that outright rebellion against him was a crime. He leaves uncertain the question of who murdered Woodstock and never says that Richard was personally responsible. The king's uncles hold perfectly correct opinions. Gaunt refuses the Duchess of Gloucester's request for vengeance, the matter being for God's decision alone. Even on his deathbed, when lamenting the state of the realm and calling Richard the landlord and not the king of England, he never preaches rebellion. And he mentions deposition only in the sense that Richard by his own conduct is deposing himself. York utters the most correct sentiments. Like the Bastard he is for supporting the existing government. And though he changes allegiance he is never for rebellion. As stated above, the gardener was against the deposition of Richard.

As well as being a study of medievalism, Richard takes his place among Shakespeare's many studies of the kingly nature. He is a king by unquestioned title and by his external graces

alone. But others have written so well on Richard's character that
I need say no more.

Lastly, for political motives, there is the old Morality theme of
Respublica. One of Shakespeare's debts in *Richard II* is to *Woodstock;* and this play is constructed very plainly on the Morality
pattern, with the king's three uncles led by Woodstock inducing
him to virtue, and Tressilian, Bushy and Green to vice. There
are traces of this motive in Shakespeare's play, but with Woodstock dead before the action begins and Gaunt dying early in it
the balance of good and evil influences is destroyed. Bushy,
Green and Bagot, however, remain very plainly Morality figures
and were probably marked in some way by their dress as abstract
vices. If Shakespeare really confused Bagot with the Earl of Wiltshire (according to a conjecture of Dover Wilson) he need not
be following an old play heedlessly: he would in any case look
on them all as a gang of bad characters, far more important as a
gang than as individuals, hence not worth being careful over
separately. Once again, as in the earlier tetralogy, England herself, and not the protagonist, is the main concern. Gaunt speaks
her praises, the gardener in describing his own symbolic garden
has her in mind. As part of the great cycle of English history covered by Hall's chronicle the events of the reign of Richard II
take their proper place. But here something fresh has happened.
The early tetralogy had as its concern the fortunes of England in
that exciting and instructive stretch of her history. *Richard II*
has this concern too, but it also deals with England herself, the
nature and not merely the fortunes of England. In *Richard II* it
is the old brilliant medieval England of the last Plantagenet in
the authentic succession; in *Henry IV* it will be the England not
of the Middle Ages but of Shakespeare himself. We can now see
how the epic comes in and how *Richard II* contributes to an
epic effect. Those works which we honour by the epic title
always, among other things, express the feelings or the habits of
a large group of men, often of a nation. However centrally
human, however powerful, a work may be, we shall not give it
the epic title for these qualities alone. It is not the parting of
Hector and Andromache or the ransoming of Hector's body that
make the *Iliad* an epic; it is that the *Iliad* expresses a whole way
of life. Shakespeare, it seems, as well as exploiting the most

central human affairs, as he was to do in his tragedies, was also impelled to fulfil through the drama that peculiarly epic function which is usually fulfilled through the narrative. Inspired partly perhaps by the example of Daniel and certainly by his own genius, he combined with the grim didactic exposition of the fortunes of England during her terrible ordeal of civil war his epic version of what England was.

This new turn given to the History Play is a great stroke of Shakespeare's genius. Through it he goes beyond anything in Hall or Daniel or even Spenser. Hall and Daniel see English history in a solemn and moral light and they are impressive writers. Spenser is a great philosophical poet and epitomises the ethos of the Elizabethan age. But none of these can truly picture England. Of the epic writers Sidney in *Arcadia* comes nearest to doing this. It is indeed only in patches that authentic England appears through mythical Arcadia, but that it can this description of Kalander's house in the second chapter of the book is sufficient proof:

> The house itself was built of fair and strong stone, not affecting so much any extraordinary kind of fineness as an honourable representing of a firm stateliness: the lights doors and stairs rather directed to the use of the guest than to the eye of the artificer, and yet, as the one chiefly heeded, so the other not neglected; each place handsome without curiosity and homely without loathsomeness; not so dainty as not to be trod on nor yet slubbered up with good fellowship; all more lasting than beautiful but that the consideration of the exceeding lastingness made the eye believe it was exceedingly beautiful.

This expresses the authentic genius of English domestic architecture.

Of this great new epic attempt *Richard II* is only the prelude. What of England it pictures is not only antique but partial: the confined world of a medieval courtly class. In his next plays Shakespeare was to picture (with much else) the whole land, as he knew it, in his own day, with its multifarious layers of society and manners of living.

Leonard F. Dean

FROM *RICHARD II* TO *HENRY V:*
A CLOSER VIEW

It has been urged in recent years that many of the features and the essential themes of Shakespeare's English history plays were derived from his chronicle sources. This view naturally stresses the considerable amount of popular history in the plays—the patriotic pageantry and spectacle, the orthodox moral and political lessons, the stock characterization of good and bad rulers, wise old counselors and parasitic flatterers. It stresses particularly the theme which is so strong in Hall's Chronicle, the interpretation which asserts that England was happy under Edward III, that Richard II was a weak king, that his deposition by Henry IV was politically necessary and led to a moment of heroic order under Henry V, but that the deposition also brought down God's wrath in the form of the Wars of the Roses, and that peace and divine blessing were restored with the defeat of the bad king Richard III and the subsequent union of Lancaster and York through the marriage of Elizabeth and Henry VII, which founded the Tudor dynasty. J. Dover Wilson sums it up: "Hall furnished the frame and stretched the canvas for the whole Shakespearian cycle, *Richard II* to *Richard III*."[1]

One difficulty with this stress on Shakespeare's closeness to his chronicle sources is that it tends to reduce him to a Tudor propagandist. But there is more here, insists A. P. Rossiter, than the "moral history of the Lancastrian House . . . and the happy ending in the dawn of Tudarchy." A "pattern is *there,* and it is like Edward Halle's," but "Halle's theory is naive," and Shakespeare cannot be "quite as naive as all that."[2] Another difficulty is that in order to generalize about a pattern (like the Tudor myth) running through the plays it is necessary to stand so far away that they merge into something known vaguely as the History Play. Only by coming close to the plays can one experience their particular pleasures and learn how a great poet may go beyond the naïvetés of popular history to his own profundities.

2

When one does come close to *Richard II*, the opening scenes do not sound like the work of a man who knew that he was writing the "first act" of a cycle dramatizing a clear and accepted theory of history. On the contrary, these scenes give the impression of a writer "thinking" his way into his subject. The first scene and its continuation in the third (derived from Hall) are history as spectacle: a royal hearing on charges of treason and a trial by combat; but the necessarily ceremonial language and behavior of spectacle muffle character and theme. The fourth act hints that the real Richard has been play-acting in the spectacular scenes, and that he is therefore bad because he is Machiavellian; but this is not in fact developed to become the key to his character. In the second scene and elsewhere we are told or reminded that Richard is a murderer (of Gloucester) and that he is a bad ruler in the popular sense: addicted to foreign fashions, misled by parasites, guilty of unjust taxation; but again all this is less clear and prominent than it might easily have been. It is perhaps not until Gaunt's great speech on England early in Act II that Shakespeare gives the impression of sensing the true mode and meaning of the play. Gaunt describes England as a fallen world: "This other Eden, demi-paradise . . . is now bound in with shame." The movement is toward the history play as ironic drama: "a vision of what in theology is called the fallen world," where "tragedy's 'this must be' becomes irony's 'this at least is.' "[3] It is a Cold War view of man and the state in which no one is perfect and no one wins. It is opposed to the dreams of popular history (it even implies that happy people have no history) and to its simplifications (professional historians feel that this is Shakespeare's most "truthful" history).

With this in mind one may look back at the confused opening scenes and sense meanings that are only implicit at best. The spectacular ceremonies may illustrate, though imperfectly, a prevailing malaise in which the forms of society are inoperative and disconnected from the realities of power and character. When a country's ruler is himself a murderer, an infected creature of the fallen world rather than the Lord's lieutenant on earth, a fundamental irony exists, and loyal subjects like Gaunt and the widow of Gloucester can only complain helplessly to God. The distance between the ideal pattern and the fallen fact may be felt behind the dying Gaunt's unrealistic determination to give "wholesome counsel" to Richard, the "unstaid youth." Counsel from one generation to another that would be heeded and fruitful in a more heroic context is irrelevant in this ironic mode, and the irrelevance is simply underscored by York's well-meant advice: "The King is come. Deal mildly with his youth; / For young hot colts being rag'd do rage the more." Here and elsewhere honest elder statesmen like York are stultified. He becomes, as he says, a "neuter." His maxims are turned by circumstances into rootless platitudes. He is so perplexed as he attempts to deal with the unroyal Richard and the usurping Bolingbroke that actors have been misled into playing him as a comic figure. Equally misleading is the attempt to equate him with the undervalued modern parliamentarian: "The politician who saves his country by turning his coat is God's most precious gift to a people which prefers a change of government to a revolution."[4] The real effect of his role, an appropriate supporting part in ironic drama, is one of pathetic helplessness. He always, appealingly, wants things to be better than they can be in the fallen world of this play.

Although by this point in the play (Act II) one may feel that Shakespeare has begun to sense a viable meaning and tone in his chaotic material, it is not until Richard's return from Ireland early in Act III that he finds the best means of developing and dramatizing his intuitions. The chief means, very simply, are those for which he became pre-eminent: the dramatic portrayal of character and the expression of theme through the contrast of characters. Starting with the basic but simple contrast between Richard, an anointed king who is ruining his country, and Boling-

broke, a treasonous usurper who is an efficient ruler, Shakespeare
first expands and deepens the character of Richard. The psychological features of the portrait were first persuasively described by Coleridge (in 1813):

> His faults spring entirely from defect of character . . .
> continually increasing energy of thought, and as constantly
> diminishing power of acting. . . . A man with a wanton-
> ness in feminine shew, feminine *friendism*, intensely woman-
> like love of those immediately about him. . . . Constant
> overflow of feelings; incapability of controlling them; waste
> of that energy which should be reserved for action in the
> passion and effort of resolves and menaces, and the conse-
> quent exhaustion. . . . Above all, the seeking refuge in de-
> spair, so characteristic of inward weakness. . . . Exhaustion
> counterfeiting quiet; and yet the habit of kingliness, the
> effect of flattery from infancy, constantly producing a sort of
> *wordy* courage which betrays the inward impotence. The
> consequent alternation of unmanly despair and of un-
> grounded hope; and throughout the rapid transition from
> one feeling to its opposite.[5]

To this basic outline, Dowden in 1875 added two points which
have been often repeated or developed: that Richard is a would-
be artist and something of an actor.

> Richard, to whom all things are unreal, has a fine feeling
> for "situations." Without any of true kingly strength or dig-
> nity, he has a fine feeling for the royal situation. . . . In-
> stead of comprehending things as they are, and achieving
> heroic deeds, he satiates his heart with the grace, the tender-
> ness, the beauty, or the pathos of the situations. Life is to
> Richard a show, a succession of images; and to put himself
> into accord with the aesthetic requirements of his position
> is Richard's first necessity.[6]

The psychological aspect of Richard's character, so acutely
analyzed by Coleridge and many others since, is certainly vivid
and important. We watch his behavior on the coast of Wales with
the knowledge that Bolingbroke's successful invasion has left him

with the name of King only, and this ironic circumstance (the title without the reality, the separation of royal symbol and substance) is a proper setting for neurotic display. Clearly Richard, as the physically sick Gaunt had earlier insisted, is the one who is "sick" and plays too nicely with his name. Here and elsewhere, we find ourselves led by the characters around him to respond to his neuroticism in realistically familiar ways: we are by turns ill at ease, embarrassed, ready with sensible advice and admonition, unwillingly tolerant, silently critical and impatient. His language, particularly, is a sign and part of his unbalanced personality. In addition to the extravagance of his expression, with its self-damaging rationalizing and subjectivism, there is his painful habit of elaborating explicit comparisons. They have to be endured not only by his necessarily tight-lipped enemies, but also by us, and our sympathy turns into resentment.

But the psychological aspect of Richard's character is only one part of his role in the play. When it is stressed to the point of making us forget the rest of Shakespeare's full composition, the result is only a sophisticated version (the king as neurotic) of the popular stereotype of the Bad Ruler. The stage-Richard has tended to illustrate this kind of simplification. One important effect which may be lost when the character of Richard is interpreted in a narrowly psychological fashion is his special relation to the Shakespearian tragic hero. There are tragic qualities in the role which are constantly undercut and thwarted, and this is a part of the play's basic irony. This is missed by Coleridge and others because in dwelling on his neuroticism they tend in effect to scold him for not being more manly and royal, as if the play would be more "successful" if it moved toward a psychological resolution of emotional balance and adjustment. But ironic drama succeeds in realizing itself (and here also in interpreting history) to the extent that it dramatizes ethical dilemmas through juxtaposing imperfect values. Thus while Richard's theatrically extravagant language does indeed make us feel that he is emotionally unstable, it may also remind us that violence and hyperbole characterize the speech of the tragic hero; and remembering this, we may observe that the excessive and unsupported rhetoric with which Richard asserts the divinity of kingship not only proves his lack of realism, but also serves like the tragic hero's assertion of transcendent values to counter the forces in the play for a lesser kind of order, such as York's efforts at accommodation or Bolingbroke's effective military government. These forces have their own identifying speech—prosaic, literal, close-mouthed, carefully public and politic—which is in constant contrast with Richard's emotional language.

Similarly, Richard's neuroticism is not only a crippling weakness, but it is also a version of the tragic hero's "madness," and it therefore implies a special kind of power and insight. It is associated with an intuitive awareness about the outcome of events and an acuteness in analyzing the motives of others. By contrast it makes normal people, especially Bolingbroke and Northumberland, appear blunted and insensitive. It seems to force them to face up to the truth about themselves and their ultimate designs, and to say with its intense and peculiar honesty that they are superior only because they do not know or reveal their deeper beings. Richard's intuitive sensing of the motives of Bolingbroke is characteristic: "He helplessly divines Bolingbroke's nebulous purpose and perhaps even shapes that purpose by expressing his willingness to surrender his crown before Bolingbroke, so far as we can see, has consciously entertained the idea of taking it."[7] In the distance, with all its great differences, is the tragic "madness" of Hamlet, which helps him to penetrate the depersonalized court of Claudius and to force it to face its poisoned self. A recognition of the partial resemblance of Richard to Hamlet intensifies our sense of Richard's full character and of the confining ironies of the play itself.

All this and more, by general agreement, is most richly realized in the deposition scenes. Here what could easily remain mere spectacle is charged with dramatic significance by having Richard and Bolingbroke attempt to impose on each other and on the situation their contrary views of its personal and historical meaning. It is as if two plays were contending for the stage. Bolingbroke is already king in fact, but no ceremony will redeem a usurpation; consequently he must attempt, in totalitarian fashion, to ratify or justify his act by staging a confession and renunciation from Richard. "Fetch hither Richard, that in common view/ He may surrender; so we shall proceed/ Without suspicion." This kind of play must be well-made: language and emotion have to be carefully controlled, and nothing spontaneous can be allowed to interfere with the prearranged effects. Bolingbroke's part is to be as patient, just, and royal as possible. The unsympathetic task of forcing Richard to read over the list of his crimes (so that the audience, the commoners, will be satisfied) is naturally delegated to Northumberland. Richard's crimes are real, and Bolingbroke is indeed a more efficient ruler, but there is an inevitable element of mummery in the forced confession, and this affects our judgment and prepares us to feel with Richard what it means to be manipulated and dehumanized. ("What must the king do now?") In this way another side of Richard's theatricality comes into view: he play-acts not to disguise or excuse himself but "to suffer everything that this role demands of him."[8] He deposes himself, as it were, "in some long, agonizing ceremony."[9] The play that he imposes on Bolingbroke's insists that everyone on the stage and in the theater feel with him what it means to be degraded and destroyed. It is natural and appropriate that his "play" should seem improvised rather than well-made, moving on a deep level from image to image, calling as the need develops for stage props like the mirror—a symbol of truth-telling as well as of vanity.[10]

As Richard and Bolingbroke contend for the "stage" it is still clear, however, that they are only parts of Shakespeare's full drama, which is neither the play of the restoration of legal rights and order (as Bolingbroke would have it), nor the play of the betrayal and sacrifice of the anointed king (as Richard insists). The problem-breeding balance of ironic drama and of history viewed as irony is still maintained. The weak side of Richard's theatricality is still present: the emotions of the "suffering king entering the world of the dispossessed" are discussed as well as felt, and a part of his role is that of the stage actor caught removing his make-up ("Alack, why am I sent for . . .") or studying his lines ("I hardly yet have learned . . .").[11] More important and more deeply ironic is the continued association of Richard with something radically opposed to order. He is emotionally sloppy, incapable of keeping his form, the most un-English (or un-Roman) of English kings, and this is given a painful emphasis by his occasional realization that he is laughed at for his excesses. He has been a callous perverter and destroyer of the legal forms, the parchment bonds and the charters of time, which give one kind of order and security to society. Finally, his relationship to time, or the meaning his career gives to time, is that of a movement toward formlessness, dissolution, nothingness. This movement is expressed through plot and character most obviously, but also through metaphors which reverse their implications so that the fertile earth becomes the dirt of the grave, the blood of national unity and royal succession becomes the gore of civil strife, and so on.[12] This movement is more than a "death-wish," more even than the recognition that the only Lancastrian retirement plan for a deposed king is murder; it is finally a disbelief in the expressive validity of all "tradition, form, and ceremonious duty." By contrast, Bolingbroke's mummery at the deposition has this much virtue: it permits him to act as well as to play-act, and is at least lip service to the necessity in society of some recognized formal manner of behavior.

Bolingbroke's relation to time, and his character and role generally, are not easy to define. It has been suggested that the obscurity of his motives and the relative flatness of his character are a sign that he is instinctively opportunistic, but this suggestion soon becomes circular since opportunism is by definition a "tacit vice"[13] and its motives cannot therefore be openly dramatized. A related suggestion is that the real Bolingbroke is hidden in the public role—an allegedly inevitable effect of high office on private worth,[14] but this is always in danger of growing into a satiric leveling interpretation ("We know who you really are up there.") which is not clearly supported by the play. It has been suggested, further, that we tend to feel the presence of "character" only where personality exceeds dramatic role[15] and that Bolingbroke seems characterless in comparison with Richard because he is perfectly functional, is only what he has to do in the play and nothing more. Perhaps these and other suggestions are ways of saying that despite Bolingbroke's personal and political success in the play he is as much an inhabitant of its confining ironies as is Richard. Neither is free.

By his self-deposition Richard does appear, momentarily, to be free. He is free to turn on the crudely insistent Northumberland: "No lord of thine, thou haught, insulting man,/ Nor no man's lord." He is free because he has no name or title still to lose; yet the irony persists: within this freedom he can move not toward growth and self-realization, but only toward the nothingness of death. When he looks into the mirror, he foresees that the final "substance" is the "silence in the tortur'd soul"; and the conclusion of his prison soliloquy is that "Nor I nor any man that but man is/ With nothing shall be pleas'd, till he be eas'd/ With being nothing." "Richard's actual death is courageous, or perhaps perfunctory, but it does not alter this."[16] Nor does Richard's death really free Bolingbroke. His "success" is confined and discolored: "Lords, I protest, my soul is full of woe/ That blood should sprinkle me to make me grow." To ask if he is sincere in his protestation is not quite relevant. He is not a suavely insincere villain like Claudius; he is caught, rather, in the ironic circumstances which underlie the mode of the play, and therefore at this moment his voice of necessity is public and obscure.

Only one person is free from the enveloping ironies: Prince Hal. He is reported to be living in the taverns, and when told of the "triumphs" to be held at Oxford, "His answer was, he would unto the stews/ And from the common'st creature pluck a glove/ And wear it as a favor; and with that/ He would unhorse the lustiest challenger." This is a new tone, strong and cocky, a voice derived from another legend invented by the people, whose perennial instinct is to find its young heroes in lucky, off-beat places outside of the grayness of ironic history. We may infer that the nature of such a hero and how he enters history and changes its mode are to be the subjects of the plays to follow, and that the hero's success will "show more goodly" by being placed against the "sullen ground" of *Richard II*.

3

But *I Henry IV* is far richer artistically and thematically than anyone leaving *Richard II* could ever foresee. The opening, to be sure, is not unexpected. King Henry asserts that violent change has been brought under administrative control and that the nation will be spiritually unified in a holy crusade, but the familiar ironies contradict his assertions. This action closes with Henry breaking off plans for the crusade, assigning duties and making appointments in an effort to patch things up, and regretting the irresponsible behavior of his absent son. Then, suddenly, the executive's desk becomes an alehouse bench and we are with Hal and his "loose" companions. Falstaff is of course the unforesee-able element. "Now, Hal, what time of day is it, lad?" The tone is easy and familiar, that of an equal, and therefore under the circumstances a mixture of presumption and toadyism. The concern about time implies the active man of affairs, but since this is belied by the facts before us, the effect, coming so soon after Henry's busyness, is unsettling. Hal reminds Falstaff what time really means to him: sack, capons, and bawds, the acceptance of an endless present rather than the Court's management of the present in an effort to control the future. The repartee is alive with puns and triple meanings, all bespeaking a leisure for verbal playfulness whose freedom to relish meaning is in contrast with the constrictive political tone of the court. This counterpointing of mode and language between Court and Tavern is enriched by the fat comic's favorite routine—"his quick evasions, when you expect him surprised," as Dryden put it. Hal soon corners him with the dry comment: "I see a good amendment of life in thee; from praying to purse-taking." A pause, and then Falstaff in a voice of affected surprise and self-righteousness slips out of the corner: "Why, Hal, 'tis my vocation, Hal. 'Tis no sin for a man to labor in his vocation." It is a gag-line with reverberations, the first of many. It points at Hal, who as a wayward crown prince is in no position to criticise a backslider. It points at King Henry, a former rebel whose newly-seized royal vocation obliges him to put down more recent rebels. It points in general toward the radical complexities not quite hidden by the conservative ideal of a social order derived from the biblical injunction: "Let every man abide in the same vocation wherein he was called" (I Cor. vii.20, Geneva Bible).

In the last act this subtle counterpointing of Court and Tavern moves toward stage allegory. The Falstaffian commentary simplifies into a gross burlesque of chivalric honor and heroics, and at the same time Hal comes full front as the uncomplicated embodiment of gallant knighthood. The problem now is not how to get one's mind all round Falstaff, as Empson puts it,[17] but all round the play itself. Can one respond fully both to Hal's victory over Hotspur and to Falstaff's stabbing of the corpse? Perhaps an actor playing Falstaff can only suggest through exaggerated comic behavior that we must reduce the seriousness of our attention and co-operate in subordinating Falstaff to Hal. At least it seems clear in theory that the contrasting modes and perspectives in the play are to find their unity in Hal, but the stresses within the play are still felt when one tries to participate in the experience of being a character like Hal. We are led into the experience formally through Hal's opening soliloquy ("I know you all . . ."). This sounds like a hero's version of the familiar "I am determined to be a villain"; but "I promise to be a hero" makes a difficult demand upon us because it asks us to experience Hal's initial doubleness without any feeling of duplicity or hypocrisy, and thereby to accept something which is outside of conventional moral categories. An added strain is felt in experiencing with Hal what it means to have one's character formed indirectly through acquiring only the virtues of others. These virtues are defined, dramatically, by contrasts. Hal ends his soliloquy, for example, with the cryptic promise that he will show his true self and redeem time "when men think least I will." Then as Hal leaves, the King enters and says strongly: "I will from henceforth rather be myself,/ Mighty, and to be feared, than my condition,/ Which hath been smooth as oil. . . ." The King is asserting that he is most himself when he is most awesomely majestic, but we understand that as a political administrator he must in fact be himself by being alternately ruthless or conciliatory as the situation demands. It is a matter of timing. But a true hero must be superior to this, and so the play by this and other contrasts asks us to imagine through Hal an extraordinary relation to time and a unique way of being one's self. We are accustomed to the notion that a chief of state is a kind of resolution of pressures and limited interests, but in Hal (Henry V to be) Shakespeare is attempting to dramatize for our acceptance the less believable idea of a chief of state who is a resolution of virtues. Many have preferred to imagine a crown prince whose waywardness is really an education in which he is becoming acquainted with his people, learning to speak their language, and gaining the maturity and experience he will need when he comes to the throne. There is some support for this in the play, but there is stronger reason to think of Hal as being perfect from the start. He is always the sun, to use the traditional imagery of his opening soliloquy; he is not the product of the clouds (of experience) which he permits for the moment to "smother up his beauty from the world." All this makes radical demands on us as well as on Shakespeare. The sharp juxtaposition of dramatic modes forces him beyond the prevailingly realistic limits of his art, and carries us out of the world.

The clash of modes is somewhat disguised, however, by an overlying tone which is often associated (especially by middle-aged males) with the earlier Falstaff. This Falstaff, in Alfred Harbage's words, "has the appeal of the minor miracle—the old hulk that will not sink, the hollow trunk that always rides out one more storm. . . ."[18] He embodies the social virtues of humor, warmth, and undemanding good fellowship (what Auden naughtily calls Charity[19]). Although Falstaff is related to Hal and the political side of the play in ways which have been noticed, and is certainly our fatherly mentor in helping us see through the studied attitudes and impressive rationalizations of our betters, he also, as parodist and impresario, guides us to a joyful acceptance of the wonderfully reliable way in which the members of the human race play their parts. 'Tis indeed no sin for man, woman, or child to labor in these vocations. We remember Hotspur's fine scorn of the splendidly prissy messenger from court, or the King's resoundingly royal rage against the rebels, or the brilliantly despicable way in which Worcester and Northumberland needle Hotspur while pretending to soothe him. Or we remember the domestic scenes. There is the aplomb with which Falstaff plays the title role in an Elizabethan tavern version of *Life With Father*. The comfortable master in his own house, he forgives the Hostess when he should apologize to her, orders her around with an easy masculine assurance ("Go, make ready breakfast . . ."), and makes her the affectionate subject of his bawdy jokes. The Hostess in turn is devoted to Falstaff, problem though he is, protects him against his enemies, and is spellbound in admiration at his endless talents ("O the Father, how he holds his countenance!") Or there is that other householder, Hotspur, the dream of a husband who never grows old and prudent, who one moment rejects his wife with a fine transparent show of masculine independence, and the next moment teasingly threat-

ens to make love to her in public. Again, we remember the minor
characters—the carriers, for example, complaining in the chill
dark about the lousy condition of Elizabethan trucker stops; or
Glendower, a proper Welshman, insisting darkly on his magical
birth and powers. And along with them, filling in the background,
are the characters created through imitation and parody by Falstaff, "the many men and manners," in Mark Van Doren's words,
whom he "suddenly, without warning, decides to be."[20] From this
view, in short, the play is like a great genre painting done in a
warm light. As history, it is more profoundly popular than the
chronicles, and its patriotism, if that is still the right word, is
genial and all-embracing.

4

Many have wished that Falstaff were at hand in *Henry V* to debunk the jingoism and to override the frustrating contradictions
in tone between ironic realism and the heroic. But *Henry V* has
its own kind of comedy, with its own expressive purpose. The
play as narrative is a traditional heroic story about men away
from home at war. It is a male frontier society, and its characteristic comedy is a form of the practical joke. This kind of humor
runs through *Henry V* and unifies its best scenes. An early, ele-
mentary example comes in scene ii when the present from the
Dauphin, the "tun of treasure," is discovered to be a barrel of
tennis balls, and Henry counters this practical joke (and its in-
sinuation about his frivolous youth) with some tough references
to cannon balls. The outline of the practical joke is implicit in
the trick by which Henry leads the traitors Cambridge, Scroop,
and Grey to condemn themselves to death. The practical joke in
its physical form is most at home, as might be expected, in the
camp. The obvious examples are the farcical scene in which
Fluellen forces Pistol to eat leeks, and the more elaborate episode
which begins with the exchange between Williams and the disguised king. Here and elsewhere the humor arising from the
basic pattern of the practical joke takes the form of comedy as
contest. It is a kind of one-upmanship, a sparring to keep fit and
to test the limits of endurance. Men are trained, judged, and
sorted out by being put on the spot. This differs from the critical

comedy of Falstaff "cornered" because his best capping rejoinders question the very premises of society; whereas here the jokes serve to identify and enhance the hero and to support the society he leads. In addition, the comedy arising from the practical joke is attached by its bursting exuberance, its rough-and-tumble, and its tension to male comraderie. Henry turns the uneven joke against the honest Williams into an expression of rough affection. Fluellen, the butt of good-natured joshing about his leek, is moved by the indwelling emotion of fellowship to blurt out his affection: "By Jeshu, I am your majesty's countryman, I care not who knows it. I will confess it to all the world. . . ."

These comic patterns, tones, and purposes are elevated in the play's finest scenes and joined with other elements to become a rich heroic composition. The first of these scenes is iv.i, the English camp on the eve of the battle of Agincourt. Henry, disguised in Erpingham's cloak and alone for a moment, encounters first Pistol and then Fluellen with Gower. Each gives a sample of his characteristic routine. Pistol at his best is the master of the ample gesture and the sonorous phrase. He first enters the play at the beginning of Act ii, newly married to the Hostess, and within eight lines he has drawn his sword, affecting to be grievously insulted at the suggestion that he and his Nell are what they are: shady tavernkeepers. As he orders Nym to leave the Hostess alone and marry Doll Tearsheet, the drab creatures are wonderfully inflated by his rhetoric: "Fetch forth the lazar kite of Cressid's kind./ Doll Tearsheet she by name, and her espouse./ I have, and I will hold, the quondam Quickly/ For the only she. . . ." The incongruities are warmly comic; there is something engaging about Pistol's indomitable effort to make things more heroic than they are. He has style. And it is Henry's style, his air of being equal to life, that Pistol, the expert on style, now saluates: "I kiss his dirty shoe, and from heart-string/ I love the lovely bully. . . ." Henry parts from him with good-natured understanding (your name "sorts well with your fierceness"), and Fluellen and Gower enter. Fluellen is an earnest man. He has taken on himself the burden of maintaining at least a semblance of military order in these slack latter days. He shakes his head in despair as he reprimands Gower for raising his voice—there was "no tittle taddle or pibble babble in Pompey's camp." Fluellen is a comically predictable worrier, but we know his inner worth, and our understanding is voiced by Henry: "Though it appear a little out of fashion,/ There is much care and valour in this Welshman." The lovely bully whom Pistol admires for his style can also tell a good man like Fluellen beneath an unstylish exterior.

Now comes the crucial, testing encounter between Henry and the common soldiers, Bates, Court, and Williams. The movement of the play is toward the climax of the heroic mode, whose premises and effects are the opposite of everything that is skeptical and questioning, and yet this antithetical note is now precisely what Shakespeare intrudes. What are we doing? ask the soldiers. Why are we here? The contrast of modes is shocking, but this time the contrast is controlled. The soldiers' skepticism seems to be one of the voices of Falstaff, the outrageous one which debunks honor and prefers life to its dead counterfeit. They know well enough, they tell the disguised Henry, that if the king is cornered he will play royal possum by getting himself ransomed. When they are dead and can't look, he will drop the talk about honor and show himself as eager as they are to be warm in bed or even up to his neck in cold river water rather than in this narrow place where they may be washed off at the next tide. The soldiers force the play out of the realm of heroic drama, as it were, and into the realism of the ironic problem play. The discussion of the war which follows is predictably inconclusive. No causes are ever quite just when viewed realistically, and no soldiers are ever spotless. The soldiers imply that they will fight and die if they can be shown that the war is just, but this in ordinary human terms they can never be shown; and they do not really want to be. Their real desire is to be natural, to be freed from the seemingly artificial demands of unquestioning heroism. At the conclusion of this movement, the soldiers, though still unanswered (because there can be no realistic answer), nevertheless do draw themselves up, re-enter the mode of heroic drama, and pledge their loyalty and their lives.

This pattern is now paralleled in Henry's soliloquy. He likewise leaves the heroic mode and enters the debate of the problem play by applying to his royal role the debunking analysis of a Falstaff. As he examines the trappings and ceremonies of kingship in the manner of Falstaff catechizing honor, he can find no more reason than could the common soldiers for continuing an artificial heroic existence. In ordinary human terms there can never be perfect agreement between royal appearance and substance; nor does Henry really want to prove to himself that there can be. Like the soldiers, he, too, is feeling sorry for himself. He also wants to be natural, and he looks longingly toward the warm bed and undemanding role of the peasant. Then, completing the pattern, Henry likewise re-enters the heroic mode, and pledges his loyalty and life to his commander, the Lord. Many have complained that with the return to the heroic, Henry loses the human appeal, the little touch of Harry in the night, which makes him so attractive as he mingles with the soldiers or reflects on the burdens and perplexities of the throne. But a heroic king gains reality as a character finally not from skeptical introspection or increasing self-consciousness (in the manner of many modern heroes), but from heroic speech and action. The momentary relaxation in this scene from the heroic to the ironic (and the latter's more "human" appeal) is a way of defining and dramatizing the difference between the two modes and of gaining our emotional sympathy for the heroic to the point of feeling it as near-tragedy: an image of the weary, unintelligible weight borne by men at their unquestioning best.

The king and his soldiers having put each other to the test, the action now moves toward the final battle, where the traditional features of heroic comedy (the testing, the "surprise" reversal, and the male affection enlarging into devotion to a common cause) reach a climax. The pace is at first deliberate (as in the walk-down). The spectator is allowed to contemplate the fearful odds and anticipate the "joke" on the enemy. The English are outnumbered five to one, and they have been further weakened by a hard winter, a Valley Forge of cold and sickness. On the one side is the multitude of French, glittering in the sun; on the other is the little band of English, their helmets rusty, sitting like "fixed candlesticks" on their "poor jades," who "Lob down their heads, dropping the hides and hips,/ The gum downroping from their pale-dead eyes,/ And in their pale dull mouths the gimmal bit/ Lies foul with chewed grass, still and motionless." But these scarecrows, as Henry says and we know, are "warriors for the working-day." The battle comes to its incredible end, and along the way, in one close-up after another, are acted out the controlling themes which Henry voices so strongly and movingly in his Saint Crispian speech. All who take part in this action are "gentled" by it and enter into a classless comradeship.

This sketchy essay must end, but perhaps the point is clear enough. The attempt to simplify Shakespeare's English history plays into an example of the History Play with a single over-riding theme obstructs our appreciation of the actual variety of dramatic mode and structure in the plays, their thematic richness, and the remarkable effects which occur when contrasting modes within a play interact co-operatively. We are "better educated" by Shakespeare, as Northrop Frye puts it,[21] than by his sources.

NOTES

1. Intro. to *King Richard II* (Cambridge, 1939), p. liv.
2. *Angel With Horns* (New York, 1961), p. 44.
3. Northrop Frye, *Anatomy of Criticism* (Princeton, 1957), p. 285.
4. John Palmer, *Political Characters of Shakespeare* (London, 1948), p. 143.
5. *Shakespearean Criticism*, ed. T. M. Raysor (Harvard, 1930), I, 148-51.
6. Edward Dowden, *Shakespeare* (1872), Capricorn reprint (1962), p. 194.
7. James A. S. McPeek, "Richard and His Shadow World," *The American Imago*, 15 (1958), 204.
8. W. H. Clemen, *The Development of Shakespeare's Imagery* (1951), Dramabook reprint, p. 55.
9. Walter Pater, *Appreciations* (London, 1889), p. 198.
10. Peter Ure, Intro. to *King Richard II*, New Arden edition (Harvard, 1956), p. lxxxii.
11. Travis Bogard, "Shakespeare's Second Richard," *PMLA*, LXX (1955), 205-6.
12. See Richard Altick, "Symphonic Imagery in *Richard II*," *PMLA*, LXII (1947), 339-65.

13. Brents Stirling, "Bolingbroke's 'Decision,'" *Shakespeare Quarterly*, ii (1951), 30.

14. Palmer, *passim*.

15. Robert Langbaum, *The Poetry of Experience* (London, 1957), p. 169.

16. Ure, p. lxxxiii.

17. *Some Versions of Pastoral* (1935), New Directions reprint (1960), p. 105.

18. *William Shakespeare* (New York, 1963), p. 208.

19. "The Fallen City," *Encounter*, xiii (1959), 27ff.

20. *Shakespeare* (1939), Doubleday Anchor reprint (1953), pp. 107-14.

21. "Characterization in Shakespearian Comedy," *Shakespeare Quarterly*, iv (1953), 271.

Brents Stirling

"OR ELSE WERE THIS A SAVAGE SPECTACLE"

MODERN READERS are prone to find the tragedy of Brutus in his rigid devotion to justice and fair play. Many members of the Globe audience, however, believed that his virtues were complicated by self-deception and doubtful principle. In sixteenth-century views of history the conspiracy against Caesar often represented a flouting of unitary sovereignty, that prime point of Tudor policy, and exemplified the anarchy thought to accompany "democratic" or constitutional checks upon authority. Certain judgments of Elizabethan political writers who refer to Brutus are quite clear upon this point.[1] Although naturally aware of his disinterested honor and liberality, contemporary audiences could thus perceive in him a conflict between questionable goals and honorable action, a contradiction lying in his attempt to redeem morally confused ends by morally clarified means. The Elizabethan tragedy of Brutus, like that of Othello, is marked by an integrity of conduct which leads the protagonist into evil and reassures him in his error.

The distinction between modern and Elizabethan views of *Julius Caesar* is not the point of our inquiry, but it is a necessary beginning, for the older view of Brutus determines both the symbolic quality and the structure of the play. I hope to show that a sixteenth-century idea of Brutus is as thoroughly related to Shakespeare's art as it is to his meaning.

When a dramatist wishes to present an idea, his traditional method, of course, is to settle upon an episode in which the idea

From *Unity in Shakespearian Tragedy: The Interplay of Theme and Character*, 1956, pp. 40-54. Copyright 1956 by Columbia University Press. Reprinted by permission of the author and the publisher.

arises naturally but vividly from action and situation. Such an
episode in *Julius Caesar* is the one in which Brutus resolves to
exalt not only the mission but the tactics of conspiracy: having
accepted republicanism as an honorable end, he sets out to
dignify assassination, the means, by lifting it to a level of rite
and ceremony.[2] In II.i, as Cassius urges the killing of Antony as
a necessary accompaniment to the death of Caesar, Brutus declares that "such a course will seem too bloody . . . ,/ To cut
the head off and then hack the limbs." With this thought a sense
of purpose comes over him: "Let's be sacrificers, but not butchers,
Caius." Here his conflict seems to be resolved, and for the first
time he is more than a reluctant presence among the conspirators
as he expands the theme which ends his hesitation and frees his
moral imagination:

> We all stand up against the spirit of Caesar,
> And in the spirit of men there is no blood;
> Oh, that we then could come by Caesar's spirit,
> And not dismember Caesar! But, alas,
> Caesar must bleed for it! And, gentle friends,
> Let's kill him boldly, but not wrathfully;
> Let's carve him as a dish fit for the gods,
> Not hew him as a carcass fit for hounds.

This proposed conversion of bloodshed to ritual is the manner
in which an abstract Brutus will be presented in terms of concrete art. From the suggestion of Plutarch that Brutus' first error
lay in sparing Antony, Shakespeare moves to the image of
Antony as a limb of Caesar, a limb not to be hacked because
hacking is no part of ceremonial sacrifice. From Plutarch's description of Brutus as high-minded, gentle and disinterested,
Shakespeare proceeds to the Brutus of symbolic action. Gentleness and disinterestedness become embodied in the act of "un-
wrathful" blood sacrifice. High-mindedness becomes objectified
in ceremonial observance.

A skeptical reader may ask why the episode just described is
any more significant than a number of others such as Brutus'
scene with Portia or his quarrel with Cassius. If more significant,
it is so only because of its relation to a thematic design. I agree,
moreover, that Shakespeare gains his effects by variety; as a

recognition, in fact, of his complexity I hope to show that the structure of *Julius Caesar* is marked by reference both varied and apt to Brutus' sacrificial rite, and that this process includes expository preparation in earlier scenes, emphasis upon "mock-ceremony" in both earlier and later scenes, and repeated comment by Antony upon butchery under the guise of sacrifice—ironical comment which takes final form in the parley before Philippi.

Derived in large measure from Plutarch, but never mechanically or unselectively, the theme of incantation and ritual is thus prominent throughout *Julius Caesar*, and this is no less true at the beginning than during the crucial episodes of Acts II and III. In the opening scene of the play we are confronted with a Roman populace rebuked by Marullus for ceremonial idolatry of Caesar:

> And do you now put on your best attire?
> And do you now cull out a holiday?
> And do you now strew flowers in his way
> That comes in triumph over Pompey's blood?

For this transgression Marullus prescribes a counter-observance by the citizens in immediate expiation of their folly:

> Run to your houses, fall upon your knees,
> Pray to the gods to intermit this plague
> That needs must light on this ingratitude.

To which Flavius adds:

> Go, go, good countrymen, and for this fault,
> Assemble all the poor men of your sort;
> Draw them to Tiber banks, and weep your tears
> Into the channel, till the lowest stream
> Do kiss the most exalted shores of all.

And after committing the populace to these rites of atonement for their festal celebration of Caesar, the two tribunes themselves leave to remove the devotional symbols set up for his welcoming. "Go you . . . towards the Capitol;/ This way will I. Disrobe the images/ If you do find them decked with ceremonies./ . . . let no images/ Be hung with Caesar's trophies." It is the hope of Flavius that these disenchantments will make Caesar "fly an ordinary pitch,/ Who else would soar above the view of men."

Act I, scene ii is equally unusual in carrying the theme of ritual. It is apparent that Shakespeare had a wide choice of means for staging the entry of Caesar and his retinue; yet he selects an entry based upon Plutarch's description of the "feast Lupercalia" in which the rite of touching or striking barren women by runners of the course is made prominent. Caesar, moreover, after ordering Calpurnia to be so touched by Antony, commands: "Set on; and leave no ceremony out." It can be said, in fact, that the whole of this scene is written with ceremonial observance as a background. Its beginning, already described, is followed by a touch of solemnity in the soothsayer's words; next comes its main expository function, the sounding of Brutus by Cassius, and throughout this interchange come at intervals the shouts and flourishes of a symbolic spectacle. When the scene is again varied by a formal reentry and exit of Caesar's train, Casca remains behind to make a mockery of the rite which has loomed so large from off-stage. Significantly, in Casca's travesty of the ceremonial crown-offering and of the token offering by Caesar of his throat for cutting, Shakespeare has added a satirical note which does not appear in Plutarch.

The process, then, in each of the two opening episodes has been the bringing of serious ritual into great prominence, and of subjecting it to satirical treatment. In the first scene the tribunes denounce the punctilio planned for Caesar's entry, send the idolatrous crowd to rites of purification, and set off themselves to desecrate the devotional images. In the second scene a multiple emphasis of ceremony is capped by Casca's satire which twists the crown ritual into imbecile mummery. At this point, and in conformity with the mood set by Casca, occurs Cassius' mockery in soliloquy of Brutus:

> Well, Brutus, thou art noble; yet I see
> Thy honorable mettle may be wrought
> From that it is dispos'd; therefore it is meet
> That noble minds keep ever with their likes;
> For who is so firm that cannot be seduc'd?

The next scene (i.iii) is packed with omens and supernatural portents, a note which is carried directly into ii.i where Brutus, on receiving the mysterious papers which have been left to prompt his action, remarks,

> The exhalations whizzing in the air
> Give so much light that I may read by them.

Appropriately, the letters read under this weird glow evoke his first real commitment to the "cause":

> O Rome, I make thee promise
> If the redress will follow, thou receivest
> Thy full petition at the hand of Brutus!

Now appear his lines on the interim "between the acting of a dreadful thing / And the first motion" in which "the state of man / Like to a little kingdom, suffers then / The nature of a insurrection." This conventional symbolizing of political convulsion by inward insurrection is followed by the soliloquy on conspiracy:

> O, then by day
> Where wilt thou find a cavern dark enough
> To mask thy monstrous visage? Seek none, Conspiracy!
> Hide it in smiles and affability.

The conflict within Brutus thus becomes clear in this scene. First, the participant in revolution suffers revolution within himself; then the hater of conspiracy and lover of plain dealing must call upon Conspiracy to hide in smiling courtesy.

We have now reached the critical point (ii.i.154ff.) to which attention was first called, an outward presentation of Brutus' crisis through his acceptance of an assassin's role upon condition that the assassins become sacrificers. Already a theme well established in preceding scenes, the idea of ritual is again made prominent. As the soliloquy on conspiracy closes, the plotters gather, and the issue becomes the taking of an oath. Brutus rejects this as an idle ceremony unsuited to men joined in the honesty of a cause and turns now to the prospect of Caesar's death. This time, however, honorable men do need ceremony,

ceremony which will purify the violent act of all taint of butchery and raise it to the level of sacrifice. But although Brutus has steadied himself with a formula his conflict is still unresolved, for as he sets his course he "unconsciously" reveals the evasion which Antony later will amplify: to transmute political killing into ritual is to cloak it with appearances. We began with Brutus' passage on carving Caesar as a dish for the gods; these are the lines which complete it:

> And let our hearts, as subtle masters do,
> Stir up their servants to an act of rage,
> And after seem to chide 'em. This shall make
> Our purpose necessary and not envious;
> Which so appearing to the common eyes,
> We shall be called purgers, not murderers.

The contradiction is interesting. In an anticlimax, Brutus has ended his great invocation to ritual with a note on practical politics: our hearts shall stir us and afterward seem to chide us; we shall thus "appear" to the citizenry as purgers, not murderers.

Shakespeare never presents Brutus as a demagogue, but there are ironical traces of the politician in him which suggest Covell's adverse picture of Roman liberators.[3] It is curious, in fact, that although Brutus is commonly thought to be unconcerned over public favor, he expresses clear concern for it in the passage just quoted and in III.i.244-51, where he sanctions Antony's funeral speech only if Antony agrees to tell the crowd that he speaks by generous permission, and only if he agrees to utter no evil of the conspiracy. Nor is Brutus' speech in the Forum wholly the nonpolitical performance it is supposed to be; certainly Shakespeare's Roman citizens are the best judges of it, and they react tempestuously. Although compressed, it scarcely discloses aloofness or an avoidance of popular emotive themes.

Act II, scene ii now shifts to the house of Caesar, but the emphasis on ritual continues as before. With dramatic irony, in view of Brutus' recent lines on sacrificial murder, Caesar commands, "Go bid the priests do present sacrifice." Calpurnia who has "never stood on ceremonies" (omens) is now terrified by them. News comes that the augurers, plucking the entrails of an offering, have failed to find a heart. Calpurnia has dreamed

that smiling Romans have laved their hands in blood running
from Caesar's statue, and Decius Brutus gives this its favorable
interpretation which sends Caesar to his death.

The vivid assassination scene carries out Brutus' ritual pre-
scription in dramatic detail, for the killing is staged with a
formalized approach, ending in kneeling, by one conspirator
after another until the victim is surrounded. This is met by a
series of retorts from Caesar ending in "Hence! Wilt thou lift up
Olympus," and the "sacrifice" is climaxed with his "Et tu Brute!"
The conspirators ceremonially bathe their hands in Caesar's
blood, and Brutus pronounces upon "this our lofty scene" with
the prophecy that it "shall be acted over / In states unborn
and accents yet unknown!"

The mockery in counterritual now begins as a servant of
Antony enters (III.i.121) and confronts Brutus:

> Thus, Brutus, did my master bid me kneel,
> Thus did Mark Antony bid me fall down;
> And being prostrate, thus he bade me say:
> Brutus is noble, wise, valiant, and honest.

Here a threefold repetition, "kneel," "fall down," and "being
prostrate," brings the ceremonial irony close to satire. Following
this worship of the new idol by his messenger, Antony appears
in person and with dramatic timing offers himself as a victim.
In one speech he evokes both the holy scene which the conspirators so desired and the savagery which underlay it:

> Now, whilst your purpled hands do reek and smoke,
> Fulfill your pleasure. Live a thousand years,
> I shall not find myself so apt to die;
> No place will please me so, no mean of death,
> As here by Caesar, and by you cut off.

The murder scene is thus hallowed by Antony in a manner
which quite reverses its sanctification by the conspirators. Brutus, forbearing, attempts to mollify Antony with his cherished
theme of purgation:

> Our hearts you see not. They are pitiful,
> And pity to the general wrong of Rome—

As fire drives out fire, so pity pity—
Hath done this deed on Caesar.

Antony's response is again one of counterceremony, the shaking
of hands in formal sequence which serves to make each conspirator stand alone and unprotected by the rite of blood which
had united him with the others. The assassins had agreed as a
token of solidarity that each of them should stab Caesar. Antony
seems to allude to this:

> Let each man render me his bloody hand.
> First, Marcus Brutus, will I shake with you;
> Now, Caius Cassius, do I take your hand;
> Now, Decius Brutus, yours; now yours, Mettellus;
> Yours, Cinna; and, my valiant Casca, yours;
> Though last, not least in love, yours, good Trebonius.
> Gentlemen all,—alas what shall I say?

It is then that Antony, addressing the body of Caesar, suddenly
delivers his first profanation of the ritual sacrifice:

> Here wast thou bay'd brave hart;
> Here didst thou fall; and here thy hunters stand,
> Sign'd in thy spoil, and crimson'd in thy lethe.

And lest the allusion escape, Shakespeare continues Antony's
inversion of Brutus' ceremonial formula: the dish carved for
the gods is doubly transformed into the carcass hewn for hounds
with further hunting metaphors of Caesar as a hart in the forest and as "a deer strucken by many princes." Brutus agrees to
give reasons why Caesar was dangerous, "or else were this a
savage spectacle," and the stage is set for what may be called
the play's chief counterritual. Only Brutus, who planned the
rite of sacrifice, could with such apt irony arrange the "true
rites" and "ceremonies" which are to doom the conspiracy.

> I will myself into the pulpit first
> And show the reason of our Caesar's death.
> What Antony shall speak, I will protest
> He speaks by leave and by permission,
> And that we are contented Caesar shall
> Have all true rites and lawful ceremonies.

But exactly after the manner of his speech announcing the ritual sacrifice (ii.i) Brutus concludes again on a note of policy: "It shall advantage more than do us wrong."

Next follows Antony *solus* rendering his prophecy of "domestic fury and fierce civil strife" symbolized in Caesar's ghost which will

> Cry "Havoc," and let slip the dogs of war,
> That this foul deed shall smell above the earth.

The passage is similar in utterance, function, and dramatic placement to Carlisle's prophecy on the deposition of Richard II, and for that reason it is to be taken seriously as a choric interpretation of Caesar's death. Significantly, the beginning lines again deride Brutus' erstwhile phrase, "sacrificers but not butchers":

> O, pardon me, thou bleeding piece of earth,
> That I am meek and gentle with these butchers!

It is unnecessary to elaborate upon the Forum scene; Antony's oration follows the speech of Brutus with consequences familiar to all readers. But there is an element in Antony's turning of the tables which is just as remarkable as the well-known irony of his references to "honorable men." If we remember that Shakespeare has emphasized ritual at various planes of seriousness and of derision, the conclusion of Antony's speech to the populace will link itself with the previous theme. For here Antony reenacts the death of Caesar in a ritual of his own, one intended to show that the original "lofty scene" presented a base carnage. Holding Caesar's bloody mantle as a talisman, he reproduces *seriatim* the sacrificial strokes, but he does so in terms of the "rent" Casca made and the "cursed steel" that Brutus plucked away with the blood of Caesar following it. Again, each conspirator had struck individually at Caesar and had symbolically involved himself with the others; for the second time Antony reminds us of this ritual bond by recounting each stroke, and his recreation of the rite becomes a mockery of it. Brutus' transformation of blood into the heady wine of sacrifice is reversed both in substance and in ceremony.

For the "realists" among the conspirators what has occurred can be summed up in the bare action of the play: the killing of Caesar has been accomplished, but the fruits of it have been spoiled by Brutus' insistence that Antony live and that he speak at Caesar's funeral. "The which," as North's Plutarch has it, "marred all." With reference to Brutus, however, something much more significant has been enacted; the "insurrection," the contradiction, within him has taken outward form in his attempt to purify assassination through ceremony. This act, not to be found in Plutarch,[4] symbolizes the "Elizabethan" Brutus compelled by honor to join with conspirators but required by conscience to reject Conspiracy.

We have followed the ritual theme in *Julius Caesar* from early scenes to the point of Antony's oration, at which it is completely defined. There remains, however, a terminal appearance of the theme in the first scene of Act V. The ultimate clash between the idealism of Brutus and Antony's contempt for it comes during the parley on the eve of Philippi, at which Antony again drives home the old issue of ceremonial imposture. Brutus has observed that his enemy wisely threats before he stings; the reply is Antony's last disposition of the sacrificial rite:

> Villains, you did not so when your vile daggers
> Hack'd one another in the sides of Caesar,
> You show'd your teeth like apes, and fawn'd like
>   hounds,
> And bow'd like bondmen, kissing Caesar's feet;
> Whilst damned Casca, like a cur, behind
> Struck Caesar on the neck.

Antony invokes the "hacking" which Brutus earlier foreswore, and he again inverts the cherished formula of sacrifice: once more the dish carved for gods becomes the carcass hewn for hounds. Over the body of Caesar he had previously employed the hunting-hound figure ("Here wast thou bay'd, brave hart."); the apes, the hounds, and the cur of these lines complete his vengeful irony of metaphor.

What, finally, is to be inferred from Antony's concluding passage on "the noblest Roman of them all"? Commonly found there is a broad vindication of Brutus which would deny an ironical interpretation. When Antony's elegiac speech is read plainly, however, its meaning is quite limited: it declares simply that Brutus was the only conspirator untouched by envy, and that, in intention, he acted "in a general honest thought / And common good to all." The Elizabethan view of Brutus as tragically misguided is thus consistent with Antony's pronouncement that he was the only disinterested member of the conspiracy. But Brutus is not to be summed up in an epitaph; as the impersonal member of a conspiracy motivated largely by personal ends, he sought in a complex way to resolve his contradiction by depersonalizing, ritualizing, the means.

Shakespeare's achievement, however, is not confined to the characterization of a major figure, for we have seen that the ceremonial motive extends beyond the personality of Brutus into the structure of the play. Exposition stressing the idea of ritual observance leads to the episode in which Brutus formulates the "sacrifice," and clear resolution of the idea follows in event and commentary. Structural craftsmanship thus supplements characterization and the two combine, as in *Richard II*, to state the political philosophy implicit in the play.

NOTES

1. See the discussion in J. E. Phillips's *The State in Shakespeare's Greek and Roman Plays* (New York, 1940), pp. 172ff. Mr. Phillips quotes at length from such typical spokesmen as Sir Thomas Elyot and Thomas Craig. His analysis of *Julius Caesar* on this basis is also illuminating. See also the present author's *The Populace in Shakespeare* (New York, 1949), p. 147, for a condemnation by William Covell of Romans who aroused civil dissension by covering their purposes "with the fine terms of a common good, of the freedom of the people, of justice. . . ." The parallel with Brutus is a very close one, and Covell, moreover, explicitly avows a topical relation of such Roman history to the civil tensions of Elizabethan England.

2. My article on the ritual theme in *Julius Caesar* (*PMLA*, LXVI, pp. 765ff.) appeared in 1951 as an early draft of this chapter. Some of my principal observations have been repeated by Ernest

Schanzer in a recent essay ("The Tragedy of Shakespeare's Brutus," *ELH* (March, 1955), pp. 1ff.; see pp. 6-8).

3. See the reference and quotation in note 1.

4. A reference at this point to Plutarch will serve both to clarify my meaning and to allay some natural doubts concerning the dramatist's intention. While it is true that the ritual murder of Caesar is Shakespeare's own contribution, the expository preparation for it in Act I comes from an episode in Plutarch in which Antony concludes the Lupercalian rites by offering a laurel crown twice to Caesar, and in which the tribunes are described as desecrating ritual offerings (*Shakespeare's Plutarch*, I, 92-3; see also II, 19-20). Hence we have basic ritual materials for Shakespeare's first two scenes present in one convenient block of his source which also offered a convenient beginning for the play. Does this prevent us from attaching significance to the unusual presence of ritual elements in the exposition scenes? I believe it does not, for two reasons. First, the choice of source material by a dramatist is itself significant; Shakespeare could have started the play with other episodes in Plutarch or with scenes of his own invention. Secondly, it is immaterial whether he began *Julius Caesar* with this episode in his source and, because of its wealth of ritual detail, was led to the theme of ritualized assassination, or whether he began with the theme and chose source materials for exposition which agreed with it. In either case the same remarkable unity between earlier and later parts of the play would have been achieved, and it is this unity which is important. Guesses about its origin in the playwright's composition are profitless. We do know that Shakespeare's Brutus plans the killing of Caesar as ritual, while Plutarch presents it as the very opposite of this. Plutarch's description of the assassination emphasizes, in fact, its resemblance to the hunting down of an animal, the very effect Brutus seeks explicitly to avoid in the "carcass-hounds" figure, and the one which Antony magnifies in his counteremphasis of imagery drawn from hunting. North notes it thus: "Caesar turned him nowhere but he was stricken at by some . . . and was hacked and mangled among them, as a wild beast taken of hunters." (*Shakespeare's Plutarch*, I, 101-2.)

Helen Gardner

HAMLET AND THE TRAGEDY OF REVENGE

THE ESSENCE of any tragedy of revenge is that its hero has not created the situation in which he finds himself and out of which the tragedy arises. The simplest of all tragic formulas, that a tragedy begins in prosperity and ends in misery, does not fit revenge tragedies. When the action opens the hero is seen in a situation which is horrible, and felt by him and the audience to be intolerable, but for which he has no responsibility. The exposition of such plays does not display the hero taking a fatal step, but the hero confronted with appalling facts. This is as true in Argos as it is in Denmark. But in Elizabethan revenge plays it is not merely the initial situation which is created by the villain. The denouement also comes about through his initiative. It is not the result of a successfully carried out scheme of the revenger. The revenger takes an opportunity unconsciously provided for him by the villain. Given this opportunity, which he seems unable to create for himself, he forms his scheme on the spur of the moment. Thus, in *The Spanish Tragedy*, Lorenzo, believing himself safe and that the secret of Horatio's murder lies buried with Serberine and Pedringano, feigns reconcilement with Hieronymo and invites him to provide a play for the entertainment of the court. By means of this play Hieronymo achieves his vengeance and brings to light the secret crime of Lorenzo. Similarly, in *Titus Andronicus*, which is obviously modelled on *The Spanish Tragedy*, although it exceeds it in horrors, the denouement comes about because Tamora believes she can deal with the old mad Titus and, through him, with his dangerous son

From "The Historical Approach" in *The Business of Criticism*, 1959, pp. 41-51. Copyright © 1959 by Oxford University Press. Reprinted by permission of the Clarendon Press, Oxford.

Lucius who threatens her and her husband, the Emperor. Confident in her scheme, she delivers herself and her sons into Titus' hands. Up to the point when she calls upon him, disguised as Revenge, Titus has done nothing but indulge in wild gestures of grief and distraction; just as Hieronymo has done nothing to avenge his son before Lorenzo's initiative suggests to him a way of destroying his enemies and revealing their wickedness. Again, in a play written after *Hamlet*, Tourneur's *The Revenger's Tragedy*, the Duke himself asks Vendice, whose mistress he has poisoned because she would not yield to him, to find him a new mistress. He himself arranges the place, a hidden pavilion, and allows his courtiers to believe that he has gone away, so as to ensure secrecy. He thus provides Vendice with the perfect place and time for his vengeance. It seems as if in plays of this kind it was a necessary part of the total effect that the villain should be to some extent the agent of his own destruction. As initiator of the action he must be the initiator of its resolution. The satisfaction of the close included to a less or greater degree the sombre satisfaction which the Psalmist felt at the spectacle of the wicked falling into pits which they had digged for others. Here, obscurely, the hand of heaven could be felt, as Raleigh felt it in the bloody pageant of history:

> Oh, by what plots, by what forswearings, betrayings, oppressions, imprisonments, tortures, poysonings, and under what reasons of State, and politique subtlety, have these forenamed Kings, both strangers, and of our owne Nation, pulled the vengeance of GOD upon themselves, upon theirs, and upon their prudent ministers! and in the end have brought those things to passe for their enemies, and seene an effect so directly contrary to all their owne counsels and cruelties, as the one could never have hoped for themselves, and the other never have succeeded, if no such opposition had ever been made. GOD hath said it and performed it ever: *Perdam sapientiam sapientium; I will destroy the wisedome of the wise.*[1]

"In the end" the wicked will destroy themselves and "purposes mistook" will fall on "the inventors' heads." The hero waits for his opponent, as if for a signal, and the initiative and activity which Johnson expected from the hero of a play seems not to have been required from heroes in situations of this kind. This conception of a hero who is committed to counter-action, and to response to events rather than to the creation of events, is very powerfully rendered by Tourneur in the exposition of *The Revenger's Tragedy*. The personages of court pass across the stage, while Vendice, holding in his hands the skull of his dead mistress, comments on the parade of vicious power and wealth. He is waiting for "that bald Madam, Opportunity."

When we turn back from reading these plays to *Hamlet* we see that Shakespeare has very greatly developed this basic element in the revenge play of his day. He has developed it to make clear what in them is confused by sensationalism, and by that moral indignation which so easily converts itself to immorality. Great writers perceive what is only half perceived by their lesser contemporaries and express what in them finds only partial or imperfect expression. In other revenge plays, once the signal is given, the revenger produces a scheme of horror by which he destroys his opponent. He becomes an agent, bent on fulfilling the hateful Senecan maxim that crimes are only to be avenged by greater crimes. The irony is only mild. It is ironic that the villain, acting as if all were well, invites his destroyer to destroy him. Once invited, the hero descends with alacrity to the moral level of his opponent. The vengeance when it comes is as hideous as the original crime, or even more hideous, and the moral feelings of the audience are confused between satisfaction and outrage.[2] In the denouement of *Hamlet* the irony is profound. Claudius, who has arranged the whole performance in order to destroy Hamlet, is himself destroyed and destroys his Queen. He is "hoist with his own petard." His tool Laertes acknowledges the justice of his fate as he reveals the plot to which he had consented: "I am justly killed with mine own treachery." Claudius himself makes no such acknowledgement. He dies impenitent; there is "no relish of salvation" in his death. Kyd, with Hieronymo left alive on his hands at the end of the general holocaust, was forced to the weak expedient of making him commit suicide as the only way to preserve any sympathy for him. Hamlet dies as a victim to that constancy to his purposes which has made

him "follow the king's pleasure" throughout. The end comes because he has accepted every challenge: "If his fitness speaks,
mine is ready." Unlike Hieronymo, Titus, and Vendice, he remains to the last, in his adversary's words, "most generous, and
free from all contriving." For there is another point in which an
Elizabethan tragedy of revenge differs from the legend of Orestes
and from the original Hamlet legend. Everyone in Argos is perfectly well aware that Clytemnestra, with the help of her para-
mour, Aegisthus, murdered her husband, Agamemnon, just as in
the old story of Hamlet everyone knows that his uncle Feng is
the murderer of his father. In these ancient stories of revenge for
blood the criminals are known to be criminals by all their world.
They are not "secret men of blood." The secrecy with which Kyd
invests the murder of Horatio is carried to such fantastic lengths
that at one point in the play it appears that the world in general
does not even realize that he is dead. In *Hamlet*, as we know it,
whether it was so in the old play or not, only his murderer among
living men knows at the beginning of the action that Hamlet the
elder was murdered. *The Spanish Tragedy* is built on a powerful
moral contrast between the treacherous, subtle, politic Lorenzo
and the honest man, Hieronymo, who lives by conscience and
the law. At the crisis of the play this contrast is blurred and
Hieronymo becomes as crafty as his enemy. In *Hamlet* it is preserved to the end, and Hamlet himself is far more of an instrument and far less of an agent than are his fellow revengers.

The view that the revenger's role was essentially a waiting
role, that he was committed by the situation in which he found
himself to counter-action, and differentiated from his opponent
by lack of guile, does not answer the question "Why does Hamlet delay?" It sets it in a different light. We must still find consistency between his character and his actions, and Bradley's
statement that "the whole story turns on the peculiar character
of the hero" retains its truth. But to set *Hamlet* against other
plays of its time which handle the same kind of subject is to suggest that however much he may reproach himself with his delay,
that delay is part of a pattern which is made clear at the close.
To ask "Why in the world did not Hamlet act at once?" is to fail
to grasp the nature of the dilemma which Kyd crudely adum-
brated when he set the man of conscience and duty against the

conscienceless and treacherous villain. Hamlet's agony of mind
and indecision are precisely the things which differentiate him
from that smooth, swift plotter Claudius, and from the coarse,
unthinking Laertes, ready to "dare damnation" and cut his enemy's throat in a churchyard. He quickly learns from Claudius
how to entrap the unwary and the generous, and betters the instruction. "He will never have a better opportunity," say many
critics, when Hamlet, convinced of his uncle's guilt and hot for
vengeance, comes on Claudius on his knees. Even Browning's
ruthless tyrant, after having long schemed his enemy's destruction, shrank back and "was afraid" when his victim "caught at
God's skirts and prayed." Do we really want to see Hamlet stab
a defenceless, kneeling man? This "opportunity" is no opportunity at all; the enemy is within touching distance, but out of
reach. Hamlet's baffled rage finds an outlet in the speech which
shocked Johnson by its depth of hatred. The speech reveals more
than its speaker's character. Like many soliloquies, it is proleptic.
The moment which Hamlet here declares that he will wait for,
the real opportunity, will come. When Hamlet has gone and
Claudius has risen from his knees, and not before, we know that
Claudius has not found grace. The opportunity which Hamlet
awaits Claudius will now provide. The play has made Hamlet
certain of his uncle's guilt; it has also shown Claudius that his
guilt is no longer his own secret. If he cannot repent, he must,
for his own safety, destroy Hamlet. He will do it in his own
characteristic way, by the hand of an accomplice and by the
treacherous man's characteristic weapon, poison. And Hamlet
will destroy Claudius in his own characteristic way also: by
"rashness" and "indiscretion," and not by "deep plots." He will
catch him at the moment when his guilt has been made clear to
all the by-standers, so that as he runs the sword through him he
will do so not as an assassin but as an executioner. The dark and
devious world in which Hamlet finds himself, when he accepts
the necessity of obeying the command of the Ghost, involves all
who enter it in guilt. But Hamlet's most terrible deed, when he
allows himself to be "marshalled to knavery" and is most con-
taminated by his world, the sending of the traitors Rosencrantz
and Guildenstern to their deaths, is a spontaneous, savage response to the discovery of their treachery; and his other crime,

the killing of Polonius, with its consequence in the madness and death of Ophelia, is also unpremeditated.

In *Othello*, Iago, speaking in the role of an honest man, puts crudely to his master the code of a soldier:

> Though in the trade of war I have slain men,
> Yet do I hold it very stuff o' the conscience
> To do no contriv'd murder.

Hamlet is fittingly borne "like a soldier, to the stage," because in the secret war which he has waged he has shown a soldier's virtues. Pre-eminently he has shown the virtue of constancy. He has not laid down his arms and quitted the field. For Bradley's comment, "Two months have passed and he has done nothing," we might better say, "Two months have passed and he is still there, at his post, on guard." The play ends with a soldier's funeral. It opens with sentries at their watch, being relieved. In his four great tragedies, when his imagination was working at its highest pitch, Shakespeare relates his beginnings to his ends particularly closely. Granville-Barker pointed out how *King Lear* ends as it began with Lear and his three daughters on the stage and with the old king hanging on the hope of words from Cordelia's lips. Any writer dramatizing Cinthio's story of the Moor of Venice would end with the midnight scenes of the attempted murder of Cassio and the death of Desdemona. Shakespeare has invented a great midnight opening to balance this close, with brawling in the streets followed by the midnight scene before the Senate, where, with the approval of Venice, Othello is united to Desdemona, as in the last scene he is united to her in death before the eyes of the envoys of Venice. *Macbeth* begins and ends with battles. It opens with the epic narrative of the defeat of the thane of Cawdor who had rebelled, and closes with the defeat of the thane of Cawdor who had usurped. And here there is contrast. The first thane confessed his treasons "very freely" and died well, giving up his life, "the dearest thing he owed," "as 'twere a trifle": his successor in the title, Macbeth, fought desperately to the last to preserve a life which had become meaningless to him. The opening and the close of *Hamlet* have the same kind of relation to each other. The soldier on guard, who cannot leave his post until he is relieved or given permission from above, is a metaphor for the soul in this world which comes very easily to Renaissance writers. Its source is Cicero's gloss on the "secret doctrine" which Socrates appealed to in his argument against suicide in the *Phaedo*.[3] The Red Cross Knight uses it against Despair:

> The souldier may not move from watchfull sted
> Nor leave his stand, untill his Captain bed.

And Donne, speaking of this world as "the appointed field," refers to the same commonplace when he chides the "desperate coward" who yields to the foes of him

> who made thee to stand
> Sentinell in his worlds garrison.

The play of *Hamlet* continually recurs to the thought of suicide, and the temptation to give up the battle of life. Hamlet's first soliloquy opens with the lament that the Almighty has "fixed his canon 'gainst self-slaughter,' and his last action is to snatch the poisoned cup from the lips of Horatio. Within this frame of soldiers on the watch, being relieved, and of a soldier's laying to rest, I do not believe that the Elizabethans thought that they were witnessing a story of personal failure. Nor do I think that we should do so either, unless we are certain of what, in this situation, would be success.

The tragedy of *Hamlet*, and of plays of its kind, of which it is the supreme example, does not lie in "the unfitness of the hero for his task," or in some "fatal flaw." It is not true that a coarser nature could have cleansed the state of Denmark, some "Hotspur of the North": "he that kills me some six or seven of Scots at a breakfast, washes his hands, and says to his wife, 'Fie upon this quiet life! I want work.' " The tragedy lies in the nature of the task, which only the noble will feel called on to undertake, or rather, in the nature of the world which is exposed to the hero's contemplation and in his sense of responsibility to the world in which he finds himself. *Hamlet* towers above other plays of its kind through the heroism and nobility of its hero, his superior power of insight into, and reflection upon, his situation, and his capacity to suffer the moral anguish which moral responsibility brings. Hamlet is the quintessence of European man, who holds that man is "ordained to govern the world according to equity and righteousness with an upright heart," and not to renounce the world and leave it to its corruption. By that conception of man's duty and destiny he is involved in those tragic dilemmas with which our own age is so terribly familiar. For how can man secure justice except by committing injustice, and how can he act without outraging the very conscience which demands that he should act?

It will have been apparent for some time that I am coming round to a point where I am demonstrating the historical nature of my own answer to my question. Although I have gone to the Elizabethans to ask how *Hamlet* appeared to audiences which had applauded *The Spanish Tragedy* and *Titus Andronicus,* it is the moral uncertainties and the moral dilemmas of my own age which make me unable to see *Hamlet* in terms of the hero's failure or success in the task which the Ghost lays upon him.

> For this same lord,
> I do repent: but heaven hath pleas'd it so,
> To punish me with this, and this with me,
> That I must be their scourge and minister.

Hamlet, speaking over the body of one of his victims, Polonius, speaks for all those called on to attempt to secure justice, the supporters of "just wars" as well as those who fight in them. In trying to set *Hamlet* back into its own age, I seem to have found in it an image of my own time. The Elizabethan Hamlet assumes the look of the Hamlet of the twentieth century.

That the answers we find are conditioned by our own circumstances does not destroy their value. *Hamlet* is not a problem to which a final solution exists. It is a work of art about which questions can always be asked. Each generation asks its own questions and finds its own answers, and the final test of the validity of those answers can only be time. Johnson, Coleridge, Bradley, all tell us things about *Hamlet* which are consistent with the play as we read it. A critic today cannot hope for more than that his questions and answers will seem relevant, and will continue to seem relevant, to others who read and ponder the play. The reward of the historical approach is not that it leads us to a final and infallible interpretation.

NOTES

1. Preface to *The History of the World*, 1614.
2. It has been suggested by F. T. Bowers (*Elizabethan Revenge Tragedy*, 1940) that we are intended to lose sympathy with Hieronymo when, ignoring the command "Vengeance is mine," he turns to plots himself and undertakes his murderous play. But the final speech of the Ghost makes it quite clear that to Kyd the characters remained to the end divided into sheep and goats. "Good Hieronymo slaine by himselfe" is to be conducted with the innocent Isabella and his accomplice Bel-Imperia to the Elysian fields, while the rest of the cast are to be haled off to Tartarean regions by Revenge.
3. "Vetat Pythagoras injussu imperatoris, id est dei, de praesidio et statione vitae decedere" (*De Senectute*, 20); cf. *Phaedo*, 62.

W. H. Clemen

THE IMAGERY OF *HAMLET*

THE surprisingly new possibilities of language which make this
play appear a turning-point in the development of Shakespeare's
style [1] seem to have their origin in the personality of Hamlet.
The new language comes from him, in him it attains to perfection. The language of the King and the Queen, of Laertes and
Polonius, although subtly adapted to their character, still treads
the well-worn paths; it is less novel, because the people by
whom it is spoken are not in need of a new form of expression—
on the contrary, they may be more aptly characterized by a
conventional mode of speech. But Hamlet's nature can only
find expression in a wholly new language. This also applies to
the imagery in the play. It is Hamlet who creates the most significant images, images marking the atmosphere and theme of
the play, which are paler and less pregnant in the speech of
the other characters. Hamlet's way of employing images is
unique in Shakespeare's drama. When he begins to speak, the
images fairly stream to him without the slightest effort—not as
similes or conscious paraphrases, but as immediate and spontaneous visions.[2] Hamlet's imagery shows us that whenever he
thinks and speaks, he is at the same time a visionary, a seer, for
whom the living things of the world about him embody and
symbolize thought. His first monologue may show this; the short
space of time which lies between his father's death and his
mother's remarriage is to him a series of pictures taken from
real life:

From *The Development of Shakespeare's Imagery*, 1951, pp. 106-
18. Copyright 1951 by Harvard University Press. Reprinted by permission of Harvard University Press and Methuen and Co., Ltd. The title
has been changed from *Hamlet* by the editor.

> A little month, or ere those shoes were old
> With which she follow'd my poor father's body
> Like Niobe, all tears:
>
> (I. ii. 147)

> Ere yet the salt of most unrighteous tears
> Had left the flushing in her galled eyes,
>
> (I. ii. 154)

or a little later, addressed to Horatio:

> the funeral baked meats
> Did coldly furnish forth the marriage tables.
>
> (I. ii. 180)

These are no poetic similes, but keen observations of reality. Hamlet does not translate the general thought into an image paraphrasing it; on the contrary, he uses the opposite method: he refers the generalization to the events and objects of the reality underlying the thought. This sense of reality finds expression in all the images Hamlet employs. Peculiar to them all is that closeness to reality which is often carried to the point of an unsparing poignancy.[3] They are mostly very concrete and precise, simple and, as to their subject matter, easy to understand; common and ordinary things, things familiar to the man in the street dominate, rather than lofty, strange or rare objects.[4] Illuminating in this connection is the absence of hyperbole,[5] of great dimensions in his imagery. In contrast to Othello or Lear, for example, who awaken heaven and the elements in their imagery [6] and who lend expression to their mighty passions in images of soaring magnificence, Hamlet prefers to keep his language within the scope of reality, indeed, within the everyday world. It is not spacious scenery and nature which dominate in Hamlet's imagery, but rather trades and callings, objects of daily use, popular games and technical terms; his images are not beautiful, poetic, magnificent, but they always hit their mark, the matter in question, with surprisingly unerring sureness. They do not waft the things of reality into a dreamworld of the imagination; on the contrary, they make them truly *real*, they reveal their inmost, naked being. All this, the wealth of realistic observation, of real objects, of associations taken

from everyday life, is enough to prove that Hamlet is no abstract
thinker and dreamer. As his imagery betrays to us, he is rather
a man gifted with greater powers of observation than the others.
He is capable of scanning reality with a keener eye and of pene-
trating the veil of semblance even to the very core of things.
"I know not seems."

At the same time, Hamlet's imagery reveals the hero's wide
educational background, his many-sidedness and the extraordinary range of his experience.[7] That metaphors taken from
natural sciences are specially frequent in Hamlet's language
again emphasizes his power of observation, his critical objective way of looking at things.[8] But Hamlet is also at home in
classical antiquity or Greek mythology,[9] in the terminology of
law,[10] he is not only familiar with the theatre and with acting
—as everyone knows—but also with the fine arts,[11] with falconry
and hunting,[12] with the soldier's trade and strategy,[13] with the
courtier's way of life. All these spheres disclosing Hamlet's personality as that of a "courtier, soldier and scholar" (in Ophelia's
words, iii. i. 159) are evoked by the imagery which, however,
turns them to living account by a fit application to situations,
persons and moods. Hamlet commands so many levels of expression that he can attune his diction as well as his imagery
to the situation and to the person to whom he is speaking. This
adaptability and versatility is another feature in Hamlet's use
of language which can also be traced in his imagery.

At the same time, this wide range of imagery can, in certain
passages, serve to give relief to his conflicting moods, to his
being torn between extremes and to the abruptness of his
changes of mood. This characteristic which has been particularly
emphasized and partly attributed to "melancholy" by L. L.
Schücking and John Dover Wilson,[14] also expresses itself in
the sudden change of language and in the juxtaposition of passages which are sharply contrasted in their diction. With no
other character in Shakespeare do we find this sharp contrast
between images marked by a pensive mood and those which
unsparingly use vulgar words and display a frivolous and sar-
castic disgust for the world.[15]

Let us consider further how Hamlet's use of imagery reflects
his ability to penetrate to the real nature of men and things

and his relentless breaking down of the barriers raised by hypocrisy. Many of his images seem in fact designed to unmask men; they are meant to strip them of their fine appearances and to show them up in their true nature. Thus, by means of the simile of fortune's pipe, Hamlet shows Rosencrantz and Guildenstern that he has seen through their intent, and thus he unmasks Rosencrantz when he calls him a "sponge," "that soaks up the king's countenance" (IV. ii. 16). He splits his mother's heart "in twain," because he tells her the truth from which she shrinks and which she conceals from herself. And again it is by means of images that he seeks to lead her to a recognition of the truth. He renews the memory of his father in her by means of that forceful description of his outward appearance which could be compared with Hyperion, Mars and Mercury. On the other hand, another series of comparisons seeks to bring home to his mother the real nature of Claudius:

> a mildew'd ear,
> Blasting his wholesome brother.
>
> (III. iv. 64)

> a vice of kings;
> A cutpurse of the empire and the rule,
> That from a shelf the precious diadem stole,
> And put it in his pocket!

> .   .   .   .   .

> A king of shreds and patches,
>
> (III. iv. 98)

So Hamlet sees through men and things. He perceives what is false, visualizing his recognition through imagery.

Hamlet's imagery, which thus calls things by their right names, acquires a peculiar freedom from his feigned madness. Hamlet needs images for his "antic disposition." He would betray himself if he used open direct language. Hence he must speak ambiguously and cloak his real meaning under quibbles and puns,[16] images and parables. The other characters do not understand him and continue to think he is mad, but the audience can gain an insight into the true situation. Under the protection of that mask of "antic disposition," Hamlet says more

shrewd things than all the rest of the courtiers together.[17] So
we find the images here in an entirely new role, unique in
Shakespeare's drama. Only the images of the fool in *King Lear*
have a similar function.

Hamlet suffers an injustice when he is accused of merely
theoretical and abstract speculation which would lead him away
from reality. His thoughts carry further than those of others,
because he sees more and deeper than they, not because he
would leave reality unheeded. It is true that his is a nature
more prone to thought than to action; but that signifies by no
means, as the Hamlet critics would often have us believe, that
he is a philosopher and dreamer and no man of the world.
When, in the graveyard scene, he holds Yorick's skull in his
hand, he sees *more* in it than the others, for whom the skull is
merely a lifeless object. And precisely because he is more
deeply moved by the reality and significance of these earthly
remains, his fantasy is able to follow the "noble dust of Alexander" through all its metamorphoses. The comparisons which
spring from this faculty of thinking a thing to the end, as it
were, derive in fact from a more intense experience of reality.

It is a fundamental tenet of Hamlet criticism that Hamlet's
over-developed intellect makes it impossible for him to act. In this
connection the following famous passage is generally quoted:

> And thus the native hue of resolution
> Is sicklied o'er with the pale cast of thought,
> And enterprises of great pith and moment
> With this regard their currents turn awry,
> And lose the name of action.—
>
> (III. i. 85)

The customary interpretation of this passage, "reflection hinders
action," does it an injustice. For Hamlet does not say "reflection
hinders action," he simply utters this image. The fact that he
does not utter that general maxim, but this image, makes all the
difference. For this image is the unique and specific form of
expression of the thought underlying it, it cannot be separated
from it. If we say "reflection hinders action," we make a false
generalization; we replace a specific formulation by an apothegm.
And thereby we eradicate in this passage that quality which is

peculiarly Shakespeare's or, what is more, peculiarly Hamlet's. Here the image does not serve the purpose of merely casting a decorative cloak about the thought; it is much rather an intrinsic part of the thought.

"Reflection hinders action"—this phrase carries in it something absolute, something damning. We sense a moralizing undertone. Action and reflection are thus conceived of as two mutually inimical abstract principles. But not so in Shakespeare's metaphorical language. "Native hue of resolution" suggests that Shakespeare viewed resolution as an innate human quality, not as a moral virtue to be consciously striven after. But the Hamlet-criticism of the nineteenth century saw the problem in this light of a moral virtue. We see, then, that a careful consideration of Shakespeare's imagery may sometimes correct false interpretations.[18]

"Reflection hinders action." Polonius, the sententious lover of maxims, could have said this, for a general saying carries no sense of personal obligation; it places a distance between the speaker and what he would say. But just as it is characteristic of Polonius to utter banalities and sententious effusions,[19] so, too, it is characteristic of Hamlet, to express even those things which would have permitted of a generalizing formulation, in a language which bears the stamp of a unique and personal experience.

Hamlet sees this problem under the aspect of a process of the human organism.[20] The original bright colouring of the skin is concealed by an ailment. Thus the relation between thought and action appears not as an opposition between two abstract principles between which a free choice is possible, but as an unavoidable condition of human nature. The image of the leprous ailment emphasizes the malignant, disabling, slowly disintegrating nature of the process. It is by no mere chance that Hamlet employs just this image. Perusing the description which the ghost of Hamlet's father gives of his poisoning by Claudius (I. v. 63) one cannot help being struck by the vividness with which the process of poisoning, the malicious spreading of the disease, is portrayed:

> And in the porches of mine ears did pour
> The leperous distilment; whose effect

> Holds such an enmity with blood of man
> That swift as quicksilver it courses through
> The natural gates and alleys of the body,
> And with a sudden vigour it doth posset
> And curd, like eager droppings into milk,
> The thin and wholesome blood: so did it mine;
> And a most instant tetter bark'd about,
> Most lazar-like, with vile and loathsome crust,
> All my smooth body.
>
> (I. v. 63)

A real event described at the beginning of the drama has exercised a profound influence upon the whole imagery of the play. What is later metaphor, is here still reality. The picture of the leprous skin disease, which is here—in the first act—described by Hamlet's father, has buried itself deep in Hamlet's imagination and continues to lead its subterranean existence, as it were, until it reappears in metaphorical form.

As Miss Spurgeon has shown, the idea of an ulcer dominates the imagery, infecting and fatally eating away the whole body; on every occasion repulsive images of sickness make their appearance.[21] It is certain that this imagery is derived from that one real event. Hamlet's father describes in that passage how the poison invades the body during sleep and how the healthy organism is destroyed from within, not having a chance to defend itself against attack. But this now becomes the *leitmotif* of the imagery: the individual occurrence is expanded into a symbol for the central problem of the play. The corruption of land and people throughout Denmark is understood as an imperceptible and irresistible process of poisoning. And, furthermore, this poisoning reappears as a *leitmotif* in the action as well—as a poisoning in the "dumb-show," and finally, as the poisoning of all the major characters in the last act. Thus imagery and action continually play into each other's hands and we see how the term "dramatic imagery" gains a new significance.

The imagery appears to be influenced by yet another event in the action underlying the play: Hamlet feels himself to be sullied by his mother's incest which, according to the conception of the time, she committed in marrying Claudius. For him this is a

poisoning idea which finds expression in his language. Professor
Dover Wilson has defended the reading of the Second Quarto
with convincing arguments: [22]

> O, that this too too sullied flesh would melt,
> Thaw and resolve itself into a dew!
>
> (I. ii. 129)

It is therefore probable that this idea is present in Hamlet's mind
at many moments when images of decay and rot appear in his
language.

The *leitmotif* occasionally appears in a disguised form at a
point where it seems to have no real connection with the main
issue of the play, for instance, in the following passage:

> So, oft it chances in particular men,
> That for some vicious mole of nature in them,
> As, in their birth—wherein they are not guilty
> Since nature cannot choose his origin—
> By the o'er growth of some complexion,
> Oft breaking down the pales and forts of reason,
> Or by some habit, that too much o'er-leavens
> The form of plausive manners, that these men,
> Carrying, I say, the stamp of one defect,
> Being nature's livery, or fortune's star,
> Their virtues else—be they as pure as grace,
> As infinite as man may undergo—
> Shall in the general censure take corruption
> From that particular fault: the dram of eale
> Doth all the noble substance of a doubt
> To his own scandal.
>
> (I. iv. 23)

Hamlet has spoken of the excessive revels and drinking-bouts
among his people and has said that this was disparaging to the
Danes in the eyes of the other peoples. Then follows this general
reflection. The question arises: why does Hamlet speak in such
detail of these matters here? For at this point in the play he has
as yet heard nothing of his uncle's murderous deed. And still he
touches in this speech upon that *leitmotif* of the whole play; he

describes how human nature may be brought to decay through a tiny birth-mark, just as from one "dram of evil" [23] a destructive effect may spread over the whole organism. "O'er-leavens" already points to "sicklied o'er," and, as in the passage discussed, the notion of the human body is in the background. As in later passages, the balance of the powers in man is the theme here, and "corruption," a basic motif in the whole play, already makes its appearance. This general reflection on gradual and irresistible infection is made in passing, as it were. Thus Shakespeare makes use of every opportunity to suggest the fundamental theme of the play. When the King says to Laertes in the fourth act:

> There lives within the very flame of love
> A kind of wick or snuff that will abate it;

the same motif occurs again: corruption through a "dram of evil."

The following passage, too, from Laertes' words of warning to his sister, has never been examined for its value as "dramatic presaging."

> The canker galls the infants of the spring,
> Too oft before their buttons be disclosed,
> And in the morn and liquid dew of youth
> Contagious blastments are most imminent.
>
> (i. iii. 39)

It is no mere chance that this sententious little image,[24] which is so neatly woven in and so conventional, touches upon a motif later to be worked out more clearly. The worm in the bud, like ulcer and eruption, is also an irresistible force destroying the organism from within. Light is cast upon this early passage when, in the last act, it is said of Claudius: "this canker of our nature" (v. ii. 69). But here we still know nothing of the coming developments. The image is a faint warning, preparing the way, together with other hints, for the future.

The Pyrrhus episode [25] which the first Player recites before Hamlet contains features which are also of importance for the theme of the play. For here it is related of Pyrrhus with vigorous emphasis how "Aroused vengeance sets him new a-work" (ii. ii. 510). For Hamlet it must be a gentle warning that vengeance calls forth so bloody a deed in another without delay. On the other hand, the previous lines described Pyrrhus as being in suspense, unable to act, "neutral to his will" as Hamlet still is:

> So, as a painted tyrant, Pyrrhus stood,
> And like a neutral to his will and matter,
> Did nothing.
>
> (II. ii. 502)

The mention of "strumpet Fortune" and the picture of her broken wheel rolled "down the hill of heaven" at the end of this passage, is likewise a hint; in the third act this image of the wheel plunging down from the height, reappears in the conversation between Rosencrantz and the King:

> The cease of majesty
> Dies not alone; but, like a gulf, doth draw
> What's near it with it: it is a massy wheel,
> Fix'd on the summit of the highest mount,
> To whose huge spokes ten thousand lesser things
> Are mortised and adjoin'd; which, when it falls,
> Each small annexment, petty consequence,
> Attends the boisterous ruin.
>
> (III. iii. 15)

Through these images, which are also spun out from a more general reflection, the coming catastrophe is already significantly foreshadowed.

The imagery in Shakespeare's tragedies often shows how a number of other images are grouped around the central symbol which expresses the same idea, but in quite other terms. Several degrees, as it were, of the metaphorical expression of a fundamental idea may be distinguished. Besides images which express a motif with the greatest clarity and emphasis, we find others which utter the thought in a veiled and indirect manner. An examination of the way in which the images are spread over the play, can reveal how subtly Shakespeare modifies and varies according to character and situation.

The most striking images of sickness, which Miss Spurgeon has already listed, make their first appearance, significantly enough, in the second half of the play, and most notably in the scene

in which Hamlet seeks to bring his mother to a change of heart.
Here the plainness and clarity of the images is meant to awaken
the conscience of the Queen; they can scarcely be forceful
enough; "let me wring your heart," Hamlet has said at the beginning of the meeting. In the first part of the play the atmosphere
of corruption and decay is spread in a more indirect and general way. Hamlet declares in the first and second acts how the
world appears to him:

> . . . Ah fie! 'tis an unweeded garden,
> That grows to seed; things rank and gross in nature
> Possess it merely.
>
> (I. ii. 135)

> . . . and indeed it goes so heavily with my disposition that this
> goodly frame, the earth, seems to me a sterile promontory, this
> most excellent canopy, the air, look you, this brave o'erhanging
> firmament, this majestical roof fretted with golden fire, why, it
> appears no other thing to me than a foul and pestilent congrega-
> tion of vapours.
>
> (II. ii. 309)

The image of weeds, touched upon in the word "unweeded," is
related to the imagery of sickness in Shakespeare's work. It
appears three times in *Hamlet*. The ghost says to Hamlet:

> And duller shouldst thou be than the fat weed
> That roots itself in ease on Lethe wharf,
>
> (I. v. 32)

In the dialogue with his mother, this image immediately follows
upon the image of the ulcer:

> And do not spread the compost on the weeds,
> To make them ranker,
>
> (III. iv. 151)

Images of rot, decay and corruption are especially numerous in
the long second scene of the second act. There are, for example,
Hamlet's remarks on the maggots which the sun breeds in a dead
dog (II. ii. 181), on the deep dungeons in the prison Denmark
(II. ii. 249), on the strumpet Fortune (II. ii. 240), who reappears

in the speech of the first Player (II. ii. 515), his comparison of himself with a whore, a drab and a scullion (II. ii. 614).

Seen individually, such images do not seem to be very important. But in their totality they contribute considerably to the tone of the play.

NOTES

1. On the style in *Hamlet* see L. L. Schücking, *The Meaning of Hamlet*, London, 1937, I. i. and I. iv.

2. The spontaneous and unpremeditated character of Hamlet's imagery will become obvious through a comparison with Claudius' language. Claudius' speeches are studied and give the impression of having been previously prepared. His images often are consciously inserted. Dr. Schmetz notes that while Claudius often uses comparisons, linking object and image by "as" or "like," Hamlet's imagination fuses both into a metaphor (cf. IV. i. 40-44, IV. v. 94-6 with III. 83-4, III. 407-8). Further examples for Claudius' comparisons: III. iii. 41; IV. vii. 15; IV. xx. 88. This is, of course, only one aspect of the manifold differences between Claudius' and Hamlet's language. The whole problem has been exhaustively dealt with in Dr. Schmetz's study. For the difference between the imagery of Claudius' public and that of his private language, and for further distinguishing features in Claudius' imagery see Una Ellis-Fermor, *The Frontiers of Drama*, London, 1945, p. 88.

3. This, as Dr. Schmetz notes, gives to Hamlet's language sometimes a brutal violence that expresses itself in the use of forceful metaphors: "For I mine eyes will rivet to his face" (III. ii. 90), "Let me wring your heart" (III. iv. 35).

4. After completion of the manuscript, the author became acquainted with Professor Mikhail M. Morozow's article, "The Individualization of Shakespeare's Characters Through Imagery" (*Shakespeare Survey*, Vol. II, Cambridge, 1949, pp. 83-106). Professor Morozow's more systematic and comprehensive examination of the content of all of Hamlet's images can throw new light on the statesments made above and adds a number of acute observations, which have a bearing on the theory put forward in this chapter. Morozow also emphasizes the realistic, common and

popular nature of Hamlet's imagery, his faculty to "see right through people" and his closeness to the common people which does not exclude his scholarship and humanist education.

5. If he makes use of hyperbole in v. i. 304 (at Ophelia's grave) it is to parody Laertes' hyperbolic diction.

6. Hamlet, too, invokes God and the heavenly powers, but these invocations never take the form of grandiose images, they are mostly brief and often restricted to mere references (cf. I. ii. 132, 150, 195; I. v. 92; I. iv. 85; v. ii. 343, 355).

7. For the following cf. Dr. Schmetz's study and Professor Morozow's article.

8. Cf. III. i. 119; I. v. 22, 27, 29; III. iv. 147. For the disease-imagery see below.

9. E.g. I. ii. 140, 149, 153; III. ii. 89, 294; III. iii. 56-8; v. i. 306, 315.

10. v. i. 107 sqq.

11. E.g. his images taken from musical instruments, III. ii. 75.

12. II. ii. 397; III. ii. 361; II. ii. 458.

13. Hamlet speaks of the "pales and forts of reason" (I. iv. 28), wonders whether his mother's heart is "proof and bulwark against sense" (III. iv. 37; cf. III. iv. 208).

14. Cf. L. L. Schücking, The Meaning of Hamlet, London, 1937. Hamlet edition (English-German), Leipzig, 1941. J. D. Wilson, What Happens in Hamlet, Cambridge, 1935.

15. There are many instances for these contrasts in Hamlet's language. Cf. the transition from the famous monologue in III. i. 56 to his conversation with Ophelia in the same scene (a parallel change in III. ii) or cf. IV. iii. 22; v. i. 230 sqq. Dr. Schmetz notes the following instances of Hamlet's use of vulgar words: "true-penny" (I. v. 150); "old mole" (I. v. 161); "drab" (II. ii. 623); "carrion" (II. ii. 184); "Jowls it to the ground" (v. i. 82); "Knocked about the mazard" (v. i. 95). For further instances of Hamlet's use of coarse and common images see Morozow's article, loc. cit., p. 95.

16. Through John Dover Wilson's edition of Hamlet (Cambridge, 1934) many of these puns and quibbles which so far had remained unintelligible (or were falsely understood) have been cleared up. On the importance of quibbles in Hamlet see John Dover Wilson's Introduction, p. xxxiii, sqq.

17. Edward Dowden noted this: "Madness possesses exquisite immunities and privileges. From the safe vantage of unintelligibility he can delight himself by uttering his whole mind and sending forth his words among the words of others, with their meaning disguised, as he himself must be, clothed in an antic garb of parable, dark sayings which speak the truth in a mystery" (*Shakespeare, His Mind and Art,* 1877, p. 145). Cf., too, John Dover Wilson's Introduction to *Hamlet,* p. xl.

18. Cf. Spurgeon, *Shakespeare's Imagery,* pp. 318-19.

19. Cf. Edward Dowden: "his wisdom is not the outflow of a rich or deep nature, but the little, accumulated hoard of a long and superficial experience. This is what the sententious manner signifies" (*Shakespeare, His Mind and Art,* p. 142). Professor John W. Draper, reviewing the divergent interpretations of Polonius' character, gives him a far more favourable treatment and considers him "not far removed from the Elizabethan ideal of what a courtier, what a father, what a 'Worthie Priuie Counceller' should be" (*The Hamlet of Shakespeare's Audience,* Durham, 1938, p. 53).

20. For the contemporary scientific background of the disease-imagery in *Hamlet* see John W. Draper, *The Humors and Shakespeare's Characters,* Durham, N. C., 1945.

21. Spurgeon, *Shakespeare's Imagery,* p. 316 sqq.

22. Cf. the note on this passage on p. 151 of John Dover Wilson's edition of *Hamlet* (Cambridge, 1934): " 'Sullied flesh' is the key to the soliloquy and tells us that Hamlet is thinking of the 'kindless' incestuous marriage as a personal defilement. Further, 'sullied' fits the immediate context as 'solid' does not. There is something absurd in associating 'solid flesh' with 'melt' and 'thaw'; whereas Shakespeare always uses 'sully' or 'sullied' elsewhere (cf. *Henry IV,* II. iv. 84; *Winter's Tale,* I. ii. 326) with the image, implicit or explicit, of dirt upon a surface of pure white; and the surface Hamlet obviously has in mind here is snow, symbolical of the nature he shares with his mother, once pure but now befouled."

23. The emendation *evil* has been accepted by several editors, e.g. by John Dover Wilson in the *New Shakespeare* edition.

24. Dr. Schmetz points out that this use of sententious diction betrays a certain immaturity in Laertes, just as his apostrophes

at the sight of the mad Ophelia in IV. v. 155 reveal a hollow
pathos, or as his hyperboles at Ophelia's grave impress us as
theatrical bombast (v. i. 274).

25. A new and important interpretation of the "Player's Speech"
is given by Harry Levin, "An Explication of the Player's Speech,"
The Kenyon Review, XII, 2, 1950.

Maynard Mack

THE WORLD OF *HAMLET*

MY SUBJECT is the world of *Hamlet*. I do not of course mean Denmark, except as Denmark is given a body by the play; and I do not mean Elizabethan England, though this is necessarily close behind the scenes. I mean simply the imaginative environment that the play asks us to enter when we read it or go to see it.

Great plays, as we know, do present us with something that can be called a world, a microcosm—a world like our own in being made of people, actions, situations, thoughts, feelings and much more, but unlike our own in being perfectly, or almost perfectly, significant and coherent. In a play's world, each part implies the other parts, and each lives, each means, with the life and meaning of the rest.

This is the reason, as we also know, that the worlds of great plays greatly differ. Othello in Hamlet's position, we sometimes say, would have no problem; but what we are really saying is that Othello in Hamlet's position would not exist. The conception we have of Othello is a function of the characters who help define him, Desdemona, honest Iago, Cassio, and the rest; of his history of travel and war; of a great storm that divides his ship from Cassio's, and a handkerchief; of a quiet night in Venice broken by cries about an old black ram; of a quiet night in Cyprus broken by sword-play; of a quiet bedroom where a woman goes to bed in her wedding sheets and a man comes in with a light to put out the light; and above all, of a language, a language with many voices in it, gentle, rasping, querulous, or foul, but all counterpointing the one great voice:

From *The Yale Review*, XLI (1952), 502-23. Copyright 1952 by the Yale University Press. Reprinted by permission of the author and the publisher.

Put up your bright swords, for the dew will rust them.

> O thou weed
> Who art so lovely fair and smell'st so sweet
> That the sense aches at thee. . . .

> Yet I'll not shed her blood
> Nor scar that whiter skin of hers than snow,
> And smooth as monumental alabaster.

> I pray you in your letters,
> When you shall these unlucky deeds relate,
> Speak of me as I am; nothing extenuate,
> Nor set down aught in malice; then must you speak
> Of one that loved not wisely but too well;
> Of one not easily jealous, but being wrought,
> Perplex'd in th' extreme; of one whose hand,
> Like the base Indian, threw a pearl away
> Richer than all his tribe. . . .

Without his particular world of voices, persons, events, the world that both expresses and contains him, Othello is unimaginable. And so, I think, are Antony, King Lear, Macbeth—and Hamlet. We come back then to Hamlet's world, of all the tragic worlds that Shakespeare made, easily the most various and brilliant, the most elusive. It is with no thought of doing justice to it that I have singled out three of its attributes for comment. I know too well, if I may echo a sentiment of Mr. E. M. W. Tillyard's, that no one is likely to accept another man's reading of *Hamlet*, that anyone who tries to throw light on one part of the play usually throws the rest into deeper shadow, and that what I have to say leaves out many problems—to mention only one, the knotty problem of the text. All I would say in defense of the materials I have chosen is that they seem to me interesting, close to the root of the matter even if we continue to differ about what the root of the matter is, and explanatory, in a modest way, of this play's peculiar hold on everyone's imagination, its almost mythic status, one might say, as a paradigm of the life of man.

The first attribute that impresses us, I think, is mysteriousness.

We often hear it said, perhaps with truth, that every great work of art has a mystery at the heart; but the mystery of *Hamlet* is something else. We feel its presence in the numberless explanations that have been brought forward for Hamlet's delay, his madness, his ghost, his treatment of Polonius, or Ophelia, or his mother; and in the controversies that still go on about whether the play is "undoubtedly a failure" (Eliot's phrase) or one of the greatest artistic triumphs; whether, if it is a triumph, it belongs to the highest order of tragedy; whether, if it is such a tragedy, its hero is to be taken as a man of exquisite moral sensibility (Bradley's view) or an egomaniac (Madariaga's view).

Doubtless there have been more of these controversies and explanations than the play requires; for in Hamlet, to paraphrase a remark of Falstaff's, we have a character who is not only mad in himself but a cause that madness is in the rest of us. Still, the very existence of so many theories and counter-theories, many of them formulated by sober heads, gives food for thought. *Hamlet* seems to lie closer to the illogical logic of life than Shakespeare's other tragedies. And while the causes of this situation may be sought by saying that Shakespeare revised the play so often that eventually the motivations were smudged over, or that the original old play has been here or there imperfectly digested, or that the problems of Hamlet lay so close to Shakespeare's heart that he could not quite distance them in the formal terms of art, we have still as critics to deal with effects, not causes. If I may quote again from Mr. Tillyard, the play's very lack of a rigorous type of causal logic seems to be a part of its point.

Moreover, the matter goes deeper than this. Hamlet's world is preëminently in the interrogative mood. It reverberates with questions, anguished, meditative, alarmed. There are questions that in this play, to an extent I think unparalleled in any other, mark the phases and even the nuances of the action, helping to establish its peculiar baffled tone. There are other questions whose interrogations, innocent at first glance, are subsequently seen to have reached beyond their contexts and to point towards some pervasive inscrutability in Hamlet's world as a whole. Such is that tense series of challenges with which the tragedy begins: Bernardo's of Francisco, "Who's there?" Francisco's of Horatio and Marcellus, "Who is there?" Horatio's of the ghost, "What art thou . . . ?" And then there are the famous questions. In them the interrogations seem to point not only beyond the context but beyond the play, out of Hamlet's predicaments into everyone's: "What a piece of work is a man! . . . And yet to me what is this quintessence of dust?" "To be, or not to be, that is the question." "Get thee to a nunnery. Why wouldst thou be a breeder of sinners?" "I am very proud, revengeful, ambitious, with more offences at my beck than I have thoughts to put them in, imagination to give them shape, or time to act them in. What should such fellows as I do crawling between earth and heaven?" "Dost thou think Alexander look'd o' this fashion i' th' earth? . . . And smelt so?"

Further, Hamlet's world is a world of riddles. The hero's own language is often riddling, as the critics have pointed out. When he puns, his puns have receding depths in them, like the one which constitutes his first speech: "A little more than kin, and less than kind." His utterances in madness, even if wild and whirling, are simultaneously, as Polonius discovers, pregnant: "Do you know me, my lord?" "Excellent well. You are a fishmonger." Even the madness itself is riddling: How much is real? How much is feigned? What does it mean? Sane or mad, Hamlet's mind plays restlessly about his world, turning up one riddle upon another. The riddle of character, for example, and how it is that in a man whose virtues else are "pure as grace," some vicious mole of nature, some "dram of eale," can "all the noble substance oft adulter." Or the riddle of the player's art, and how a man can so project himself into a fiction, a dream of passion, that he can weep for Hecuba. Or the riddle of action: how we may think too little—"What to ourselves in passion we propose," says the player-king, "The passion ending, doth the purpose lose"; and again, how we may think too much: "Thus conscience does make cowards of us all, And thus the native hue of resolution Is sicklied o'er with the pale cast of thought."

There are also more immediate riddles. His mother—how could she "on this fair mountain leave to feed, And batten on this moor?" The ghost—which may be a devil, for "the de'il hath power T' assume a pleasing shape." Ophelia—what does her behavior to him mean? Surprising her in her closet, he falls to such perusal of her face as he would draw it. Even the king at his prayers is a riddle. Will a revenge that takes him in the purging of his soul be vengeance, or hire and salary? As for himself, Hamlet realizes, he is the greatest riddle of all—a mystery, he warns Rosencrantz and Guildenstern, from which he will not have the heart plucked out. He cannot tell why he has of late lost all his mirth, forgone all custom of exercises. Still less can he tell why he delays: "I do not know Why yet I live to say, 'This thing's to do,' Sith I have cause and will and strength and means To do't."

Thus the mysteriousness of Hamlet's world is of a piece. It is not simply a matter of missing motivations, to be expunged if only we could find the perfect clue. It is built in. It is evidently an important part of what the play wishes to say to us. And it is certainly an element that the play thrusts upon us from the opening word. Everyone, I think, recalls the mysteriousness of that first scene. The cold middle of the night on the castle platform, the muffled sentries, the uneasy atmosphere of apprehension, the challenges leaping out of the dark, the questions that follow the challenges, feeling out the darkness, searching for identities, for relations, for assurance. "Bernardo?" "Have you had quiet guard?" "Who hath reliev'd you?" "What, is Horatio there?" "What, has this thing appear'd again tonight?" "Looks 'a not like the king?" "How now, Horatio! . . . Is not this something more than fantasy? What think you on 't?" "Is it not like the king?" "Why this same strict and most observant watch . . . ?" "Shall I strike at it with my partisan?" "Do you consent we shall acquaint [young Hamlet] with it?"

We need not be surprised that critics and playgoers alike have been tempted to see in this an evocation not simply of Hamlet's world but of their own. Man in his aspect of bafflement, moving in darkness on a rampart between two worlds, unable to reject, or quite accept, the one that, when he faces it, "to-shakes" his disposition with thoughts beyond the reaches of his soul—comforting himself with hints and guesses. We hear these hints and guesses whispering through the darkness as the several watchers speak. "At least, the whisper goes so," says one. "I think it be no other but e'en so," says another. "I have heard" that on the crowing of the cock "Th' extravagant and erring spirit hies To his confine," says a third. "Some say" at Christmas time "this

bird of dawning" sings all night, "And then, they say, no spirit
dare stir abroad." "So have I heard," says the first, "and do in
part believe it." However we choose to take the scene, it is clear
that it creates a world where uncertainties are of the essence.

Meantime, such is Shakespeare's economy, a second attribute
of Hamlet's world has been put before us. This is the problematic
nature of reality and the relation of reality to appearance. The
play begins with an appearance, an "apparition," to use Marcellus's term—the ghost. And the ghost is somehow real, indeed the
vehicle of realities. Through its revelation, the glittering surface
of Claudius's court is pierced, and Hamlet comes to know, and
we do, that the king is not only hateful to him but the murderer
of his father, that his mother is guilty of adultery as well as incest.
Yet there is a dilemma in the revelation. For possibly the apparition *is* an apparition, a devil who has assumed his father's shape.

This dilemma, once established, recurs on every hand. From
the court's point of view, there is Hamlet's madness. Polonius
investigates and gets some strange advice about his daughter:
"Conception is a blessing, but as your daughter may conceive,
friend, look to 't." Rosencrantz and Guildenstern investigate and
get the strange confidence that "Man delights not me; no, nor
woman neither." Ophelia is "loosed" to Hamlet (Polonius's vulgar
word), while Polonius and the king hide behind the arras; and
what they hear is a strange indictment of human nature, and a
riddling threat: "Those that are married already, all but one, shall
live."

On the other hand, from Hamlet's point of view, there is
Ophelia. Kneeling here at her prayers, she seems the image of
innocence and devotion. Yet she is of the sex for whom he has
already found the name Frailty, and she is also, as he seems either
madly or sanely to divine, a decoy in a trick. The famous cry—
"Get thee to a nunnery"—shows the anguish of his uncertainty. If
Ophelia is what she seems, this dirty-minded world of murder,
incest, lust, adultery, is no place for her. Were she "as chaste as
ice, as pure as snow," she could not escape its calumny. And if
she is not what she seems, then a nunnery in its other sense of
brothel is relevant to her. In the scene that follows he treats her
as if she were indeed an inmate of a brothel.

Likewise, from Hamlet's point of view, there is the enigma of the king. If the ghost is *only* an appearance, then possibly the king's appearance is reality. He must try it further. By means of a second and different kind of "apparition," the play within the play, he does so. But then, immediately after, he stumbles on the king at prayer. This appearance has a relish of salvation in it. If the king dies now, his soul may yet be saved. Yet actually, as we know, the king's efforts to come to terms with heaven have been unavailing; his words fly up, his thoughts remain below. If Hamlet means the conventional revenger's reasons that he gives for sparing Claudius, it was the perfect moment not to spare him—when the sinner was acknowledging his guilt, yet unrepentant. The perfect moment, but it was hidden, like so much else in the play, behind an arras.

There are two arrases in his mother's room. Hamlet thrusts his sword through one of them. Now at last he has got to the heart of the evil, or so he thinks. But now it is the wrong man; now he himself is a murderer. The other arras he stabs through with his words—like daggers, says the queen. He makes her shrink under the contrast he points between her present husband and his father. But as the play now stands (matters are somewhat clearer in the bad Quarto), it is hard to be sure how far the queen grasps the fact that her second husband is the murderer of her first. And it is hard to say what may be signified by her inability to see the ghost, who now for the last time appears. In one sense at least, the ghost is the supreme reality, representative of the hidden ultimate power, in Bradley's terms—witnessing from beyond the grave against this hollow world. Yet the man who is capable of seeing through to this reality, the queen thinks is mad. "To whom do you speak this?" she cries to her son. "Do you see nothing there?" he asks, incredulous. And she replies: "Nothing at all; yet all that is I see." Here certainly we have the imperturbable self-confidence of the worldly world, its layers on layers of habituation, so that when the reality is before its very eyes it cannot detect its presence.

Like mystery, this problem of reality is central to the play and written deep into its idiom. Shakespeare's favorite terms in *Hamlet* are words of ordinary usage that pose the question of appearances in a fundamental form. "Apparition" I have already mentioned. Another term is "seems." When we say, as Ophelia says of Hamlet leaving her closet, "He seem'd to find his way without his eyes," we mean one thing. When we say, as Hamlet says to his mother in the first court-scene, "Seems, Madam! . . . I' know not 'seems,'" we mean another. And when we say, as Hamlet says to Horatio before the play within the play, "And after, we will both our judgments join In censure of his seeming," we mean both at once. The ambiguities of "seem" coil and uncoil throughout this play, and over against them is set the idea of "seeing." So Hamlet challenges the king in his triumphant letter announcing his return to Denmark: "Tomorrow shall I beg leave to see your kingly eyes." Yet "seeing" itself can be ambiguous, as we recognize from Hamlet's uncertainty about the ghost; or from that statement of his mother's already quoted: "Nothing at all; yet all that is I see."

Another term of like importance is "assume." What we assume may be what we are not: "The de'il hath power T' assume a pleasing shape." But it may be what we are: "If it assume my noble father's person, I'll speak to it." And it may be what we are not yet, but would become; thus Hamlet advises his mother, "Assume a virtue, if you have it not." The perplexity in the word points to a real perplexity in Hamlet's and our own experience. We assume our habits—and habits are like costumes, as the word implies: "My father in his habit as he liv'd!" Yet these habits become ourselves in time: "That monster, custom, who all sense doth eat Of habits evil, is angel yet in this, That to the use of actions fair and good He likewise gives a frock or livery That aptly is put on."

Two other terms I wish to instance are "put on" and "shape." The shape of something is the form under which we are accustomed to apprehend it: "Do you see yonder cloud that's almost in shape of a camel?" But a shape may also be a disguise—even, in Shakespeare's time, an actor's costume or an actor's role. This is the meaning when the king says to Laertes as they lay the plot against Hamlet's life: "Weigh what convenience both of time and means May fit us to our shape." "Put on" supplies an analogous ambiguity. Shakespeare's mind seems to worry this phrase in the play much as Hamlet's mind worries the problem of acting in a world of surfaces, or the king's mind worries the meaning of Hamlet's transformation. Hamlet has put an antic disposition on, that the king knows. But what does "put on" mean? A mask, or a frock or livery—our "habit"? The king is left guessing, and so are we.

What is found in the play's key terms is also found in its imagery. Miss Spurgeon has called attention to a pattern of disease images in *Hamlet,* to which I shall return. But the play has other patterns equally striking. One of these, as my earlier quotations hint, is based on clothes. In the world of surfaces to which Shakespeare exposes us in Hamlet, clothes are naturally a factor of importance. "The apparel oft proclaims the man," Polonius assures Laertes, cataloguing maxims in the young man's ear as he is about to leave for Paris. Oft, but not always. And so he sends his man Reynaldo to look into Laertes' life there—even, if need be, to put a false dress of accusation upon his son ("What forgeries you please"), the better by indirections to find directions out. On the same grounds, he takes Hamlet's vows to Ophelia as false apparel. They are bawds, he tells her—or if we do not like Theobald's emendation, they are bonds—in masquerade, "Not of that dye which their investments show, But mere implorators of unholy suits."

This breach between the outer and the inner stirs no special emotion in Polonius, because he is always either behind an arras or prying into one, but it shakes Hamlet to the core. Here so recently was his mother in her widow's weeds, the tears still flushing in her galled eyes; yet now within a month, a little month, before even her funeral shoes are old, she has married with his uncle. Her mourning was all clothes. Not so his own, he bitterly replies, when she asks him to cast his "nighted color off." "Tis not alone my inky cloak, good mother"—and not alone, he adds, the sighs, the tears, the dejected havior of the visage —"that can denote me truly."

> These indeed seem,
> For they are actions that a man might play;
> But I have that within which passes show;
> These but the trappings and the suits of woe.

What we must not overlook here is Hamlet's visible attire, giving the verbal imagery a theatrical extension. Hamlet's apparel now is his inky cloak, mark of his grief for his father, mark also of his character as a man of melancholy, mark possibly too of his being one in whom appearance and reality are attuned. Later, in his madness, with his mind disordered, he will wear his costume in a corresponding disarray, the disarray that Ophelia describes so vividly to Polonius and that producers of the play rarely give sufficient heed to: "Lord Hamlet with his doublet all unbrac'd, No hat upon his head; his stockings foul'd, Ungarter'd, and down-gyved to his ankle." Here the only question will be, as with the madness itself, how much is studied, how much is real. Still later, by a third costume, the simple traveler's garb in which we find him new come from shipboard, Shakespeare will show us that we have a third aspect of the man.

A second pattern of imagery springs from terms of painting: the paints, the colorings, the varnishes that may either conceal, or, as in the painter's art, reveal. Art in Claudius conceals. "The harlot's cheek," he tells us in his one aside, "beautied with plastering art, Is not more ugly to the thing that helps it Than is my deed to my most painted word." Art in Ophelia, loosed to Hamlet in the episode already noticed to which this speech of the king's is prelude, is more complex. She looks so beautiful—"the celestial, and my soul's idol, the most beautified Ophelia," Hamlet has called her in his love letter. But now, what does beautified mean? Perfected with all the innocent beauties of a lovely woman? Or "beautied" like the harlot's cheek? "I have heard of your paintings too, well enough. God hath given you one face, and you make yourselves another."

Yet art, differently used, may serve the truth. By using an "image" (his own word) of a murder done in Vienna, Hamlet cuts through to the king's guilt; holds "as 'twere, the mirror up to nature," shows "virtue her own feature, scorn her own image, and the very age and body of the time"—which is out of joint—"his form and pressure." Something similar he does again in his mother's bedroom, painting for her in words "the rank sweat of an enseamed bed," making her recoil in horror from his "counterfeit presentment of two brothers," and holding, if we may trust a stage tradition, his father's picture beside his uncle's. Here again the verbal imagery is realized visually on the stage.

The most pervasive of Shakespeare's image patterns in this

play, however, is the pattern evolved around the three words, show, act, play. "Show" seems to be Shakespeare's unifying image in *Hamlet*. Through it he pulls together and exhibits in a single focus much of the diverse material in his play. The ideas of seeming, assuming, and putting on; the images of clothing, painting, mirroring; the episode of the dumb show and the play within the play; the characters of Polonius, Laertes, Ophelia, Claudius, Gertrude, Rosencrantz and Guildenstern, Hamlet himself—all these at one time or another, and usually more than once, are drawn into the range of implications flung round the play by "show."

"Act," on the other hand, I take to be the play's radical metaphor. It distills the various perplexities about the character of reality into a residual perplexity about the character of an act. What, this play asks again and again, is an act? What is its relation to the inner act, the intent? "If I drown myself wittingly," says the clown in the graveyard, "it argues an act, and an act hath three branches; it is to act, to do, to perform." Or again, the play asks, how does action relate to passion, that "laps'd in time and passion" I can let "go by Th' important acting of your dread command"; and to thought, which can so sickly o'er the native hue of resolution that "enterprises of great pitch and moment With this regard their currents turn awry, And lose the name of action"; and to words, which are not acts, and so we dare not be content to unpack our hearts with them, and yet are acts of a sort, for we may speak daggers though we use none. Or still again, how does an act (a deed) relate to an act (a pretense)? For an action may be nothing but pretense. So Polonius readying Ophelia for the interview with Hamlet, with "pious action," as he phrases it, "sugar [s] o'er The devil himself." Or it may not be a pretense, yet not what it appears. So Hamlet spares the king, finding him in an act that has some "relish of salvation in 't." Or it may be a pretense that is also the first foothold of a new reality, as when we assume a virtue though we have it not. Or it may be a pretense that is actually a mirroring of reality, like the play within the play, or the tragedy of *Hamlet*.

To this network of implications, the third term, play, adds an additional dimension. "Play" is a more precise word, in Elizabethan parlance at least, for all the elements in *Hamlet* that

pertain to the art of the theatre; and it extends their field of
reference till we see that every major personage in the tragedy
is a player in some sense, and every major episode a play. The
court plays, Hamlet plays, the players play, Rosencrantz and
Guildenstern try to play on Hamlet, though they cannot play on
his recorders—here we have an extension to a musical sense. And
the final duel, by a further extension, becomes itself a play, in
which everyone but Claudius and Laertes plays his role in
ignorance: "The queen desires you to show some gentle entertainment to Laertes before you fall to play." "I . . . will this
brother's wager frankly play." "Give him the cup."—"I'll play
this bout first."

The full extension of this theme is best evidenced in the play
within the play itself. Here, in the bodily presence of these travel-
ing players, bringing with them the latest playhouse gossip out
of London, we have suddenly a situation that tends to dissolve
the normal barriers between the fictive and the real. For here on
the stage before us is a play of false appearances in which an
actor called the player-king is playing. But there is also on the
stage, Claudius, another player-king, who is a spectator of this
player. And there is on the stage, besides, a prince who is a
spectator of both these player-kings and who plays with great
intensity a player's role himself. And around these kings and that
prince is a group of courtly spectators—Gertrude, Rosencrantz,
Guildenstern, Polonius, and the rest—and they, as we have come
to know, are players too. And lastly there are ourselves, an audience watching all these audiences who are also players. Where,
it may suddenly occur to us to ask, does the playing end? Which
are the guilty creatures sitting at a play? When is an act not
an "act"?

The mysteriousness of Hamlet's world, while it pervades the
tragedy, finds its point of greatest dramatic concentration in the
first act, and its symbol in the first scene. The problems of
appearance and reality also pervade the play as a whole, but
come to a climax in Acts II and III, and possibly their best
symbol is the play within the play. Our third attribute, though
again it is one that crops out everywhere, reaches its full development in Acts IV and V. It is not easy to find an appropriate
name for this attribute, but perhaps "mortality" will serve, if we

remember to mean by mortality the heartache and the thousand natural shocks that flesh is heir to, not simply death.

The powerful sense of mortality in *Hamlet* is conveyed to us, I think, in three ways. First, there is the play's emphasis on human weakness, the instability of human purpose, the subjection of humanity to fortune—all that we might call the aspect of failure in man. Hamlet opens this theme in Act I, when he describes how from that single blemish, perhaps not even the victim's fault, a man's whole character may take corruption. Claudius dwells on it again, to an extent that goes far beyond the needs of the occasion, while engaged in seducing Laertes to step behind the arras of a seemer's world and dispose of Hamlet by a trick. Time qualifies everything, Claudius says, including love, including purpose. As for love—it has a "plurisy" in it and dies of its own too much. As for purpose—"That we would do, We should do when we would, for this 'would' changes, And hath abatements and delays as many As there are tongues, are hands, are accidents; And then this 'should' is like a spendthrift's sigh, That hurts by easing." The player-king, in his long speeches to his queen in the play within the play, sets the matter in a still darker light. She means these protestations of undying love, he knows, but our purposes depend on our memory, and our memory fades fast. Or else, he suggests, we propose something to ourselves in a condition of strong feeling, but then the feeling goes, and with it the resolve. Or else our fortunes change, he adds, and with these our loves: "The great man down, you mark his favorite flies." The subjection of human aims to fortune is a reiterated theme in *Hamlet*, as subsequently in *Lear*. Fortune is the harlot goddess in whose secret parts men like Rosencrantz and Guildenstern live and thrive; the strumpet who threw down Troy and Hecuba and Priam; the outrageous foe whose slings and arrows a man of principle must suffer or seek release in suicide. Horatio suffers them with composure: he is one of the blessed few "Whose blood and judgment are so well co-mingled That they are not a pipe for fortune's finger To sound what stop she please." For Hamlet the task is of a greater difficulty.

Next, and intimately related to this matter of infirmity, is the emphasis on infection—the ulcer, the hidden abscess, "th' imposthume of much wealth and peace That inward breaks and

shows no cause without Why the man dies." Miss Spurgeon, who
was the first to call attention to this aspect of the play, has well
remarked that so far as Shakespeare's pictorial imagination is
concerned, the problem in *Hamlet* is not a problem of the will
and reason, "of a mind too philosophical or a nature temperamentally unfitted to act quickly," nor even a problem of an
individual at all. Rather, it is a condition—"a condition for which
the individual himself is apparently not responsible, any more
than the sick man is to blame for the infection which strikes and
devours him, but which, nevertheless, in its course and development, impartially and relentlessly, annihilates him and others,
innocent and guilty alike." "That," she adds, "is the tragedy of
Hamlet, as it is perhaps the chief tragic mystery of life." This is
a perceptive comment, for it reminds us that Hamlet's situation
is mainly not of his own manufacture, as are the situations of
Shakespeare's other tragic heroes. He has inherited it; he is "born
to set it right."

We must not, however, neglect to add to this what another
student of Shakespeare's imagery has noticed—that the infection
in Denmark is presented alternatively as poison. Here, of course,
responsibility is implied, for the poisoner of the play is Claudius.
The juice he pours into the ear of the elder Hamlet is a combined poison and disease, a "leperous distilment" that curds "the
thin and wholesome blood." From this fatal center, unwholesomeness spreads out till there is something rotten in all Denmark.
Hamlet tells us that his "wit's diseased," the queen speaks of her
"sick soul," the king is troubled by "the hectic" in his blood,
Laertes meditates revenge to warm "the sickness in my heart," the
people of the kingdom grow "muddied, Thick and unwholesome
in their thoughts"; and even Ophelia's madness is said to be "the
poison of deep grief." In the end, all save Ophelia die of that
poison in a literal as well as figurative sense.

But the chief form in which the theme of mortality reaches
us, it seems to me, is as a profound consciousness of loss. Hamlet's father expresses something of the kind when he tells Hamlet
how his "[most] seeming-virtuous queen," betraying a love which
"was of that dignity That it went hand in hand even with the
vow I made to her in marriage," had chosen to "decline Upon a
wretch whose natural gifts were poor To those of mine." "O Ham-

let, what a falling off was there!" Ophelia expresses it again, on hearing Hamlet's denunciation of love and woman in the nunnery scene, which she takes to be the product of a disordered brain:

> O what a noble mind is here o'erthrown!
> The courtier's, soldier's, scholar's, eye, tongue, sword;
> Th' expectancy and rose of the fair state,
> The glass of fashion and the mould of form,
> Th' observ'd of all observers, quite, quite down!

The passage invites us to remember that we have never actually seen such a Hamlet—that his mother's marriage has brought a falling off in him before we meet him. And then there is that further falling off, if I may call it so, when Ophelia too goes mad—"Divided from herself and her fair judgment, Without the which we are pictures, or mere beasts."

Time was, the play keeps reminding us, when Denmark was a different place. That was before Hamlet's mother took off "the rose From the fair forehead of an innocent love" and set a blister there. Hamlet then was still "Th' expectancy and rose of the fair state"; Ophelia, the "rose of May." For Denmark was a garden then, when his father ruled. There had been something heroic about his father—a king who met the threats to Denmark in open battle, fought with Norway, smote the sledded Polacks on the ice, slew the elder Fortinbras in an honorable trial of strength. There had been something godlike about his father too: "Hyperion's curls, the front of Jove himself, An eye like Mars . . . , A station like the herald Mercury." But, the ghost reveals, a serpent was in the garden, and "the serpent that did sting thy father's life Now wears his crown." The martial virtues are put by now. The threats to Denmark are attended to by policy, by agents working deviously for and through an uncle. The moral virtues are put by too. Hyperion's throne is occupied by "a vice of kings," "a king of shreds and patches"; Hyperion's bed, by a satyr, a paddock, a bat, a gib, a bloat king with reechy kisses. The garden is unweeded now, and "grows to seed; things rank and gross in nature Possess it merely." Even in himself he feels the taint, the taint of being his mother's son; and that other taint, from an earlier garden, of which he admonishes

Ophelia: "Our virtue cannot so inoculate our old stock but we shall relish of it." "Why wouldst thou be a breeder of sinners?" "What should such fellows as I do crawling between earth and heaven?"

"Hamlet is painfully aware," says Professor Tillyard, "of the baffling human predicament between the angels and the beasts, between the glory of having been made in God's image and the incrimination of being descended from fallen Adam." To this we may add, I think, that Hamlet is more than aware of it; he exemplifies it; and it is for this reason that his problem appeals to us so powerfully as an image of our own.

Hamlet's problem, in its crudest form, is simply the problem of the avenger: he must carry out the injunction of the ghost and kill the king. But this problem, as I ventured to suggest at the outset, is presented in terms of a certain kind of world. The ghost's injunction to act becomes so inextricably bound up for Hamlet with the character of the world in which the action must be taken—its mysteriousness, its baffling appearances, its deep consciousness of infection, frailty, and loss— that he cannot come to terms with either without coming to terms with both.

When we first see him in the play, he is clearly a very young man, sensitive and idealistic, suffering the first shock of growing up. He has taken the garden at face value, we might say, supposing mankind to be only a little lower than the angels. Now in his mother's hasty and incestuous marriage, he discovers evidence of something else, something bestial—though even a beast, he thinks, would have mourned longer. Then comes the revelation of the ghost, bringing a second shock. Not so much because he now knows that his serpent-uncle killed his father; his prophetic soul had almost suspected this. Not entirely, even, because he knows now how far below the angels humanity has fallen in his mother, and how lust—these were the ghost's words— "though to a radiant angel link'd Will sate itself in a celestial bed, And prey on garbage." Rather, because he now sees everywhere, but especially in his own nature, the general taint, taking from life its meaning, from woman her integrity, from the will its strength, turning reason into madness. "Why wouldst thou be a breeder of sinners?" "What should such fellows as I do crawling between earth and heaven?" Hamlet is not the first young man to have felt the heavy and the weary weight of all this unintelligible world; and, like the others, he must come to terms with it.

The ghost's injunction to revenge unfolds a different facet of his problem. The young man growing up is not to be allowed simply to endure a rotten world, he must also act in it. Yet how to begin, among so many enigmatic surfaces? Even Claudius, whom he now knows to be the core of the ulcer, has a plausible exterior. And around Claudius, swathing the evil out of sight, he encounters all those other exteriors, as we have seen. Some of them already deeply infected beneath, like his mother. Some noble, but marked for infection, like Laertes. Some not particularly corrupt but infinitely corruptible, like Rosencrantz and Guildenstern; some mostly weak and foolish like Polonius and Osric. Some, like Ophelia, innocent, yet in their innocence still serving to "skin and film the ulcerous place."

And this is not all. The act required of him, though retributive justice, is one that necessarily involves the doer in the general guilt. Not only because it involves a killing; but because to get at the world of seeming one sometimes has to use its weapons. He himself, before he finishes, has become a player, has put an antic disposition on, has killed a man—the wrong man—has helped drive Ophelia mad, and has sent two friends of his youth to death, mining below their mines, and hoisting the engineer with his own petard. He had never meant to dirty himself with these things, but from the moment of the ghost's challenge to act, this dirtying was inevitable. It is the condition of living at all in such a world. To quote Polonius, who knew that world so well, men become "a little soil'd i' th' working." Here is another matter with which Hamlet has to come to terms.

Human infirmity—all that I have discussed with reference to instability, infection, loss—supplies the problem with its third phase. Hamlet has not only to accept the mystery of man's condition between the angels and the brutes, and not only to act in a perplexing and soiling world. He has also to act within the human limits—"with shabby equipment always deteriorating," if I may adapt some phrases from Eliot's *East Coker*, "In the general mess of imprecision of feeling, Undisciplined squads of emotion." Hamlet is aware of that fine poise of body and mind, feeling and thought, that suits the action to the word, the word to the action; that acquires and begets a temperance in the very torrent, tempest, and whirlwind of passion; but he cannot at first achieve it in himself. He vacillates between undisciplined squads of emotion and thinking too precisely on the event. He learns to his cost how easily action can be lost in "acting," and loses it there for a time himself. But these again are only the terms of every man's life. As Anatole France reminds us in a now famous apostrophe to Hamlet: "What one of us thinks without contradiction and acts without incoherence? What one of us is not mad? What one of us does not say with a mixture of pity, comradeship, admiration, and horror, Goodnight, sweet Prince!"

In the last act of the play (or so it seems to me, for I know there can be differences on this point), Hamlet accepts his world and we discover a different man. Shakespeare does not outline for us the process of acceptance any more than he had done with Romeo or was to do with Othello. But he leads us strongly to expect an altered Hamlet, and then, in my opinion, provides him. We must recall that at this point Hamlet has been absent from the stage during several scenes, and that such absences in Shakespearean tragedy usually warn us to be on the watch for a new phase in the development of the character. It is so when we leave King Lear in Gloucester's farmhouse and find him again in Dover fields. It is so when we leave Macbeth at the witches' cave and rejoin him at Dunsinane, hearing of the armies that beset it. Furthermore, and this is an important matter in the theatre—especially important in a play in which the symbolism of clothing has figured largely—Hamlet now looks different. He is wearing a different dress—probably, as Granville-Barker thinks, his "seagown scarf'd" about him, but in any case no longer the disordered costume of his antic disposition. The effect is not entirely dissimilar to that in *Lear*, when the old king wakes out of his madness to find fresh garments on him.

Still more important, Hamlet displays a considerable change of mood. This is not a matter of the way we take the passage about defying augury, as Mr. Tillyard among others seems to think. It is a matter of Hamlet's whole deportment, in which I feel we may legitimately see the deportment of a man who has been "illuminated" in the tragic sense. Bradley's term for it is fatalism, but if this is what we wish to call it, we must at least acknowledge that it is fatalism of a very distinctive kind—a kind that Shakespeare has been willing to touch with the associations of the saying in St. Matthew about the fall of a sparrow, and with Hamlet's recognition that a divinity shapes our ends. The point is not that Hamlet has suddenly become religious; he has been religious all through the play. The point is that he has now learned, and accepted, the boundaries in which human action, human judgment, are enclosed.

Till his return from the voyage he had been trying to act beyond these, had been encroaching on the role of providence, if I may exaggerate to make a vital point. He had been too quick to take the burden of the whole world and its condition upon his limited and finite self. Faced with a task of sufficient difficulty in its own right, he had dilated it into a cosmic problem— as indeed every task is, but if we think about this too precisely we cannot act at all. The whole time is out of joint, he feels, and in his young man's egocentricity, he will set it right. Hence he misjudges Ophelia, seeing in her only a breeder of sinners. Hence he misjudges himself, seeing himself a vermin crawling between earth and heaven. Hence he takes it upon himself to be his mother's conscience, though the ghost has warned that this is no fit task for him, and returns to repeat the warning: "Leave her to heaven, And to those thorns that in her bosom lodge." Even with the king, Hamlet has sought to play at God. *He* it must be who decides the issue of Claudius's salvation, saving him for a more damnable occasion. Now, he has learned that there are limits to the before and after that human reason can comprehend. Rashness, even, is sometimes good. Through rashness he has saved his life from the commission for his death, "and prais'd be rashness for it." This happy circumstance and the unexpected arrival of the pirate ship make it plain that the roles of life are not entirely self-assigned. "There is a divinity that shapes our ends, Roughhew them how we will." Hamlet is ready now for what may happen, seeking neither to foreknow it nor avoid it. "If it be now, 'tis not to come; if it be not to come, it will be now; if it be not now, yet it will come: the readiness is all."

The crucial evidence of Hamlet's new frame of mind, as I understand it, is the graveyard scene. Here, in its ultimate symbol, he confronts, recognizes, and accepts the condition of being man. It is not simply that he now accepts death, though Shakespeare shows him accepting it in ever more poignant forms: first, in the imagined persons of the politician, the courtier, and the lawyer, who laid their little schemes "to circumvent God," as Hamlet puts it, but now lie here; then in Yorick, whom he knew and played with as a child; and then in Ophelia. This last death tears from him a final cry of passion, but the striking contrast between his behavior and Laertes's reveals how deeply he has changed.

Still, it is not the fact of death that invests this scene with its peculiar power. It is instead the haunting mystery of life itself that Hamlet's speeches point to, holding in its inscrutable folds those other mysteries that he has wrestled with so long. These he now knows for what they are, and lays them by. The mystery of evil is present here—for this is after all the universal graveyard, where, as the clown says humorously, he holds up Adam's profession; where the scheming politician, the hollow courtier, the tricky lawyer, the emperor and the clown and the beautiful young maiden, all come together in an emblem of the world; where even, Hamlet murmurs, one might expect to stumble on "Cain's jawbone, that did the first murther." The mystery of reality is here too—for death puts the question, "What is real?" in its irreducible form, and in the end uncovers all appearances: "Is this the fine of his fines and the recovery of his recoveries, to have his fine pate full of fine dirt?" "Now get you to my lady's chamber, and tell her, let her paint an inch thick, to this favor she must come." Or if we need more evidence of this mystery, there is the anger of Laertes at the lack of ceremonial trappings, and the ambiguous character of Ophelia's own death. "Is she to be buried in Christian burial when she wilfully seeks her own salvation?" asks the gravedigger. And last of all, but most pervasive of all, there is the mystery of human limitation. The grotesque nature of man's little joys, his big ambitions. The fact that the man who used to bear us on his back is now a skull that smells; that the noble dust of Alexander somewhere plugs a bunghole; that "Imperious Caesar, dead and turn'd to clay,

Might stop a hole to keep the wind away." Above all, the fact that a pit of clay is "meet" for such a guest as man, as the grave-digger tells us in his song, and yet that, despite all frailties and limitations, "That skull had a tongue in it and could sing once."

After the graveyard and what it indicates has come to pass in him, we know that Hamlet is ready for the final contest of mighty opposites. He accepts the world as it is, the world as a duel, in which, whether we know it or not, evil holds the poisoned rapier and the poisoned chalice waits; and in which, if we win at all, it costs not less than everything. I think we understand by the close of Shakespeare's *Hamlet* why it is that unlike the other tragic heroes he is given a soldier's rites upon the stage. For as William Butler Yeats once said, "Why should we honor those who die on the field of battle? A man may show as reckless a courage in entering into the abyss of himself."

A. P. Rossiter

THE PROBLEM PLAYS

MY SUBJECT is "The Problem Plays" and it is not entirely of my own choice. One can choose to talk about a single play; but over such a matter as the grouping of *Troilus and Cressida, Measure for Measure* and *All's Well*—their labelling in a separate category —a lecturer to-day is not a free man. His audience has certain expectations; and I am sure that (having had the temerity to come for such a title), you will be deeply disappointed if I do not contrive to send you away with heads full of glooms, disillusions, moral dilemmas and artistic perplexities, vexed questions of human psychology and behaviour; and, above all, if I fail to leave these plays as "problematical" as either you or I found them, or more so.

Do not be uneasy: I have every hope of upsetting you (one way or another) before I have done. I cannot promise that each and all will emerge saying "I am wrapp'd in dismal thinkings," as the King does in *All's Well;* but I shall do my best to catch at some of the qualities of this queer trio of middle-period pieces which we agree to bracket as "Problems."

But first: why put these three plays together—*The Tragedie of Troilus and Cressida* (as it is called on its three pages in the Folio; the Quartos call it *The famous Historie* . . .) and two comedies—and call them "Problem Plays"? When my grandmother read them in Dr. Bowdler's *Family Shakespeare* ("in which . . . those words and expressions are omitted which cannot with propriety be read in a family"), there were no such things. Nor were there when my father read Dowden (1875).

From *Angel with Horns,* Theater Arts Books and Longmans, Green, & Co., 1961, 108-28. Reprinted by permission.

The title "Problem-Plays" as applied to certain of the works of Shakespeare can in fact be dated very accurately. It was devised by F. S. Boas in his *Shakspere and His Predecessors* (1896), but when it started it meant *four* plays—and the fourth was *Hamlet*. Boas considered that all were concerned with sophisticated, "artificial" societies, rotten-ripe, in which "abnormal" conditions of mind and feeling are expected, and "intricate cases of conscience" demand "unprecedented methods" of solution (the adjectives show that *Hamlet* came first in Boas's mind). He continued by saying "we move along dim untrodden paths, and at the close our feeling is neither of simple joy nor pain; we are excited, fascinated, perplexed, for the issues raised preclude a completely satisfactory outcome."[1] Then, having said that the fifth-act adjustments of *All's Well* and *Measure for Measure* are not solutions, and that in *Troilus and Cressida* and *Hamlet* there is no such "partial settlement of difficulties . . . we are left to interpret their enigmas as best we may," he concluded thus: "Dramas so singular in theme and temper cannot be strictly called comedies or tragedies. We may therefore borrow a convenient phrase from the theatre of to-day and class them together as Shakespere's problem-plays."[2]

The date of Boas's book was 1896. "The theatre of to-day" means the stage of the dramatic revival under the influence of Ibsen: the theatre of William Archer, Shaw and Pinero; and, later, of Granville-Barker. The label "Problem Plays" retains still *some* of its Ibsenite smell. The Ibsenite-Fabian slant comes out very nicely in Shaw's Preface to *Plays Pleasant and Unpleasant* (1898), where the assumption is that Shakespeare would have been an Ibsen if he had had the chance:

> Shakespear . . . has left us no intellectually coherent drama, and could not afford to pursue a genuinely scientific method in his studies of character and society, though in such unpopular plays as All's Well, Measure for Measure, and Troilus and Cressida, we find him ready and willing to start at the twentieth century if the seventeenth would only let him. (*Preface*, p. ix)

Clearly Shaw *thinks* of these as "problem plays," though he does not use the term. In Sir Walter Raleigh's *Shakespeare*[3] they are

"later and darker comedies" (p. 162), though he scouts the idea
of a Shakespeare who wrote them in a phase of despondency or
pessimism. In 1910, in his article in the *Encyclopaedia Britan-
nica*,[4] E. K. Chambers put all the weight of his authority behind
quite a different view. They are "the three bitter and cynical
pseudo-comedies." *All's Well* "drags the honour of womanhood in
the dust"; *Troilus and Cressida* confounds the ideals of heroism
and romance; and in *Measure for Measure* "the searchlight of
irony is thrown upon the ways of Providence itself."

I mention Chambers's article for two reasons. First, it tersely
states one view of these plays (in an extreme form); and, secondly, it seems to have given the spur to Professor W. W. Lawrence, of Columbia University, whose *Shakespeare's Problem
Comedies*, published in 1931, is mainly responsible for the currency of the label "Problem." Lawrence made it "Comedies" to
exclude *Hamlet*. None the less, the formula "Problem Plays"
established itself in the 1930's, and you may think that implies it
is a bit "dated."

Since then—in the last twenty-five years—more has been written on these three plays than in the whole of the eighteenth and
ninteenth centuries. Broadly speaking, there are two main group-
ings of critical opinion. One rejects the view of E. K. Chambers,
and will have nothing to do with Shakespearian biography in
connection with these plays; the other insists that these *are*
"bitter comedies," as they were called by Dr. Dover Wilson (*The
Essential Shakespeare*, 1932, p. 119), from whom let me quote:
"The note of them all is disillusionment and cynicism, the air is
cheerless and often unwholesome, the wit mirthless, the bad characters contemptible or detestable, the good ones unattractive"
(p. 116). The centre of this group is still Sir E. K. Chambers, who
wrote of *Measure for Measure* as a "remorseless analysis which
probes the inmost being of man and strips him naked before the
spectators while he—

> Plays such fantastic tricks before high heaven,
> As make the angels weep,"

commenting "It is the temper of the inquisitor; and you can but
shudder as a soul is brought into the torture-chamber and shriv-
els to nothingness before some sharp test of circumstance."[5]

The opposition to this point of view is harder to sketch without distortion. W. W. Lawrence's line was to argue that "All's well that ended well for the Elizabethan audience." His book adopts "the historical method," and its main plank is that Shakespeare—like Kipling's 'Omer—was only staging traditional stories (some of vast antiquity).

> When 'Omer smote 'is bloomin' lyre
> 'E'd 'eard men sing by land an' sea;
> An' wot 'e thought 'e might require
> 'E went an' took . . . the same as me!

Lawrence's rejection of biography is uncompromising: "there is no evidence that the problem comedies were composed . . . for the gratification of Shakespeare's aesthetic interests, or to give expression to his views on conduct and morality."[6] "They were written in the first place to entertain . . . and must in part be judged according to the immediate effects which they were designed to produce upon spectators." That is an extreme point of view. It sounds all right until you reflect that we have not a single word of evidence about how the Elizabethan audience took any of these plays.[7]

The weakness of "the historical method" stands out when Lawrence tells us we must "base our primary conclusions upon definite and tangible evidence" (all right so far), "discarding as far as possible the emotional and moral effect which the plays produce upon us today" (p. 13). There is, no doubt, much virtue in "as far as possible"; but if we *do* succeed in "discarding" the emotional effect of a play, I fail to see what we are left talking about. Of course, what he means is that it would be simply a blunder to ascribe to Bertram your or my feelings if we were suddenly imprisoned in wedlock for the duration of Her Majesty's pleasure; or to see in Helena the "Unwomanly Woman" of *The Quintessence of Ibsenism*. There are many ways in which Elizabethan or Jacobean feelings and thoughts are demonstrably different from ours; and it is the business of scholars to tell us where these matter. But inasmuch as Shakespeare's plays have only "lived" because his mind was *not* limited to that different world, the limiting-terms of Lawrence are a great deal *too* limiting.

One main conclusion he reaches is to throw doubt on the

grouping of the three plays in a "period," and therefore on what
C. J. Sisson (in a British Academy lecture of 1934) called "the
Mythical Sorrows of Shakespeare." In both critics you see the
reaction against the nineteenth-century assumption that a man's
personal experience can be read in his works, and his spiritual
autobiography traced, as it can be in, say, *The Prelude*, or in
Keats. In particular, the "disillusion" of the Sonnets—the faithless
friend, the inconstant mistress—cannot, Lawrence maintains, be
held to have any real connection with the men and women of
the Problem Comedies or with the mood of these plays (p. 229).[8]

The other turning-point of criticism was in 1937: R. W. Chambers's British Academy paper, *The Jacobean Shakespeare and
Measure for Measure*.[9] On the one hand, it is a direct attack on
Sir E. K. Chambers and Dover Wilson and their adherents. Lawrence and Sisson are brought into an alliance, the aims of which
are:

(1) to cast doubt on the distressing and morally disturbing
things which had been seen in the play;

(2) to question the irony which "disillusioned" critics were
accused of having invented: especially over the "cynical happy
ending" (and that of *All's Well* also. See p. 29).[10] And

(3) to question (with Sisson) that there ever was any 'fer-
ment of doubt and bitterness of disillusion" in Shakespeare's
mind. Towards the end of it Chambers wrote, "I realise how
deeply fixed by generations of repetition, is the dogma of Shakespeare's disillusioned early Jacobean period, 'in the Depths.'"
After mentioning Sisson and the "Mythical Sorrows" he concluded: "Shakespeare's career is that of an artist. Let us study
his plays as the works of art which we know them to be, rather
than weave baseless conjectures concerning details of a biography
which we can never know" (p. 59).

The *positive* side of the paper was none the less actively concerned with what amounts to spiritual biography—of an "opti-
mist" and Christian cast. *Measure for Measure* emerges as "a play
of forgiveness" (anticipating the Last Plays), and Shakespeare's
"philosophy" of 1604 as "more definitely Christian than that of
The Tempest" (p. 54). Why should we not see his career as "a
continuous progress to the Heights?" Why not, indeed? But that
is as much biographical criticism as "Never does Shakespeare

seem more passionately to identify himself with any of his characters than he does with Isabel, as she pleads for mercy" (pp. 36-7). With "Judge not . . ." on the same page, the official (British Academy) Christian Shakespeare was launched.

True, in 1910 E. K. Chambers had seen "Providence" in *Measure for Measure* (under the searchlight of irony). Yet I think there is no doubt that R. W. Chambers had read Wilson Knight's *Wheel of Fire* (1930) and its essay on *"Measure for Measure and the Gospels,"* though he never mentions it (in 1937 T. S. Eliot, who wrote the book an Introduction, was still a suspicious character). Whether you say, "O Father Abraham, what these Christians are!" or not, it is certain that a cloud of Christian witnesses arises from Wilson Knight or R. W. Chambers, or both combined; and probable that you have only to wait for a complete Christian interpretation of all the "Problems." Far be it from me to talk Shakespearian theology: but the Christianity of Dr. T. S. Eliot is not that of Dr. Billy Graham nor that of Dr. Donald Soper; and the Christian interpretations are as various as contradictory. I shall mention an extreme case by and by: Mr. Roy Battenhouse on *Measure for Measure* (1946). In the meantime, let me remark that it is perfectly possible to set to work on *Hamlet* with certain set prepossessions, and to show that it is about "the misery of man without God" (Pascal), up to the time when Hamlet first recognizes that there *is* "a divinity that shapes our ends"; and that this is followed by the full conversion implicit in "there is a special providence in the fall of a sparrow" (cf. Matt. x. 29): the Prince's redemption being tactfully suggested by Horatio's farewell, "And flights of angels sing thee to thy rest!" The bulk of the play can then be seen to be concerned with the pomps and vanities of this wretched world, and the ineluctable unhappiness of those who cannot look beyond it.

Forgive me if I seem only to scoff. I do not doubt that Jacobean England was "a Christian society" in the sense that modern England is not; and that Christian commonplaces, allusions, images, biblical phrases and parallels lay all apt to Shakespeare's producing hand: as many of them did to my father's tongue (he was not a parson); and I have watched them dying out during my lifetime. But when I find up-to-date Shakespearian interpreters so emphatic, and so certain about significances which were totally missed by such great and discerning critics—*and* Christians —as Johnson and Coleridge, I take leave to lift an eyebrow. I do not doubt that William Shakespeare was a "Christian," and when I say "scepticism" in this lecture I never intend "agnosticism." Shakespeare was a Christian, yes; but so, beyond any shadow of doubt, was the great sceptic Montaigne.

To return to our Problems. There is a real division of opinion between those who find them "bitter," "disillusioned," "*navrant,*" even "cynical" (i.e. predominantly *negative*), and those who find them either undisturbing (as Lawrence does), or containing positives adequate to make it absurd to ascribe them to any phase or stage of "disillusion," "despondency" or the like.

Since some critics wedge off *Troilus and Cressida* from the rest (Dr. Leavis, for example, rejects any conjunction of it with *Measure for Measure*), the question immediately arises: "How far can we justifiably make a separate group of these plays?" One thing we must not lose sight of is that they come from the period of Shakespeare's greatest versatility: a versatility unmatched by any other artist of any sort whatsoever. If you can imagine a being capable of producing within seven years *Così fan tutte* and the Fifth Symphony, Verdi's *Falstaff* and *Don Giovanni,* the Kreutzer Sonata and *La Belle Hélène,* then you are some way towards imagining what it meant to have written between 1597-8 and 1604 the twelve plays which include *2 Henry IV* and *Julius Caesar* and *Hamlet, Much Ado, As You Like It, Twelfth Night* and *The Merry Wives of Windsor,* our three "Problem Comedies" and *Othello.* And all this by the time "forty winters" had besieged his brow. In a genius of this prodigality, "pouring (his) bounties forth/ With such a full and unwithdrawing hand," it is only human frailty that sets us looking for simple straight-line, step-by-step "development." "Improvement makes straight roads," said Blake; "but the crooked roads without improvement are the roads of Genius."

If these dozen plays are read "without prejudice," we find, I believe, that we experience a certain uneasiness and a consequent uncertainty of interpretation in *2 Henry IV* (and not only about the rejection of Falstaff); and that while it is missing in the "great comedies" (as in *1 Henry IV*), it is variously present in all three "plays of the Hamlet period"—as they might be called—

and not entirely absent from *Othello*. I shall not attempt to summarize what I have said on *2 Henry IV;*[11] but uncertainties about the nobility of Nobles and about the geniality of some of the humour are so evident in the criticisms of that play that I can say, "Never mind about 'ambivalence': there must be much ambiguity in the piece, or the qualified interpreters would not be so much at variance about it." Exactly the same applies to *Hamlet*, where the Prince speaks a good deal of "satire"; to the Problem Plays (where one main question is, "How seriously do we take the 'satirical' lights in which many, perhaps most, of the characters are placed?"); *and* to *Othello* (where Dr. Leavis's essay[12] convincingly brings out some things which leave an uneasiness in the mind and are missed entirely in Bradley).

I suggest that a label for the causes of these feelings might be *the tragi-comic view of man:* a view which splits the world today, and gives us the "totalitarian" attitude *versus* the end-product of a European tradition which *was* chivalric and Christian. I mean by this any or all of the following, or any combination of these distinguishable attitudes:

1. A refusal or failure wholly to credit the dignity of man, and the significance that that gives the individual in tragedy.

2. An emphasis (comic, derisive, satiric) on human shortcoming, even when man is engaged in great affairs. There is a touch or more of this in Caesar: he is never *comic* (though you can see how he could be made so), but much the least *dignified* of Shakespeare's rulers.

3. Any trend towards suggesting that there is usually another side to all human affairs, and that the "other side" to the serious, dignified, noble, famous and so forth, is comic. This implies a scepticism of man's worth, importance and value; and may range from the quizzical through the ironical to the cynical. Hamlet's commentaries on men and affairs run through the whole gamut. The pure comic of Shakespeare's comedy is never met in the "comic relief" of the tragedies (contrast, for example, Jonson's *Catiline*): the comic relief of Shakespearian tragedy is "tragicomic," with many of the qualities found in the Problem Plays.

4. Any trend in the direction of expressing unhappiness, disappointment, resentfulness or bitterness about human life, by inverting these feelings and presenting the causes of them as

matter for laughter or jest (which may mean "mirthless laughter," as in the indecent Sonnets): i.e. offering the comic, but
giving it a grating quality which excludes geniality and ensures
disturbing after-thoughts.

5. A corresponding attitude towards traditionally funny subjects which insinuates that in some way they are serious, or that
the stock response to them by-passes pain at human shortcom-
ings or wickedness; or that this stock response depends on a lack
of sympathy or insight which an author can make us aware of
without abolishing the comic situation.[13]

As the name suggests, there is something equivocal in the nature of the tragi-comic. I do not mean the simple or *"Much Ado
About Nothing"* kind of dramatic tragi-comedy, in which a situation which has promised to be "tragic" is switched to a happy
ending (usually with some unconvincing *coup de théâtre*); although two of these plays operate on something like that pattern.
I mean, rather, a kind of drama in which the contemplation of
man is on the one hand held back from the "admiration" and
"commiseration" (as Sidney put it) of tragedy; and on the other,
denied the wholehearted (or heart-whole) enjoyments of human
irrationality and human sentiment of comedy. Tragi-comedy is
an art of inversion, deflation and paradox. Its subject is tragi-
comic man; and my repetition is not tautology, because genuine
tragi-comedy is marked by telling generalizations about the subject, *man*, of a seriousness which is unexpected in comedy and
may seem incongruous with it.

Let me first give two examples of what is *not* tragi-comic.
Twelfth Night is about human sentiment and irrationality, and
what "every wise man's son doth know"; and it is not very important to know that an Elizabethan proverb said "The wise man
has a Fool for his son." Orsino is "sentimentally" in love with
Olivia. That is contrasted by juxtaposition and interweaved with
Viola's being "passionately" in love with Orsino. Sir Andrew
"imagines" he loves Olivia; and Malvolio is even more fancifully
in love with her too, and can be fooled into believing his passion
is reciprocated. Yet out of all this promising display of human
gullibility (the irrationality of sentiment) *nothing whatsoever* is
thrust at us by way of generalization about mankind. No sensitive
spectator can identify himself with Malvolio or Sir Andrew; al-

though this is not to say that there is *no* feeling for Malvolio—
that he is only the comic gull. The play is not in the least tragi-
comic; but parts of it are from a man who *could* write tragi-
comedy, had probably written some already, was going to write
more. Now consider *Much Ado* (1598). It *looks* like tragi-comedy, but we have only to read it beside *All's Well* to see the
difference. The Hero-Claudio plot is potentially tragic, perhaps;
but nearly all of it is soft-pedalled, "shot" out of focus, in comparison with Beatrice and Benedick. It is about seeming and being in love, or, more comprehensively, about misunderstandings
and delusions, most of them *verbal*. These misunderstandings,
miscomprehensions and incomprehensions are "serious" on the
Hero side; "high-comic" in the Beatrice-Benedict plot; and "farcical" in Dogberry (but still the farce of misapprehension and non-
comprehension. "You shall comprehend all vagrom men," say
the Standing Orders to the constabulary of Messina. Shakespeare
carries out the instructions.) Considering the volte-face which
Shakespeare demanded of our feelings at the end of *All's Well*,
there might seem a possibility that, in the Church-scene, Claudio
should plunge to the depths with Troilus—

> This Hero? No—this is Borachio's Hero!
> If beauty have a soul, this is not she. . . .

But the tone of the whole play forbids it. Claudio's outburst,
"Out on the seeming,[14] I will write against it" is theatrical hysteria, very different from the hysteria of Troilus. Yet *Much Ado*
does give valuable help in attuning the ear and mind and heart
to the tragi-comic tone. From which of the Problem Comedies
have I extracted these general comments on man?

> O, what men dare do! What men may do! What men daily do,
> not knowing what they do!

> O, what authority and show of truth
> Can cunning sin cover itself withal!

The second might well be Isabella in *Measure for Measure;* the
first is exactly paralleled in *All's Well* (in Helena's lines on men's
pursuit of lust and their after-hatred for the thing they "love").
Both are from the Church-scene in *Much Ado* (IV. i. 18 and 34).

They sound the tragi-comic note; momentarily, then gone. It is no tone of the play as a whole. We react perhaps like Leonato: "Are these things spoken, or do I but dream?" (IV. i. 65). When we turn to the thoroughly tragi-comic plays, Don John's reply takes on its full weight: "Sir, they are spoken, and these things are true."

I hope I have clarified what I meant by "telling generalizations about man," and tuned you in somewhat to their peculiar reverberant capacity. Beyond this I have no concern with *Much Ado*. A shift of tone—a deepening of Hero, more depth to Claudio—would shift it across a line that demarcates *All's Well*. But the tonal change would have to be general, and the implicit overall view of mankind very different indeed. "Sir, they are spoken, and these things are true." The implication is that they are disagreeable things. Suppose we take that to our three Problem Plays? No one will deny that they hold much that is unpleasant.

Troilus and Cressida is about the hollowness of the seeming glories of war, the hollowness of seeming heroes (Achilles, Ajax), and disillusion in romantic love. Troilus loves a woman who is "unworthy," yet Cressida is so real a creature that he also looks "an enthusiastic young fool" (Boas); and sympathy with him is drastically mitigated, even withered, by the dramatic context, in which the whole Trojan War is also about a woman who is unworthy. The theme of the play slowly emerges, on patient study, as the disorderly house of man (amorous and military), turned into chaos by the egoisms of pride and lust. The love-theme is debased by the sniggering "humorist" Pandarus, the war filthily besmirched by the snarling clown Thersites. The last word is given to Pandarus, and is about procuring, brothels and venereal disease (of which he has advertised himself as a victim seven scenes from the end, when he delivers Cressida's letter). Ulysses speaks much wisdom, but it is true only negatively of the humans in the play; and his shrewdness is totally ineffectual in action. The whole is an acrid comedy of deflation, making a searching inquiry into manly honour, the illusions of sex and the deceiving power of women. There are the makings of tragic issues in Troilus betrayed, but the greatness of tragedy is nowhere. Hector is a great shadow. Ulysses would do well as a tragedy-commentator; but in the near-tragic betrayal-scene he is present only to miss the true point of Troilus's agony. One effect of this is an irony like that of some of the more tormented Sonnets (e.g. 137, 141-2, 148), in which subjective and objective views of the Dark Lady's lust and treachery are counterpointed. The Time-theme of the Sonnets is also strongly present in the play. On the comic side Pandarus is droll, but debases what he touches; the "comic relief" centring in Thersites is comedy without a sense of humour: a willing suspension of indignation or hurtness at human indignity, gullibility, meanness, lustfulness and folly. This "two-clown pattern" is constant throughout the play.

Measure for Measure is about seeming justice in conflict with the rank reality of sex: about honour in the guise of "the demigod Authority." We are invited to "see,/ If power change purpose, what our seemers be" (the Duke at I. iii. 53). As the Authority himself puts it, the virtuous-seeming Angelo:

> O place, O form,
> How often dost thou with thy case, thy habit,
> Wrench awe from fools, and tie the wiser souls
> To thy false seeming! (II. iv. 12-15)

Under the robes and furred gowns "blood" is "blood": that is, lust is lust. The main plot of the attempted moral rape of the nun-to-be by the seeming Justice is backed by an extensive revelation of the seething base vitality of the lower orders, mainly in the bawdy trade: observed with a kind of sardonic affection, and presented with great gusto of expression (frequently lewd, extensively indecent, occasionally brutally obscene). With the absconded Duke we are led to the exploration of a demoralized world, in which, as elsewhere in Shakespeare, rampant sexuality *means* disorder and chaos. The themes of justice and sex are twisted tight together by the Gilbertian law which makes the begetting of life (by Claudio on Julietta) the getting of death.[15] And, from the suburbs, Pompey the pimp has the humane sanity to imply that it *is* Gilbertian, with his innocent inquiry: "Does your worship mean to geld and splay all the youth of the city?" (II. i. 218). Lucio, the loose-spoken gentleman-clown, takes much the same view.

That is the purpose of these humorists: one side of them stands for a world of vileness; the other exploits the Clown's function of switching a theme into a violently contrasted light.[16] The humanity of the base-born, the lack of it in the lofty, is one of the play's running paradoxes. Isabella, admirable in strength as she is, is not immune from Langland's "Chastity without Charity is chained in hell." Angelo (the name is patently ironical: he puns on it himself) is law or legalism, rather than justice. His hard, prim, precise ruling by the book is not felt to be just, because his rule makes all offences the same size; and to think of incontinence or fornication as if it were murder does violence to all normal human feelings. Again, once tempted, he is only seeming-justice and utterly vulnerable to the Biblical commonplace glanced at in the title: the exemplar of "man, proud man,/ Dress'd in a little brief authority" . . . playing the "fantastic trick" of condemning in others what is far worse in himself. There is further emphasis on the "inequity" of the law, in that *legally* here, there is no difference between the incontinence of two agreed lovers and the forcing of a nun-to-be by blackmail.

Once conquered by lust and wilfulness, Angelo sinks deep into evil. Having enjoyed his sexual victory, as he thinks, he still executes the brother whose life was purchased with the sister's honour. A trick keeps the brother alive, but—since murder lies in the intention—Angelo the man is a murderer, even though Angelo the Authority is only carrying out the sentence of the law. The first half of the play is full of subtle casuistry like that. If there were nothing else to make this a "play of the Hamlet period," there is the undeniable fact that, next to the Prince of Denmark, Isabella and Angelo are in a class by themselves as Shakespearian intellectuals—with Ulysses next on the list. I am only using "character-approach" to bring out the quality of keen argumentative or speculative inquiry, especially into the nature of man. The Duke, disguised as Friar, generalizes with sombre finality on this in the strong set speech, "Be absolute for death" (III. i. 5 f.): a speech packed with sceptic deflations of human pride and self-importance, doubts of human validity, and insistence on man's servitude to time and circumstance; and most un-Friarly lacking in the faintest whisper of a Christian hope, or even an urge towards penitence. (Presumably this is why the

Christian interpreters give it so very little attention.) Those who want a "pessimist" Shakespeare will make the most of this speech; and those who want to soft-pedal or mute the disturbing notes will do the opposite.[17]

Measure for Measure is tragi-comic in two distinguishable senses. In the first half it moves swiftly towards tragic calamity, twisting deeper and deeper into the quick; then the observer Duke turns *Deus ex machina*, and the puppet-master makes all dance to a happy ending, with a lot of creaking.[18] It seems needless to argue about this: particularly the abrupt conversion of Isabella and the deep damnation of her marrying-off to the Duke (as many worthy minds have found it; although others have as solemnly argued, "she was not *really* a nun"). It is enough to say, This is the trick-switch type of tragi-comedy, in which a potentially tragic situation is knocked on the head with a *coup de théâtre* (which the Christian interpreters read as a *coup* by divine Grace).

I lack time to argue with them. But surely Dr. Tillyard is right in his objection to all the "allegorical" interpretations of the play. Whether the Duke is Providence (Wilson Knight and R. W. Chambers); Rightful Authority conducting "a controlled experiment" in moral education (F. R. Leavis); or a secular analogy of the Incarnation (Roy Battenhouse, in *PMLA*, 1946, 1029-59[19]): no matter what these special pleaders argue, Tillyard's objection remains:

> The simple and ineluctable fact is, that the tone in the first half . . . is frankly, acutely human, and quite hostile to the tone of allegory or symbol. And, however much the tone changes in the second half, nothing in the world can make an allegorical interpretation poetically valid throughout. (*Shakespear's Problem Plays*, p. 123)

It is true that in his study of *All's Well* Dr. Tillyard does consider *en passant* the hypothesis of a morality framework in which Bertram stands for Unregenerate Man and Helena for Heavenly Grace. But he very wisely does not press it, and even if he had, would never take it to the length of "allegorical interpretation." The inescapable objection to this would be that Helena speaks indeed of "the great'st Grace lending Grace" apropos of curing the *King,* but is given not a syllable to suggest that she is furthermore intending the (moral) cure of Bertram. The allegorical interpreter must therefore slip in an undistributed middle term: Helena has her will with the King, who is restored to health. This is therapeutic. *Therefore* Helena stands for something miraculous. This cannot be found in the play, and must be imposed from outside. The difference between what Dr. Tillyard thinks possible and what allegorists offer is that Tillyard is concerned with what *may* have been in Shakespeare's mind (a sort of *Gestalt*); the others with what they must claim to have been communicated to Shakespeare's *audience.* The contrast is clear in *The Winter's Tale:* Leontes' repentance is duly sign-posted; but would anyone "interpret" Paulina as "Grace"—a Mrs. Julia Shuttlethwaite removed from *The Cocktail Party* to Sicilia?

The other sense in which the play is tragi-comedy depends on the parallel running of the same themes in two incongruous tones. The "tragic" sex-plot of Angelo and Isabella is commingled with low-life comic stuff, involving Pompey, Mrs. Overdone and Lucio, not only in their bawdy or business relations, but also in connection with the operations of summary justice in the underworld—the sphere of operation of Constable Elbow, whose wife was (he avows) never "respected" with man, woman or child. Sex, justice and mercy are the serious themes: with the comics, sex is seen only as bawdy and justice made the sport of buffoons. The crude jesting on venereal disease (which some have tried to reject as "interpolation") seems to me to belong with this deflationary "other side to the picture." Here, as in *Troilus and Cressida,* lust is a major issue; and in the evaluation of lust (especially commercialized lust), this unpleasant fact of nature has its place. It also appears in *All's Well* and *Hamlet* ("pocky corpses") and in *2 Henry IV* ("A pox of this gout! or, a gout of this pox!" etc.): an interesting coincidence, if that is all it is?

However, the greatest scandal about *Measure for Measure,* one shared with *All's Well,* is irremovable. I mean "the bed-trick": a term which has become current for a "stagy" interlude in which a man beds with a lady in the dark, and commits himself to the very law he imagines he is breaking with impunity. He thinks he is committing fornication, while the lady (who is not the lady he took her for) knows that she is achieving consummation. Such is the final predicament of both Angelo (with Mariana) and Bertram (with Helena); and the two plays are certainly alike in making a tortuous trial-scene of the penultimate *exposé* by the conniving females. The exposure of the iniquity and meanness of both men is not "tragic," yet it jars discordantly with the comedy-ending in marriage: in both cases not to the women of their choice. In *Measure for Measure* the "low" comic key constantly erupts in the trial-scene (v. i.), in the witty but improper comments of Lucio." Know you this woman?" asks the Duke. "Carnally, she says," Lucio answers. This is comic inversion: the serious sex-situation of one "plane" is a smart bawdy jest on another.

The difficulty about both bed-tricks and trick-endings is that the psychological realism, the complexity of shifting and sharply contrasted viewpoints, the *inquiringness* of so much of both plays, eggs us on to ask questions about the *minds* of the participants in these theatrical devices. We know we should not: enough critics have told us it is dramatically "improper"; but curious and probing inquisition into human feelings and into the nature of man and woman is so much in the atmosphere that, in a sense, Shakespeare has set our wits to work making our own "problems." That these problems centre largely on sex has nothing to do with the changed viewpoint of the twentieth century. The exposures of Cressida, of Angelo, of Bertram (and, I might add, of Queen Gertrude by her son) suffice to show how strong the sex-theme is in these four plays. And *Othello* is to follow. Both tones on this subject—the serious and condemnatory *and* the bawdy or comic-derisive—are matched in the "unpleasant" Dark Lady Sonnets (127-152: with possibly a sort of preview in 40-42), which our recent critics are showing signs of thinking much better of than their forbears could.[20]

I am *not* insinuating Shakespearian biography in making this connection; but lust, "the expense of spirit," is central to all these plays. I must say "lust," because there is in every one of them a, to my mind, pointed absence of *normal sexual love:* a self-fulfilling mutual enjoyment of man in woman (and woman in man) which is generative as much to mind and being as in body, and the very opposite of a frustration. "You cannot call it

love . . . ," says Hamlet. No, indeed. But to turn "sex" into a
label in Shakespeare's "Plays Unpleasant" is not adequate. They
have other important terms or themes in common, and all have
some echo or parallel in *Hamlet*.

1. They share a common evaluation of conventionally accepted "nobilities": noble heroes in *Troilus and Cressida* (and
the nobility of courtly love); Authority-in-ermine in *Measure
for Measure;* a gentleman of family in *All's Well*. All are deflated; and with the deflations there runs concurrently the critical
devaluation of man at large. Yet "Man delights not me—no, nor
woman neither" is again too simple a summing-up: even for its
speaker, who readily admires man in Horatio, Fortinbras and
Laertes, "a very noble youth."

2. Interpolated into the critical-analytical patterns we find
"ideal" figures who check our prattle of "cynicism," "satire" or
"misanthropy": Greek and Trojan chivalrically fraternizing; Hector; Ulysses in his degree-speech, perhaps; the Duke in his quasi-
regal moments; the Isabella who talks Christian charity so movingly; and in *All's Well* the King and the conjured spirit of
Bertram's father. To these one might add Hamlet, son of the
majesty of buried Denmark, the noble Prince: as contrasted with
the other Hamlet, the bitter carping wit, the satirical rogue, the
wag who brutally mocks Ophelia. I said "interpolated." All are
as if inset or *montage* figures, so that in their context they appear
out-of-phase; distanced, like Yeats's "things that look/ Out of
some old picture-book"; wish-fulfilments, perhaps, not realities.
But that is not quite it either: rather they are counter-statements
of "what man might be" counterpoised with what he is, like the
tragic and the comic tones of the play.

3. Surely it is needless to insist that these plays involve us in
discoveries, always of a bad reality beneath the fair appearances
of things: revelations, painful in the extreme—and we are *made
to feel the pain*—of the distressing, disintegrating possibilities of
human meanness (ignobility and treachery, craft and selfishness)
inflicted on Hamlet, Isabella, Troilus and, in a slighter way,
Helena. *All's Well* hardly cuts deep enough to be called even
potentially tragic; though perhaps it may be so to a woman. Yet
all these have good reason to be "cruelly disappointed in humanity," and this strikes home emotionally—more directly than re-

flective generalizations on man. We should not merely watch, but *wince* at the shock that Isabella meets when Angelo and Claudio fling the mire of masculinity in her cloistered-virtuous face. The wrenching emotional twists of *Othello* do not begin in *Julius Caesar;* rather, in the tragi-comedy of *Troilus.*

4. All the Problem Plays are profoundly concerned with seeming and being: and this can cover both sex and human worth (each claiming nobility). Combine this with what I have just said about "disintegrating" discoveries, and, with a wider generalization, you can say that they share a quality which can be called *maskedness:* not only because "unmasking" describes so many of the actions, but because the total effect of all three (or four) plays together is to present a world of appearances (very close to a realistically observed reality), capable of opening—like a masque-set transformation-scene—and disclosing something totally different. This maskedness brings doubt, mixed feelings, an "edgy" curiosity, a kind of fear.

The fear is of the incalculable nature of man: or of the infinite incalculability of the answers to the question, "What is man, *really?*" I do not pretend to know whether Shakespeare wrote these plays to bother our heads and make our hearts quaver: I do not even claim he may, in the writing of them, have been trying to un-perplex his own. I say only, "They *do* bother us." And I feel sure that the suave critics who smooth everything over are responding, like Lafeu's modern philosophers in *All's Well,* to "an unknown fear": ". . . we have our philosophical persons to make modern and familiar things supernatural and causeless. Hence is it that we make trifles of terrors, ensconcing ourselves into seeming knowledge when we should submit ourselves to an unknown fear" (II. iii. 1-6).

"Terrors" is too strong a word, no doubt. But Doubt—the true Montaignian doubt (*Que sçay-je?*)—has its own "unknown fear" when the scepticism is about the maskedness of man. For a final shot at the overall qualities of the Problem Plays, I throw out the term *shiftingness.* All the firm points of view or *points d'appui* fail one, or are felt to be fallible: in Ulysses, Isabella, Helena; even in Order, as represented by the Duke. Hence the "problem"-quality, and the ease with which any critic who takes a firm line is cancelled out by another. To pursue this shiftingness I should have to explore at length the world of the 1590's: of Donne, of

Chapman, Marston, Jonson and the young Middleton. But this much I can say: it was a world in which human experience, thought and feeling seemed only describable in terms of *paradox:* the greatest of all, man himself. Any of them might have said, with Donne: "O to vex me Contraries meet in one," or

> This man, so great, that all that is, is his,
> Oh what a trifle, and poore thing he is!
> (*The first Anniversary*, ii. 169-70)

Either is a tragi-comic statement.

Like Donne's love-poems, these plays throw opposed or contrary views into the mind: only to leave the resulting equations without any settled or soothing solutions. They are all about "*X's*" that do not work out. *Troilus and Cressida* gives us a "tragedy-of-love" pattern that is not tragic (nor love?); *All's Well* a "happy ending" that makes us neither happy nor comfortable; *Measure for Measure* a "final solution" that simply does not answer the questions raised.

To catch the full range of Shakespeare's tragi-comic utterance, we must start with *Henry IV* (Part 1 gives the essential tragi-comic *pattern*), and follow him through the ambiguities of *Troilus and Cressida* and *Measure for Measure*[21] to the uncertainties of *Othello*. We shall then no longer be content with an eternal triangle of three "Problem Plays."

NOTES

1. *Shakspere and His Predecessors*, p. 345.
2. Ibid.
3. In the "English Men of Letters" series, 1907.
4. 11th edn., Vol. xxiv, p. 785.
5. *Shakespeare, A Survey*, 1925, quoted by Dover Wilson, above, pp. 122-3.
6. *Shakespeare's Problem Comedies*, p. 13.
7. Unless we think that *The Phoenix* tells us how Middleton took *Measure for Measure*. The advertisement to the Quarto *Troilus and Cressida* says nothing much.
8. Although that mood, as he says, is marked by "preoccupation with the darker sides of life, serious and searching analysis of character and conduct, and drastic realism" (p. 231).

9. Reprinted in *Man's Unconquerable Mind*, 1939.

10. This attacks an article in *The Times Literary Supplement* of October 1921.

11. See pp. 55-7.

12. "Diabolic Intellect and the Noble Hero," *Scrutiny*, December 1937 (reprinted in *The Common Pursuit*, 1952, p. 136).

13. Cf. G. B. Shaw on stock jokes in *The Quintessence of Ibsenism*: "The mask of laughter wears slowly off the shames and the evils; but men finally see them as they really are" (3rd edn., 1922, p. 176); and later: "Falstaff develops into an enormous joke and an exquisitely mimicked human type. Only in the end the joke withers. The question comes to Shakespeare: *Is* this really a laughing matter? Of course there can be only one answer" (p. 177).

14. Knight's conjecture, accepted by the Editors of the New Cambridge edn.

15. See pp. 154-5.

16. As Pompey here switches it downwards:

> Yonder man is carried to prison.

Mrs. Overdone: What has he done?

> *Pompey:* A woman.

For Claudio, tragic calamity; but that is how the world sees it— a word and a jest (as Yeats said of Helen and *her* scandal).

17. W. W. Lawrence and E. M. W. Tillyard, for example, leave it undiscussed.

18. In Act IV there is also a marked change of style, surprisingly unnoted by Dr. Leavis ("Measure for Measure": *The Common Pursuit*, p. 160): the only *competent* critic to be satisfied with the ending.

19. Mr. Battenhouse is certain that, since Vincentio is the Duke's real name and Lodowick his assumed one, and the first means "conqueror" and the second "famous warrior," Shakespeare had in mind Isaiah, ch. ix. 6: "and his name shall be called Wonderful, Counsellor, The mighty God, The everlasting Father, The Prince of Peace."

20. Donne is largely the reason: the Donne who curiously and sceptically inquired into the patterns of love and lust.

21. L. C. Knights' "Troilus and Cressida Again" (*Scrutiny*, Autumn 1951, pp. 144-57) is a good guide here.

Willard Farnham

TROILUS IN SHAPES
OF INFINITE DESIRE

WHEN Shakespeare wrote *Troilus and Cressida* his imagination
was full of cross-currents. In twentieth-century critical opinion
about the play there are currents even more at odds. Their forces
seem bent upon canceling each other out. In a way it can be
understood why a reviewer of the 1960 Stratford-upon-Avon
production of *Troilus and Cressida* could find that what its author provides is "merely a collection of beautiful speeches" and
that a good producer of the piece must provide on the stage "the
shape which Shakespeare himself missed."[1]

In this essay I confine myself to one poetic concern of Shakespeare's imagination within the play, a concern which creates
shapes of infinite desire for the forming of Troilus. It works
strongly and surely, despite cross-currents, to make two figures of
Troilus in one. It serves to give Troilus the lover and Troilus the
warrior a recognizable distinctness at the same time that it gives
them a bond of substance. What one sees in the result must have
bearing upon one's finding of shape in the play as a whole.

There will be an advantage in looking first at Troilus the lover.
When Shakespeare makes Troilus tell Cressida that in love "the
will is infinite and the execution confin'd," and that "the desire is
boundless and the act a slave to limit" (III. ii. 88-90), we see
concentric circles of application.[2] One is the circle of those
"pretty encounters" to which Pandarus is immediately to lead
the lovers and which Troilus has not long before envisioned in no
ordinary way. He has thought of these encounters as about to
take place in Elysian fields where he "may wallow in the lily

From *Shakespeare Quarterly*, xv (1964), 257-64. Reprinted by
permission.

beds/ Propos'd for the deserver." In this circle there is a fleshly core of limitless desire, and it is the sexual act that we must take to be the slave to limit.

Beyond this is a circle where the desirous courtly lover becomes all fire and air as he pictures impossible deeds that will prove his merit to his beloved. Troilus, becoming forgetful of his lily beds, takes us into this farther realm by speaking of bounds set to those "undertakings" of love in which "we vow to weep seas, live in fire, eat rocks, tame tigers—thinking it harder for our mistress to devise imposition enough than for us to undergo any difficulty imposed."

And beyond that is still another circle where, again to draw upon words of Troilus, desire even challenges mutability and strives to convert love into a "fair faith" by which beloved as well as lover will keep

> constancy in plight and youth,
> Outliving beauties outward, with a mind
> That doth renew swifter than blood decays.
> (III. ii. 168-70)

Here at last is "a winnowed purity in love." But even as he attains to thought of it Troilus says in ominous sadness:

> But, alas,
> I am as true as truth's simplicity
> And simpler than the infancy of truth.
> (III. ii. 175-7)

What we find here is poetry of that special flight of the human spirit toward the limitless which our postclassical western world has made much of and has embodied, often dramatically, in some deeply meaningful culture-icons. Of such figures the Tamburlaine and the Faustus of Marlowe are good, if unsubtle, Elizabethan examples. Different from them though he is in many ways, the Troilus of Shakespeare in one way stands with them. His vision of infinite will or boundless desire matched with human action fated to suffer indignity by confinement or slavery is of their kind. It serves well as a reminder of the hold that the concept of infinity has had upon our western Christian world, whether in religion, in astronomy and mathematics, or in thought and feeling generally. Troilus is created within the frame of Renaissance infinitization of man's quest on earth. We find in the Marlovian Tamburlaine a hero who can link a restless "climbing after knowledge infinite," for which Nature teaches us all to have "aspiring minds," with his own climbing after "an earthly crown," that "ripest fruit of all." We find in the Shakespearian Troilus a hero who can aspire in love toward something not in any Marlovian hero's ken. The Renaissance urge to infinitize man's earthly quest is of course very different from what Erwin Panofsky calls a tendency the mystic has "to infinitize the ego because he believes in the self-extinction of the human soul in God."[3] With some simplicity this Renaissance urge can present the celestial cosmos as measureless. With less simplicity it can in painting from the beginning of the fourteenth century onward make use of perspective, which, as Panofsky says, is an interpretation of space that gives visual expression to the concept of the infinite by making the perspective vanishing point the projection of the point in which parallels intersect (pp. 16-17).

As a figure of infinite desire in love Troilus makes out that he is simple. He stands for the truth that is the keeping of faith and says:

I with great truth catch mere simplicity.
(IV. iv. 106)

But of course he is not by any means all simple. The complexity that appears in the poetry given to Troilus when we put together such words of his as "great truth," "true as truth's simplicity," "mere simplicity," and "simpler than the infancy of truth" defies final statement. It goes beyond irony that is undoubtedly there to something that transforms irony by working opposites toward oneness.

We should look back to Troilus' "imaginary relish" of lily beds in Elysium. To beds of asphodel (the asphodel being literally enough a kind of lily) Pandarus as Charon is to carry the deserver of what by all classic connotations is to be noble bliss. But there Troilus is to "wallow." What this word "wallow" brings with it achieves nothing short of a declaration of war upon the imagery in which it is set. Its dominant connotations are unavoidably those of animal action, often under befouling conditions, and we are bound to feel at a loss about them so long as we try to keep Troilus the lover an uncomplicated creation. A Troilus simpler than truth's infancy who with orthodox poetic elevation is in the full cry of aspiration toward love's Elysium is not to be allowed suddenly and casually to image its enjoyment as a wallowing. We cannot make him ironist enough for that. Nor does it help to make him nothing more than a base sensualist who is suddenly revealed in his true nature by such imaging. The expression of something else in him is far too important poetically to be discarded. The idealistic Troilus does exist—dramatically because poetically—but he does not exist to speak that word "wallow." The Troilus who actually speaks the word also exists, just as surely. But he could not have being without the other. The fullness of truth is that Troilus is indeed to wallow, though at the same time he will take his idealism to bed with him and though in fact he can never lose it. The unsimple Troilus says bluntly to the simple that such is to be. Such is what can happen to man in a world where the aspiration of love is called upon often enough to undergo what the flesh devises as its contribution to the range of love's experience. The unsimple Troilus can be a mocking Troilus but he is a very knowing one, who is certainly not without earnestness.

In the soliloquy that follows we find the unsimple Troilus taking inspiration from the simple for a transformation of sensual wallowing into a sensual flight toward the infinite. This is mockery so much in earnest that it tends to join with earnestness mocked. The flight rises from an anticipation by the simple Troilus that would once more give his coming possession of Cressida a classic-poetic elevation. The "sweet" expectation "enchants" his sense as he wonders what effect the tasting of "Love's thrice-repured nectar" will have upon him. At that point the flight takes form. The unsimple Troilus seizes from his simple other self this contemplation of delectable sweetness and whirls it into a presentiment of a sweetness so extreme that it will take a form monstrous and terrible:

> Death, I fear me;
> Sounding destruction; or some joy too fine,
> Too subtile-potent, tun'd too sharp in sweetness
> For the capacity of my ruder powers.

> I fear it much; and I do fear besides
> That I shall lose distinction in my joys,
> As doth a battle when they charge on heaps
> The enemy flying.

(III. ii. 23-30)

These images draw love's sensation toward a point where separateness within being can no longer exist—where, as we might
say, parallel lines at last come together in infinity. For man's
"ruder powers," which make his love a slave to limit, this is a
refinement beyond bearing. Yet it starts in homely senses of the
flesh like the one that belongs to "the wat'ry palate." What
Shakespeare does here and elsewhere to make the Troilus of
infinite desire in love reach toward the abolition of distinctions
reminds one of lines in which John Donne has it that

> separation
> Falls not on such things as are infinite,
> Nor things which are but one, can disunite.

Donne comes to the wording of these lines by way of the image
of married love in which

> one glorious flame
> Meeting Another, growes the same,

and in which the two flames

> To an unseparable union growe.[4]

We have considered some basic imagery of infinite desire for
Troilus as lover. We have now to look at some of such imagery
for Troilus as warrior. With surety of touch Shakespeare unites in
Troilus a lover's vision with a warrior's, through a poetry of infinity at the center of the character creation, and yet gives differences to these visions that go deep.

Basic imagery for Troilus the warrior comparable to that just
considered for Troilus the lover is found in the Trojan debate on
whether the war should be ended by the giving up of Helen to
the Greeks. Here Troilus becomes a figure of honor, whatever he
is earlier in the play when, out of his absorption in love, he speaks
of the war as fought by "fools on both sides." His contribution to

the debate is a full poetic statement of a concept of honor developed from imagery of the infinite. Contrast is quickly apparent between this figure and the Troilus figure of love. This figure shows nothing of a tendency we have just found in Troilus the lover to play two parts, one simple and one unsimple. It reveals only a simple Troilus of the most utter consistency.

Priam starts the debate by asking Hector whether Helen should be surrendered, and Hector by his reply sets Troilus on his course. Hector concludes that Helen is "not ours nor worth to us" and asks:

> What merit's in that reason which denies
> The yielding of her up?
>
> (II. ii. 24-25)

Troilus rises at once beyond finite considerations and beyond reason:

>   Fie, fie, my brother!
> Weigh you the worth and honour of a king
> So great as our dread father in a scale
> Of common ounces? Will you with counters sum
> The past-proportion of his infinite?
> And buckle in a waist most fathomless
> With spans and inches so diminutive
> As fears and reasons? Fie, for godly shame!

Thus he comes to a vision of boundlessness for the will of honor to match his vision of boundlessness for the will of love. It is to be noted, both here and later on, that Troilus in what he says of honor never declares or assumes that the act is a slave to limit whereas the will is infinite. With love it must be thus. With honor, on the other hand, there is freedom of execution for the spirit that has infinite desire. In the debate Troilus sets out confidently to carry all before him. And he does carry all before him, so much so that he wins Hector over to his side and shapes Trojan policy in accordance with his conviction, after receiving some help from Paris that is not too free from involvement of personal interest.

But it is not only that there is no tension now between infinite will and finite act. Infinity itself for Troilus is now but simple measurelessness. There is nothing like a drawing of separatenesses toward conjunction in infinity, such as we have seen in the case of love. There is only a scheme of things where when honor does not guide there is base finite calculation according to "fears" and according to a justification of fears by "reason" but where when honor does guide there is infinite surety and a plain path to travel. The plain path is one of truth. In the way of honor, just as in the way of love, truth is for Troilus an archaic matter out of the feudal and chivalric age. It is loyalty, fidelity, constancy, steadfastness. It means keeping one's word to the death when one has solemnly promised adherence to a person or a cause. It means a reality that lies in the word one has given and not in the changing array of "facts" in one's surrounding world, which may appear, but according to Troilus can do no more than deceitfully appear, to make the given word of no validity.

It seems to be natural for some critics to condemn Troilus the warrior as though he were speaking only out of our own time and speaking most meaningfully to those in our own time who are antipathetic to the professional fighting man. It is revealing enough to put this Troilus now and then in modern dress, since some part of him looks forward to our age out of an earlier age. But he is not merely a modern "militarist" any more than Troilus the medieval and Renaissance courtly lover is merely a modern sensualist having trouble with a mistress who is susceptible to other men. His upholding of honor can today perhaps too easily be made to count against him rather than for him. Though on this score Hector can be thought "more culpable," Troilus can be joined with him in culpability for a "love of honour" that is an "obsession" and a "personal indulgence."[5] A love of honor looked upon as a personal indulgence would seem to be a love of fame. We owe it to Shakespeare to remember that love of honor in his hands can very plainly be love of a virtue for itself as well as love of fame for the practice of that virtue.[6] Troilus and Hector are not without a Renaissance love of honor as public esteem but they show also a love of honor as something more, which can be condemned as personal indulgence only at the risk of making all personal integrity into personal indulgence.[7] The ruling idea of honor is most certainly not an idea of fame in these lines of Troilus'

> Manhood and honour
> Should have hare hearts, would they but fat their thoughts
> With this cramm'd reason.
>
> (II. ii. 47-9)

Infinite will does make Troilus absolute for honor, at whatever cost not only to his own life but likewise to other lives. The extremes to which he goes in this way make it all the more notable that when he talks of honor he never plays the detached choric part to comment ironically upon himself. He never expresses a mock-rueful realization that in his pursuit of honor he with his "great truth" catches "mere simplicity." Of his being true in love he says to Cressida when she questions him about it:

> Who? I? Alas, it is my vice, my fault!
>
> (IV. iv. 104)

But when honor is his theme he never takes such liberty with his faith in the virtue of truth as to look at truth in two ways and make it a vice as well as a virtue. In the crucial Trojan debate his argument is that Priam's honor is the honor of Troy because Priam as king *is* Troy and is ultimately responsible for sending out the Trojan expedition that captured Helen. But there was a Trojan council before the departure of the expedition and this participated in the decision to send it. It gave "full consent." So all Troy made the choice solemnly. By such an election promises are made that in honor are unbreakable and effects are produced on human life and on human values that in honor are irreversible. Such an election is like marriage. In honor one does not divorce one's wife although the "will" come to "distaste what it elected." (In other words, odd as it may sound to anyone who thinks of the speaker as having an "affair" with Cressida, there is honor in faithful marriage of which faithful courtly love knows the peculiar virtue.) At this point in the debate Cassandra comes in to cry of destruction fated for Troy unless it lets Helen go. Of course she moves Troilus not at all. No fear of destruction, even fear of inevitable destruction, should "deject the courage" of honable Trojan minds.

When Hector makes his sudden about-face to take a stand on the side of Troilus and Paris because, as he declares, the "joint and several dignities" of the Trojans are after all a decisive consideration, it would seem that we are called upon not to condemn Hector for first seeing truth and then being false to it but rather to understand that he sees, and that we ourselves should see, validity in two truths, one out of a modernity of tough-minded reason (a late Renaissance modernity, if we like) and one out of a chivalric past. The idea of the first truth he develops himself. The idea of the second he allows Troilus to develop. It is well in accord with other unsimple things in *Troilus and Cressida* that he insists his own contribution to the debate has been offered "in way of truth" even as he turns to embrace the truth urged by Troilus. The warring truths of honor and reason undergo being brought together in Hector's recognition of both and become one complex truth of honesty (*honestas*) where integrity knows not only a loyalty to persons and causes that have been given pledges but also a loyalty to more general principles that can be clarified by intellect. The fact that Hector can choose but one of these loyalties as a guide to action thus becomes an expression of human limitation in putting truth into practice.

One of the most memorable of the unsimple things in the play is found near the end in Troilus' vision of a Cressida who is and is not Cressida. When we come upon this we know that we are once more observing the Troilus for whom infinity is not mere measurelessness. It is the Troilus who has to deal with truth in the way of love, not in the way of honor. He is finding that when love is drawn out by man to the farthest extent of his understanding it can produce opposites which become baffling oxymorons. But it is not the ruefully ironic or mocking Troilus that we now see. It is one filled with the agony of discovery that his foreboding about attainment with Cressida of "winnowed purity in love" was all too well founded. The oxymoron of Cressida's being "secretly open" with Diomed, which is presented to him as he stands hidden with Ulysses, makes him perceive a more essential oxymoron of lying truth:

> But if I tell how these two did coact,
> Shall I not lie in publishing a truth?
>   (v. ii. 118-19)

Troilus here is trying to conquer both time and disunity. In thought, by process of reason, he constructs an infinity which is a realm of timelessness as well as of oneness. In this realm of infinite truth Cressida cannot change from true to false any more than she can suffer division into Troilus' Cressida and Diomed's. But his reason wavers in the construction as it attempts to hold together as a single reality the Cressida infinitely desired by himself and the Cressida finitely won by Diomed. It is thus that he comes to exclaim:

> Bifold authority! where reason can revolt
> Without perdition, and loss assume all reason
> Without revolt: this is, and is not, Cressid!
>
> (v. ii. 144-6)

After coming to full realization of his powerlessness before a falsity in Cressida already accomplished he does not hesitate. When he tears up her letter and throws it to the wind he surrenders her and her untrue love completely to the eddying medium of time as to their proper element:

> Go, wind, to wind! there turn and change together.
>
> (v. iii. 110)

Thus in his pursuit of love Troilus as a figure of infinite desire suffers defeat. Aspiring toward truth in love he undergoes, with greater pain than he has ever foreboded, a slavery to limit. He finds as he explores love that it has doublenesses. In the finite world even the truest of infinite desire cannot make these doublenesses yield to what he calls "rule in unity itself." The least subtle of them comes from the fact that for love to be at all there must be two beings who remain separate no matter how far they go toward oneness.

Yet in his pursuit of honor Troilus as a figure of infinite desire does not suffer defeat at all. One who is inclined to make *Troilus and Cressida* into an unqualified tragedy may be given pause by a consideration of its last scene. This ending of the drama belongs to Troilus the warrior. In a sense it is no ending at all because it implies so much still to come, and its very inconclusiveness, its failure to bound the action, gives it all the more surely to a Troilus unconquered. The infinite aspiration of Troilus in honor, which Shakespeare has created as a poetic counterpart of his aspiration in love and which is just as much a shaper of his action, is here all that remains of moving force in Troilus. It is not weakened by working alone in him. It makes him "dare all imminence that gods and men/ Address their dangers in" as he looks off into the distance, in which there is to be honor sustained unfailingly in spite of what he recognizes as the "sure destructions" of Troy and himself.

This is the Troilus who sees infinity as mere measurelessness. He is a man who in his kind of infinite desire is able to prevail. Troilus the lover loses himself on his search for the winnowed purity of faith-keeping and one may even say that in a sense he dies if one wishes to have for him a tragedy in Elizabethan terms. But Troilus the warrior finds what the other misses. He comes to know by trial that the grasp of man the individual upon faith-keeping can be sure, however unsure the grasp upon it may be of the paired man and woman in love.

There is irony in the way this Troilus prevails and in the fact that it is he and not the other Troilus who prevails. In the light of reason the irony draws power from all that is said in the play about reason and anti-reason, for his prevailing is seen to be by anti-reason. The irony also draws power from a dramatic pattern within the play that Shakespeare found place for in other plays. In *Hamlet* there is irony in the fact that Hamlet himself, who is the greater spirit, is overthrown where Fortinbras, the plain man of war, prevails. About *Timon of Athens* one can say the same thing with Timon substituted for Hamlet and Alcibiades for Fortinbras. What we find in *Troilus and Cressida* is not, as in these plays, a hero who falls tragically while another man who is a lesser spirit rises to a place of leadership that the hero could not achieve. Yet we find the same irony essentially. In *Troilus and Cressida* the hero is both the greater figure and the lesser, all within himself. Troilus the lover, the greater Troilus because greater in human reach, falls tragically. Troilus the warrior (in accord with tradition in the line of Dares) rises to lead Troy in outfacing the "discomfort" of Hector's death. This Troilus who prevails is an estimable man within the framework of honor, as

294   SHAKESPEARE: MODERN ESSAYS IN CRITICISM

we are meant not to forget. But while the other Troilus speaks of having "mere simplicity" and is by no means so simple as he would be thought, this Troilus is simple in all truth.

NOTES

1. Harold Hobson, *The Sunday Times,* July 31, 1960.
2. Shakespeare quotations are from the text of G. L. Kittredge.
3. *Gothic Architecture and Scholasticism* (New York, 1957), p. 15.
4. "An Epithalamion, Or, mariage Song on the Lady Elizabeth and Count Palatine being married on St. Valentines day," *The Poems of John Donne,* ed. H. J. C. Grierson (Oxford, 1912), I, 128-9.
5. The words quoted are Alice Walker's in her edition of *Troilus and Cressida* (Cambridge, 1957), pp. xiii, xxviii.
6. See, for example, Curtis Brown Watson, *Shakespeare and the Renaissance Concept of Honor* (Princeton, New Jersey, 1960), pp. 206 ff.
7. Recent opinion which works against such condemnation is to be found in: William R. Bowden, "The Human Shakespeare and Troilus and Cressida," *Shakespeare Quarterly,* VIII (1957), 167-77; Richard C. Harrier, "Troilus Divided," *Studies in the English Renaissance Drama,* ed. Josephine W. Bennett, Oscar Cargill, and Vernon Hall, Jr. (1959), pp. 142-56; David Kaula, "Will and Reason in *Troilus and Cressida*," *Shakespeare Quarterly,* XII (1961), 271-83.

Arthur Sewell

TRAGEDY AND THE "KINGDOM OF ENDS"

THERE IS, I believe, a logical connexion—I will not say, development—discernible in the three great tragedies, in terms of which
Shakespeare is seen to treat this debate between that which is
temporal and that which is metaphysical, in three different
modes. One mode was to set side by side in the play, separate
from each other, secular society—as it is apprehended in the
comedies and, perhaps, the histories but seen now as "immoral"
—and a single human soul. This is done in *Othello*. A second
mode was to follow the single human soul into the darkness,
where reality and morality are cancelled, and where the soul
seeks but never finds identity in the dark recesses of his own
being. This is done in *Macbeth*. A final and supreme mode was
to see that world in which the hero seeks identity as wholly involved with the life of society, and to move for a moment towards the vision of a kind of identity which comes to men when
they are members of each other. This is done in *King Lear*.

In the opening scenes of *Othello* the sense of society is strongly
emphasized. Othello lives and loves in a society as particularized,
as concrete, as the society depicted in *The Merchant of Venice*.
It is much the same kind of society, too; its values and behaviours
are of the same sort, they belong to the same Venice. But they
are no longer seen *from within*, but from without, and hence
differently. They themselves come up now for judgement. It is
a society, indeed, which has also something in common with the
society of *Measure for Measure*. Natural man is similarly at odds
with social order, and there is a licence in men's conduct which

From *Character and Society in Shakespeare*, 1951, pp. 91-121.
Reprinted by permission of the Clarendon Press, Oxford.

social disapproval barely contains and privily condones. It is this sense of a particular and restricted society which gives to *Othello* a general quality different from that of *Macbeth* or *King Lear;* something not so grand, something less universal in its range. In *Othello* we are aware of a human community closely contained within its own meannesses, hypocrisies, and greeds. Part of the tragedy consists in the reduction of the large spirit of Othello to the petty dimensions of the society in which he moves.

Professor Wilson Knight has suggested that one of the notable things about this play is the separateness of the "worlds" in which the major characters live. And superficially, perhaps, it looks as though Iago's world is quite opaque to Desdemona's and Desdemona's to Othello's. But only superficially. Surely Desdemona and Iago belong to the same world, to the same Venice. Desdemona is not less truly Brabantio's daughter than Roderigo is Iago's dupe. I think she has been imagined as a citizen of that world. This does not mean that she must be full citizen as perhaps Iago is. It means, rather, that her world implies Iago's world and Iago's hers.

For there is little relation between Othello's valuation of fidelity and hers. She takes her valuation from that very same world in which Iago has turned cynic. His cynicism is the natural corollary of her innocence, and they belong to the same level of human being. Her innocence has, indeed, as little true spiritual value—it has a like charm—as Eve's before the Fall.

There is, however, a significant separateness of "worlds" in *Othello;* it is the separateness of Othello's world from that to which all the other characters equally belong. In an earlier section I pointed out the difference between Othello's world and Iago's. It must now be suggested that Iago's world is the world of Venice, to which all the Venetians were born and in which they were imagined. It is more than that. It is society as Shakespeare now presented it. The central recommendation of society, so conceived, is cynically summed up in Iago's "Put money in thy purse." It is a world in which soldiers compete for office and prestige. It is a world in which, as Emilia well knows, men will do each other's offices in the women's beds. It is a world in which lust flaunts its finery and is not abashed. It is a world, indeed, from which spirit has been drained, and all is measured by use and entertainment and position. It is a kingdom of means, not ends.

We do not judge this society by any standard to which any actual society might attain. We do not set against it an ideal society towards which an actual society might asymptotically move. In judging the society in this Venice, we make a judgement on the very nature of all society whatsoever. We see that this society is, in fact, representative of society in general; and that society in general sets up use against value, expediency against integrity, prestige against principle, behaviour against moral being. In *Othello*, two worlds are set in opposition: the world set in time and inhabited by the Venetians; the world of the spirit, in terms of which we apprehend Othello. For this reason, in the bulk of the play, these Venetians are seen by Shakespeare from the outside, they are seen as they behave; whereas Othello is seen from within, he is seen as he is.

Othello is, in one respect, an extremely simple play, for the conflict between "value" and "use" is set out in its most extreme terms. Othello, in his deepest spirit, knows very little of use; Iago nothing of value. Othello's thought and feeling at the beginning of the play are free from the pressures of temporal things; they have a purity and spontaneity which remind us of an early innocence. There is a sense, indeed, in which Othello is at first imagined as without original sin, and self-regarding impulses in him are not yet touched with guilt, but—so undivided is he from the world he makes for himself—these very impulses are transmuted and (to speak in Christian terms) of themselves turn God-ward. They are naturally innocent.

In *Othello*, indeed, is re-enacted the Fall of Man; and Othello himself has that superiority of spiritual being over Desdemona which Adam had over Eve. Iago is the Tempter, but in conspiracy with him is all Venice and all the Venetians. They very aptly make that world within which fallen man confined himself. Othello is brought by Iago—and, perhaps in another way, by Desdemona—to indulge himself, to surrender himself to self-regarding impulses which are all infected and diseased by the meaner expectations and vanities which society may breed in our flesh. He becomes subject to the very itches of the flesh, and jealousy degrades his love so that it becomes no more than lust. As to Adam, so to Othello, "Chaos is come again." Hoodwinked by Iago, he leaves the true domain of value and comes down, shedding all the bravery of his spirit, into Iago's world, where value is unknown; into Desdemona's world, where (except through him as by Eve through Adam) value has never yet been known.

Chaos comes indeed to Othello. But what comes after? What vision does "character" fulfil at the end of the play?

Perhaps the first observation we must make, in answering this question, is that in the closing scene Othello becomes very much aware of his audience. Even if it is wrong to accuse him of "cheering himself up," it is at least true that he appears to be "setting himself right"; and in the process of "setting himself right" he seems to lose something of the distinction he once had and the authority he once exercised amongst the Venetians. Iago's work, in a measure, has been successful, and Othello has lost both innocence and grace. He seeks to restore the proper love of himself by recalling what he has been in the past; and to do this is to come down to the level of the Venetians. And, of course, he fails.

But perhaps that is the wrong way to speak of the matter. After Othello has discovered his fatal error—and perhaps even before—there is a change in the mode in which his character is presented. Shakespeare seems no longer to "dart himself forth." He seems, indeed, to have ceased altogether that kind of charac- ter-creation of which I have spoken earlier in this essay—when, in language, a human soul seeks identity in his encounter with the universe. Othello now seeks no such identity. Shakespeare pre- sents him; and Othello no longer seems to be fashioning his identity and settling his vision from moment to moment in words. He is as he is presented. The settlement he is making now is with society, not with the universe. The provenance of the images and their reinforcement are now to be found in social and secular experiences and assessments. Rhetoric now persuades, and no longer reveals. Vision is of a different kind and employs another mode, a more oblique mode, of character-presentation. Shakespeare, we may say, is now outside Othello's spirit and the presentation is now third-personal. He shows forth Othello to the audience in a certain light. And this light is secular light, plain social daylight. Othello is fallen man, indeed, but Shakespeare—all metaphysical consideration now put aside—exhibits him, even excuses him, to the social judgement—as though he would say: He has done the state some service, and that is something. He has shown valour in war, and, but for being tried intolerably, he has shown loyalty in love. Some pre-eminence amongst men he must be judged to have had—pre-eminence amongst men.

It was, I have said, Iago's filthy function to bring Othello down to the level of the Venetians. So well does he succeed that at the end of the play it is the social judgement that comes into its own again. Society, we may suppose, is not absolutely represented in Iago. Valour and devoted love are values which society must respect, if it would continue itself. But something has vanished like a dream—the glory and the grandeur of the universe to which we had once thought that Othello had belonged. The tale of fallen man is complete, and, for my part, I find here as yet no hint of regeneration or redemption.

Not one of the central images in *Macbeth* is regulative; not one steadies us for life in society. And this can be said of no other of Shakespeare's plays. In *Othello* we are continually reminded in Cassio, in Iago, even in Othello himself by image and idea of a world of social obligation and expectation. In *King Lear* order in society is apprehended with the same actuality as the threat of chaos, whether in society or the individual. It is true that in *Othello* the accepted, the external, world is hard and harsh with cynicism and the test of use, but we never lose the sense of the actuality of that world. And in *Lear* the animal imagery is balanced and criticized by the images of clothes. Bestial individualism is set against the needs and imperatives of life in civilized society. But in *Macbeth* we are never so steadied by inescapable reminders from the actual world, and we lose the sense of that ethical and political order which is expressed in social institutions.

It was inevitable, then, that at least one of the central images should be the image of blood, for blood is the symbol both of life and death, the principle of energy within. It has deep significance in sacrifice and sacrament. The pulse of the blood sets

the rhythm of our beings, and its movement records and expresses every chance and change of the spirit. Both joy and horror
affect it; and the dry skin or the parched lips are only secondary
appearances of these affections of the blood. There could be no
other image which so strikingly marked that moment in the development of Shakespeare's vision in which, with all its implications, he saw and imagined the workings of the human spirit
absolutely from within.

The image recurs time and again in *Macbeth*. Duncan's first
words are:

> What bloody man is that?

Lady Macbeth calls upon the spirits "that tend our mortal
thoughts":

> Make thick my blood.

She bids her husband

> smear
> The sleepy grooms with blood.

But Macbeth looks at his hangman's hands and cries out:

> Will all great Neptune's ocean wash the blood
> Clean from my hand?

Lennox cries of the murdered grooms:

> Their hands and faces were all badged with blood,

and of Duncan it is said:

> His silver skin lac'd with his golden blood.

During the banquet scene Macbeth speaks much of blood:

> Blood hath been shed ere now.
> It will have blood; they say, blood will have blood.
> 　　　　　　　I am in blood
> Stepp'd in so far that, should I wade no more,
> Returning were as tedious as go o'er.

And, towards the end, Lady Macbeth walks in her sleep, making as though she would wash her hands;

> Yet who would have thought the old man to have had so much blood in him?
> Here's the smell of blood still.

With the evocation of these images the social sense has nothing to do.

Similarly there are many images of night and sleep. These again are not regulative or descriptive; they evoke in us the very act of annihilating real and solid things, of making blurred the outlines of objects, of mantling the surfaces with darkness. Lady Macbeth calls on night in her opening soliloquy:

> Come, thick night,
> And pall me in the dunnest smoke of hell,
> That my keen knife see not the wound it makes,
> Nor heaven peep through the blanket of the dark,
> To cry, "Hold, hold."

At night reality loses its noted order;

> The night has been unruly; where we lay,
> Our chimneys were blown down.
> . . . the obscure bird
> Clamour'd the livelong night.

The murder of Duncan is done near midnight. Throughout the third act of the play we expect the night.

> Come, seeling night,
> Scarf up the tender eye of pitiful day;
> And with thy bloody and invisible hand
> Cancel and tear to pieces that great bond
> Which keeps me pale! Light thickens; and the crow
> Makes wing to the rooky wood;
> Good things of day begin to droop and drowse
> While night's black agents to their preys do rouse.

Before night comes, but with night in the air, Banquo is murdered;

> The west yet glimmers with some streaks of day.

And something of the common experience of nightfall is reported in the words of the first murderer:

> Now spurs the lated traveller apace
> To gain the timely inn.

When the guests have left the banquet-hall, Macbeth asks:

> What is the night?

And Lady Macbeth tells him:

> Almost at odds with morning, which is which.

The witches belong to the night; they are "secret, black and midnight hags." And it is at night, fearfully, that Lady Macbeth walks in her sleep.

I find it difficult to set down the significance of the images of sleep. In sleep the spirit returns to its elemental resting-place and in a natural rhythm the energies are given pause. In sleep, too, reality is suspended and its demands on us are for the time being quiet. But there may be, too, a sleep which is no sleep but a waking, when the spirit is troubled, and wayward impulses find speech and chance expression. Sleep of this kind is a twilight kingdom, in which we dwell with things half-real. The images of sleep, then, in *Macbeth*, have not a simple but a complex significance. They are an expression of the half-wish to cancel reality; they show within the very anarchy of energy a nostalgia for rest. They represent that ultimate abrogation of the external world in which either the untroubled heart is at rest or else the troubled spirit stirs and mutters and is afraid.

For Macbeth there is to be no more the sweetness of sleep;

> Methought I heard a voice cry, "Sleep no more!
> Macbeth doth murder sleep!"

And this sleep is "innocent," it is a

> Sleep that knits up the ravell'd sleave of care,
> The death of each day's life, sore labour's bath,
> Balm of hurt minds, great nature's second course,
> Chief nourisher in life's feast.

Duncan knows such a sleep in death;

> Wake Duncan with thy knocking! I would thou couldst.
>> Duncan is in his grave:
> After life's fitful fever he sleeps well.

At the end of the banquet scene Lady Macbeth says to her husband:

> You lack the season of all natures, sleep.

And Macbeth replies:

> Come, we'll to sleep.

We remember all this of sleep when Macbeth asks of the doctor,

> Canst thou not minister to a mind diseased,
> Pluck from the memory a rooted sorrow,
> Raze out the written troubles of the brain,
> And with some sweet oblivious antidote
> Cleanse the stuff'd bosom of that perilous stuff
> Which weighs upon the heart?

Terror and unrest come, too, with these images of sleep, as though in sleep this perilous stuff may have at its mercy the deeps of the spirit and all the mind. Banquo first mentions this helplessness in sleep, when he says:

> And yet I would not sleep; merciful powers,
> Restrain in me the cursed thoughts that nature
> Gives way to in repose!

The grooms must have been disturbed by dreams, when one laughed in his sleep and one cried "Murder!" After the murder, Macbeth will risk anything rather than

> sleep
> In the affliction of these terrible dreams
> That shake us nightly.

Lady Macbeth in "a most fast sleep" rises from her bed, throws her nightgown upon her, takes forth paper, writes upon it, reads it, afterwards seals it, and again returns to bed.

Nothing in the play is what it seems; nothing belongs to its own "law of kinde." In *Macbeth*, "fair is foul and foul is fair"; pleasantly-sited castles are the settings for dreadful murder;

> by the clock, 'tis day,
> And yet dark night strangles the travelling lamp;

a man may be not of woman born; and Birnam Wood can come to Dunsinane.

This leads me to mention the emphasis laid in the play on phantasmal experience, on illusion, on half-appearance. The energy of inner imagining seems very often to be too much for solid reality; and the world of Macbeth becomes a world of shadows, of visitations from a space other than this. The eye conjures beings out of the very air; and things real dissolve into unreality. Neither the eye nor the ear can be wholly believed and all assurance is lost.

Banquo asks of the witches:

> I' the name of truth,
> Are ye fantastical, or that indeed
> Which outwardly ye show?

And when they have vanished he says:

> The earth hath bubbles, as the water has,
> And these are of them. Whither are they vanished?

Macbeth gives him his answer:

> Into the air; and what seemed corporeal melted
> As breath into the wind.

Certainly the dagger which Macbeth sees before he goes in to murder Duncan is "fantastical." When he would clutch it, he clutches empty air. He has it and he has it not. It is "a dagger of the mind, a false creation," and yet it is in form as "palpable" as that which now he draws. In the "dagger" soliloquy, the images of sleep and the images of dreams are joined with fantastical imaginings—and with night:

> Now o'er the one half world
> Nature seems dead, and wicked dreams abuse

The curtained sleep; witchcraft celebrates
Pale Hecate's offerings, and withered murder,
Alarum'd by his sentinel, the wolf,
Whose howl's his watch, thus with his stealthy pace,
With Tarquin's ravishing strides, towards his design,
Moves like a ghost.

What has all this to do with character? In the first place, we
can surely say that what goes on in Macbeth's mind when he
fears that he will sleep no more, when he knows that "blood will
have blood," when Nature in half the world seems dead to him,
is just as revealing, though differently, as the practical question
which he puts to himself: Shall I kill a king? We can say more:
we can say that killing a king would be a small and merely public matter, were it not that to kill a king involves Macbeth in less
palpable encounters, which find their mimesis in the poetry. To
kill a king was the first act—and what followed may be thought
of as a catalogue of crimes, but, more truly, is apprehended as an
ever closer encounter with darkness.

Early in the play Macbeth is in some doubt: he hesitates on
the very brink of action. The theme of his soliloquy, "If it were
done, &c.," is the theme of "judgement here," something that
has to do not with moral conscience, but with the fear of consequences. This fear has puzzled a large number of critics in the
past, and if we inquire, What is it Macbeth really fears? we shall
be hard put to it to find an answer. One would not suppose that
he fears physical punishment. By his own hypothesis he does not
fear death. What then? The answer is that he fears nothing in
particular. He fears that unknown chain of consequences which
(once we think of them) may make us tremble before any act
whatsoever. The fear phrases itself but does not define itself for
Macbeth as a judgement, as the return of the poisoned chalice to
his own lips. But the fear is, in fact, something fundamental and
more deeply rooted in the general condition of man; it is the
fear, or the distrust, or the moral uncertainty, which attaches
itself to any act whatsoever. It is precisely the same fear which
prevented Hamlet from killing the king. It is the Either/Or of
our human being.

But in *Macbeth* the matter is a little different. The play is not a play about doubt or indecision; it is a play about those ineluctable processes which follow decision. It is not irrelevant to point out here that Shakespeare deliberately distorted the historical facts. The historical Macbeth reigned well, as far as we know, for ten years after the murder. Our Macbeth is from the moment of the act an exile from the daylight. We can be sure, then, that Shakespeare, as by way of supreme experiment, takes as the hypothesis of his play an extreme case of a man's delivery of himself, through action, to darkness, to chaos. Macbeth, as a tragic hero, is a man with a capacity, one might almost say a taste, for damnation. This capacity, as Mr. Eliot once pointed out, is not so very different from a capacity for salvation. *Macbeth* is a terrible play because its business is to give us some notion of what that damnation is which a man embraces when he is, indeed, man enough for it.

Whereas in *Othello* we witness the Fall of Man, in *Macbeth* we have a study (not, as Mr. Stewart would have us suppose, of a man) of Fallen Man; Man, who, because he is fallen, cannot reject the discipline of daylight without involving himself in utter darkness. And how vision reveals itself in *Macbeth* may be conveniently illustrated from the two main soliloquies in the play, one at the beginning, the other at the end. In the soliloquy just mentioned, when Macbeth hesitates before the act, order (the order of civil institutions and decent hospitalities) is still actual for him. He remembers that Duncan is his king, his kinsman, and his guest. In the same speech he remembers "virtue" and "angels" and "heaven's cherubin"; and although I do not think these argue a Christian "philosophy" in the play, they do at least indicate that Macbeth is not yet committed to the darkness. Something still tells him that "institutions are necessary," and, although he does not say so, necessary perhaps to salvation. Towards the end of the play—the hypothesis has worked itself out—all sense of actuality and order is lost. Life has become "a tale told by an idiot, full of sound and fury, signifying nothing."

But vision does not rest there, for while Shakespeare may not here affirm Divine Order, he certainly could not accept a godless existentialism. This is as far as vision, discovering itself in and through Macbeth, could go; but now it changes its mode, as it does at the end of *Othello*. In these last moments Macbeth, not perhaps for himself but for us, is brought back to the daylight world. Social order, daylight order, reasserts itself. He himself admits that the juggling fiends have paltered with him in a double sense, and, as he confesses this, he opens his eyes to the world and to his audience. He becomes a man once again behaving in the presence of men, and that is how Shakespeare represents him. One social virtue he can still exhibit, not redeeming him, but giving him distinction and pre-eminence—the virtue of courage, however desperately called upon. His vision no longer matters, except in so far as we judge it and find it wanting. But his courage matters, for men should be brave. And yet, in a sense, it is wrong to say that his vision no longer matters: for through it we have been brought to the edge of nothingness and dissolution. And it is as men who have been so near that edge that we hear at last the mention of "measure, time, and place."

King Lear is the play in which Shakespeare returns once again to see man as a human soul, not in opposition to society, not rejecting society, but finding in society the sphere of fulfilment. Order is now seen, for the first time, and perhaps imperfectly, "not merely negative, but creative and liberating." It is a vision of society very different from that discovered in *Othello*. In *Othello* we cannot suppose that society is ever moral or good. Othello and Iago die, but future Othellos will find themselves betrayed in Venice, and future Iagos will still prey upon its profligates. In *King Lear* the conflict is no longer apprehended as a conflict between the individual and society; the conflict is now within society itself. Disorder in the human soul is both the agent and the product of disorder in society. Social order is the condition, as it is the resultant, of sweet and affirmative being, without which man relapses into a beastly and self-destructive individualism.

The play gives an impression of towns and villages and castles, on which the barren moor and the wild marshland are ever ready to encroach. Outside the walls lies the realm of brutishness, of animals and roots, of standing pools and naked madmen. Certain of the characters become exiles from comfort, from decent living, from politeness. Lear, in the wind and the rain and the thunder, and in the hovel, is such an exile. So is Edgar, in the rags of Tom o'Bedlam. So are the fool and, afterwards, the blind Gloucester. The beastly life is very close, near neighbour to civilized man; and man has not much to do to resume the life of the beast.

He has only to cast off his clothes—for in this symbolism Shakespeare dramatically anticipates Carylye. Clothes alone divide men from the animals:

> Is man no more than this? Consider him well. Thou owest the worm no silk, the beast no hide, the sheep no wool, the cat no perfume. Ha! here's three on's are sophisticated! Thou art the thing itself: unaccommodated man is no more but such a poor, bare, forked animal as thou art: Off, off, you lendings! Come, unbutton here.

And when Lear flings off his clothes we may remember his words to Regan earlier in the play:

> O, reason not the need: our basest beggars
> Are in the poorest thing superfluous:
> Allow not nature more than nature needs,
> Man's life is cheap as beast's: thou art a lady;
> If only to go warm were gorgeous,
> Why, nature needs not what thou gorgeous wear'st,
> Which scarcely keeps thee warm.

Brutish nature is made actual for us in the frequent mention of animals, especially those who prey upon each other. And disorder in humanity is symbolized in rank and wayward weeds which seem ever to encroach on the cultivated field.

The imagery of clothes—and many other things in the play—reinforce the notion that in society "institutions are necessary"; and character in the play is certainly conceived in terms of social rank and function, as well as in terms of the family. We expect trouble, indeed, when at the beginning of the play we learn that Lear intends to continue rank without function, has subscribed his power, and confined it merely to "exhibition," and would manage those "authorities" which he has given away. The bastardy of Edmund ("there was good sport at his making") has such results that we see a "fault," where a woman has "a son for her cradle ere she [has] a husband for her bed." Ironically enough, it is an insistence on the rightness and reasonableness of institutions which gives some point to the sisters' complaint that Lear's hundred retainers are intolerably more than "nature" needs. There is nothing in the play to cast suspicion upon the rightness of external order—there is much in the play to make us feel that without it we are lost, to affirm that not discipline, but indiscipline destroys. But there is also much to support the view that even discipline will destroy where it is not involved in self-discipline and in love.

King Lear—this is a large claim to make—is the only one of Shakespeare's plays in which personal relationship is treated as an end and not as a means; the only play in which personal relationships seem to determine character rather than to have an effect upon character. It is not merely that, say, in *Hamlet* the relationships between Hamlet and his mother and Hamlet and Ophelia are subsidiary in the major vision of the play; it is rather that what these characters are, and especially Hamlet, in his personal relationships, is important and enriches the vision, but the relationship in itself plays no necessary part in that vision and is incidental to it.* We may think that Ophelia's kind of love is a betrayal and that Hamlet's spirit is the more embittered: but what concerns us is not that Hamlet should have loved Ophelia but that by love he should be so embittered. In *King Lear*, however, all the characters are conceived—and this is central to the vision—in their relationships with other people, in their relationships with each other, and society is a vital complex of such relationships. In *King Lear*, then, not only is individual character differently conceived, but also living society itself.

The question is one of priority, not psychological but imaginative. In *Hamlet* (to continue the example) the nature of personal relationship is dependent on the nature of the characters: in *King Lear*, in a large measure, the nature of the character is revealed in the personal relationship. In *Hamlet* relationship and character are separable: in *King Lear* they are wholly bound up with each other. So it is that in *King Lear* personal relationships are the field of character-fulfilment.

* Family relationships are not the same, of course, as personal relationships.

None other of Shakespeare's plays contains such moving and dramatic references to personal loyalty and love. This play opens with the grand and, perhaps, grotesque announcement of the major theme in Lear's demand that his daughters shall declare their love. I do not find this opening difficult to accept; it is a bold enlargement of that morbidity which can poison affection, when affection gives nothing and asks everything. Lear's need to be told is matched by the two elder daughters' readiness in the telling; and it is seen, not wholly but in part, for what it is, in Cordelia's inability to tell. There follow immediately many variations of the theme; for Burgundy personal relationship is a matter of use, whereas to the King of France it is a matter of value. Kent is loyal, Goneril and Regan whisper together because, for a while, their interests are in common. The King of France finds words for the theme, when he says:

> Love is not love
> When it is mingled with regards that stand
> Aloof from the entire point.

More subtly and more movingly, Cordelia's conduct quickens and illuminates the vision; for her love, which cannot speak, has some regards—she cannot help it—which stand "aloof from the *entire* point." She is to blame, although she can do no other, for keeping herself blameless.

There is no need to rehearse the way in which Shakespeare deepens and develops this vision in the creation of his characters in *King Lear*. One or two of the minor characters catch a vivid if momentary life from it. I think of the servant who bids Cornwall hold his hand:

> I have served you ever since I was a child,
> But better service have I never done you
> Than now to bid you hold.

Or of the old man who brings the blinded Gloucester to Edgar:

> O my good lord!
> I have been your tenant, and your father's tenant,
> These fourscore years.

Such a man sweetens and fortifies institutions with loyalty and service. Loyalty is found in Oswald, too—and in Kent. Lear himself—although this is too large a matter to do more than hint at—insists on his hundred followers, but comes to the moment when he bids the fool go first into the hovel; thinks of "poor naked wretches"; will make a little society of affection in prison with Cordelia; thanks a gentleman for undoing his button. And is not something darker suggested, related to this same vision, when the two sisters both desire Edmund?

> Yet Edmund was belov'd;
> The one the other poison'd for my sake
> And after slew herself.

The weeds, after all, spring from the same soil as the "sustaining corn."

Personal relationships, however, are conceived in two ways—in loyalty and consideration which are owed according merely to the "bond," and in that going out of oneself which makes of love and loyalty something more than is demanded by the bond. So, in the first Act, Lear does a terrible thing to Cordelia; he inhibits in her that love which has no need of a bond. So we apprehend that moral behaviours are inseparably bound up with each other, hers with his, for it is Lear who puts Cordelia in the position of relying merely on the bond. In similar fashion, Kent's honesty shows a loyalty something more than his commitment—and this honesty has in it a bluntness something more than the mere requirement of its occasion. There is, indeed, throughout the play a deep sense of the evil that must mix with goodness—and of the "reason" that may mix with evil; and Shakespeare makes it clear that the admixture of good with evil, of evil with "reason," is both proof and product of the fact that, morally, we are members of each other. There is, indeed, in *King Lear,* a kind of irony which is not, to any important extent, to be found in any other play: the irony which lies in the contradiction between the rightness of what is said and the wrongness of its being said by that particular character, or in that particular situation, or in that particular manner. Lear is old, and his age is full of changes, but his daughters should not say so. There is no reply—no reply but "Nothing"—to Lear's request that Cordelia should outdo her sisters in protestation of her love; but Cordelia should not make that reply. Kent should warn the king, but loyalty asks for more mannerly phrasing. The vision that is discovered in character in the early part of the play is that vision which sees, in all its complexities, the play in conduct of mere "reason" and "rightness," at odds with that other play of something more than "reason," something more than "rightness." So much is this the theme of the first Act that we may risk the judgement that this is what the play is about. Nature, we are to learn, needs more than reason gives.

Except for the King of France, the first Act shows all the other characters—this is the manner in which they were conceived—determining their conduct and their speech either by self-regarding "reason" or by a sense of "rightness" which has in it something of self-regard. At any rate, conduct in them is determined, in one way or another, according merely to the need or the letter, and, because of this, has in it an admixture of evil and necessary imperfection. Whether the regard for self be "proper" or "improper," at the beginning of the play the impulse in conduct is almost universally self-regarding, or has in it something self-regarding as a presiding element. Something in self, something inhibitory in the conduct of another combining with something in self, prevents a "going out" of the self. Even where the spirit is generous, it is forced to seek refuge in "reason," in the letter, and is thereby frustrated and impoverished. At the end of the play, however, conduct—again in one way or another—becomes something more than "reason" needs. There is, for example, a kind of generosity, a certain "going out" of the self, in Goneril, when she says, "I have been worth the whistle." There is, in this, release from the self, and much more than "reason" needs. So, too, in Edmund's "Yet Edmund was belov'd"; and it is significant that this is followed immediately by something very much like remorse for others. Edmund—and Goneril, too, for that matter—shows himself for a moment as man enough to be damned. When Lear thinks of the "poor naked wretches," there is a most subtle play on all these themes—for such compassion in him has been in the past more than reason has seemed to need and is now a "going out" of himself; and yet in this compassion there is a higher reason, which shows the heavens "more just."

Reason and compassion come together at last, when Kent says of the king:

> Vex not his ghost: O! let him pass; he hates him
> That would upon the rack of this rough world
> Stretch him out longer.

And, a little later:

> I have a journey, sir, shortly to go;
> My master calls me, I must not say no.

The movement of the play seems to be from conduct (and character) in which reason is governed by self-regard, to conduct (and character) in which reason is transformed by compassion. In an image, this compassion becomes a healing and medicinal balm. So the third servant says of Gloucester:

> I'll fetch some flax and whites of eggs
> To apply to his bleeding face.

And Cordelia of her father:

> O my dear father! Restoration hang
> Thy medicine on my lips, and let this kiss
> Repair those violent harms that my two sisters
> Have in thy reverence made!

That was one way of representing compassion.

"Institutions are necessary," but they are administered by men, and, necessary though they are, they are no guarantee against viciousness and evil. Lear, in his madness, has a terrible picture of what may lie beneath the façade of social and political institutions, and for a moment we have a vision of all society itself, in its forms and customs, rotten and hypocritical. It is a picture of society in which institutions are all false-seeming, and justice itself is so perverted that it lends itself as a disguise to those very ills on which it passes judgement. The image of clothes is still used by Shakespeare:

> Through tatter'd clothes small vices do appear;
> Robes and furred gowns hide all.

Here is society, as Lear in his madness sees it, without grace, without sweetness. The law conceals what it cannot prevent, and, by stealth, luxury goes to it, pell-mell. As we envisage such a society, we have a physical nausea, which makes us wish, like Lear, "an ounce of civet" to sweeten our imaginations. We have raised the stone and seen the maggots. Shakespeare never gave us a clearer clue—and there is another in that travesty of justice as Lear arraigns the joint-stools in the hovel—to the vision of the play from which the characters draw their identities.

But it is not a merely secular society in which these characters are conceived to have their being. Nor, on the other hand, do I think it can be said (even through allegory) to be a society understood in terms of Christian theology. Nevertheless, to put the matter quite simply, we certainly get the impression in the play that the characters are imagined not only as members of each other but also as members of a Nature which is active both within themselves and throughout the circumambient universe. Man is nowhere so certainly exhibited as a member of all organic creation and of the elemental powers. Man's membership of society is more than legal, is more than political, because it is subtended in a wider membership, in which plants and animals, the wind and the thunder, are also included. And is it too extravagant to suggest that this natural universe is, in the earlier part of the play, peopled not only by men but also by beings of a primitive pagan belief—by Hecate, by Apollo, by Jupiter, by "the gods"; and that the dominion of these beings is, in the action of the play, superseded? Is it, indeed, too extravagant to suggest that in the play we have a veritable change in dispensation? That, at any rate, is the impression given as the imagery changes and one store of images gives way to another. What the final dispensation is, however, it is difficult to determine, for Shakespeare seems not to specify it. The most we can say is that, like the promise of rain in Mr. T. S. Eliot's *The Waste Land,* there are moments and images towards the end of *King Lear* which give promise of grace and benediction.

It is hard, then, to understand how *King Lear* can ever have been taken to be "the most Senecan of all Shakespeare's tragedies." Even Mr. Eliot, while seeking to suggest that there is "much less and much more" than Senecan Stoicism in the play, agrees that "there is [in it] a tone of Senecan fatalism; *fatis agimur.*" I should have thought that of all Shakespeare's tragedies this statement is least true of *King Lear.* It cannot be argued, surely, that we are to take as true for the whole play Gloucester's statement:

> As flies to wanton boys, are we to the gods:
> They kill us for their sport.

The characters seem to me to be self-active and responsible, and even the idea that "ripeness is all" is scarcely resignation as Seneca might have understood it. What might be mistaken for resignation is, indeed, something very different, and not at all Senecan; I mean the humility which manifests itself unmistakably in Lear, in Edgar, in Albany, at the end of the play. Goneril's "I have been worth the whistle" and Edmund's "Yet Edmund was belov'd" have in them something of the element which Mr. Eliot has called "cheering oneself up"; but they are more than that. Moreover, these utterances come too late, in a moment too desperate, for them to be dismissed merely as the speech of Pride. Not Pride, indeed, but Humility, which is the "reverse" of the stoical attitude, is the most memorable principle at the end of the play; but we could never have known what this Humility was, had we not learned also something about Pride. True humility, moreover, goes hand in hand with compassion, and so it is in the closing scenes of *King Lear.* Does not the play look forward to Dostoievsky, rather than back to Seneca?

In general, the tragic hero is conceived as pursuing a settlement not only with secular society but also with his universe. Settlement with society is not enough; for he must also find for himself an identity which, while giving him mastery over his temporal problems, justifies that mastery with a more than temporal sanction. The nature of his settlement with his universe is determined in the pursuit of settlement itself. In this sense it is true to say that Shakespeare had no "philosophy." It is no prefabricated universe with which the hero seeks to find accommodation; it is no prefabricated universe which at his peril and cost he ignores. The Christian categories never preside over the vision, although, naturally enough, the vision is impregnated with Christian sentiment. Tragedy finds its origin not in a Christian idea of imperfection but in "Renaissance anarchism."

Only through grace, perhaps, if at all, can man find blessedness; and Shakespearian tragedy is tragedy simply because in it Fallen Man seeks to find rehabilitation in "infiniteness"—but without grace. The tragedy is in the failure, and perhaps the failure is general to the case of Man. The tragic character (and in this there is no Senecan "cheering oneself up") will not resign himself to confinement in the secular world; but he has no certitude of status in a world more absolute. We cannot judge the tragic character in terms of our temporal moralities; neither can we schematize those mysteries of redemption which might at last exempt him from such judgements. He believes that he belongs to this world and he believes that he does not. He would jump the life to come—and yet he dare not. He comes to know that "the readiness is all," but that same ripeness, which releases him from the importunities of this world, discovers for him no other. Shakespearian tragedy is the product of the change in men's minds— the Renaissance change—by which men came to feel themselves separate from God; by which, indeed, the idea of God receded from men's habitual certitudes and became no more and often less than an intellectual construction, a merely credible hypothesis, a Being remote and not certainly just or beneficent, perhaps the Enemy. In a world where anarchism was of recent development and men had not yet resigned themselves to a disabling opportunism man's perennial hunger for metaphysical being prompted Shakespeare to create supreme drama out of the question, How shall man find the intersection between that which is in time and that which is out of time? Or, to put the matter simply, and I do not think too simply, What shall we do to be saved?

Elmer Edgar Stoll

SOURCE AND MOTIVE IN
MACBETH AND *OTHELLO*

*The best tragedy—highest tragedy in short—is that of the
worthy encompassed by the inevitable.*

THOMAS HARDY

SHAKESPEARE, of course, has, like the Greeks—unlike the Bourbon
French—no *règles*, neither rule nor formula. But for all that, why
in *Othello* and *Macbeth*, two of the great tragedies that are not
histories and that apparently are not in any measure *rifacimenti*
of previous plays, does he, in the matter of motivation, deviate
so widely and so similarly from his source?

• • • •

What in *Macbeth* he has omitted and what substituted Sir Arthur
Quiller-Couch has made admirably clear, but has not considered
the reasons for this or the similarity of procedure in *Othello*. In
Holinshed's Chronicle there is the suggestion that, cut off by the
nomination of Malcolm as successor to the throne from his own
expectations, Macbeth had for his usurpation "a juste quarell so
to do (as he tooke the matter)." The crown was then not strictly
hereditary, and "by the old lawes of the realme, if he that should
succeed were not of able age to take the charge upon himselfe,
he that was next of blood should be admitted." [1] "Did Shakespeare use that one hint, enlarge that loophole?" asks Sir Arthur.
"He did not."

Instead of using a paltry chance to condone Macbeth's guilt, he seized on it and plunged it threefold deeper . . .

He made this man, a sworn soldier, murder Duncan, his liege-lord.

He made this man, a host, murder Duncan, a guest within his gates.

He made this man, strong and hale, murder Duncan, old, weak, asleep and defenceless.

He made this man commit murder for nothing but his own advancement.

He made this man murder Duncan, who had steadily advanced him hitherto, who had never been aught but trustful, and who (that no detail of reproach might be wanting) had that very night, as he retired, sent, in most kindly thought, the gift of a diamond to his hostess.

To sum up: instead of extenuating Macbeth's criminality, Shakespeare doubles and redoubles it. [*Shakespeare's Workmanship* (Holt, N. Y., 1930), pp. 19-20.]

And yet Macbeth is the protagonist, the hero, with whom as such, for the right tragic effect, there must, naturally, be some large measure of sympathy. So, having thus put him much farther beyond the reach of our sympathy than in the original, what does the dramatist then do but (indirectly) bring him back within it—in general, by the power of poetry, in particular, by the exhibition of the hero's bravery and virtue at the beginning, by emphasizing the influence of the supernatural presented, and of his wife's inordinate ambition distinctly mentioned, in the source.

There are additional devices which Sir Arthur dwells upon, such as the flattening of the other characters—that the hero and heroine may stand out in high relief, to absorb our interest and (presumably on the principle considered in the preceding chapter) our sympathy also; and such as the keeping of the murders, as the ancients do, in the background, off the stage. "There is some deep law in imaginative illusion," says Watts-Dunton,[2] "whereby the identification of the spectator's personality is with the active character in most dramatic actions rather than the passive." We share the emotions, the perturbations, of Macbeth and his Lady, as even of Clytemnestra and Phaedra, because they are the impassioned doers and speakers, constantly in the foreground; and it is with their ears that we hear the owl and the cricket, the voices in the castle and the knocking at the gate. And still more clearly than in the veiling of the horrors the method is that of the ancients. The central complication—the contrast—is that recommended by Aristotle,[3] the *good* man doing the dreadful deed, though not unwittingly, nor quite unwillingly either. As with the ancients, again, he is under the sway of fate; for the Weird Sisters and his Lady—"burning in unquenchable desire to beare the name of a queene" [4]—together amount to that.

This, of course, is not what we ordinarily call motivation, not psychology. For both—the narrative or external motivation and the internal—there was, positively and negatively, better provision in Holinshed—not only the "juste quarell (as he took the matter)" but also "the feeble and slouthfull administration of Duncane," [5] no treachery or violation of the laws of hospitality in the killing, and the just and efficient rule (for ten years) in the sequel.[6] *La carrière ouverte aux talents,* and Macbeth had the justification of Napoleon, of Cromwell. But not Shakespeare's Macbeth.

Nor is this what we call drama, either, as it is ordinarily practiced today. It is as in Aristotle,—situation first and motivation or psychology afterwards, if at all. The effect is emotional, with which psychology or even simple narrative coherence often considerably interferes. To Schiller's neglect of careful motivation, and in a day of psychology and philosophy both, Goethe even attributes his superiority on the stage.[7] Shakespeare sometimes neglects it because it can be counted upon as familiar; sometimes, as with Hamlet's feigning of lunacy and Lear's dividing of the kingdom, because, the motive in the old play not being a good one, it is better that it should be omitted or only hinted at; but in Macbeth the omission is for a positive purpose, and the contravention of psychological probability is so as well. Here, as generally in Shakespeare, *Coriolanus* being only a partial exception, character is not its own destiny, the action is not exclusively derived from it. For Shakespeare "a human being" is *not,* as in Galsworthy's words or as in his own and his fellows' practice, "the best plot there is." To his minor characters the words better apply. The hero's conduct, at the heart of the action, is often not in keeping with his essential nature but in contrast with it.

Manifestly, and, if not forthwith, certainly upon a moment's consideration, by all the motives prompting or circumstances attending the murder of Duncan that have been omitted, the big, sharply outlined, highly emotional contrast in the situation of a good man doing the deed of horror would be broken or obscured. If Macbeth had been thwarted or (to use Holinshed's word) "defrauded," as having, at this juncture, a better title to the throne than Malcolm, or had thought himself better fitted to rule; or, again, if Duncan had not borne his faculties so meek and been so clear in his great office, as in the tragedy but not the chronicle he is; why, then, Macbeth's conduct in killing him would have been more reasonable and more psychologically in keeping, to be sure, but less terrible, less truly tragic. Even if Duncan had been less affectionate and generous, less admiring and confiding, still the hero's conduct would have been less truly tragic! There is positive need of "the deep damnation of his taking off." For the tragedy is of the brave and honorable man suddenly and squarely—fatally, too—turned against the moral order. Sir Arthur compares him to Satan about to engage in the temptation: "Evil, be thou my good." Or "Fair is foul and foul is fair," as the Weird Sisters have it, which Macbeth on his first appearance echoes—

So foul and fair a day I have not seen.

And that situation, no question, is a contrast big and sharp enough.

Sir Arthur does not, indeed, pause to take notice how unpsychological the change here is. Others besides fallen archangels have so turned about, but evil they do not continue to call evil. Macbeth so does. He has scarcely a word of ambition beforehand, not a word of delight in the power when attained. As Mr. Firkins and even Mr. Bradley have noticed, it is the deterrents that he dwells upon, not the incentives; it is the spectral bloody dagger that he sees, not a glittering crown; it is "withered murder" that he follows to the chamber, not the call to sovereign sway and masterdom. In horror he commits the crime, even as he is to remember it. There is no satisfaction but only torment in the thought of it. The conscience in him, before and after, is that of a good man, not that of the man who can do such wickedness;

first the voice of God, then either that or else—"accuser of mankind"!—the devil's.[8] It is Macbeth himself that considers the "deep damnation," and neither before nor after does he deceive himself, as the good turning to wickedness necessarily do. But the contrast is kept clear and distinct; and the emotional effect —that the whole world has acknowledged.

If, on the other hand, Shakespeare had kept to history, to reality and psychology! If he had followed Holinshed—made more of Macbeth's grievances, dilated on Duncan's unfitness and his own fitness to rule, without bringing on his head the blood of an old man, asleep, his benefactor and guest! If he had dwelt on reasons for committing instead of not committing the crime! And if afterwards he had expressed the psychologically natural or appropriate opinions upon his own conduct, excusing or palliating it, perhaps even justifying it! If in short Macbeth (and his Lady, too, who invokes the powers of evil at the outset and is tormented by conscience at the end) had acted more like the human beings we know of; why, then we should have had decidedly less of contrast and excitement, of imaginative and emotional power generated and discharged, of poetry and drama.

2

The treatment of the material in *Othello,* probably an earlier play, is somewhat the same. In Cinthio there is no warrant for introducing the supernatural; but in Shakespeare's hands the villain takes the place of Fate—of the Weird Sisters and the Lady —and more completely than is usual in the tragedy of the Renaissance. He is a devil in the flesh, as Booth played him, as Coleridge and Lamb implied, and George Woodberry, J. J. Chapman, Lytton Strachey, John Palmer, not to mention others, have put it explicitly.[9] Iago himself practically acknowledges it in the soliloquies—"Hell and night," "Divinity of hell! when devils will the blackest sins put on"—and on that point apparently he and Othello at the end are agreed:

> If that thou beest a devil, I cannot kill thee—
> [*wounds* IAGO]
> I bleed, sir, but not kill'd.

Before that, to be sure, the Ancient is misapprehended by everybody; yet as Fate, as master of the show, he is holding nearly all the strings of the action in hand, and leading both heroine and hero to destruction. In the victim now, not the victimizer, is the great change; but from good to evil only under a complete delusion—"be thou my good" he neither says nor thinks, and the prince of villains himself has no need to say it. For again, as in *Macbeth*, the motives are dispensed with. The Ensign of the *novella* is deprived of the internal incentives to his wickedness, and the Moor relieved of the traits which might have provoked or somewhat warranted it.

As Professor Wolfgang Keller notices, the villainy is "better motived" in the source. That is, more plausibly, more realistically. Not a devil in the flesh, a "black angel," as Mr. Chapman calls him, Cinthio's Ensign is still of "the most depraved nature in the world" (*della più scelerata natura che mai fosse huomo del mondo*). But as such he has provocation enough. He is a rejected suitor, and really suspects the Captain (Shakespeare's Cassio) of being the favored one. Against both him and the lady he has a grudge; his love for her is turned to the "bitterest hate"; whereas in the tragedy his love for Desdemona and her intrigue with Cassio are, like Cassio's and Othello's with Emilia, pretexts and afterthoughts. There he has need of these. His genuine reason for resentment is against Othello, but only for promoting Cassio above him, and against Cassio (incidentally) for being promoted. In soliloquy, as always in drama, the truth will out. "I hate the Moor," he mutters,

> *And it is thought* abroad that 'twixt my sheets
> He has done my office.

And the next moment the pretext is made still plainer: "I know not if't be true, but I for mere suspicion in that kind will do as if for surety." [10]

So the Ensign is deprived of his motive as much as the Thane of Glamis—as much as Richard III of his, which was ambition, or as Goneril and Regan of theirs, which was envy,[11]—but without an external Fate to relieve him of the burden of his iniquity. He carries it indeed, like the Weird Sisters, lightly enough; and the Aristotelian contrast of the good man doing the deed of horror is presented in his victim, who, however, unlike Macbeth, is guilty only of a mistake in judgment—the *hamartia*—and is far from uttering Satan's cry. Othello never loses our sympathy, as Macbeth, despite the poignant presentation of his sufferings, cannot but in some measure do.

What is almost quite as important to the emotional effect—to the steep tragic contrast—as the apparently unmitigated wickedness of Iago, is, as in the Caledonian tragedy, the nature of the victim and the circumstances of the crime. As we have seen, Shakespeare's Moor has changed places with his wife in the villain's enmity. Love turned to hatred is too ambiguous and appealing a passion—it is that, moreover, into which the Moor himself is precipitated, and, as Strachey observes, the villain's must not be anything of a parallel. For the contrast, again, it must not be. Moreover, though Cinthio's Moor is given some noble and attractive traits, especially at the outset, Shakespeare's is both there and throughout on a far higher level of intelligence and feeling. He is not a stupid dupe or a vulgarly vindictive cuckold. He is not the man to call the informer in to do the killing, or the concealing of it afterwards. For his own safety, Shakespeare's, unlike Cinthio's Moor, shows no concern. Nor is there, for that matter, the slightest evidence in his conduct or his utterance, nor in the woman's either, of the love Iago suspects between him and Emilia—no more than there is in Iago's own conduct or utterance, indeed, of his own love for Desdemona—though of late there has been a fairly prominent critic to say there is.[12] That would be like thinking, with some Germans, that Hamlet had betrayed Ophelia, for which, to be sure, there is a little evidence, though far from enough; or with some Frenchmen, that Lady Macbeth, as, reenacting in memory the deed of blood, she whispers, "to bed, to bed! there's knocking at the gate . . . to bed, to bed, to bed," she, having enticed her husband, is now for rewarding him. On the contrary, the black man is made the grandest and noblest of Shakespeare's lovers; and it is only through Iago's overwhelming reputation for honesty and sagacity, the impenetrableness of his mask together with the potency of his seductive arts, that he is led astray and succumbs. For the highest tragic effect it is the great and good man that succumbs. Like other supreme artists, Shakespeare has here created his own world, which holds together. Like Corneille (*les grands sujets de la tragédie doivent toujours aller au delà du vraisemblable*) Goethe holds that *in den höheren Regionen des künstlerischen Verfahrens, hat der Künstler ein freieres Spiel, und er darf sogar zu Fiktionen schreiten.*[13] This Shakespeare boldly does. No one else sees through Iago, including his own wife; so Othello, for not seeing, is no gull or dupe. In the matter of the Ancient's cleverness in maneuver and also of his success in hypocrisy the English is a little indebted to the Italian writer; but the Ensign's wife does see through him and only for fear of him holds her tongue.

3

In both *Macbeth* and *Othello*, then, it is the whole situation that is mainly important, not the character; it is the reciprocal matter of motivation (whether present or missing), of defects or qualities in both victim and victimizer together. Here lies the chief point of the present discussion. What if Shakespeare's Macbeth and Duncan had been like Holinshed's, or like Henry IV and Richard II, or like Cromwell and Charles I? And as I have elsewhere said, "How the scope and stature of Iago's wickedness (and of Othello's virtue) would be limited by any adequate grudge!" [14] How they would be also by a credulous or suspicious nature—a predisposition or a psychology—in the hero! Against that Shakespeare has guarded not only by Iago's impregnable reputation and by his all-prevailing arts but also by Othello's own reputation for capability and for virtue. (A world of reputation and circumstance here, not of motive!) Before the temptation begins, as in *Macbeth*, but much more fully and felicitously, the Moor has not only in his own right but through the admiration of everybody (and here even of the villain been firmly established in our good opinion and our sympathies. So with Desdemona, too, and she is not deceitful or supersubtle as Mr. Shaw would have her, not enough so "to strengthen the case for Othello's jealousy"; the dramatic preparations are emotional, not analytical and psychological, primarily for the situation, not the character. And both women, Emilia at the last and Desdemona once the action is well started, are shocked at the discoveries they make in their husbands. But she is justified, when hers gives signs of jealousy, in being unable to believe it; "not easily jealous" he himself says (where a Shakespearean hero, or his best friend, is expected to know and everything comes to light) at the end. Even Iago, hearing that Othello is angry, exclaims,

> and is he angry?
> Something of moment, then. I will go meet him.
> There's matter in't indeed, if he be angry.

And in the fourth act, when the jealous rage is fully upon him, Lodovico, newly come from Venice, is moved to wonder and to grief.

> Is this the nature
> Whom passion could not shake? whose solid virtue
> The shot of accident nor dart of chance
> Could neither graze nor pierce?

"He is much chang'd," Iago coolly, and still not superfluously, replies. So he is, until, in the last scene, by Emilia's disclosures and Iago's self-betraying resentment, he recovers something of his old stately and generous self.

Macbeth too is changed, but for once and all. Othello had suffered from an overpowering delusion, and has just now, he thinks, performed an act of justice. Macbeth, not deluded, has come under the dominion of evil, his "eternal jewel given to the common enemy of man." Neither change is probable. In neither is there much of what can be called psychology. In life neither person would really have done what he did. In both tragedy and comedy, however, that is not exactly what is to be expected: for a Henry IV, a Cromwell, we should turn to history, not the stage. What is expected is what from life we do not get—enlargement, excitement, another world, not a copy of this. And that airy edifice, an imaginative structure, is the emotionally consistent story or situation as a whole,—the conduct of characters both active and passive, perhaps also a motiving both external and internal, but in any case an interplay of relations or circumstances as important as the motives themselves; not to mention the apportionment of emphasis or relief whether in the framework or the expression, the poetry that informs both, and the individuality of the speech, which, real, though poetical, leads one to accept and delight in the improbable things said or done. "It is when their minds (those of the audience) are preoccupied with his personality," says Dr. Bridges of Macbeth, "that the actions follow as unquestionable realities." [15] Not merely, that is, when the actions proceed from the character; and the convincing quality of the speech is only a participating element in the consistent overpowering imaginative and emotional effect of the whole.

4

"In tragedy and comedy both," I have said elsewhere, "life must be, as it has ever been, piled on life, or we have visited the theater in vain." It is not primarily to present characters in their convincing reality that Shakespeare and the Greeks have written, nor in an action strictly and wholly of their doing, but to set them in a state of high commotion, and thus to move and elevate the audience in turn. And here I fall back upon the authority of Mr. Santayana, a philosopher (but also a poet and critic) who, without my knowledge until of late,[16] expressed, though from a different point of view, similar opinions before me:

> Aristotle was justified in making the plot the chief element in fiction; for it is by virtue of the plot that the characters live, or, rather, that we live in them, and by virtue of the plot accordingly that our soul rises to the imaginative activity by which we tend at once to escape from the personal life and to realise its ideal. . . .

And as the eminent critic proceeds, he maintains that poetry is not

> at its best when it depicts a further possible experience, but when it initiates us, by feigning something which as an experience is impossible, into the meaning of the experience which we have actually had.

And that is partly because "in the theater," as the producer Mr. Robert Edmond Jones has assured us, "the actual thing is never the exciting thing. Unless life is turned into art on the stage it stops being alive and goes dead." [17] It is by the excitement that the meaning is brought home to us. And that is true, as in the next chapter we shall see, even without a stage or without poetry, as in Dickens, who, according to Chesterton, "could only make his characters probable if he was allowed to make them impossible."

NOTES

1. *Boswell-Stone's Holinshed* (1896), p. 25. Sir Arthur's quotation, preceding, is curtailed: "for that Duncane did what in him lay to defraud him of all maner of title and claime, which he might, in time to come, pretend unto the crowne."

2. *Harper's* (November, 1906), p. 818. Touched on in the preceding chapter and in note 10 there.

3. *Poetics, cap.* 13, 14.

4. *Boswell-Stone's Holinshed* (1896), p. 25.

5. Ibid., p. 32. Cf. p. 20: "At length, Macbeth speaking much against the kings softnes and overmuch slacknesse in punishing offenders. . . ."

6. Ibid., p. 32: "he set his whole intention to maintaine justice and to punish all enormities and abuses which had chanced," etc.; "made manie holesome laws and statutes for the publike weale."

7. Eckermann (Castle), 1, 400.

8. Cf. below, chap. xvi.

9. For their opinions see my *Shakespeare and Other Masters*, pp. 233, 238, 243-4.

10. Cf. *Shakespeare and Other Masters*, pp. 236-8, for the way that his suspicions become convictions.

11. In the old *King Leir*, envy of Cordelia's beauty, cf. E. E. Kellett, *Suggestions* (1923), p. 38. For Richard, cf. Brandl, *Shakespeare* (1937), p. 120.

12. It is of course not enough to urge the probabilities upon us —that a healthy and vigorous soldier of the time would lead "a *man's* life," and that Emilia was none too good for taking up with him. As I have repeatedly reminded my readers, no character in fiction has a private life, beyond the reach of the writer, which a character in a biography or history, on the other hand, has, not being the writer's own creation. And in Shakespearean drama, as in the ancient or the classical French, none has the

"past" or the "love life" that is more readily expected, and so more easily suggested, today. Cf. chap. VIII, above.

13. Eckermann, April 18, 1827.—I hope Corneille here does not go beyond the endurable.

14. *Shakespeare and Other Masters*, p. 245.

15. *The Influence of the Audience on Shakespeare's Drama.*

16. *Poetry and Religion* (1900). Cf. my *Shakespeare and Other Masters*, p. 369. The passage here quoted is as in the *Works* (Scribner, N. Y., 1936) ii.

17. *The Dramatic Imagination* (1941), p. 82 (quoted by W. W. Lawrence, *Modern Language Review*, October 1942, p. 424).

Robert B. Heilman

WIT AND WITCHCRAFT:
AN APPROACH TO *OTHELLO*

THE CRITIC who proposes a reading of *Othello* may hope for it
that it will appear at least to illuminate some of the parts and at
most to contribute to the understanding of the sum of the parts.
If *Othello* is not the most complex of the tragedies, the problem
of its over-all form is still a large one, and he who aspires to a
full account of the creative relationship of all the parts [1] must
be content if he seems generally to be moving in the right direction. The theory of the whole that proceeds from an examination
of the parts will at best be a distant cousin of the drama; such
wit as the critic may have can but follow the witchcraft of the
dramatist (to take Iago's words out of context) from afar. But
the cousin may help identify the drama, the wit tell how the
witchcraft has gone. At the same time the critic, whatever he
imparts, must at many points duplicate and parallel his predecessors while essaying to be himself; so he runs the double risk of
not encompassing the novelty which will absolve him of the suspicion of merely repeating what oft was thought, or of falling
into innovations which in other quarters will seem dubious because such things were never thought.

The parts which make up the whole are numerous and diverse.

From *The Sewanee Review*, LXIV, 1 (Winter 1956), 1-4, 8-10,
copyright 1956 by the University of the South; and *Arizona Quarterly*
(Spring 1956), pp. 5-16. Reprinted by permission of the author and
the editors, with new transitional material supplied by the author.
The ideas in this essay are among those developed by Mr. Heilman in
Magic in the Web: Action and Language in Othello, copyright 1956 by
the University of Kentucky Press; used by permission.

Othello is a part. Iago is a part. Iago's deception of Roderigo is a part. Iago's remarks on reputation, Desdemona's incredulity at the sexual misbehavior of wives, Emilia's revulsion against Iago, Cassio's drunken babbling are parts. All recognitions and reversals, all thoughts and feelings of characters are parts. The night-time in which most of the major actions occur is a part. Iago's use of *honesty* is a part. All the uses of *honesty* are a part. All the metaphors of medicine and disease, the images from army life, the language of light and dark are parts.

The point is to keep the idea of the part flexible and inclusive, as a step toward adequate freedom in the description of structure. A view of the parts begotten of a preoccupation with gross anatomy will yield a coarse and constricted account of structure. On the other hand, compiling an unlimited serial list of parts would be futile. The main thing is to be aware of a part in all its relational possibilities.[2] Othello's farewell to arms (III.3.348ff.) is relevant to the specific situation of the moment, to Othello's personality generally, to Shakespeare's conception of the modes of response to disaster possible to human beings. Emilia's picking up the handkerchief helps advance the action by contributing to Iago's deception of Othello, but it is also relevant to her character and to Shakespeare's conception of the modes of wifely devotion and marital relationship (not to mention its relations by contrast with actions of Desdemona and Bianca and of Emilia herself later). The theories of sex which Iago advances to Roderigo are relevant to his purpose of controlling Roderigo, to his modes of thought generally, and to Shakespeare's awareness of the whole realm of philosophies of love.

For working criticism, the broad categories of the parts whose relatedness is to be observed are two: plot and poetry. We might again borrow Iago's words for metaphor and speak of the wit and witchcraft of the dramatist: the conscious designing and articulating; and the mysterious endowing of many parts—especially the poetic language—with dramatic value and meaning far in excess of the minimal logical requirements of the occasion: the magic in the web. This is less a theory of composition than an effort to suggest different aspects of the play that are only theoretically separable. Let us put it another way. If love is what *Othello* is "about," *Othello* is not only a play about love but a

poem about love.[3] It has parts which interact in the mode of
"pure" drama—people having such and such an effect on each
other, irrespective of whether they communicate in verse, prose
or pantomime; it also has parts which interact in the manner of
a poem. Again, this is a theoretical separation: the characters
have such and such an effect by means of the words they speak;
and conversely, an analysis of the words they speak involves the
student regularly in a consideration of the "action" and interaction of the speakers. Yet when the dramatist has his characters
speak in poetic language, he vastly complicates their communication with each other and with us. Figure, rhythm, poetic order do
not merely make "more vivid" or "heighten" a literal prose statement that is otherwise unchanged; they constitute a fundamentally different statement by the introduction of the nuance,
overtone, feeling, association, implication, and extension characteristic of them; in other words, by subtly carrying us beyond
the finiteness, one-dimensionalism, and contextual restrictions of
the pure statement determined only by the strict logical requirements of the immediate situation. When Othello summons Desdemona and dismisses Emilia, "Leave procreants alone . . . ;
/Cough or cry hem if anybody come./ Your mystery, your mystery! . . ." (IV.2.28-30), he not only dismisses Emilia, accuses
Desdemona of infidelity, and betrays his own insane bitterness,
but he converts the marriage into a brothel arrangement in
which all three are involved, and by so doing establishes imaginative lines of connection with the role of Bianca and particularly with the Iago philosophy of sexual conduct. If we take all
the lines of one character out of context and consider them as
a unit, we have always a useful body of information; but if, when
we study Iago's lines, we find that he consistently describes himself in images of hunting and trapping, we learn not only his
plans of action but something of his attitude to occasions, to his
victims, and to himself; and beyond that there is fixed for us an
image of evil—one of those by which the drama interprets the
human situation. When Othello says he threw away a "pearl,"
we recall that Brabantio, in acceding to Desdemona's departure,
called her "jewel"; when Desdemona says she would rather have
lost her purse than the handkerchief, we recall that Iago, who
has stolen the handkerchief, has spoken of stealing a purse; we

spontaneously make these connections, and, even if we go no further, our reading has brought forth linkings that cannot be expunged; but we often do go further, and seek out the formal order that is exemplified in these images that leap out of their own contexts and carry our imaginations into other parts of the play.[4] When to these we add many other instances in which poetic language, functioning doubly or triply, takes us beyond specific moments of action into others and on into general areas of character, feeling, and thought, we find that we have an immensely complicated verbal structure with which we must come to terms—the "poem about love," as I have called it. We are trying to describe what Traversi called "a new kind of dramatic unity." [5]

In pursuit of this dramatic unity we must inevitably take account of one notable characteristic of Shakespeare's verbal drama—its repetitiveness of images and likewise of abstract words. After Emilia has three times incredulously asked, "My husband?" Othello demands, "What needs this iterance, woman?" (v.2.150). We all must play Othello to Shakespeare's Emilia: "iterance" forces itself upon us as a critical problem. The dramatist cannot conspicuously repeat words and rely upon figures of the same class (e.g. clothes, military life) without catching our eye and raising a question about what goes on. We are hardly likely to attribute this recurrency to the artist's carelessness or failing resourcefulness or to stop at description—an inert lexicon of repetitions. When editors devotedly multiply cross references to dictional or rhetorical echoes and anticipations, they act, one assumes, more from a sense of relationship than from a delight in coincidence. Speaking of *Antony and Cleopatra*, Professor Clemen uses a phrase that is valid for other plays: "this symbolical meaning of certain sequences of imagery." [6] As Paul Goodman puts it, Shakespeare's "profusion of images is so handled through a long play that it forms a systematic structure and is part of the plot." He elaborates on

a method that is characteristically Shakespearean: this is to present a line of thought by an independent development of the system of imagery. Put formally: when several characters independently and throughout the play employ the same system of images, the diction becomes an independent part of the plot implying a thought, action, etc., whatever is the principle of the system. For it is not in character for different characters to use the same images.[7]

I suspect that it *may* be "in character for different characters to use the same images," which can be a device for suggesting similarities or even contrasts among them; or if the images belong dominantly to one character in one part of the play, and to another in another part, the change may be an important mark of dramatic progression, as when the almost pre-emptive use of animal imagery passes in mid-play from Iago to Othello. But beyond all its possible uses in characterization, recurrent diction has still other functions. Goodman's phrase "independent development" is the key. For though speeches are in one sense not separable from the characters, in another sense they do become disengaged from particular speakers and enter the general verbal fund of the play. (The more rich and profuse the language, the more this is likely to be true, just as the more rich and powerful the literary work, the more likely it is to become disengaged from its own times, however much these times may be needed for exegetic purposes, and to enter the general timeless fund of literary possessions.) Reiterative language is particularly prone to acquire a continuity of its own and to become "an independent part of the plot" [8] whose effect we can attempt to gauge. It may create "mood" or "atmosphere": the pervasiveness of images of injury, pain, and torture in *Othello* has a very strong impact that is not wholly determined by who uses the images. But most of all the "system of imagery" introduces thoughts, ideas, themes —elements of the meaning that is the author's final organization of all his materials.[9]

II

Before coming directly to the forming of the love-theme that differentiates *Othello* from other Shakespeare plays that utilize the same theme, I turn arbitrarily to Iago to inspect a distinguishing mark of his of which the relevance to thematic form in the play will appear a little later. When Iago with unperceived scoffing reminds Roderigo, who is drawn with merciless attraction to the unreachable Desdemona, that love effects an unwonted nobility in men, he states a doctrine which he "knows" is true but in which he may not "believe." Ennoblement by love is a real possibility in men, but Iago has to view it with bitterness and to try to undermine it. With his spontaneous antipathy to spiritual achievement, he must in principle deny the mysterious transformation of personality; instinctively he is the observer of all these habits that suggest infinite corruptibility as the comprehensive human truth. He is the believer in shrewd observation and in corruption in whose credo, which is not altogether unique, man is a union of lusting, folly, and plotting.

Good sense, hard sense, common sense, no nonsense, rationality—all these terms, we may suppose, are ones which Iago might consider as defining his perspective. As he plays against Othello with his game of honest and loving friend, he uses words that put him on that side of the fence. First he can't tell Othello his "thoughts" (about Cassio) because of his "manhood, honesty," or *"wisdom"* [10] (III.3.153-54); a little later he finds *"reason"* to tell them (193). Othello considers him *"wise"* (IV.1.75). While privately Iago may deny his love and kid his honesty, he takes his brains seriously. "Thus do I ever make my *fool* my purse," he boasts; to spend time with Roderigo otherwise, "Mine own gain'd *knowledge* should profane" (I.3.389-90). Othello is to be treated like an *ass* (I.3.408; II.1.318). Iago applies the term *fool* successively to Roderigo (II.3.53), Cassio (II.3.359), Desdemona (IV.1.186), and Emilia (IV.2.148), and condescends to fools "credulous" and "gross" (III.3.404; IV.1.46). His view of himself as the clearheaded manipulator of gulls is significantly unchallenged despite the barrage of derogatory rhetoric eventually aimed at him. He remains the "smart man," apt in "deals," scornful of "suckers."

It is more fun for the smart man if his victim thinks he is using *his* head with especial acuteness. Early in the big deception scene (III.3.93ff.) on which all the subsequent action turns, Iago urges Othello "that your *wisdom* yet" should "take no notice" of Iago's "unsure observance" (148-51); later he repeats, "Nay, but be *wise*" (432). The idea that he is being sharp goes to Othello's head; he resolves to be *"cunning* in my patience" (IV.1.91), and he queries erring Desdemona, "Are you *wise?*" (IV.1.245). With his new wisdom he murders his unwise wife, and Emilia tells him what he has become: "O *gull!* O *dolt! / As ignorant* as dirt! . . . O thou *dull* Moor, . . . what should such a *fool /* Do with so good a wife?" (V.2.163-234). How does Iago try to stop this confessional outburst which will ruin him? By commanding Emilia, "Be *wise,* and get you home" (223). Here he cannot induce that wisdom that serves his own end; the sharp-eyed engineer of folly in others now by necessity collapses into senseless abuse and violence. But Othello's reproach to himself, "O fool! fool! fool!" (323), inadequate a self-judgment as it is, acknowledges Emilia's indictment and, inadvertently, the success of Iago's plot to make him "egregiously an ass." After all this, Othello's "lov'd not wisely" is unconsciously an understatement.

Making a fool of someone else is an aesthetic demonstration of intellectual superiority. It is implicitly partial, temporary; a comic episode after which life goes on. Let this exploit in self-aggrandizement expand with the full pressure of passion, and the attack becomes an ultimate one against sanity: Iago's design to put Othello "into a jealousy so strong / That judgment cannot cure," driving him "even to madness" (II.1.310-11, 320). It is the extreme revenge possible to the man of "reason," a chaos that logically extends and completes the other modes of chaos which Iago instinctively seeks, in a variety of ways, at all stages of the action. Twice again he speaks of Othello's madness as a likelihood or as a formal objective (IV.1.56, 101), and his program works well enough to make Lodovico inquire about Othello's mental soundness (IV.1.280) and to make Othello express a doubt about his own sanity (V.2.111). Madness spreads: Emilia fears lest Desdemona "run mad" (III.3.317), Othello cries to her that he is "glad to see you mad" (IV.1.250), and she in turn fears his "fury" (IV.2.32). But the planned madness eventually recoils upon its creator: "What, are you mad?" is Iago's response when Emilia tells the truth about what he has done (V.2.194).

Such points in the auxiliary theme of madness (a slender anticipation of what will be done in *Lear*) mark the course of rational Iago. Insofar as he identifies rationality and wisdom with his own purposes, he is close enough to Everyman; but he is sharply individualized, and at the same time made the representative of a recognizable human class, when the drama reveals that his purposes require the irrationalizing of life for everyone else. Of the insights that create Iago, none is deeper than the recognition that a cool rationality may itself bring about or serve the irrational. Though Brabantio, awakened by the nocturnal outcries in front of his house, thinks that Iago has "lost" his "wits" and that Roderigo comes "in madness" (1.1.92, 98), their universal technique of matching half-truths to latent fears makes him give up his sane conclusions and accept their distorted history of what has happened to Desdemona, so much so that he then attributes "a judgment maim'd and most imperfect" (1.3.99), i. e., failure of mind, to anyone who takes a different view of the situation. Here Iago simply has to make Brabantio as irrational as possible; shortly he has to curb Roderigo's irrationality, or rather, to convert it from a less to a more serviceable form, from suicidal despair to the sexual pursuit of Desdemona. Now for the first step in this conversation Iago utilizes the traditional argument of the "authority of . . . our wills" and of "one scale of reason to poise another of sensuality"; "But we have reason to cool our raging motions, our carnal stings, our unbitted lusts; . . ." (1.3.329-36). If in one sense this is the devil talking Scripture, in another it is Iago paying tribute to a faculty that he values deeply. He is the self-conscious possessor of brain-power. But reason has many functions, and the critical utility of this passage is that it points to the distinction between the ostensible and the real functions that Iago assigns to reason. In no way does he press Roderigo really to apply reason to his emotional ailment, to diagnose it and moderate and perhaps cure it; on the contrary he assures him that his cause "hath . . . reason" (373) and encourages him to found his hopes on Desdemona's sharing in a universal unregeneracy which Iago quite evidently believes is subject to rational control by no one. But more than that we see that Iago has not the slightest thought of using reason to "cool" his own "raging motions," "carnal stings," and "unbitted lusts": reason is rather the agent of his unbitted lusts and of the raging motions of his hate. It is in their behalf that he reasons with Roderigo; his reason is instrumental, serving his own unreason by playing upon Roderigo's. When he mentions the rumor that his wife Emilia has been unfaithful with Othello, he hurries on to say, "I know not if't be true" (394); rather he intends to act on "mere suspicion," just to make sure. His mind is used not to determine the truth but to convert into action a feeling not founded in truth. This is a basic Shakespearian definition of evil: the sharp mind in the service of uncriticized passion. And the final irony, as Shakespeare sees it, is that the owner of the sharp mind is eventually destroyed by the passion his mind serves.

We see the innermost mechanism of this rational instrument when the Iago-Roderigo relationship comes to its last phase. Like several of the major characters, Roderigo is able at times to assess his own headwork: once he almost resolves to give up the lecherous pursuit of Desdemona and to return to Venice with "a little more wit" (II.3.374); he is angrily aware that he has "foolishly suffer'd" and he suspects that he is "fopp'd" (IV.2.182, 197). Iago retorts by praising Roderigo for both his brains (". . . your suspicion is not without *wit* and *judgment*") and his moral quality (214-19). The recurrent irony for Roderigo is that he cannot rely on his own good sense but falls back instead on Iago's version of what is good sense for him. Here comes the payoff. When once again Iago asserts that there is a way of sleeping with Desdemona, Roderigo's reply is, "Well, what is it? Is it within *reason* and compass?" (223-4). Is it "reasonably practical"? No other question, no other issue of sanction or value. How many philosophic frills are being got rid of, and how far down to positive bedrock this is getting, appears when Iago reveals the program: kill Cassio. Roderigo is still shockable. Iago soothes him, "Come, stand not amaz'd . . ." (245), and offers a cure for "amazement": "I will show you such a necessity in his death that you shall think yourself bound to put it on him" (245-6). To this promise of logical demonstration Roderigo responds in the same key: "I will hear further *reason* for this" (251). Iago makes good his promise, "And you shall be satisfied" (252), for when Roderigo is finally lying in wait to kill Cassio, he sums up the rationale of the project:

> I have no great devotion to the deed,
> And yet he hath given me satisfying *reasons*.
> *'Tis but a man gone*.   (v.1.8-10)

Despite his moral hesitancy, Roderigo has found "satisfying reasons" for committing murder and thinking it a way to Desdemona's bed. In this climax of persuasion to evil, Iago's "reason" mediates between his own uncontrollable irrational drives and those of Roderigo. The rational serving one irrationality and appearing to serve another while playing selfishly upon it: this sums up, and sums up archetypally, the fundamental operating methods of the Iago way of life.

" 'Tis but a man gone" is pure Iago thought. It does away with every value or imperative or speculation that "man" or the death of man traditionally evokes, and it makes "a man" simply a neutral instance of a category, a statistical item, an object that can be acted on without moral responsibility. The philosophy " 'Tis but a man gone" (of which there are contemporary manifestations in whole political systems, in demagogic practices of our own, in some methods of business and advertising and even abstract thought, in propaganda) is consistent with Iago's reductive contention, which he develops at length, that love is no more than unstable sexual appetite; his declaration that "there is more sense" in a "bodily wound" than in "reputation," which he says is a chimera; his skepticism about "honour," which he implies is unreal because unseen; and even, in a slightly different way, with his contempt for Cassio's theoretical knowledge, "Mere prattle, without practice" (1.1.26). Theory of any kind may open the door to values that transcend the immediately utilitarian. "Iago's is a pragmatic world, and his imagery finds its authority in social usage," as Arthur Sewell has said. Iago says tacitly, "Let's get down to facts," that is, the tangible and the visible. (Seen from a slightly different perspective, he has affiliations with the anti-metaphysical thinker, the extremist in semantics, the constitutional debunker.)

III

Reason as an ally of evil is a subject to which Shakespeare keeps returning, as if fascinated, but in different thematic forms as he

explores different counter-forces. In *Macbeth* the rational effort
to minimize the killings done for ambition's sake runs finally into
the force of conscience. In *Lear*, rationalized self-seeking is coun-
terbalanced by all the fidelities implied in *pietas*. And in *Othello*?
Although Iago, as we saw, does not take seriously the ennobling
power of love, he does not fail to let us know what he does take
seriously. When, in his fake oath of loyalty to "wrong'd Othello,"
he vows "The execution of his wit, hands, heart" (III.3.466),
Iago's words give a clue to his truth: his heart is his malice, his
hands literally wound Cassio and kill Roderigo, and his wit is the
genius that creates all the strategy. How it enters into the dialectic of structure, or the thematic form, is made clear in one
of Iago's promises to Roderigo that he shall have Desdemona:
"if sanctimony and a frail vow betwixt an erring barbarian and
a supersubtle Venetian be not too hard for my wits and all the
tribe of hell, thou shalt enjoy her" (I.3.362-6). "Tribe of hell"
is somewhat rhetorical; the real antagonist is "my wits"—set
against the rival power of love, which he cannot tolerate. But
even beyond Iago's own conscious battle, his brains against a
vow of love, there is a symbolic conflict in the heart of the drama.
And for this symbolic conflict Iago, again assuaging the pain of
Roderigo, gives us a name by the words he chooses:

> Thou know'st we work by wit, and not by witchcraft;
> And wit depends on dilatory time.

> (II.3.378-9)

Wit and *witchcraft*: in this antithesis is the symbolic structure,
or the thematic form, of *Othello*. By *witchcraft*, of course, Iago
means conjuring and spells to induce desired actions and states
of being. But as a whole the play dramatically develops another
meaning of *witchcraft* and forces upon us an awareness of that
meaning: *witchcraft* is a metaphor for love. The "magic in the
web" of the handkerchief, as Othello calls it (III.4.69), extends
into the fiber of the whole drama. Love is a magic bringer of
harmony between those who are widely different (Othello and
Desdemona), and it can be a magic transformer of personality;
its ultimate power is fittingly marked by the miracle of Desdemona's voice speaking from beyond life, pronouncing forgiveness
to the Othello who has murdered her (V.2.124-5). Such events

lie outside the realm of "wit"—of the reason, cunning, and wisdom on which Iago rests—and this wit must be hostile to them. Wit must always strive to conquer witchcraft, and there is an obvious sense in which it should conquer; but there is another sense in which, though it try, it should not and cannot succeed; that, we may say, is what *Othello* is "about." Whatever disasters it causes, wit fails in the end: it cuts itself off in a demonic silence before death (Iago's "last words" are "I will never speak word"—v.2.304), while witchcraft—love—speaks after death (Desdemona's last farewell).

Between the poles of wit and witchcraft, all the major characters in the play find their orientation. Emilia looks at a good deal of life through the Iago wit, but yields to the love for Desdemona which transforms her into a sacrificial figure. Under the influence of the Iago wit, Cassio, acting through Desdemona's friendly love, tries to high-pressure Othello into a charity (a revocation of his dismissal) that could come only spontaneously. Roderigo falls under the witchcraft of love, but, instead of letting it take effect as it might, to bring him death or renunciation, chooses Iago's wit game and plays for what he cannot have. Emilia and Desdemona, dying, are not creatures of wit: what we have called witchcraft has led them to a trans-rational achievement of spirit.

The conflict of Desdemona and Iago for Othello can be called the conflict of love and hate, or the conflict of two different potentialities in the soul where both reside. It may also be called the conflict of wit and witchcraft for Othello. Though Othello seems to be all the naïveté of Everyman, and Iago to be all his calculatingness and slyness, Othello gives himself more to wit than to witchcraft because he and Iago, though in different degrees, have much in common—a histrionic bent, an inadequate selfhood that crops up in self-pity and an eye for slights and injuries, an uncriticized instinct to soothe one's own feelings by punishing others (with an air of moral propriety), the need to possess in one's own terms or destroy, an incapacity for love that is the other side of self-love. All this is in another realm from that of witchcraft. When Othello decides to follow Iago and be "wise" and "cunning," he adopts a new code: he will "see" the facts, get the "evidence," "prove" his case against Desdemona, and execute "justice" upon her. This is the program of "wit." Now this is not only utterly inappropriate to the occasion on which, under Iago's tutelage, Othello elects to use it, nor is it simply one of several possible errors; rather he adopts an attitude or belief or style which is the direct antithesis of another mode of thought and feeling which is open to him. He makes that particular wrong choice which is the logical opposite of the right choice open to him. He essays to reason when reason is not relevant: he substitutes a disastrous wit for a saving witchcraft. He could reject Iago's "proof" against Desdemona "by an affirmation of faith," as Winifred Nowottny has put it, "which is beyond reason, by the act of choosing to believe in Desdemona." Othello, the prime beneficiary of witchcraft, might win all its gifts had he the faith that would open him to its action; but he is short on faith, is seduced by wit (the two actions are simply two faces of the same experience), and ruined. He knew the first miracle of love, the thing given without claim, but cut himself off from the greater miracle, the transformation of self into a giver. His final failure is that, though he comes to recognize that he has been witless, he is never capacious enough in spirit to know how fully he has failed or how much he has thrown away. He never sees the full Desdemona witchcraft.

In the light of Desdemona's spiritual wealth—the unfailing love that continues into forgiveness of her murderer—we can understand Iago as a spiritual have-not. Like the have-not in the realm of things who in a materially oriented culture suffers from envy and malice, the spiritual have-not lives in characteristic vices that Shakespeare has analyzed with many-angled perception. The analogy between the material and the spiritual have-not is confirmed by a line in *Lear*, Edmund's "Let me . . . have lands by wit," and by Iago's own addiction to actual theft (of Roderigo's gifts meant for Desdemona). If the analogy fails at one point—that the achievement of spiritual wealth depends on the individual and cannot be essentially helped by external accidents or blocked by external obstacles—that failure only underscores the failure of the spiritual have-not. His modes of action are exhaustively canvassed in Shakespeare's plot and in the poetry of the play. Wit is Iago's instrument to compensate for what he does not have. He perversely hates and yet lusts after what he does not have (Desdemona as a person, and as a symbol of love), and he undertakes to disparage it, minimize it, debunk it, and destroy it. Rule-or-ruin becomes rule-by-ruining. He must fashion the world after his own image: "And knowing what I am, I know what she shall be" (IV.1.74). So it pleases him to trap (he repeatedly uses the language of hunting and trapping) those who are unlike himself, by proclaiming virtues which he does not possess ("honest Iago," the friend of all), confusing the appearance of things seeming to act in one way (as light-bringer and physician during the two nocturnal brawls which he stirs up) while acting in another (making things "dark," wounding and killing). Noisiness and vulgarity of style become him, though as a skilled actor he can simulate the amiable, contained, and discreet adviser and consoler. His most far-reaching method is to seduce others philosophically—to woo them from assumptions in which their salvation might lie (faith in the spiritual quality of others), to baser assumptions that will destroy them (their freedom to act in the light of the accepted unregeneracy of all about them). Iago the moral agent is akin to Iago the philosopher: there is a common element in stealing purses, stealing good names, and stealing ideas needed for survival.

In sociological terms we might allegorize Iago as the criminal type, in political as the self-seeking divisive force or the patriot-eer or the power-seeker who will pay any price, in cultural as the mass-mind, in psychological as all the impulses that lead to despair of human possibility, in moral as envy or hate or spiritual hardness (versions of pride), in mythical as The Enemy— the universal destroyer of ultimate values. Before all these, he is simply a human being, the apparent friend and lover of everybody. We think of these diverse tentative formulations only because he is so variously and richly set before us as the final outcome when certain potentialities of Everyman are freed to develop fully. There is no single way into this extraordinary characterization. As the spiritual have-not, Iago is universal, that is, many things at once, and of many times at once. He is our contemporary, and the special instances of his temper and style —as distinct from the Iagoism to which all men are liable—will be clear to whoever is alert to Shakespeare's abundant formulations. Seen in a limited and stereotyped form, he is the villain of all melodrama. He is Elizabethan—as Envy or Machiavel. And to go further back still, we see in how many parts of Dante's *Inferno* he might appear. He could be placed among the angry and violent. But his truer place is down among those who act in fraud and malice—the lowest category of sinner who on earth had least of spiritual substance and relied most on wit. Here we might put him on a higher level with the panders, but again it is when we reach the lower level that he is summoned more strongly, not once but by group after group: the hypocrites, the thieves, the evil counselors, the sowers of dissension, and, at the very bottom of the eighth circle, the impersonators and false witnesses. Finally, in the ninth and last circle, "damn'd beneath all depth in hell," come the treacherous. And here at last we go beyond time into our timeless myths of evil.

By an extraordinary composition of character Shakespeare has made Iago, literally or symbolically, share in all these modes of evil. And in Iago he has dramatized Dante's summary analysis: "For where the instrument of the mind is joined to evil will and potency, men can make no defense against it." But he has also dramatized the hidden springs of evil action, the urgency and passion and immediacy of it. He contemplates, too, the evildoer's "potency" and man's defenselessness: but these he interprets tragically by making them, not absolute, but partly dependent on the flaws or desire of the victims themselves. In the *Othello* world, Iago, seductive as he is, is not an inevitable teacher. Whoever would, could learn from Desdemona. He would have the choice of wit or witchcraft.

NOTES

1. One who is committed to a detailed study of the parts might seize protectively on Edward A. Armstrong's observation, "There is a strange psychological bias which tempts those interested in large issues to belittle detailed work," in *Shakespeare's Imagination* (London, 1946), p. 125n. Cf. G. Wilson Knight's preface to the 4th edition of *The Wheel of Fire* (London: Methuen, 1949), pp. vi-vii. In *Flaming Minister* (Durham: Duke University Press, 1953), G. R. Elliott makes a detailed commentary on individual passages and on their relationships.

2. Cf. L. C. Knights, *Explorations* (New York: Stewart, 1947), p. 31.

3. Cf. E. E. Stoll's phrase, "a tragedy which is also a poem, in which the parts 'mutually support and explain each other' . . ." This is in *Shakespeare and Other Masters* (Cambridge: Harvard University Press, 1940), p. 219. In *Poetry and Drama* (Cambridge: Harvard University Press, 1951), p. 43, T. S. Eliot speaks of the "perfection of verse drama, which would be a design of human action and of words, such as to present at once the two aspects of dramatic and musical order."

4. For numerous examples of images which link separated passages, see W. H. Clemen, *The Development of Shakespeare's Imagery* (Cambridge: Harvard University Press, 1951). Clemen makes a telling comment on the general sense of the interrelatedness of all parts which is created by the imagery (p. 224).

5. D. A. Traversi, *Approach to Shakespeare* (London, 1938), p. 14; and see his whole first chapter. Of *Othello* he says, "Plot and imagery, in fact, are fused as never before" (p. 86). Cf. his "Othello," *The Wind and the Rain*, VI (1950), 268-9. On the importance of the language spoken, the "wording," there are some relevant comments by E. E. Stoll in *Poets and Playwrights* (Minneapolis: University of Minnesota Press, 1930), pp. 5ff., 128.

6. Page 162.

7. *The Structure of Literature* (Chicago: University of Chicago Press, 1954), pp. 17, 64.

8. One might speak of an image-system as an inner organism—a part of the whole that could not exist without the whole and yet an entity having parts that function with respect to each other. This would be "a verbal drama" as distinct from "verbal drama" generally. As a created thing it does not "just happen"; nor yet, I believe, is it deliberately blue-printed and executed. One may surmise: a certain image or kind of image "comes up" for a speaker on a certain occasion; then it is felt consciously or semi-consciously to have some relevance to the import of the whole; and it continues to be used (with the varying degrees of consciousness presumably characteristic of the creative process) as a way of exploring character or mood or theme.

9. Cf. Price, *Construction in Shakespeare* (Michigan, 1951),

pp. 24 and 35ff., and George Rylands, "Shakespeare's Poetic Energy," *Proceedings of the British Academy*, xxxvii (1951), 99-119. Note his statement that the "repetition of a word in diverse contexts throughout the play, with its correlatives and associations, often gives the clue to the poetic thought, the *dianoia*, which informs the whole" (p. 102).

10. All italics are my own.

Mark Van Doren

MACBETH

THE BREVITY of *Macbeth* is so much a function of its brilliance
that we might lose rather than gain by turning up the lost scenes
of legend. This brilliance gives us in the end somewhat less than
the utmost that tragedy can give. The hero, for instance, is less
valuable as a person than Hamlet, Othello, or Lear; or Antony,
or Coriolanus, or Timon. We may not rejoice in his fall as Dr.
Johnson says we must, yet we have known too little about him
and have found too little virtue in him to experience at his death
the sense of an unutterable and tragic loss made necessary by
ironies beyond our understanding. He commits murder in violation of a nature which we can assume to have been noble, but we
can only assume this. Macbeth has surrendered his soul before
the play begins. When we first see him he is already invaded by
those fears which are to render him vicious and which are finally
to make him abominable. They will also reveal him as a great
poet. But his poetry, like the poetry of the play, is to be concerned wholly with sensation and catastrophe. *Macbeth* like *Lear*
is all end; the difference appearing in the speed with which doom
rushes down, so that this rapidest of tragedies suggests whirl-
winds rather than glaciers, and in the fact that terror rather than
pity is the mode of the accompanying music. *Macbeth*, then, is
not in the fullest known sense a tragedy. But we do not need to
suppose that this is because important parts of it have been lost.
More of it would have had to be more of the same. And the truth
is that no significant scene seems to be missing. *Macbeth* is in-

comparably brilliant as it stands, and within its limits perfect. What it does it does with flawless force. It hurls a universe against a man, and if the universe that strikes is more impressive than the man who is stricken, great as his size and gaunt as his soul may be, there is no good reason for doubting that this is what Shakespeare intended. The triumph of *Macbeth* is the construction of a world, and nothing like it has ever been constructed in twenty-one hundred lines.

This world, which is at once without and within Macbeth, can be most easily described as "strange." The word, like the witches, is always somewhere doing its work. Even in the battle which precedes the play the thane of Glamis has made "strange images of death" (I, iii, 97), and when he comes home to his lady his face is "as a book where men may read strange matters" (I, v, 63-4). Duncan's horses after his murder turn wild in nature and devour each other—"a thing most strange and certain" (II, iv, 14). Nothing is as it should be in such a world. "Who would have thought the old man to have had so much blood in him?" There is a drift of disorder in all events, and the air is murky with unwelcome miracles.

It is a dark world too, inhabited from the beginning by witches who meet on a blasted heath in thunder and lightning, and who hover through fog and filthy air as they leave on unspeakable errands. It is a world wherein "men must not walk too late" (III, vi, 7), for the night that was so pretty in *Romeo and Juliet, A Midsummer Night's Dream,* and *The Merchant of Venice* has grown terrible with ill-smelling mists and the stench of blood. The time that was once a playground for free and loving spirits has closed like a trap, or yawned like a bottomless pit. The "dark hour" that Banquo borrows from the night is his last hour on earth which has lost the distinction between sun and gloom.

> Darkness does the face of earth entomb,
> When living light should kiss it.
>   (II, iv, 9-10)

The second of these lines makes a sound that is notable in the play for its rarity: the sound of life in its normal ease and lightness. Darkness prevails because the witches, whom Banquo calls its instruments, have willed to produce it. But Macbeth is its instrument too, as well as its victim. And the weird sisters no less than he are expressions of an evil that employs them both and has roots running farther into darkness than the mind can guess.

It is furthermore a world in which nothing is certain to keep its shape. Forms shift and consistencies alter, so that what was solid may flow and what was fluid may congeal to stone.

> The earth hath bubbles, as the water has,
> And these are of them,
>
> (I, iii, 79-80)

says Banquo of the vanished witches. Macbeth addresses the "sure and firm set earth" (II, i, 56), but nothing could be less firm than the whole marble and the founded rock he has fancied his life to be. At the very moment he speaks he has seen a dagger which is not there, and the "strange infirmity" he confesses at the banquet will consist of seeing things that cannot be. His first apostrophe to the witches had been to creatures

> That look not like the inhabitants o' the earth,
> And yet are on 't.
>
> (I, iii, 41-2)

So now a dead man lives; Banquo's brains are out but he rises again, and "this is more strange than such a murder is."

> Take any shape but that, and my firm nerves
> Shall never tremble.
>
> (III, iv, 102-3)

But the shape of everything is wrong, and the nerves of Macbeth are never proof against trembling. The cardinal instance of transformation is himself. Bellona's bridegroom has been turned to jelly.

The current of change pouring forever through this universe has, as a last effect, dissolved it. And the dissolution of so much that was solid has liberated deadly fumes, has thickened the air until it suffocates all breathers. If the footing under men is less substantial than it was, the atmosphere they must push through is almost too heavy for life. It is confining, swarming, swelling; it is viscous, it is sticky; and it threatens strangulation. All of the

speakers in the play conspire to create the impression that this
is so. Not only do the witches in their opening scene wail "Fair
is foul, and foul is fair," but the military men who enter after
them anticipate in their talk of recent battle the imagery of en-
tanglement to come.

> Doubtful it stood,
> As two spent swimmers that do cling together
> And choke their art. . . .
> The multiplying villainies of nature
> Do swarm upon him. . . .
> So from that spring whence comfort seem'd to come
> Discomfort swells.
>
> (I, ii, 7-28)

Macbeth's sword is reported to have "smok'd with bloody execution," and he and Banquo were "as cannons overcharg'd with
double cracks"; they

> Doubly redoubled strokes upon the foe.

The hyperbole is ominous, the excess is sinister. In the third
scene, after what seemed corporal in the witches has melted into
the wind, Ross and Angus join Banquo and Macbeth to report
the praises of Macbeth that had poured in on Duncan "as thick
as hail," and to salute the new thane of Cawdor. The witches
then have been right in two respects, and Macbeth says in an
aside:

> Two truths are told,
> As happy prologues to the swelling act
> Of the imperial theme.
>
> (I, iii, 127-9)

But the imagined act of murder swells in his mind until it is too
big for its place, and his heart beats as if it were choking in its
chamber.

> Why do I yield to that suggestion
> Whose horrid image doth unfix my hair
> And make my seated heart knock at my ribs,
> Against the use of nature? Present fears
> Are less than horrible imaginings.

> My thoughts, whose murder yet is but fantastical,
> Shakes so my single state of man that function
> Is smother'd in surmise, and nothing is
> But what is not.
>
> (I, iii, 134-42)

Meanwhile Lady Macbeth at home is visited by no such fears. When the crisis comes she will break sooner than her husband does, but her brittleness then will mean the same thing that her melodrama means now: she is a slighter person than Macbeth, has a poorer imagination, and holds in her mind less of that power which enables it to stand up under torture. The news that Duncan is coming to her house inspires her to pray that her blood be made thick; for the theme of thickness is so far not terrible in her thought.

> Come, thick night,
> And pall thee in the dunnest smoke of hell,
> That my keen knife see not the wound it makes,
> Nor heaven peep through the blanket of the dark
> To cry, "Hold, hold!"
>
> (I, v, 51-5)

The blanket of the dark—it seems to her an agreeable image, and by no means suggests an element that can enwrap or smother. With Macbeth it is different; his soliloquy in the seventh scene shows him occupied with images of nets and tangles: the consequences of Duncan's death may coil about him like an endless rope.

> If it were done when 't is done, then 't were well
> It were done quickly. If the assassination
> Could trammel up the consequence, and catch
> With his surcease success; that but this blow
> Might be the be-all and the end-all here,
> But here, upon this bank and shoal of time,
> We'd jump the life to come. But in these cases
> We still have judgement here, that we but teach
> Bloody instructions, which, being taught, return
> To plague the inventor.
>
> (I, vii, 1-10)

And his voice rises to shrillness as he broods in terror upon the endless echo which such a death may make in the world.

> His virtues
> Will plead like angels, trumpet-tongu'd, against
> The deep damnation of his taking-off;
> And pity, like a naked new-born babe
> Striding the blast, or heaven's cherubin hors'd
> Upon the sightless couriers of the air,
> Shall blow the horrid deed in every eye,
> That tears shall drown the wind.
>   (I, vii, 18-25)

It is terror such as this that Lady Macbeth must endeavor to allay in what is after all a great mind. Her scolding cannot do so. She has commanded him to screw his courage to the sticking-point, but what is the question that haunts him when he comes from Duncan's bloody bed, with hands that can never be washed white again?

> Wherefore could not I pronounce "Amen"?
> I had most need of blessing, and "Amen"
> Stuck in my throat.
>   (II, ii, 31-3)

He must not consider such things so deeply, his lady warns him. But he does, and in good time she will follow suit. That same night the Scottish earth, shaking in a convincing sympathy as the Roman earth in *Julius Caesar* never shook, considers the grievous state of a universe that suffocates in the breath of its own history. Lamentings are heard in the air, strange screams of death, and prophecies of dire combustion and confused events (II, iii, 61-3). And the next morning, says Ross to an old man he meets,

> By the clock 't is day,
> And yet dark night strangles the travelling lamp.
>   (II, IV, 6-7)

Macbeth is now king, but his fears "stick deep" in Banquo (III, i, 50). The thought of one more murder that will give him perhaps the "clearness" he requires (III, i, 133) seems for a moment

to free his mind from its old obsessive horror of dusk and thickness, and he can actually invoke these conditions—in the only
verse he ever uses with conscious literary intention.

> Come, seeling night,
> Scarf up the tender eye of pitiful day,
> And with thy bloody and invisible hand
> Cancel and tear to pieces that great bond
> Which keeps me pale! Light thickens, and the crow
> Makes wing to the rooky wood;
> Good things of day begin to droop and drowse,
> While night's black agents to their preys do rouse.
>
> (III, ii, 46-53)

The melodrama of this, and its inferiority of effect, may warn
us that Macbeth is only pretending to hope. The news of
Fleance's escape brings him at any rate his fit again, and he
never more ceases to be "cabin'd, cribb'd, confin'd" (III, iv, 24).
He is caught in the net for good, his feet have sunk into quick-
sands from which they cannot be freed, his bosom like Lady
Macbeth's is "stuff'd" with "perilous stuff which weighs upon the
heart" (v, iii, 44-5)—the figure varies, but the theme does not.
A strange world not wholly of his own making has closed around
him and rendered him motionless. His gestures are spasmodic at
the end, like those of one who knows he is hopelessly engulfed.
And every metaphor he uses betrays his belief that the universal
congestion is past cure:

> What rhubarb, senna, or what purgative drug,
> Would scour these English hence?
>
> (v, iii, 55-6)

The answer is none.

The theme never varies, however rich the range of symbols
employed to suggest it. One of these symbols is of course the
fear that shakes Macbeth as if he were an object not human;
that makes him start when the witches call him "King hereafter,"
that sets his heart knocking at his ribs, that wrings from him
unsafe extremities of rhetoric, that reduces him to a maniac when
Banquo walks again, that spreads from him to all of Scotland

until its inhabitants "float upon a wild and violent sea" of terror
(IV, ii, 21), and that in the end, when he has lost the capacity
to feel anything any longer, drains from him so that he almost
forgets its taste (v, v, 9). Another symbol, and one that presents
itself to several of our senses at once, is blood. Never in a play
has there been so much of this substance, and never has it been
so sickening. "What bloody man is that?" The second scene
opens with a messenger running in to Duncan red with wounds.
And blood darkens every scene thereafter. It is not bright red,
nor does it run freely and wash away. Nor is it a metaphor as it
was in *Julius Caesar*. It is so real that we see, feel, and smell it
on everything. And it sticks. "This is a sorry sight," says Macbeth
as he comes from Duncan's murder, staring at his hands. He had
not thought there would be so much blood on them, or that it
would stay there like that. Lady Macbeth is for washing the
"filthy witness" off, but Macbeth knows that all great Neptune's
ocean will not make him clean; rather his hand, plunged into the
green, will make it all one red. The blood of the play is everywhere physical in its looks and gross in its quantity. Lady Macbeth "smears" the grooms with it, so that when they are found
they seem "badg'd" and "unmannerly breech'd" with gore, and
"steep'd" in the colors of their trade. The murderer who comes
to report Banquo's death has blood on his face, and the "blood-
bolter'd Banquo" when he appears shakes "gory locks" at Macbeth, who in deciding upon the assassination has reflected that

> I am in blood
> Stepp'd in so far that, should I wade no more,
> Returning were as tedious as go o'er.
>   (III, iv, 136-8)

Richard III had said a similar thing, but he suggested no veritable pool or swamp of blood as this man does; and his victims,
wailing over their calamities, did not mean the concrete thing
Macduff means when he cries, "Bleed, bleed, poor country!" (IV,
iii, 31). The world of the play quite literally bleeds. And Lady
Macbeth, walking in her sleep, has definite stains upon the palms
she rubs and rubs. "Yet here's a spot. . . . What, will these
hands ne'er be clean? . . . Here's the smell of the blood still;
all the perfumes of Arabia will not sweeten this little hand."

A third symbol, of greater potency than either fear or blood, is sleeplessness. Just as there are more terrors in the night than day has ever taught us, and more blood in a man than there should be, so there is less sleep in this disordered world than the minimum which once had been required for health and life. One of the final signs of that disorder is indeed the death of sleep.

> Methought I heard a voice cry, "Sleep no more!
> Macbeth does murder sleep. . . .
> Glamis hath murder'd sleep, and therefore Cawdor
> Shall sleep no more; Macbeth shall sleep no more."
>   (II, ii. 35-43)

Nothing that Macbeth says is more terrible than this, and no dissolution suffered by his world is more ominous. For sleep in Shakespeare is ever the privilege of the good and the reward of the innocent. If it has been put to death there is no goodness left. One of the witches knows how to torture sailors by keeping sleep from their pent-house lids (I, iii, 19-20), but only Macbeth can murder sleep itself. The result in the play is an ultimate weariness. The "restless ecstasy" with which Macbeth's bed is made miserable, and

>   the affliction of these terrible dreams
>   That shake us nightly
>   (III, ii, 18-19)

—such things are dreadful, but his final fatigue is more dreadful still, for it is the fatigue of a soul that has worn itself out with watching fears, wading in blood, and waking to the necessity of new murders for which the hand has no relish. Macbeth's hope that when Macduff is dead he can "sleep in spite of thunder" (IV, i, 86) is after all no hope. For there is no sleep in Scotland (III, vi, 34), and least of all in a man whose lids have lost the art of closing. And whose heart has lost the power of trembling like a guilty thing.

> The time has been, my senses would have cool'd
> To hear a night-shriek, and my fell of hair
> Would at a dismal treatise rouse and stir
> As life were in 't. I have supp'd full with horrors;

> Direness, familiar to my slaughterous thoughts,
> Cannot once start me.
>
> (v, v, 10-15)

Terror has degenerated into tedium, and only death can follow, either for Macbeth who lacks the season of all natures or for his lady who not only walks but talks when she should sleep, and who will not die holily in her bed.

Meanwhile, however, another element has gone awry, and it is one so fundamental to man's experience that Shakespeare has given it a central position among those symbols which express the disintegration of the hero's world. Time is out of joint, inoperative, dissolved. "The time has been," says Macbeth, when he could fear; and "the time has been" that when the brains were out a man would die, and there an end (III, IV, 78-80). The repetition reveals that Macbeth is haunted by a sense that time has slipped its grooves; it flows wild and formless through his world, and is the deep cause of all the anomalies that terrify him. Certain of these anomalies are local or specific: the bell that rings on the night of the murder, the knocking at the gate, the flight of Macduff into England at the very moment Macbeth plans his death, and the disclosure that Macduff was from his mother's womb untimely ripp'd. Many things happen too soon, so that tidings are like serpents that strike without warning. "The King comes here tonight," says a messenger, and Lady Macbeth is startled out of all composure: "Thou 'rt mad to say it!" (I, v, 32). But other anomalies are general, and these are the worst. The words of Banquo to the witches:

> If you can look into the seeds of time,
> And say which grain will grow and which will not,
>
> (I, iii, 58-9)

plant early in the play a conception of time as something which fulfills itself by growing—and which, the season being wrong, can swell to monstrous shape. Or it can find crannies in the mold and extend secret, sinister roots into dark soil that never has known them. Or it can have no growth at all; it can rot and fester in its place, and die. The conception wavers, like the courage of Macbeth, but it will not away. Duncan welcomes Macbeth to Forres with the words:

> I have begun to plant thee, and will labour
> To make thee full of growing.
>
> (I, IV, 28-9)

But Macbeth, like time itself, will burgeon beyond bounds. "Nature's germens" will

> tumble all together,
> Even till destruction sicken.
>
> (IV, i, 59-60)

When Lady Macbeth, greeting her husband, says with excited assurance:

> Thy letters have transported me beyond
> This ignorant present, and I feel now
> The future in the instant,
>
> (I, V, 57-9)

she cannot suspect, nor can he, how sadly the relation between present and future will maintain itself. If the present is the womb or seed-bed of the future, if time is a succession of growths each one of which lives cleanly and freely after the death of the one before it, then what is to prevail will scarcely be recognizable as time. The seed will not grow; the future will not be born out of the present; the plant will not disentangle itself from its bed, but will stick there in stillbirth.

> Thou sure and firm set earth,
> Hear not my steps, which way they walk, for fear
> Thy very stones prate of my whereabout,
> And take the present horror from the time,
> Which now suits with it,
>
> (II, i, 56-60)

prays Macbeth on the eve of Duncan's death. But time and horror will not suit so neatly through the nights to come; the present moment will look like all eternity, and horror will be smeared on every hour. Macbeth's speech when he comes back from viewing

Duncan's body may have been rehearsed and is certainly delivered for effect; yet he best knows what the terms signify:

> Had I but died an hour before this chance,
> I had liv'd a blessed time; for, from this instant,
> There's nothing serious in mortality.
>
> (II, iii, 96-8)

He has a premonition even now of time's disorders; of his own
premature descent into the sear, the yellow leaf (v, iii, 23); of
his failure like any other man to

> pay his breath
> To time and mortal custom.
>
> (IV, i, 99-100)

"What, will the line stretch out to the crack of doom?" he cries
when Banquo's eight sons appear to him in the witches' cavern
(IV, i, 117). Time makes sense no longer; its proportions are
strange, its content meaningless. For Lady Macbeth in her mind's
disease the minutes have ceased to march in their true file and
order; her sleep-walking soliloquy (v, i) recapitulates the play,
but there is no temporal design among the fragments of the past
—the blood, the body of Duncan, the fears of her husband, the
ghost of Banquo, the slaughter of Lady Macduff, the ringing of
the bell, and again the blood—which float detached from one
another in her memory. And for Macbeth time has become

> a tale
> Told by an idiot, full of sound and fury,
> Signifying nothing.
>
> (v, v, 26-8)

Death is dusty, and the future is a limitless desert of tomorrows.
His reception of the news that Lady Macbeth has died is like
nothing else of a similar sort in Shakespeare. When Northumberland was told of Hotspur's death he asked his grief to wait upon
his revenge:

> For this I shall have time enough to mourn.
>
> (Henry IV, 2-I, i, 136)

And when Brutus was told of Portia's death he knew how to play the stoic:

> With meditating that she must die once,
> I have the patience to endure it now.
> (*Julius Caesar*, iv, iii, 191-2)

But Macbeth, drugged beyond feeling, supped full with horrors, and tired of nothing so much as of coincidence in calamity, can only say in a voice devoid of tone:

> She should have died hereafter;
> There would have been a time for such a word.
> (v, v, 17-18)

There would, that is, if there were such a thing as time. Then such words as "died" and "hereafter" would have their meaning. Not now, however, for time itself has died.

Duncan was everything that Macbeth is not. We saw him briefly, but the brilliance of his contrast with the thane he trusted has kept his memory beautiful throughout a play whose every other feature has been hideous. He was "meek" and "clear" (i, vii, 17-18), and his mind was incapable of suspicion. The treachery of Cawdor bewildered him:

> There's no art
> To find the mind's construction in the face.
> He was a gentleman on whom I built
> An absolute trust
> (i, iv, 11-14)

—this at the very moment when Macbeth was being brought in for showers of praise and tears of plenteous joy! For Duncan was a free spirit and could weep, a thing impossible to his murderer's stopped heart. The word "love" was native to his tongue; he used it four times within the twenty lines of his conversation with Lady Macbeth, and its clear beauty as he spoke it was reflected that night in the diamond he sent her by Banquo (ii, i, 15). As he approached Macbeth's castle in the late afternoon the building had known its only moment of serenity and fairness. It was because Duncan could look at it and say:

> This castle hath a pleasant seat; the air
> Nimbly and sweetly recommends itself
> Unto our gentle senses.
>
> (I, vi, 1-3)

The speech itself was nimble, sweet, and gentle; and Banquo's explanation was in tone:

> This guest of summer,
> The temple-haunting martlet, does approve,
> By his loved masonry, that the heaven's breath
> Smells wooingly here; no jutty, frieze,
> Buttress, nor coign of vantage, but this bird
> Hath made his pendent bed and procreant cradle.
> Where they most breed and haunt, I have observ'd
> The air is delicate.

Summer, heaven, wooing, and procreation in the delicate air—such words suited the presence of a king who when later on he was found stabbed in his bed would actually offer a fair sight to guilty eyes. His blood was not like the other blood in the play, thick and fearfully discolored. It was bright and beautiful, as no one better than Macbeth could appreciate:

> Here lay Duncan,
> His silver skin lac'd with his golden blood
> (II, iii, 117-18)

—the silver and the gold went with the diamond, and with Duncan's gentle senses that could smell no treachery though a whole house reeked with it. And Duncan of course could sleep. After life's fitful fever he had been laid where nothing could touch him further (III, ii, 22-6). No terrible dreams to shake him nightly, and no fears of things lest they come stalking through the world before their time in borrowed shapes.

Our memory of this contrast, much as the doings of the middle play work to muffle it, is what gives power to Malcolm and Macduff at the end.

> Angels are bright still, though the brightest fell.
> (IV, iii, 22)

Scotland may seem to have become the grave of men and not their mother (IV, iii, 166); death and danger may claim the whole of that bleeding country; but there is another country to the south where a good king works miracles with his touch. The rest of the world is what it always was; time goes on; events stretch out through space in their proper forms. Shakespeare again has enclosed his evil within a universe of good, his storm center within wide areas of peace. And from this outer world Malcolm and Macduff will return to heal Scotland of its ills. Their conversation in London before the pious Edward's palace (IV, iii) is not an interruption of the play; it is one of its essential parts, glancing forward as it does to a conclusion wherein Macduff can say, "The time is free" (v, viii, 55), and wherein Malcolm can promise that deeds of justice, "planted newly with the time," will be performed "in measure, time, and place" (v, viii, 64-73). Malcolm speaks the language of the play, but he has recovered its lost idiom. Blood will cease to flow, movement will recommence, fear will be forgotten, sleep will season every life, and the seeds of time will blossom in due order. The circle of safety which Shakespeare has drawn around his central horror is thinly drawn, but it is finely drawn and it holds.

J. Stampfer

THE CATHARSIS OF *KING LEAR*

THE OVERRIDING critical problem in *King Lear* is that of its ending. The deaths of Lear and Cordelia confront us like a raw, fresh wound where our every instinct calls for healing and reconciliation. This problem, moreover, is as much one of philosophic order as of dramatic effect. In what sort of universe, we ask ourselves, can wasteful death follow suffering and torture? Nor is this concern an extrapolation from our own culture. It is, rather, implicit in Lear's own image, when he calls for tongues and eyes to howl "That heaven's vault should crack" (v, iii, 259), and in his despairing question:

> Why should a dog, a horse, a rat, have life,
> And thou no breath at all?
>
> (v, iii, 306-7)

The problem becomes more overwhelming when we consider that, unlike the problems Shakespeare may have inherited with the plot of *Hamlet,* this tragic ending was imposed by Shakespeare on a story which, in its source, allowed Cordelia's forces to win the war. Moreover, the massive intrusion into *King Lear* of Christian elements of providence, depravity, and spiritual regeneration make it impossible to shunt aside the ending as a coincidence of its pre-Christian setting. The antiquity of setting may have had the irrelevant effect of releasing certain inhibitions in the playwright's mind; but the playgoers in Shakespeare's audience did not put on pagan minds to see the play. Rather, the constant references to retributive justice, perhaps greater here

From *Shakespeare Survey*, Vol. 13, 1960, pp. 1-10. Copyright © 1960 by Cambridge University Press. Reprinted by permission.

than in any other of Shakespeare's tragedies, make it an issue in a way that it is not in such "pagan" plays as *Timon of Athens, Antony and Cleopatra,* and *Coriolanus.* Indeed, part of the poignance of *King Lear* lies in the fact that its issues, and the varieties of evil that it faces, are so central to Christianity, while it is denied any of the mitigation offered by a well-defined heaven and hell, and a formal doctrine of supernatural salvation.

The impression of unreconciled savagery and violence in the ending has been mitigated, in our generation, by a critical reading that would interpret Lear's last emotion as one of joy, even ecstasy, rather than one of unbearable agony. Bradley advances this reading, though hedged with a considerable qualification, in the following passage:

> And, finally, though he is killed by an agony of pain, the agony in which he actually dies is not one of pain but of ecstasy. Suddenly, with a cry represented in the oldest text by a four-times repeated "O," he exclaims:
> > Do you see this? Look on her, look, her lips,
> > Look there, look there!
>
> These are the last words of Lear. He is sure, at last, that she *lives:* and what had he said when he was still in doubt?
> > She lives! if it be so,
> > It is a chance which doth redeem all sorrows
> > That ever I have felt!
>
> To us, perhaps, the knowledge that he is deceived may bring a culmination of pain: but, if it brings *only* that, I believe we are false to Shakespeare, and it seems almost beyond question that any actor is false to the text who does not attempt to express, in Lear's last accents and gestures and look, an unbearable *joy*.[1]

Some recent critics[2] have gone much further than Bradley in an attempt to build from Lear's momentary emotion at death a "chance which doth redeem all sorrows," and make the play's ending a transfigured vision of attained salvation.

Before disputing the weight this penultimate moment in Lear's life can bear in counterbalancing all that precedes it, one must first consider whether the reading itself is defensible; for, in a sense, everything in the play hangs in the balance with Lear's death. If it is one of transfiguring joy, then one might, for all the enormous difficulties involved, affirm that a species of order is re-established. If not, however, then the impression is irresistible that in *King Lear* Shakespeare was confronting chaos itself, unmitigated, brutal, and utterly unresolved. The problems of justice and order, however interpreted, finally rest in the mystery of Lear's last moment, and not in the ambiguity of whether Edgar will or will not take over, by default, the throne of England. Like the news of Edmund's death, the problem of the succession is "but a trifle" (v, iii, 295) alongside the supreme issue of whether any "comfort" was applied by Shakespeare to the "great decay" of Lear, as was evidently applied by him to the deaths of Hamlet and to a lesser extent Othello.

Bradley and those who follow him in this matter rest their case on the observation that Lear died persuaded that Cordelia still lived. He leaves unremarked, however, the fact that this illusion is not a new and sudden turn, but recurs three or four times in the last scene. It is, indeed, the main concern of Lear's first three speeches on re-entering the stage, before he goes temporarily out of his mind:

> She's gone for ever!
> I know when one is dead, and when one lives;
> She's dead as earth. Lend me a looking glass;
> If that her breath will mist or stain the stone,
> Why, then she lives.

(v, iii, 259-63)

The tension here, and it is the underlying tension in Lear until his death, lies between an absolute knowledge that Cordelia is dead, and an absolute inability to accept it. Lear "knows when one is dead, and when one lives." His very faculties of reason and knowledge would be in question if he could not distinguish life from death. "She's gone for ever . . . She's dead as earth," he repeats over and over. If he is to grasp reality in the face of madness, it is the reality of Cordelia's death that he must grasp. But this is the one reality that sears him whenever he attempts to grasp it, and so he tries, by the test of the looking glass, to prove that she lives, despite his emphatically underlined knowledge to the contrary.

Three brief speeches by Kent, Edgar, and Albany intervene between this and Lear's next speech. One would guess that Lear is very active on stage at this point, possibly getting a looking glass, holding it up to Cordelia's lips, registering either momentary hope or immediate despair, then, when this test fails, snatching a feather and trying a second test. He would seem to be oblivious to all reality but Cordelia's body and his attempts to prove that she is alive. His second speech shows what is at stake in the effort:

> This feather stirs; she lives! If it be so,
> It is a chance which does redeem all sorrows
> That ever I have felt.
>
> (ll. 265-7)

This effort, too, fails, and Kent's painful attempt, on his knees, to wrest Lear's attention away from Cordelia only makes Lear momentarily turn on his companions with the savage outcry of "murderers" and "traitors" before trying again to prove her alive, this time by putting his ear to her lips in the thought that she might be speaking:

> A plague upon you, murderers, traitors all:
> I might have sav'd her; now she's gone for ever!
> Cordelia! Cordelia! stay a little. Ha!
> What is't thou say'st? Her voice was ever soft,
> Gentle, and low; an excellent thing in woman.
> I kill'd the slave that was a-hanging thee.
>
> (ll. 269-74)

His outcry, "Ha!," like his cry "This feather stirs," registers an illusion that Cordelia has spoken to him. This is a wilder self-deception than the thought that she has breathed, and remains with him beyond the end of the speech. His "I kill'd the slave" is said almost lovingly and protectively to Cordelia's body, as if she heard him. Thus he struggles simultaneously for sanity and for the belief that Cordelia lives. Under the strain of these two irreconcilable psychic needs, his mind simply slips and relaxes into temporary madness:

> He knows not what he says; and vain is it
> That we present us to him.
>
> (ll. 293-4)

But agonized sanity breaks through Lear's madness once more, as the words of Kent, Albany, and Edgar could not. Albany sees it rising, ominously convulsing Lear's features, and exclaims, "O, see, see!" (l. 304) as Lear cries out:

> And my poor fool is hang'd! No, no, no life!
> Why should a dog, a horse, a rat, have life,
> And thou no breath at all? Thou'lt come no more,
> Never, never, never, never, never!
>
> (ll. 305-8)

The repeated cries of "Never!" are the steady hammering of truth on a mind unable to endure it. Lear's life-blood rushes to his head. He chokes, and asks someone to undo the button of his collar (l. 309). Then, against the unendurable pressure of reality, the counterbalancing illusion that Cordelia lives rushes forth once more. Once again, it is at her lips, breathing or speaking, that he seeks life and dies:

> Do you see this? Look on her, look, her lips,
> Look there, look there! (*dies*)
>
> (ll. 310-11)

Who is to say, given this cycle of despair, insanity, and the illusion of hope, if it really matters at what point of the cycle Lear expires, or even if his last words establish it decisively? On the contrary, on purely aesthetic grounds, we have an indication from another point in Act v that all of Lear's emotions have been gathering to an unendurable head at the moment of death. Gloucester, the counterpart to Lear in the subplot, was, like him, driven out by his false offspring, tormented in the storm, and finally preserved by a faithful, though rejected child. And Gloucester's death, which is described in considerable detail by Edgar, contains just such a welter of conflicting feelings as does

Lear's, and might well be the model for understanding Lear's death:

> Never,—O fault!—reveal'd myself unto him,
> Until some half-hour past, when I was arm'd.
> Not sure, though hoping, of this good success,
> I ask'd his blessing, and from first to last
> Told him our pilgrimage; but his flaw'd heart,
> Alack, too weak the conflict to support!
> 'Twixt two extremes of passion, joy and grief,
> Burst smilingly.
>
> (v, iii, 192-9)

Gloucester's heart burst from its inability to contain two conflicting emotions, his psyche torn apart by a thunderclap of simultaneous joy and grief. And such, by aesthetic parallel, we may presume was the death of Lear, whose "flaw'd heart," too, as is evident throughout the last scene, was

> Alack, too weak the conflict to support!

But the similarity only serves to accentuate the basic difference between the two deaths. Gloucester died between extremes of joy and grief, at the knowledge that his son was miraculously preserved, Lear between extremes of illusion and truth, ecstasy and the blackest despair, at the knowledge that his daughter was needlessly butchered. Gloucester's heart "burst smilingly" at his reunion with Edgar; Lear's, we are driven to conclude, burst in the purest agony at his eternal separation from Cordelia.

There is, then, no mitigation in Lear's death, hence no mitigation in the ending of the play. On the contrary, either the play has no aesthetic unity, or everything in it, including Lear's spiritual regeneration, is instrumental to the explosive poignance of Lear's death. Nor can there be any blenching from the implications of Lear's last sane question:

> Why should a dog, a horse, a rat, have life,
> And thou no breath at all? Thou'lt come no more.
> Never, never, never, never, never!

It is only by giving Lear's death a fleeting, ecstatic joy that Bradley can read some sort of reconciliation into the ending, some renewed synthesis of cosmic goodness to follow an antithesis of pure evil. Without it, this is simply, as Lear recognized, a universe where dogs, horses, and rats live, and Cordelias are butchered. There may be mitigations in man himself, but none in the world which surrounds him. Indeed, unless Lear's death is a thoroughly anomalous postscript to his pilgrimage of life, the most organic view of the plot would make almost a test case of Lear, depicting, through his life and death, a universe in which even those who have fully repented, done penance, and risen to the tender regard of sainthood[3] can be hunted down, driven insane, and killed by the most agonizing extremes of passion.

The plot of *King Lear* is generally not read in this fashion. On the contrary, its denouement is generally interpreted as another "turn of the screw," an added, and unnecessary, twist of horror to round out a play already sated with horrors. If it is defended, it is generally on grounds like those of Lamb,[4] who contended that it was a "fair dismissal" from life after all Lear had suffered, or those of Bradley, that Lear's death is a transfiguration of joy to counterbalance all that has preceded it. Neither reading is satisfactory, Lamb's because it makes the ending, at best, an epilogue rather than a denouement to the main body of the action, Bradley's because the textual evidence points to the opposite interpretation of Lear's death. If Lear's spiritual regeneration, however, with the fearful penance he endures, is taken as the play's "middle," and his death, despite that regeneration, as its denouement, then the catharsis of *King Lear*, Shakespeare's profoundest tragedy, has as yet escaped definition. This catharsis, grounded in the most universal elements of the human condition, can be formulated only when one has drawn together some of the relevant philosophical issues of the play.

Thus, the ending is decisive in resolving the plethora of attitudes presented in the play concerning the relationship between God and man. Set side by side, out of context, and unrelated to the denouement, these attitudes, and their religious frames of reference, can be made to appear an absolute chaos. Certainly almost every possible point of view on the gods and cosmic justice is expressed, from a malevolent, wanton polytheism (IV, i, 38-9) to an astrological determinism (IV, iii, 34-5), from an amoral, personified Nature-goddess (I, ii, 1) to "high-judging

Jove" (II, iv, 231). But the very multitude, concern, and contradictory character of these references do not cancel each other out, but rather show how precarious is the concept of cosmic justice. Surely if the play's ending is an ending, and cosmic justice has hung in the balance with such matters as Goneril's cruelty (IV, ii, 46-50), Gloucester's blinding (III, vii, 99-100), and Edmund's death (V, iii, 174), it collapses with Lear's ultimate question: "Why should a dog, a horse, a rat, have life,/ And thou no breath at all?" Despite the pagan setting, the problem of theodicy, the justification of God's way with man, is invoked by so many characters, and with such concern, that it emerges as a key issue in the play. As such, either the denouement vindicates it, or its integrity is universally destroyed. In point of fact, this is implied in the deaths of Lear and Cordelia.

The force of evil, perhaps the most dynamic element in the Christian tragedies, is extended to wide dimensions in *King Lear*, where two distinct modes of evil emerge, evil as animalism, in Goneril and Regan, and evil as doctrinaire atheism, in Edmund. These modes are not to be confused. Goneril, in particular, is, from the point of view of conscience, an animal or beast of prey. She and Regan never discuss doctrine, as does Edmund, or offer motives, as does Iago. Their actions have the immediacy of animals, to whom consideration never interposes between appetite and deed. It is in this spirit that Lear compares Goneril, in a single scene (I, iv), to a sea-monster, a detested kite, a serpent and a wolf, and Albany, in another (IV, ii), to a tiger, a bear, a monster of the deep, and a fiend, as though, through them, animalism were bursting through civil society.

Edmund, on the other hand, is a doctrinaire atheist, with regard not only to God, but also to the traditional, organic universe, a heterodoxy equally horrifying to the Elizabethans. This doctrinaire atheism involves an issue as basic in *King Lear* as that of a retributive justice, and that is the bond between man, society, and nature. Here, there is no plethora of attitudes, but two positions, essentially, that of Cordelia, and that of Edmund. Cordelia's position is perhaps best expressed by Albany, after he learns of Goneril's treatment of Lear:

> That nature which contemns its origin
> Cannot be bordered certain in itself.

> She that herself will sliver and disbranch
> From her material sap, perforce must wither
> And come to desperate use.
>
> (IV, ii, 32-6)

According to Albany, an invisible bond of sympathy binds human beings like twigs to the branches of a tree. This bond is no vague universal principle, but closely rooted in one's immediate family and society. This is natural law in its most elemental possible sense, not a moral code, but almost a biochemical reaction. Hierarchical propriety is a necessity for life, like sunlight and water, its violation an act of suicide or perversion. It is Cordelia, in response to this law, who says firmly, "I love your majesty? According to my bond; no more nor less" (I, i, 94-5). This bond, the central concept of the play, is the bond of nature, made up at once of propriety and charity.

In contrast to this concept of Nature is Edmund's soliloquy affirming his doctrinaire atheism (I, ii, 1-15), where natural law is summed up in two phrases, "the plague of custom," and "the curiosity of nations." The bond of human relations, as understood by Cordelia and Albany, is a tissue of extraneous, artificial constraints. Edmund recognizes a hierarchy, but rather than growing out of society, this hierarchy goes wholly against its grain. This is the hierarchy of animal vitality, by which "the lusty stealth of nature," even in the act of adultery, creates a more worthy issue than the "dull, stale, tired bed" of marriage. And in response to Gloucester's superstitious references to the larger concept of the organic universe, Edmund repudiates any relationship between the "orbs from whom we do exist" and his own destiny (I, ii, 139-45).

Strangely enough, however, while the denouement seems to destroy any basis for providential justice, it would seem to vindicate Cordelia with regard to the bond of human nature. Thus, the death of Cornwall, Goneril, and Regan are, as Albany prophesied, the swift and monstrous preying of humanity upon itself. Cornwall is killed by his own servant; Regan is poisoned by her sister; and Goneril finally commits suicide. Even more is Cordelia vindicated in Edmund, who is mortally wounded by his brother, and then goes through a complete, and to this reader, sincere repentance before his death. Critics have expressed bewilderment at Edmund's delay in attempting to save Lear and Cordelia. They do not, however, remark the significance of the point at which Edmund acts. For it is not until Goneril confesses the poisoning of Regan and commits suicide, thus persuading Edmund that he was loved, that he bestirs himself to save Lear and Cordelia if it is not too late. Intellectual assent is not sufficient. Only to those wholly caught up in the bond of love is charity possible:

> *Edm.* Yet Edmund was belov'd:
> The one the other poison'd for my sake,
> And after slew herself.
> *Alb.* Even so. Cover their faces.
> *Edm.* I pant for life. Some good I mean to do,
> Despite of mine own nature.
>
> (v, iii, 239-44)

Herein, however, lies a sardonic paradox; for Edmund deceived himself. He was the object of lust, but was not encompassed by love. Goneril slew Regan for his sake, but it was out of lust and ambition; she was incapable of that love which brings to self-transcendence, such as Cordelia's love of Lear, or his own act of "good," in spite of his "own nature." And far from killing herself for Edmund's sake, she committed suicide, utterly alone, at the implicit threat of arrest for treason. Edmund, ever the doctrinaire logician, took false evidence of the bond of love at face value, and died as isolated as he lived. The two forms of evil in *King Lear* were ultimately opaque to one another.

But an even more sardonic paradox is implicit in Edmund's death. For Edmund, by abandoning his atheistic faith and acknowledging the power of love, accepts Cordelia's instinctual affirmation of natural law. But the denouement itself, with the gratuitous, harrowing deaths of Cordelia and Lear, controverts any justice in the universe. Chance kills, in despite of the maidenly stars. It would seem, then, by the denouement, that the universe belongs to Edmund, but mankind belongs to Cordelia. In a palsied cosmos, orphan man must either live by the moral law, which is the bond of love, or swiftly destroy himself. To this paradox, too, Shakespeare offers no mitigation in *King Lear*. The human condition is as inescapable as it is unendurable.

To so paradoxical an ending, what catharsis is possible? This question can be answered only by re-examining the structure of the plot. There can be observed, in *Hamlet*, a radical break from the mode of redemption in such earlier plays as *Romeo and Juliet*. In *Romeo and Juliet*, redemption comes when the tragic hero affirms the traditional frame of values of society, love, an appropriate marriage, peace, and the like, though society has, in practice, ceased to follow them. The result is to enhance the *sancta* of society by the sacrifice of life itself. In *Hamlet*, redemption only comes, finally, when the tragic hero spurns and transcends the *sancta* of society, and appeals to a religious mysticism into which human wisdom can have no entry, and in which, at most, "the readiness is all." The final result, however, is none the less the redemption of society and the reconciliation of the tragic hero to it; for Hamlet's last act is to cast a decisive vote for the next king of Denmark. Even *Othello*, domestic tragedy though it is, ends with the reconciliation of the tragic hero and society; and Othello's last act is an affirmation of loyalty to Venice and the execution of judgement upon himself. *King Lear* is Shakespeare's first tragedy in which the tragic hero dies unreconciled and indifferent to society.

The opening movement of *King Lear* is, then, not merely a physical exile from, but an abandonment of the formal *sancta* and institutions of society, which is pictured as even more bankrupt than in *Hamlet*. In *Hamlet*, only one man's deliberate crime corrupts the Danish state, "mining all within"; in *King Lear*, animalism, atheism, brutal ambition, superstition, self-indulgence, and lethargy all contribute to society's decay. In this opening movement of abandonment, Lear is stripped of all that majesty and reverence clothing him in the opening scene, of kingdom, family, retainers, shelter, and finally reason and clothing themselves, until he comes, at the nadir of his fortunes, to "the thing itself . . . a poor bare forked animal" (III, iv, 111-12). Romeo found his touchstone of truth against the rich texture of the Capulet feast, Lear in an abandoned and naked madman. Romeo and Juliet formed, from the first, an inviolate circle of innocence that was the fulfilment of their previous lives; Lear found no innocence until all his previous life had been stripped away from him.

In contrast to this movement of abandonment, and the basis of the second, counter-movement, stands not, as in *Hamlet*, religious mysticism, but an elemental bond that we can, in this play, indifferently call charity or natural law, one that binds man to man, child to parent, husband to wife, and servant to master almost by a biological impulse. From first to last, charity is discovered, not as the crown of power and earthly blessing, but in their despite. This theme is enunciated by France in taking Cordelia for his wife:

> Fairest Cordelia, that art most rich being poor,
> Most choice forsaken, and most lov'd despis'd!
> Thee and thy virtues here I seize upon,
> Be it lawful I take up what's cast away.
> Gods, gods! 'tis strange that from their cold'st neglect
> My love should kindle to inflam'd respect.
>
> (I, i, 253-8)

The same affirmation is made by Kent, in entering the impoverished Lear's service:

> *Lear*. If thou be'st as poor for a subject as he's for a king,
>   thou art poor enough. What wouldst thou?
> *Kent*. Service.
> *Lear*. Who wouldst thou serve?
> *Kent*. You.
> *Lear*. Dost thou know me, fellow?
> *Kent*. No, sir; but you have that in your countenance which
>   I would fain call master.
> *Lear*. What's that?
> *Kent*. Authority.
>
> (I, iv, 22-32)

Indeed, organized society dulls people to an awareness of charity, so that it is only in Lear's abandonment that he becomes bound to all men:

> Poor naked wretches, wheresoe'er you are,
> That bide the pelting of this pitiless storm,
> How shall your houseless heads and unfed sides,

> Your loop'd and window'd raggedness, defend you
> From seasons such as these? O, I have ta'en
> Too little care of this! Take physic, pomp;
> Expose thyeslf to what these wretches feel,
> That thou may'st shake the superflux to them,
> And show the heavens more just.
>
> (III, iv, 28-36)

Shakespeare could, of course, have used this more elemental level of charity or natural law as he used the force of love in *Romeo and Juliet,* to redeem and renew society. Had he chosen to do so, it would have become politically effective in Cordelia's invading army, overwhelmed the corrupt elements then in power, and restored the throne to Lear, as is suggested in Shakespeare's conventionally pious source. But society, in Shakespeare, is now no longer capable of self-renewal. And so the counter-movement of the play, the reclothing of Lear, by charity and natural law, with majesty, sanity, family, and shelter, after the most terrible of penances, does not close the play. At its close, the completion only of its dramatic "middle," Lear is utterly purged of soul, while the hierarchy of society is reduced, as at the end of *Hamlet,* to an equation of "court news" with "gilded butterflies" (v, iii, 13-14). At this point, if the universe of the play contained a transcendent providence, it should act as in the closing movement of *Hamlet,* mysteriously to redeem a society unable to redeem itself.

Shakespeare's pessimism, however, has deepened since *Hamlet,* and the deaths to no purpose of Lear and Cordelia controvert any providential redemption in the play's decisive, closing movement, so that another resolution entirely is called for. Narrowing our problem somewhat, the catharsis of any play lies in the relationship of the denouement to the expectations set up in the play's "middle." In *King Lear,* this middle movement has to do primarily with Lear's spiritual regeneration after his "stripping" in the opening movement of the play. These two movements can be subsumed in a single great cycle, from hauteur and spiritual blindness through purgative suffering to humility and spiritual vision, a cycle that reaches its culmination in Lear's address of consolation to Cordelia before they are taken off to prison (v, iii, 9-17). The catharsis of *King Lear* would seem to lie, then, in the challenge of Lear's subsequent death to the penance and spiritual transcendence that culminates the play's second movement. This challenge can be described as follows:—

All men, in all societies, make, as it were, a covenant with society in their earliest infancy. By this covenant, the dawning human consciousness accepts society's deepest ordinances, beliefs, and moral standards in exchange for a promise of whatever rewards and blessings society offers. The notion of intelligible reward and punishment, whether formulated as a theological doctrine and called retributive justice or as a psychological doctrine and called the reality principle, is as basic to human nature as the passions themselves. But given the contingency of human life, that covenant is constantly broken by corruption within and without. A man's life and that of his family are at all times hostages of his limited wisdom, his tainted morality, the waywardness of chance, and the decay of institutions. Indeed, social ritual, whether religious in character, like confession or periodic fasting, or secular, like the ceremonial convening of a legislature, is an attempt to strengthen the bond of a covenant inevitably weakened by the attrition of evil and the brute passage of time. These are all, in a sense, acts of penance, that is, acts whose deepest intent is to purge us of guilt and the fear of being abandoned, to refresh our bond with one another and with our private and collective destiny.

Lear, at the beginning of the play, embodies all that man looks forward to in a world in which, ultimately, nothing is secure. He has vocation, age, wealth, monarchy, family, personal followers, and long experience. Like Oedipus and Othello, he would have seemed to have attained, before the play begins, what men strive for with indifferent success all their lives. In this sense, Lear engages our sympathies as an archetype of mankind. And just as Othello discovers areas of experience which he never cultivated and which destroy him, Lear discovers that even in those areas he most cultivated he has nothing. Thus, like Oedipus and more than Othello, Lear activates the latent anxiety at the core of the human condition, the fear not only of unexpected catastrophe but that even what seems like success may be a delusion, masking corruption, crime, and almost consummated failure.

This opening movement, however, leads not to dissolution, exposure, and self-recognition, as in *Oedipus* and *Othello,* but to purgation. And Lear's purgation, by the end of the play's middle movement, like his gifts and his vulnerability at its start, is so complete as to be archetypal. By the time he enters prison, he has paid every price and been stripped of everything a man can lose, even his sanity, in payment for folly and pride. He stands beyond the veil of fire, momentarily serene and alive. As such he activates an even profounder fear than the fear of failure, and that is the fear that whatever penance a man may pay may not be enough once the machinery of destruction has been let loose, because the partner of his covenant may be neither grace nor the balance of law, but malignity, intransigence, or chaos.

The final, penultimate tragedy of Lear, then, is not the tragedy of *hubris,* but the tragedy of penance. When Lear, the archetype not of a proud, but of a penitential man, brutally dies, then the uttermost that can happen to man has happened. One can rationalize a passing pedestrian struck down by a random automobile; there is no blenching from this death. Each audience harbours this anxiety in moments of guilt and in acts of penance. And with Lear's death, each audience, by the ritual of the drama, shares and releases the most private and constricting fear to which mankind is subject, the fear that penance is impossible, that the covenant, once broken, can never be re-established, because its partner has no charity, resilience, or harmony—the fear, in other words, that we inhabit an imbecile universe. It is by this vision of reality that Lear lays down his life for his folly. Within its bounds lies the catharsis of Shakespeare's profoundest tragedy.

NOTES

1. A. C. Bradley, *Shakespearean Tragedy* (1924), p. 291.
2. Harold S. Wilson, *On the Design of Shakespearean Tragedy* (Toronto, 1957), p. 204; Geoffrey Bush, *Shakespeare and the Natural Condition* (Cambridge, Mass., 1956), p. 128.
3. L. L. Schücking, in his *Character Problems in Shakespeare's Plays* (New York, 1922), p. 186, cites most, though not all the evidence that can be offered to document a spiritual regeneration in Lear, only to deny it any validity in the play because, by the

comparative method, he finds no similar concern elsewhere in Shakespeare for *charitas*, or social justice. Aside from a number of relevant passages that leap to mind from other plays, the most striking parallel is in *King Lear*, itself, where Gloucester, Lear's counterpart in the subplot, makes a speech similar to Lear's prayer, though not as profound, on the poor and the wretched (IV, i, 67-74). Whatever may or may not be true in other plays, charity is apparently a prime consideration in *King Lear;* and, if so, Lear's regeneration in charity is, by Schücking's own evidence, part of the play's aesthetic movement.

4. New Variorum edition of *King Lear* (Philadelphia, 1880), p. 421.

John F. Danby

THE FOOL AND HANDY-DANDY

I PROPOSE in this chapter to isolate one aspect of the Fool. The aim is to see how far Shakespeare's larger theme—the theme of man and his society, of the two Natures and Janus-like Reason—is reflected in the shivered mirror of the Fool's verse.

The manner of that verse is gnomic and elliptic. It is an ideal idiom for twisting broken fragments into unexpected patterns. On one side it might originate in the medieval nonsense poem. The sixteenth century popular ballad still kept this alive in such scraps and oddments as the Fool sings. On the other it comes down through Shakespeare's own period of Gobbo-like confusion-mongering. It ends, in *King Lear*, as the sort of thing Blake might have taken as a model for his own octosyllables. It is not a carefree or a happy verse, for all its capering and jauntiness. It is taut with anxiety and bafflement, with distress and bitterness. It is abrupt and bewildered. It can juggle with fragments of the two Natures and the two Reasons, and then shrug off the whole business with hideous flippancy. Pain distorts the Fool's grimace, but the pain might equally mask compassion or contempt.

A passage from the Fool's first scene in the play provides a fair example of his normal idiom:

Lear:
　　When were you wont to be so full of songs, sirrah?
Fool:
　　I have used it nuncle, e'er since thou mad'st thy
　　daughters thy mothers, for when thou gav'st them

From *Shakespeare's Doctrine of Nature: A Study of King Lear,* 1949, pp. 102-13. Reprinted by permission of Faber & Faber Limited.

the rod, and put'st down thy own breeches,
Then they for sudden joy did weep,
And I for sorrow sung,
That such a King should play bo-peep,
And go the fools among.
Prithee nuncle keep a schoolmaster that can teach
thy fool to lie, I would fain learn to lie.

Lear:

An you lie, sirrah, we'll have you whipped.

(I, iv)

We might note first that the Fool is under a compulsion to tell
the truth, so that what he says has professional reliability. Second, the popular ballad material incorporated into his part is not
chosen at random: it matches his own manner, and throws new
light on what he has to say. Thirdly, very often his speeches
deliberately re-state what has already been given expression in
the play elsewhere. "Thou mad'st thy daughters thy mothers,"
for example, repeats Goneril's outburst of the scene before:

Idle old man
That still would manage those authorities
That he hath given away, now by my life,
Old fools are babes again, and must be us'd
With checks as flatteries, when they are seen abus'd.

(I, iii)

Each of these points is a commonplace of criticism: their combined force is sufficient warrant for treating the whole of the
Fool's lines as serious and homogeneous utterance. His statements have as much weight, for interpretation, as those of anyone in the play.

The most significant aspect of the Fool's verse is also illustrated in the passage. This is his habit of translating everything
into handy-dandy. (Cp. "When a man is over-lusty at legs,
then he shall wear wooden nether-stocks.")

He sees everything as a see-saw. Whichever end of the see-
saw anyone chooses, the Fool's job is to be counterweight. The
King himself is an instance of this universal handy-dandy. He
has made his daughters his mothers. Instead of wielding the rod,

he receives correction himself. Instead of remaining a ruler on the throne he has become an irresponsible child playing bo-beep. Handy-dandy is a psychological law, too:

> Then they for sudden joy did weep
> And I for sorrow sung.

The ballad lines, apart from the *King Lear* context, are merely Launcelot Gobbo silliness. In the *King Lear* context, however, they develop characteristic overtones. There is first the obvious common-sense meaning: excessive joy can make one weep, and hysterical sorrow will sometimes sing. But this in itself shows how the mind rocks perpetually between extremes, with no fixed centre of measure or control. Furthermore there is the meaning that comes from the deliberate switching of the tears and the song. The daughters have stolen the Fool's tears; he is left to sing their song. It might be a profound hypocrisy on the daughters' part—the kind of hypocrisy that steals the good man's weapons and leaves him with none but those the hypocrite has discarded. (This, of course, is Cordelia's plight when she must be dumb because the hypocrites have already made truth seem like a lie.) Hypocrisy can always seize the initiative, put truth in this false position and leave it paralysed and immobile; hypocrisy can force even truth to seem a collaborator. The Fool appears to be as callous as the sisters, they are no more cruel than he. The Fool can see it all happening, and knows exactly how it works. But his knowledge leaves him no better off. It is all an inevitable and miserable handy-dandy.

A striking thing about the Fool is that while his heart makes him belong to the Lear-party, and while his loyalty to Lear himself is unshakeable, his head can only represent to him that meaning for Reason which belongs to the party of Edmund and the Sisters. He is aware of the two common senses in the debate between Goneril and Albany. But his constant recommendation to the King and his following is a counsel of self-interest. Here is his advice to Kent:

> Let go thy hold, when a great wheel runs down a hill, lest it breaks thy neck with following. But the great one that goes upward, let him draw thee after: when a wise man

gives thee better council give me mine again: I would have
none but Knaves follow it since a Fool gives it:

> That Sir, which serves and seeks for gain,
>   And follows but for form;
> Will pack, when it begins to rain,
>   And leave thee in the storm,
> But I will tarry, the Fool will stay,
>   And let the wise man fly:
> The Knave turns Fool that runs away,
>   The Fool no Knave perdy.

(II, ii)

It is usual to claim that in instances such as this the Fool is sub-
mitting the loyalty of Lear's following to a test. He gives advice
which he knows will not be taken by the disinterested; he is a
hypocrite in a benevolent sense. This view, I think, makes the
Fool less ambiguous than he really is. As I see him, he really does
believe that to follow Lear to disaster is foolishness. Absolute
loyalty is irrational, and the Fool never suggests that there is a
supernatural sanction for such irrationality. Folly is an alternative to knavery, certainly. But that does not make it a virtue. The
third term that would rescue him from the counterbalancing
negatives is simply missing. Handy-dandy works on the ethical
level, too. It is this which separates the Fool from Albany whom
Goneril calls a "moral fool." The Fool can see no sense in the
foolish morality Albany would urge his wife to pursue. On the
other hand, Goneril's alternative is no more acceptable. The Fool
is quite clear on the point that such common sense as hers (such
wisdom) is mere knavishness. Wiseman has come to mean for
him, as for Bunyan later, worldly-wiseman. Unlike Bunyan the
Fool does not see the wiseman as a candidate for damnation.

Handy-dandy operates in society, too. The "great wheel" runs
down the hill and another is drawn upward by its very descent.
It is tempting to see behind this image some new device of
haulage machinery. (Massinger's image for the great man and
his satellites was the great wheel of a mill that makes the lesser
wheels go round. In Chapman the wheels are those of a spit.)
The wheel is probably, however, the wheel of Fortune. Either
way a strong sense pervades the lines of the individual's weakness

in the authoritarian setting for human action. The Great Man himself is as insecure as the small man. The tilted plane of society makes tug and scamble inevitable. Under such conditions the panic of save-your-own-skin will be the prevailing mood.

The Fool holds up to Lear a model of cautionary excellence. It is the hypocrite, the canny capitalist, and the self-denying puritan combined:

> Mark it, nuncle;
> Have more than thou showest,
> Speak less than thou knowest,
> Lend less than thou owest,
> Ride more than thou goest,
> Learn more than thou trowest,
> Set less than thou throwest;
> Leave thy drink and thy whore,
> And keep in a door,
> And thou shalt have more,
> Than two tens to a score.
>
> (I, iv)

Goneril has already charged Lear with the vices of the old regime, riotous "Epicurism and Lust"—the excess of those impulses which, in the mean, are sociability, comradeship, free self-expression, and love. The Fool prescribes the complementary vices of the new dispensation: a riot of acquisitiveness, self-protection, suspicion.

Again, it is impossible to say that the advice is meant only as irony. The model proposed is certainly mean and contemptible, an inversion of the grand image of the King in the scheme of natural theology. It is not one that would be freely espoused if other alternatives were open. However, the Fool doubts whether any alternative does lie open, apart from the permanent alternative of Folly.

We are tempted to think of the Fool as being on the side of some social Utopia, until we see handy-dandy applied to this, too:

> When priests are more in word, than matter;
> When brewers mar their malt with water;

> When nobles are their tailors' tutors,
> No heretics burned, but wenches' suitors;
> When every case in Law, is right;
> No squire in debt, nor no poor knight;
> When slanders do not live in tongues;
> Nor cutpurses come not to throngs;
> When usurers tell their gold i' th' field,
> And bawds, and whores, do churches build,
> Then shall the Realm of Albion,
> Come to great confusion;
> Then comes the time, who lives to see't,
> That going shall be us'd with feet.
> This prophecy Merlin shall make, for I live
>   before his time.
>
> (III, ii)

The first four lines describe the actual state of present corruption. The next four switch without warning to the coming Utopia. The two lines following manage to mix both together:

> When usurers tell their gold i' th' field,
> And bawds, and whores, do churches build.

We can read this either as total conversion or as utter unregeneracy. The confusion is completed by the last four lines. The Golden Age to come will entail the overthrow of Albion, and the last stage will return us to the point from which we start:

> Then comes the time, who lives to see't,
> That going shall be us'd with feet.

There is little hope of enlisting the Fool as a social reformer.

Handy-dandy is even applied to Time: "This prophecy," the Fool explains, "Merlin shall make; for I live before his time." Direction and purpose in history itself are lost. The motion from past to future becomes that of a wheel again.

The wheel is the key to much of the Fool's imagery. The great wheel running up and down the hill is a double wheel-image—a wheel running round in a circle. We used the image of the see-saw to explain the working of the Fool's opposites. A suspended wheel is an endless series of see-saws. The old man and

the babe, the moralist and the knave, the wise man and the fool
—these are opposites diametrically counterpoised, and then (since
the wheel always comes full circle) identified. The mechanism
is shown at work in the individual, in society, in the pattern of
the moral world, and in history itself. Man is caught in a con-
traption that bears him up and down, carries him round and
round, continually.

Edmund and the Sisters see society as a competition; and
Goneril says it is safer to fear than to trust too far. In this competitiveness there is a certain combative courage, and for them
fear is an offensive-defensive of caution. Man even as an animal
still retains a kind of dignity. He is King of the Beasts. The Fool
sees this competitiveness and fear in a different light. "He that
has a house to put's head in," he remarks, "has a good head-
piece." Or, another occasion:

> *Fool:*
>> Canst tell why an oyster makes his shell?
>
> *Lear:*
>> No.
>
> *Fool:*
>> Nor I neither; but I can tell why a snail has a house.
>
> *Lear:*
>> Why?
>
> *Fool:*
>> Why, to put's head in, not to give it away to his
>> daughters and leave his horns without a case.

(I, v)

Here he makes the fear, timidity, and the creatures nearest to
man in this general respect the close oyster and the fearful snail.
Self-interest does not only lead to an aggressive outgoing among
one's fellows. It leads also to a self-protective shrinkage within
one's shell. Man is a poor, cowering, threatened creature, and will
do well to look after himself as best he can.

The shell and the sheltering creature symbolize for the Fool
man in the carapace of his society. The compelling factor in the
image is the suggestion of the external threat. Man must defend
himself in such an environment. His mean shifts are a necessity
imposed on him by the sub-humanity of the surrounding uni-

verse, a universe constantly threatening to crush the shell men have built for themselves. It is this same sub-humanity (sensed by Kent, as well as by the Fool, as lying behind the Thunder) which amply sanctions man's inhumanity to man. Not all can be equally warm or sheltered. Those like Poor Tom who are pushed outside must blame themselves only—and the elements.

The Fool, like Hobbes, knows that "the passion to be reckoned upon is fear." Fear throbs as a motive through his human world, and beats down from the non-human world of the heavens. It is this underlying feeling which explains the Fool's sincerest piece of advice to the suffering King he accompanies over the heath. It is an example of compassion working to the same effect as cruelty: an unconscious handy-dandy. He is alone with Lear on the heath; the storm is still raging; the King has just called on the "all-shaking thunder" to

> Strike flat the thick rotundity o' th' world,
> Crack Nature's moulds, all germens spill at once
> That makes ingrateful man.
>
> (III, ii)

The Fool says:

> O nuncle, Court holy-water in a dry house, is better than this rain water out o' door. Good nuncle, in, ask thy daughters' blessing; here's a night pities neither wise men, nor fools.
>
> (III, iii)

The heath tests the breaking-points of the human beings wandering over it. This is the Fool's, and a nadir of negated humanity is reached. "Court holy-water" is the sycophancy and corruption of the time-servers that fawn on power. Under the threat of Thunder the Fool's opposition collapses. He will abjectly consent even to playing the hypocritical knave. He urges the king to accept the worst terms society can offer, the blessing of pelican daughters:

> The Knave turns Fool that runs away.

This is an ultimate bankruptcy. And it is the intellect's sincere advice. There is neither bitterness nor irony, only moral panic.

We are invited back with Lear into the corrupt world we were glad to have quitted—invited to stand by the same fire with Lady Brach, and stink.

The corrupt world is the final clue to the meaning of the Fool. He is not of tragic scope. He affirms the dignity of man neither as animal nor angelic reason. Nor has he the ennobling weakness of compassion. He remains a figure of pathos because he is so helpless—helplessly immobilized by a handy-dandy of opposites neither of which he can choose. Nor will he admit of any third ground, the possibility that knavishness might not be an ultimate, that wisdom might be redeemable, that society might be capable of re-birth. He does not survive his own grim laughter, and disappears for that reason. He could not survive, without metamorphosis, in the same context as Cordelia. He is fast in the sickening stasis of his handy-dandy.

His summary of the human situation is as follows:

He that has a house to put's head in, has a good head-piece:
>The codpiece that will house,
>Before the head has any;
>The head, and he shall louse:
>So beggars marry many.
>The man that makes his toe,
>What he his heart should make,
>Shall of a corn cry woe,
>And turn his sleep to wake.
For there never yet was fair woman, but she made mouths in a glass.

(III, ii)

This is the closest knot Shakespeare ties in the idiom he invented for the Fool, and is original for both manner and matter.

That the imagery should be both social and sexual is not chance prurience. The idea of sexual love in Shakespeare's time was approaching the end of an interesting career. It had been a relation under which to figure the ideal destiny of man, both as a person and a social agent. In Spenser, for example, love is the consummation of the whole course of virtue in man. It may be that wherever love is more than casual mating it inevitably serves as an allegory of the marriage of the individual to truth. Throughout the Elizabethan period (and in Petrarch and Dante) this liaison seems certainly to have been well established. By 1600 optimism had reached its term (maybe a nemesis for Elizabeth's over-stimulation of the cult of Gloriana). In the Shakespearean breakdown of confidence, extending to most of the human values, love was also involved. *King Lear* reflects moods that are not only anti-authoritarian, and anti-social, but also anti-sexual. Love is left with none of the Spenserian glamour (except in relation to Cordelia) and the revulsion is expressed crudely— as by Lear in his mad speeches, and by the Fool here.

The codpiece is part of the gallant's costume, and also, quite simply, the phallus. The first four lines thus describe how improvident lechering leads to disease, and how this begins a vicious circle: because the head, too (shrewd prudence and cautious provision against all the potential threats of life) becomes lousy. Once the process has started it is increasingly difficult to stop it. This is the explanation of the paradox concerning the Beggarman and his long train of doxies. He "marries" so many because he is poor (the result of an initial imprudence), and not vice versa. The four lines give a kind of condensed Rake's Progress, and the career of proud gallant becoming Abram man conforms to the mechanism of the wheel. This central idea in the lines is repeated, of course, in Poor Tom—the courtier whose vices had just been those that set the wheel turning and who becomes a naked Bedlamite.

The next four lines fuse the images of Beggarman and Courtier after another fashion. The "toe" can belong to either: it might be the Courtier's pinched in his over-tight shoes, or the Beggarman's that has burst through his boot. A sexual symbolism, paralleling "codpiece," accompanies the social reference. The toe is also (*pace* Freud) the phallus.—I take the lines to mean: "The man—rich or poor—who makes his 'toe' the centre of all his hopes, aspirations, and satisfactions, sacrificing, if he be a courtier, all real human feeling to vanity, or, if he be a beggar, squandering his emotional means in slovenly lust—this man, the composite social creature, will suffer the inevitable pain consequent on his perversity: pangs of guilty remorse that will never let him rest. Thus both extremes in society, acting in opposite

ways from opposite motives, come together in the same state—
a state of self-torment."

Handy-dandy is doubly exerted in these lines. First, one half
of society is neatly folded over the other. The quatrains seem at
first sight to be referring only to one, but are in fact applicable
to the other, too. The effect is to argue, seemingly, that haves
and have-nots are in an identical plight. Secondly, through the
intertwining of the social and sexual in the same image, the public world of community and the private world of personal emotional life are shown to interlock.

Yet a third handy-dandy remains to be noted. The poem is
about the strife between head and heart, both of them sinning
and sinned against. The first quatrain illustrates a sin against
the head: lust flouts prudence, and the unregulated instinct after
one's kind leads to disaster. The second depicts a sin against
the heart: either by the vain courtier (cultivating the externals
instead of attending to the inward things of the spirit) or
through the coney-catching beggarman (exposing and parading
his ill-shodness, yet not revealing the design and deceit in his
breast). Head and heart, like courtier and beggarman are equally
badly off. Neither is a reliable guide. Both are mutually con-
founding. The eight lines summarize the plight of a fissured
society and of a divided man: a severance that is self-perpetuat-
ing and self-aggravating. Society and man come together only
to make each other worse. This applies to rich as well as poor.
At either end of the social scale (and it is a scale with no middle)
we see a travesty of human nature—flaunting codpiece, calloused
toe, man lacerated in head and heart, in mind and body, by
disease or conscience.

To sum up, the Fool can be regarded as the consciousness of
a split society. Like man, its creator, the society is a twin-headed
monster at strife with itself. The Fool consistently uses the
imagery of disease and perversity. Complementary ill-healths
counterbalance in perpetual handy-dandy. He sees rich man and
poor man, head and heart, sympathizes with neither, yet cannot
dissociate himself from the conditions of the strife. Harsh as the
handy-dandy world of corrupt society is, there is no escape from
it: "In, nuncle, in, and ask thy daughters' blessing."

We began by observing the unconscious handy-dandy in the

Fool's own behaviour. His head thinks with the Reason of Goneril and Regan, yet what he does is directly counter to the self-interest which for them and for him is the only thing that makes sense. His greatest bit of cruelty is wrung from him by compassion. While he counsels flight, with wiseman and knave, he will not desert the king: because he is a Fool. What he does will not square with what he says, and it is a redeeming insincerity. Wilfully and blindly he holds to the Great Wheel going downhill.

The Fool, I think, stands for the unillumined head—the intellect—as Lear is the soul, and Cordelia the spirit. He can discern in his cold light the alternatives between which he cannot choose. The sort of thing he could desire he will not admit to exist. It would be too good to be true. Nature in him is an arrest of motion. His head will not allow him to descend the scale with Edmund and the Sisters, and yet it shows no sign of rushing into the natural theology of Lear and Cordelia. The Fool is incapable of Goneril's wickedness, of Lear's error and his subsequent growth, of Cordelia's faultless integration. He prefers, however, to walk in a darkness he cannot fathom rather than stay in the light of such reason as he cannot abide. The head would betray him back to Goneril's hearth, with Lady Brach. But for reasons neither he nor the head knows he follows Lear over the heath.

Robert Ornstein

THE ETHIC OF THE IMAGINATION:
LOVE AND ART IN *ANTONY AND CLEOPATRA*

WE LOSE the profounder meanings of *Antony and Cleopatra* if we insist that questions of truth and honesty are irrelevant to Cleopatra or that her splendid poetic vision is beyond reason itself. For nothing less is at stake in the final scene than the honesty of the imagination and the superiority of its truths to the facts of imperial conquest. What we share with Cleopatra is not a visionary experience but the delight of her conspiracy with the Clown that unpolicies Octavius. She is used to playing jokes on these Romans, and her skill as a comedian shines brightly in the farce of the Seleucus episode, and in the irony of her grave submission to the sole sir of the world. Even as she earlier tormented Antony with references to the immortal Fulvia ("Can Fulvia die?"), in the last act her thoughts dwell humorously on Octavia, the Roman matron, who is demurely sharpening her fingernails in anticiation of Cleopatra's arrival in Rome. There is so much laughter earlier in the play that the comedy of the last act does not surprise us. It does bother us, however, because we think that the story of Antony and Cleopatra should have been as tragic to Shakespeare as it was to the illustrators of De Casibus tales and to Shakespeare's French and English contemporaries. Or if we do not insist that it is tragic despite its final mood of joyous triumph and release, then we would have it an ironic comedy like *Troilus and Cressida,* in which ageing sensual love is shadowed by deceptions, jealousies, and fears. Ignoring the contrary evidence of the poetry, we imagine a relatively detached

From *Later Shakespeare,* ed. T. R. Brown and Bernard Harris, Stratford-upon-Avon Studies, No. 8, Edward Arnold Ltd., 1966 (first two paragraphs omitted). Reprinted by permission.

Shakespeare, who could delight in the paradoxical qualities of his lovers, but who would not have us take their professions at face value.

Most of the ironies in *Antony and Cleopatra* are not present in Plutarch's account, because they arise from the extravagant declarations and sublime aspirations which Shakespeare gives to his lovers. Antony would die a bridegroom, but his longing is prompted by the lie of Cleopatra's death, and he fails to imitate the noble Roman suicide of Eros. Cleopatra melts into lyric grief but she will not open the Monument, and so Antony must be hauled aloft to die in her arms. Then she speaks bravely of dying in the high Roman fashion but equivocates with life, charms Dolabella, and trifles with Seleucus before she shackles up all accidents. Even as we list these ironic episodes, however, we wonder if irony is the primary effect which these scenes have upon an audience. And when we take a larger view of plot we see that again and again irony is transformed into paradox by a felicitous turn of events that offers to the lovers something like the second chance given to the characters of the late romances. Though only for a dying moment, Antony and Cleopatra have the opportunity to call back yesterday, and to rediscover the love which they had thought was lost forever. Indeed, if Antony's death in Cleopatra's arms is a mocking irony, then it is an irony devoutly to be wished for.

Though some critics dwell on Antony's disillusionment, his rages more often approach the melodramatic hyperbole of Leontes' speeches than the torments of Troilus'; in fact Antony is most comic when he takes a high moral tone with his Egyptian dish and laments his Roman pillow left unpressed. We are urbane enough, of course, to admit some joking about adultery in *The Winter's Tale*. We smile at the thought of Sir Smiles fishing in his neighbour's pond because we know that Hermione is chaste. But we would have a more serious view of sexuality in *Antony and Cleopatra* because Cleopatra's innocence is only a pose and her fidelity is open to question. Why should her promiscuous past be cheerfully dismissed as "salad days"? And why should the lack of honesty in women, which is so bitter a theme in *Hamlet* and *Troilus and Cressida*, be reduced at last to the Clown's silly joke? If we assume that a personal disillusion lies behind the view of sex in the great tragedies, then we can infer from *Antony and Cleopatra* (as from the late romances) that in time Shakespeare recovered from the sexual nausea and sickness of generation expressed in *Hamlet* and *King Lear*. But biographical interpretations are at best dubious; what we find in *Antony and Cleopatra* is not a changed attitude towards sexual love, but rather a new perspective on the relations between the sexes. In his great tragedies and in the problem comedies, Shakespeare is concerned with the masculine view of sex. Hamlet's lines, for example, express a typically masculine contempt for woman's frailty and a masculine horror at the sexuality that breeds generations of sinners. Similarly Troilus and Othello are haunted by the masculine desire for sexual possession, a desire that is accompanied by the fear of loss and of the general mock. The darker side of romantic (i.e. masculine) ideals of fidelity is revealed in the anguish of the corrupted Moor, who would not keep a corner in the thing he loved for others' uses.

Where the masculine hunger is for sexual possession and domination, Cleopatra's womanly desire is to be possessed, and to triumph in surrendering. She would be taken; she would yield and feel again the weight of Antony. In his moments of rage, Antony is tormented by the thought that other men have enjoyed Cleopatra. Her womanly jealousies are of another kind: she envies in Fulvia and Octavia the title and place of a "married woman." Only superficially does the imagery of feeding in *Antony and Cleopatra* recall that of *Troilus and Cressida*, for Cleopatra's lines do not express the pang of unsatisfied appetite or of frustrate longing; her thoughts linger over the delicious memory of a fulfilment that is maternal as well as sexual. She has borne the weight of Antony in her womb as on her body; she has fed the lover and the babes at her breast. It is striking, moreover, how often Cleopatra's sexuality is an emotion recollected, not an immediate desire. Her scenes with Antony are filled with talk of war, with wranglings, and reconciliations. Only when Antony is absent is Cleopatra's thought "erotic," and then her longing is not of the flesh but of the total being, one that is rapturously satisfied by news of Antony. In an ageing Falstaff passion is merely ludicrous; but the love which survives the wrinkles and grey hairs that Shakespeare adds to Plutarch's portrait of the lovers is not quite Time's fool. The injurious gods cannot cheat Cleopatra as the stars cheat Juliet, because she has known years of love and revelry with Antony. Even the sorrow she feels in bearing his dying weight is transmuted by the memory of their earlier dyings. And if her last dream of Antony is an illusion, it is an illusion born out of the deepest reality of her experience— she is for Cydnus again.

Vaster than orgiastic memory, the past touches every character and every scene of *Antony and Cleopatra*. We hear of Antony's former greatness as a soldier, of Caesar and Pompey, Brutus and Cassius. The historical events depicted in *Julius Caesar* are recalled, and the past seems to live again in the present as Antony takes Brutus' place as Octavius' antagonist, and as once again love is opposed to imperial ambition. The ruthless impersonalism of the Triumvirate depicted in *Julius Caesar* lives on in the cold efficiency of Octavius, and the fidelity which the defeated Brutus inspired is reflected again in the deaths of Antony and Cleopatra and of those who loved them. To look back at *Julius Caesar* is to realize that Shakespeare did not expediently darken his portrayal of Rome in *Antony and Cleopatra* in order to soften our judgement of Egypt. He saw Caesar's ambition as a symptom of the decay of the Roman state, and he saw the decline of Roman political idealism as a process which had begun even before the assassination of Caesar unloosed the spirit of empire in Antony and Octavius. The end of an era of nobility was marked in *Julius Caesar* by the execution of a hundred Senators and by the suicides of Portia, Cassius, Titinius, and Brutus. In *Antony and Cleopatra* the decay of Roman idealism is so advanced that it is difficult to say whether a Roman thought is of duty or of disloyalty. Yet the decay of the Roman state is paradoxical, because it is not a melting into Egyptian softness but a hardening into the marble-like ruthlessness of the universal landlord. No trace of Brutus' stoicism remains in Octavius' Rome; the prevailing philosophy is the cynical prudence of the Fool's songs in *Lear*. Weakness is merely despised, misfortune corrupts honest soldiers, and loyalty belongs only to the rising man. The pattern of Roman history unfolds for us on Pompey's galley. At present Rome is led by men who (with the exception of Octavius) would rather feast than rule and who make treaties of convenience they do not intend to keep. The Rome that was is recalled by Pompey, who is kept from treachery, not by a personal sense of honour, but by a memory of the honour once sacred to Rome —by a nostalgia for the ethic of his father. Unable to play falsely, Pompey loses the future, which belongs to a Menas who will desert the half-corrupted Pompey, and to an Octavius, whose honour demands only the justification of unscrupulousness. Far more than in the days of Brutus, Rome is bent on empire and ruled by the sword; yet compared to the past, the present is not a time of great soldiery. The continual talk of war only emphasizes that the great military exploits live in memory. All the leaders, including Antony, deal in lieutenantry, and their lieutenants fear to win great victories. Except for the moment when Antony and Scarus beat back Octavius' legions, the battlefield is not a place where honour is won. It is a place where great men defeat themselves; it is the scene of shameful weakness or of the shameless policy that places revolted legions in the van.

The echoes of a nobler past are important because they remind us that the Rome which Octavius rules is not the eternal reality of political life. Only here and now must men like Enobarbus choose between the ways of soldiery and of personal loyalty, that were before a single path. But even as Shakespeare bounds his present scene by placing it in a larger historical framework, his use of archetypal imagery suggests that the worlds of Rome and Egypt are eternal aspects of human experience and form a dichotomy as elemental as that of male and female. The hard masculine world of Rome is imaged in sword, armour, and terms of war, in geometry and stone, and in the engineering that builds or destroys. The soft yielding feminine world of Egypt is poetically imaged as uniting the artifices of sexual temptation to the naturalness of fecundity and to the process of growth and decay which depend on sun, wind, and water. But the absolute distinctions between Rome and Egypt which the imagery enforces are qualified by the dramatic action, that reveals the extent to which these worlds are mirror images of one another and divergent expressions of the same fundamental human impulses. Although by Roman standards, Antony is unmanned, the Roman standard of masculinity is itself examined by the dramatic action and found deficient. Moreover, although Antony's decline in Egypt is from the Roman measure, his decline also measures the decay of the Roman ideal of soldiery.

The tension between image and plot in *Antony and Cleopatra* leads again and again to paradox. The patterns of imagery insist that Egypt is a Circean land of mandragora and lotus-eaters, where sensuality breeds forgetfulness of Rome and duty. But the action shows us that it is Cleopatra, the Serpent of Old Nile, not Antony, who would hear the Roman messengers; and it is Cleopatra, not Octavia, who demands her place in the war by Antony's side. Thus it may not be completely ironic that the finest Roman words of the play are spoken by Cleopatra to Antony in Act i, scene iii:

> Your honour calls you hence,
> Therefore be deaf to my unpitied folly,
> And all the gods go with you! Upon your sword
> Sit laurel victory, and smooth success
> Be strew'd before your feet!

The imagery contrasts the enduring monumental quality of Rome to the melting evanescence of Egypt. But the Roman leaders know that the marble-constancy of Rome is founded precariously on the shifting loyalties of a disaffected populace and is forever subject to the battering ram of ambition. The violent spasms of destruction common to Rome are alien to Egypt, where there is permanence in the recurring cycle of growth and decay that dungs the earth, and where the bounty of the Nile requires that nothing be cultivated except the human sensibility. While the imagery insists upon the oversophisticated appetites of Egypt, the Roman leaders tell of wars that make men drink the stale of horses and eat flesh that men die to look upon. Recurrent allusions to snare, serpent, toil, and charm depict Cleopatra as archetypal temptress and seducer. And yet there is no Egyptian snare or temptation as degrading as that which Menas offers Pompey or that which Octavius twice offers Cleopatra. How, indeed, shall we compare Cleopatra's toils with the politic duplicities of Octavius, who tries to patch a quarrel with Antony, engineers the cynical proposal of the marriage to Octavia, and breaks his treaty with Pompey and his bond with Lepidus? The lies of Egypt are amateurish compared with those of Octavius and of the trustworthy Proculeius; not one Roman speaks the truth to Cleopatra at the end except Dolabella, and he must be seduced into telling the truth.

I do not mean that we are supposed to shudder at Rome. Though its political principles have decayed, it is in other respects a healthy and capable world, led by an Octavius who is cold not inhuman, unprincipled yet eminently respectable. His ambition is not seen as an anarchic force in an ordered world; it is rather the normal bent of a society shaped by masculine ideals of politics and power. Morally there is not much to choose between Rome and Egypt; in matters of the heart and of the imagination, however, they are polar opposites. Where Antony and Cleopatra's thoughts have a cosmic poetic amplitude, the Roman measure of bigness is earthbound and philistine; its imagination stirs at thoughts of triumphal spectacle and arch. (Octavius would have the trees bear men and the dust ascend to heaven when his sister enters Rome.) Untouched by art, and unsoftened by feminine influence, the Romans pride themselves on their masculine hardness and reticence. Cold, and to temptation slow, they scorn tears and womanish emotion. Despite the protective attitude they adopt, they are cross and patronizing in their relations with women, whom they value as sexual objects and political pawns. Cleopatra rightly fears Antony's callousness because she knows that by Roman standards she is a diversion that should not be missed or overprized. The coarseness of the Roman view of sex is apparent throughout the play—in the lines of Octavius as well as Enobarbus, in Pompey's smutty jests, and in the salicious eagerness of Caesar's lieutenants to hear tales of Cleopatra. Although Enobarbus describes her lightness, her artfulness, her wit, and her infinite variety, the other Romans (like so many modern critics) can picture her only in the conventional posture of a whore, drugging Antony with cloying lascivious wassails.

In most respects the priggish Octavius is the very opposite of Antony. In his treatment of women, however, he is Antony's Roman brother. Antony adopts the pose of Cleopatra's general when he flees his Egyptian "dotage." Octavius sends Thyreus to Cleopatra with solemn assurances that her honour is unsullied. Antony babbles to Octavia about his honour when he deserts her; Octavius marries his sister to a man he despises and then wars to erase her dishonour. Octavius, like Antony, hungers for Cleopatra but his desire to possess her is more shameless and more contemptible. Indifferent to Antony's fate (he would be content if Cleopatra murders her lover), he lies to Cleopatra, cajoles her, and threatens her children in order to keep her alive so that she may be displayed as his trophy in Rome. He has no doubt that a woman like Cleopatra will be seduced into ignobleness when "want will perjure/ The ne'er-touched vestal."

Warm and generous as well as callous, Antony is able to respond to the arts of Egypt, and he is so deeply altered by his response that it is difficult to say what is Antony or when he is less than Antony or when he is himself again. A legend in his lifetime, he is the hero of fantastic exploits and the stuff of soldierly brags and mythic imaginings. Contemning his Egyptian dotage, Philo, Demetrius, and Octavius recall a plated Mars and contrast Antony's earlier feats of battle to his present wassails. But Cleopatra and Enobarbus remember another, more sensual, Antony— Plutarch's gamester and reveller, the lover of plays in *Julius Caesar,* who did not learn the arts of dissipation in Egypt or desert them when he returns to Rome. When plagued by his Roman conscience, Antony sees his salvation in a flight from Egypt; in Rome he momentarily recovers his abilty to command, which allows him to look over Octavius' head. But Antony is not reinspired by Roman ideals; on the contrary, his superiority is a personal honesty that contrasts with Octavius' devious and politic attempts to provoke a quarrel. No salvation awaits Antony in Rome because there is no honourable purpose to engage him; the Triumvirate feasts and gambles and despises the populace. The only Roman dedication is Octavius' desire to be the sole sir of the world. Moreover, if Antony's faults are Egyptian, he does not lose them in Rome, where he displays the very weaknesses that are later to destroy him: a desire to put off issues and to escape unpleasantness. In Egypt he is led by Cleopatra; in Rome he is led by Octavius' lieutenants into the foolish expediency of the marriage to Octavia. There is no point in the play, therefore, at which we can say, here Antony falls. His decline is a process that began in years past and which seems the inevitable destiny of a sensualist and opportunist who never shared Octavius' ambition to possess the entire world, but who wanted empires to play with and superfluous kings to feast and do his bidding. If we must have a reason for Antony's decline, we can say that he lost the desire before he lost the ability to command. He is never defeated in battle during the play. After the disaster at Actium, his fleet is intact and his army powerful though kings and legions desert. A doting braggart might have brushed aside the reality of his cowardice at sea; but Antony is shattered by the very trait which ennobled him in his dealings with Octavius, by an honourable shame at his failings as a leader.

It is characteristic of the handling of events in *Antony and Cleopatra* that we do not see Antony's failure of nerve at Actium; we see Canidius', Scarus', and Enobarbus' response to it, and, following that, we see Antony's reaction. Much use is made of messengers bearing tidings of conflict, disaster, and death, because this is a play of reaction rather than of action. We know Octavius, Cleopatra, Enobarbus, Pompey, and Lepidus by the way that they respond to news of Antony. And we know Antony by his response to Cleopatra and to his fading powers, by his alternating moods of depression and elation, by his moments of impotent rage or of bluster, when he will outstare the lightning, and by his reconciliations with Cleopatra. This vacillation of mood in Antony reminds us of Richard II, except that Richard's journey is towards the nihilism of endlessly circling thoughts, while Antony becomes a fuller man in his decline, more bounteous in his love and in his generosity. When he tries to express, after the second disaster at sea, his loss of soldierly identity, he convinces us that he has changed, not lost, his identity. The soldier has become a lover, the spendthrift a mine of bounty, and the callous opportunist a meditative poet.

The growth of poetic sensitivity in Antony was apparent to earlier generations of critics. It is less apparent to us, ironically, because our desire to read Shakespeare "poetically" blurs our awareness of the poetic attributes of the characters in the plays. And to avoid critical naïveté, we make artificial distinctions between the form and substance of Shakespeare's dramatic verse. When Antony compares his state to the evanescent shapelessness of clouds in a dying afternoon, we grant to him the sense of weariness and loss which the lines convey; but the heavenly imagery and the poetic sensibility revealed in this passage we reserve for Shakespeare, who, we say, merely lends Antony his poetic faculty for artistic purposes. But it is only a step from this "sophisticated" approach to Antony's speeches to the notion that the morbidity of Hamlet's soliloquies is "saved" by the nobility of Shakespeare's poetry. If we grant Hamlet the nobility of his utterances, how shall we deny Antony his poetry? Not all the characters who speak in verse are poetic. Although Octavius' lines are at times richly metaphorical, he seems to us thoroughly prosaic, because the impression of poetic sensibility in Shakespeare's characters depends upon the nature of their response to life, not on the mere presence of figurative language in their speeches. Who but a poet would see the clouds as Antony does, and who but a poet would remember this heavenly image at the point of death? Antony's leave-taking of the world is an imaginative reverie untouched by the grandiosity that marks so many of his early "poetic" declarations.

At the beginning of the play it is obvious that Antony does not know Cleopatra because he does not yet know what is evident to the audience, that his only desire is to be with this woman. We feel that the hyperbole of his early speeches is strained, because his extravagant professions of love are undercut by his harsh, grating response to news from Rome and by his sensitivity to the Roman view of Cleopatra. Though he says here is my space, he is unable to conceive of a world limited by love; and he is unaware that he uses Cleopatra to excuse his indifference to political issues. We smile at Cleopatra's role of betrayed innocence, but not at her keen perception of the emotional dishonesty of Antony's gestures of devotion and of the callousness that underlies them. She knows how easily an Antony who shrugs off Fulvia's death may desert her in turn. The first scenes show us an Antony who is caught between what he tells Cleopatra, and in part believes, and what he tells himself about her, and in part believes. In Rome he is irritated by every reference to her; he never speaks her name though his is always on her lips, and he never regards her as an equal or as having any claim upon him. When he decides to return to Egypt, he speaks of her as his pleasure.

As Antony's world shrinks, his hyperbole becomes, paradoxically, more convincing. When he is confronted by Octavius' legions, his chivalric pose becomes more than a pose, because at last he does fight for Cleopatra; and thus his arming before battle with Cleopatra's aid is more than one last parody of medieval romance. Now when Antony acts, he is aware of his pretendings; tutored by Cleopatra, he imitates after Actium her celerity in dying and, like her, he plays on the feelings of those who love him, making Enobarbus onion-eyed. His talk of death and his shaking of hands is an artful appeal to his followers' emotion and yet an honest piece of acting, because it expresses a true warmth and generosity of spirit. There are times, of course, when Antony's gestures are less honest, when he abuses Cleopatra for her treachery. But his Herclean rages are short-lived and his self-pity is untouched by genuine suffering. His despondency is always more painful to those who love him than it is to Antony, who is never deeply in conflict with himself, and who is more a spectator to, than a participant in, the final disaster at sea. His catastrophes are strangely beautiful: his gods desert to music, his loss of empire is signalled by shouts of joy in the fleets. Even at his nadir he shakes hands with Fortune as with an old familiar friend.

Whatever ironies attach to the manner of Antony's death, he is raised visually, and poetically, above the earth on which the melancholy Enobarbus sinks. The moralizing critic interprets Antony's fate as a warning to adhere to the path of reason; he forgets that Enobarbus follows reason to a fate more wretched than Antony's. Enobarbus chooses Rome lest he lose himself in Antony's dotage and like Antony be made a woman. In itself this choice is not shameful; Enobarbus' act has a hundred Roman precedents, and he has no reason—or, at least, no Roman reason—to follow a leader who can no longer command. What is shameful is Enobarbus' betrayal of himself, because he allows his reason and his honesty to square. Worse still, he goes over to Octavius knowing that to have stayed with Antony was to have "won a place in the story." Yet the place which Enobarbus wins is not as ignoble as he thinks, for we sense that his desertion of Antony is, like his death, an act of love. He leaves Antony when he can no longer bear to watch Antony's failure as a general, and he is redeemed by his response to Antony's generosity even though he has no chance to express to his master the full measure of his

devotion. The lie of Cleopatra's death saves Antony from Enobarbus' fate because it ends the lie of his rage while Cleopatra
is still alive. And Antony's failure to die in the high Roman fashion makes possible the final expression of his bounteous love, his
dying wish that she save herself by making terms with Octavius.

Between the disaster at Actium and his final reunion with
Cleopatra, Antony is the centre of the dramatic action. At the
Monument, however, the dramatic focus shifts; the dying Antony plays the chorus to Cleopatra's impassioned grief, and she is
from that moment on the supreme figure of the play. At Antony's
death, we are told, a new Cleopatra is born—the wanton temptress rises to regal majesty. But what is really new in the Cleopatra who mourns over Antony? Her royalty, her poetic sensibility, and her capacity for profound emotion were evident before; her grief is hardly surprising when, from the beginning, her
every thought is of Antony, and she is haunted by the fear of
losing him. Is it the new Cleopatra who says, "Husband, I come"?
Or is she the same Egyptian who in the first scene of the play
reveals her envy of Fulvia, the *married woman*, and her longing
to be more to Antony than his pleasure?

Only Shakespeare could have imagined that the greatest courtesan of all time hungered to be Antony's wife—to be made "an
honest woman." Only he could have dreamed of a Cleopatra who
is, despite her lies and pretendings, always emotionally honest.
When the messenger brings news of Antony's remarriage, she is
furious, but her fury is directed at the messenger, not at Antony.
If she pretends to die when Antony leaves her, it is because
their partings are a form of death which leaves only the desire to
sleep and dream of Antony. Those who read her thoughts an-
nounce that she intends to betray him when she listens to Thyreus. The text indicates only the elaborate irony of her submission and her comic surprise at Octavius' concern for her honour.
It is quite explicit, moreover, that Enobarbus is able to uncover
Cleopatra's intended treachery only because she insists that he be
present at the interview with Thyreus. How foolish of this cunning woman to plan a betrayal of Antony in the presence of Enobarbus! What we witness is not Cleopatra's duplicity but Enobarbus' jealous revenge and the confusion of rage in Antony, who

has Thyreus whipped for kissing the "kingly" hand of that "boggler" Cleopatra.

According to Plutarch, Cleopatra demanded a role in the war against Octavius because she feared that in her absence Antony and Octavius might be reconciled. Shakespeare fails to give Cleopatra a similar explicit motive. Against Enobarbus' warning and against her own nature, she insists upon bearing a charge in the war; she will have Antony fight by sea so that she may command her fleet at Actium. If Cleopatra were nothing more than the seductress whom critics describe, her desire to fight by Antony's side would seem to us incredible. It does not astonish us, however, because we see from the beginning her desire to be worthy of this Herculean Roman, and to imitate the noble Roman fashion of words and deeds. She bids a Roman farewell to Antony in the first act even as she seeks a Roman death in the last act. Her desire to be a Roman wife, which becomes explicit at her death, leads Cleopatra to attempt at Actium the role of Fulvia, the only part she plays falsely before Antony.

Like Antony, Cleopatra does not die in the high Roman fashion; and though she earns the title of Antony's wife she remains more Egyptian than Roman, more various than marble-constant. Timidity, vanity, and womanly fears plague her Roman resolution; she dies a sensual creature of the Nile, artful, theatrical, jealous to the end of Antony. Part of the mystery of her death is the fullness with which it expresses the multiplicity of her nature. She is Antony's mistress and his wife, the graceful courtesan and the tender mother, the great queen and the simple lass. Her drowsiness is at once sensual, maternal, and child-like, for though she nurses her imaginary babes, she is, as so many times before, very like a child, who plays now at being mother, and who is dressed in a royal costume to surprise Octavius. Her crown slips, but Charmian mends it before she too plays.

More than a triumph over Octavius, Cleopatra's death is a triumph over her own fears and over a deeply rooted instinct for life. She is not, however, in love with death though she allows it to commit a loving act upon her; she dreams of life and of Antony. And though she makes a fellow-conspirator of the worm which will eat her, she knows it is not worth the feeding; she knows too the horror of physical decay, which she has envisioned before in striking images of fly-blown bodies. Her death will not be a melting into eternal natural change; it will be a change into changelessness that robs Octavius of his victory and that mocks his immortal longings. He thinks that Cleopatra's "life in Rome/ Would be eternal in our triumph" and he meditates in his last speech on the glory he has won by the deaths of the lovers. But it is paltry to be Caesar, whose quest of fame earns an ignominious place in the story.

Cleopatra's sense of the comedy of imperial ambition is not a new intuition that reaches "beyond the tragic." The paltriness of Caesar was evident to the youthful Shakespeare, whose sonnets contrast the vital power of art to the lifeless marble and gilded monuments of princes. There are echoes of the sonnets, I think, in the antithesis of Egypt and Rome, and in the depiction of a love which finally admits not even the impediment of death. The themes of the sonnets are also relevant to the echoes in the final scene of Capulet's Monument, where another pair of lovers found in death the marriage union which life denied. As *Romeo and Juliet* draws to a close, we sense that the true memorial to the lovers is not the gilded statues which Montague and Capulet promise to raise, but Shakespeare's play. And we know that Cleopatra will live in art because she fashions her own incomparable memorial, the scene in the Monument, which overshadows the mythic wonder of Cydnus. It is the artist in Cleopatra who stirs Shakespeare's deepest imaginative sympathies and who receives the immeasurable bounty of his artistic love, which is immortality itself.

We need not turn *Antony and Cleopatra* into an allegory of art to see that its final paradox is the final paradox of Donne's "Canonization": though deserted by those who observe Octavius' face, the lovers die and rise the same, and prove mysterious by their love. The defect of their passion becomes perfection because ultimately theirs is not a sublunary love; their "faults" shine like the unchanging stars. Donne's lover is a poet who builds in sonnets' pretty rooms, and who fashions the legend of his love in immortal verse. Cleopatra is an artist who fashions out of her life a legend that is unfit for hearse or for Octavius' half-acre tombs. Her "place in the story" is beside the legendary figures who live in ancient myth. She is another Thetis, an Isis, a Venus, a Dido; Cupids and Nereides attend her, the winds are enamoured of her, and she is wooed by Phoebus and, at last, by Death himself. She teaches a plated Mars an artful way of loving; and she turns this demi-Atlas after death into a very god who spreads the masculine seed of his inexhaustible bounty over the earth. In her mythopeic imagination Antony bestrides the ocean, making cities on the waves, and creating empires through a divinely prodigal carelessness—he drops realms and islands out of his pockets.

The foolish Clown is right after all. The biting of Cleopatra's worms is immortal, because it brings a death that lives in the artistic imagination. She dies in the last scene of Shakespeare's play as she has died so many times before in Plutarch, in medieval "tragedy," and in Renaissance plays and poems. And because Shakespeare has written, she will die many times again and be staged over and over to the show—so long as men can breathe or eyes can see, Cleopatra is again for Cydnus. The terms *act, play*, and *show* are not metaphorical when applied to her, because she is in her essential being an actress. Her poses are too extravagant to decive; they are meant to bewitch and captivate by their infinite variety. She will not allow herself to be carted through the streets of Rome in the posture of a whore or to be staged to the show in vulgar Roman fashion. But as if she knows that her destiny is art, she dons her robes and prepares one last dazzling scene that draws a gasp of admiration from Octavius. We have seen her metamorphoses before—her sudden changes from tears to laughter, from pettiness to regality, and from sickness to health. None of them is comparable, however, to the metamorphosis of her death, which turns life into art.

As early as the sonnets, Shakespeare knew that the enemy of love is not time or death; these can only refine its worth. Love's adversary is the unfeeling heart—those who are "as stone / Unmoved, cold and to temptation slow." He can accept a world of mutability in *Antony and Cleopatra*, as in the tragedies and the late romances, because it offers the possibility of renewing change, in later generations, and in the heart of a Lear, an Antony, or a Leontes. Shakespeare does not retreat in his later plays from the exalted humanism of his tragedies, which stresses the irreplaceableness of a Cordelia; he does not find comfort in a naturalistic faith in the continuance of life. The security of *Antony and Cleopatra* and of the late romances is founded on the paradox of tragic art, which depicts immeasurable loss and yet preserves forever that which the artist supremely values. Although great creating Nature may reincarnate some of the rareness of Hermione in Perdita, the true miracle of *The Winter's Tale* is Paulina's art, which preserves and enriches the wonder of Hermione herself.

In Shakespeare's great tragedies illusion and seeming are opposed to moral reality. But in Cleopatra's artful spectacle as in the masques of Prospero and Paulina, illusion and reality intermingle. Sober realists may agree with Dolabella that the Antony whom Cleopatra ecstatically recalls is only a dream of her imagination; they forget, however, that Dolabella, like Cleopatra, is only a dream of Shakespeare's imagination. The triumph of love and art in *Antony and Cleopatra* will not allow us to believe that Shakespeare, who celebrated in the sonnets the miracle of poetry, expressed in Prospero's lines a disillusioned awareness of the vanity of his dramatic art. After a lifetime spent in creating the magic of the stage, Shakespeare must have known that the "idle" dreamlike play of an artist's imagination is the deepest reality of his experience, if not a clue to the fundamental reality of all experience:

> We are such stuff
> As dreams are made on, and our little life
> Is rounded with a sleep.

Oscar James Campbell

CORIOLANUS

IN *Coriolanus* we have Shakespeare's second and more successful experiment in tragical satire. The structure which in *Timon of Athens* was bare and almost crude has here become a suitable form in which to cast the Roman aristocrat's story. Yet the construction of this last of Shakespeare's tragedies has been almost universally deplored. Critics, realizing that its pattern is very different from the one which the poet employed in his great tragedies, have agreed to brand it as inept. A. C. Bradley, for example, believes that the author's unintentional departure from his usual practice accounts for the failure of the play to produce a sound tragic effect.[1] This usually acute critic did not allow for the fact that Shakespeare, at this time a thoroughly experienced dramatist, might have deliberately experimented with new dramatic structures.

It is natural enough to judge *Coriolanus* by the standards of conventional tragedy; in the first Folio it is entitled *The Tragedy of Coriolanus*. Bernard Shaw was one of the first to see that the play was not a tragedy at all. He solves the problem of *Coriolanus* by propounding a witty paradox. "It is," he asserts, "the greatest of Shakespeare's comedies." This perverse statement suggests the proper approach to the play. Shakespeare did not attempt to give *Coriolanus* the structure of a conventional tragedy. Neither in his presentation of the central figure nor in his construction of the plot does he follow orthodox tragic principles. Instead of enlisting our sympathy for Coriolanus, he deliberately alienates it. Indeed he makes the figure partly an

From *Shakespeare's Satire*, 1943, pp. 198-216. Copyright 1943 by Oxford University Press, Inc. Reprinted by permission.

object of scorn. Instead of ennobling Coriolanus through his fall
and death, he mocks and ridicules him to the end. In brief, he
fills the tragedy so full of the spirit of derision that the play can
be understood only if it be recognized as perhaps the most successful of Shakespeare's satiric plays.

II

Shakespeare found the materials for his play in Plutarch's *Life
of Coriolanus,* but he gave the historical events a meaning entirely his own. For Plutarch they yielded a lesson in political restraint and patriotism. As he tells the story continual war has
reduced the plebs to dire poverty. Indeed their misery is so
great that they demand a change in their constitution—the creation of new officers to be called tribunes, who are to redress
the wrongs of the people. This agitation contains a threat of
revolution. But the peril is averted because the senate is wise
enough to send to the plebs "certain of their pleasantest old
men" to discuss the grievances of the commoners. These ambas-
sadors agree to the creation of the new officers and induce the
plebs to join with the patricians in the defense of Rome against
a foreign enemy.

Shakespeare completely changes the significance of these
events. His play opens "in the midst of a riot staged by the
mutinous masses," who are starving because of a shortage of
wheat. For their misery they blame not the drought, which is
the real cause of the famine, but their governing class, the
patricians, and, in particular, Coriolanus, the leader and mouthpiece of the aristocrats. They hate him for the contempt he has
always shown them. Coriolanus in his very first speech proves
that their charge is just, for he addresses them as:

> dissentious rogues
> That, rubbing the poor itch of your opinions,
> Make yourself scabs.
>
> (I. i. 168-70)

This unsavory figurative language is characteristic of most of
the utterances of the haughty patrician. On the occasion in
question the vituperative torrent is interrupted by a messenger

who brings Coriolanus an order to lead the Roman army against the Volscians and Aufidius their leader. Since carnage is his natural element, he responds to this call with enthusiasm. But even the heroism he summons for the battle cannot temper his fundamental brutality. When at the first onslaught of the enemy his soldiers flee in disorder, he berates them with characteristically foul speech. By insults rather than encouragement he drives his men back into the fray, where he does deeds of superhuman valor, defeats Aufidius in single combat, and brings complete victory to his army.

On his return to the capital, the populace greets him with wild acclaim and the senators at once nominate him for consul. He craves the office, but his whole nature flares into revolt against the convention which demands that he stand in the market place and beg the plebians for their votes. However, at the insistence of his dominating mother he submits to the humiliation of this electioneering. Though his appeal is filled with disdain, it seems to succeed. But after he has come through his ordeal and gone home, the tribunes persuade the crowd that he has mocked them. If they possess any self-respect, they will at once revoke their "ignorant election." This they do and drive Coriolanus into the rage which the tribunes anticipate and exploit.

When they inform him of the people's change of heart, he insults them with mounting violence, until they call in a "rabble of plebians" and precipitate a brawl. In the course of this uproar the people and their officers are driven off. Later they return to find that Coriolanus has been persuaded by his mother to allay their anger with fair speech. But his amenity does not divert them from their intention to drive him into one of his fits of uncontrollable rage. They call him traitor, and to the word he reacts as they had planned. He looses upon them a torrent of abuse. This stimulates the rabble to shout for his banishment, and in the words of Coriolanus they "whoop" him out of Rome. Through his uncontrollable rage he has been manipulated into a course of action which is to lead to his self-destruction.

Then he goes straight over to the enemy, and although he treats all the Volscians with overbearing arrogance, his military genius enables him to lead their conquering army to the very gates of Rome. There various representative citizens meet him with desperate pleas to spare his native city. They find him adamant. As a last resort his mother, Volumnia, accompanied by his wife Virgilia and his small son, is sent out to confront him. She feels sure that she can force him to abandon his dire purpose, for she well knows her irresistible influence upon the man who in many respects is still her little boy. She wisely does not ask him to rejoin the Roman forces, but merely to force Aufidius to make peace. Coriolanus is deaf to his mother's entreaties but cannot hold out against her anger. He yields in the flurried terror of a frightened child.

Returning to the Volscian army, Coriolanus induces Aufidius to "frame convenient peace." By thus snatching the fruits of complete victory from the Volscians, he wins the undying resentment of their leader, who lays a clever trap to catch and destroy the haughty Olympian schoolboy. He knows how to stimulate Coriolanus to one of his characteristic fits of wild anger. He uses the same method which the tribunes had found effective, and insults him publicly. In the presence of a crowd of confederates he brands him as a traitor to his adopted country. The accusation has the desired effect. Coriolanus throws into the teeth of the Volscians his former triumphs over them and raises their resentment to the killing point. Then, though the Lords of Corioli protest, the Volscian plebians fall upon Coriolanus and kill him.

III

From this brief resumé of the action it should be clear that *Coriolanus*, like all Shakespeare's other history plays, embodies some of the author's political ideas. Some critics, to be sure, hesitate to attribute any definite political views to him. The idolators of the early nineteenth century and their modern representatives are responsible for this transcendental attitude toward their hero. Shakespeare, they proudly assert, was not of an age, but of all time. Of all movements in a given era, political squabbles are the most ephemeral. Therefore to the idolators an assertion that Shakespeare expressed positive political opinions even in his chronicle history plays was the rankest heresy. A. C. Bradley expressed their view when he wrote, "I think it extremely hazardous to ascribe to him [Shakespeare] any political feeling at all and ridiculous to pretend to any certainty on the subject." [2] This betrays a strange view of the dramatist's art. He, less than any other man of letters, dares to retire to an ivory tower, remote from the social interests of his contemporaries, in order to allow the trade winds from eternity to blow through his philosophic mind. Shakespeare based his profound studies of human motive and human passion upon a realistic appraisal of the various milieux in which his characters came to life; and of all the environments in which human beings must live, the political organization most interested Shakespeare and his contemporaries. The problems of Tudor politics obsessed them.

The usual view is that in *Coriolanus* Shakespeare expresses his contempt for the common man and his conviction that political power in the hands of the mob always brings disaster to the state.[3] More recently critics have looked at the other side of the picture and discerned in Coriolanus' conduct an exposure of the brutal methods that dictators in every age must employ to retain their absolute power.[4] Each of these apparently contradictory views is partly correct. Though Shakespeare is not in this play showing his contempt for the common man, he is nevertheless expressing his vigorous disapproval of democracy. In common with all political theorists of his age, he regarded it as the absence of all government—a form of organized disorder.[5]

But he does not lay all the blame for the social chaos on the plebs and its leaders. To his mind Coriolanus is equally guilty. He is a bad ruler. In the many volumes that the fifteenth and sixteenth centuries devoted to the education of a prince, the supreme magistrate—usually the king—is admonished to regard his subjects as his children and to be a father to them. He must sympathize with their trials and dangers and feel keenly his responsibility for their welfare. He must follow the example set by Henry V toward his soldiers in Shakespeare's play of that name. But Coriolanus acts in a manner diametrically opposed. He hates the people. On almost every occasion in which he meets them face to face he berates them and curses them vilely. Inevitably he finds them hostile and recalcitrant to his leadership —brave and efficient though it be in battle. Instead of correcting

their faults, he goads them to anarchy by his hostility and violence. Coriolanus is thus as much responsible as the plebs for
the political débâcle.

As a political *exemplum* the play presents a case of violent
political disorder and reveals its causes. The trouble lies in the
fact that no civil group performs its prescribed duties properly.
As a result the divinely revealed pattern for the state is disrupted
and society reels toward primal chaos. This lesson could not be
clearly taught in the terms of tragedy. With its interest concentrated upon the tragic career of Coriolanus the man, an audience
might easily ignore the political significance of the play. But the
satiric form gave Shakespeare an opportunity to treat derisively
both the crowd and Coriolanus, between whose "endless jars"
the commonweal was sorely wounded. A careful analysis of the
play will show how skillfully the political teaching, the central
theme of every Elizabethan history play, has been fitted to the
satiric form of the drama.

IV

The play opens with a picture of a mutinous mob, in this way
establishing immediately the atmosphere of social turmoil which
is to exercise its destructive power throughout the action and to
form a natural milieu for the subversive forces in the little world
of Coriolanus' passions. In the midst of the uproar Menenius appears. He is the chief of the many commentators and expositors
in this play who serve as Shakespeare's mouthpiece. He performs
this service with a fussy garrulity that is intended to rouse our
laughter. Later in the play he explains that he is "a humorous
[i.e. crotchety] patrician and one that loves a cup of hot wine
with not a drop of allaying Tiber in 't . . . One that converses
more with the buttock of the night than with the forehead of
the morning. What I think, I utter, and spend my malice in my
breath" (II. i. 51-8 *passim*). The character of this speech, particularly its unsavory metaphors, stamps Menenius as Shakespeare's variant of the now familiar buffoonish commentator.
Like Carlo Buffone he says right things in the wrong way, thus
giving to his comments a kind of outrageous pertinence.

His first speech to the crowd only partly reveals these charac-

teristics. In order to persuade it to cease its revolutionary uproar, he tells the fable of the rebellion which the other members
of the body once raised against the belly,

> That only like a gulf it did remain
> I' the midst o' th' body, idle and unactive,
> Still cupboarding the viand, never bearing
> Like labor with the rest.
>
> (I. i. 101-4)

But the belly replies that by sending rivers of blood to all parts
of the body it serves as the source of the health and the very
life of the whole organism. The belly, it appears, stands in this
parable for the senators, and for Coriolanus in particular, because in Rome he and his fellow patricians exercised the functions of the king. The mutinous members of the body represent
the plebians.

The audience would have regarded this figure of the belly and
its functions as a speech designed to characterize Menenius—to
stamp him as a garrulous old man. But they would also recognize it as a conventional way of stating a familiar principle of
current political philosophy. It would seem like a page torn from
almost any political primer. Because both the plebs and Coriolanus disregard the principles illustrated in Menenius' parable
they bring disaster to Rome and to themselves. The people, in
seeking to exercise the functions of a ruler, were permitting "the
foot to partake in point of preëminence with the head." They
were instituting a form of democracy which was universally regarded as a monstrous body of many heads.[5] Coriolanus himself
employs this figure to describe the proletariat. As he stands outside the gate of Rome, whence he has been driven by the mob,
he exclaims

> The beast
> With many heads butts me away.
>
> (IV. i. 2-3)

Elsewhere in the play he calls the plebs Hydra.[6] Through the
repeated use of such familiar figurative language the author impressed his historical lesson upon his audience. No member of
it could fail to recognize the drama as an exhibition of the forces

of democracy at their destructive work. The most obvious lesson that the drama is designed to teach is, then, as follows: The people should never be allowed to exercise any of the functions proper to a ruler. That way lies anarchy. But the career of Coriolanus is to constitute an equally impressive warning: No ruler must act as cruelly and brutally toward his subjects as does this man. He is more of a slave driver than a kind father. Such a magistrate is always an architect of social confusion.

v

A character cast to play such an admonitory role cannot be treated like an ordinary tragic hero. And Shakespeare deals with Coriolanus from the moment of his first appearance through the whole course of the play to the catastrophe in a manner directly opposite to the one he invariably adopted for his real tragic protagonists. In the first place he endows all his true tragic heroes with many noble traits which appear and reappear through the play. In particular he puts into the mouths of other characters words of praise for the hero as they knew him before he became a slave to one of the subversive passions. Shakespeare also puts into his hero's mouth reflective soliloquies which reveal his struggles between good and evil, and win our sympathetic understanding even while he is losing his battle with destiny. Then, as his protagonist stands at the very brink of the catastrophe, the poet allows him to utter a poignant speech which recalls to the minds of the spectators the loftiness of his nature before he had been caught in the net of his tragic fate. Finally, after the hero's death some character who has survived the holocaust is likely to utter a brief encomium or a benediction upon the soul of the dead man.

These dramatic characteristics are all clearly illustrated in the tragedy of *Hamlet*. In this play Shakespeare finds numerous opportunities to describe his hero's nature before it was overwhelmed with grief and melancholy. Ophelia's lament is the most famous of these portraits of the uncorrupted Hamlet:

> O, what a noble mind is here o'erthrown!
> The courtier's, scholar's, soldier's eye, tongue, sword,

> The expectancy and rose of the fair state,
> The glass of fashion and the mould of form,
> The observ'd of all observers—quite, quite down.
>   (III. i. 158-62)

The same innate gentleness shines through Hamlet's colloquies with the friends of his youth. It comes out clearly in his talks with Horatio, and only a little less appealingly in his conversations with his renegade friends Rosencrantz and Guildenstern.

But it is on the eve of his death that Shakespeare allows the best in Hamlet's nature to reveal itself in a final burst of splendor. He generously forgives Laertes. And he appeals to Horatio's loyalty in terms of idealistic friendship. Shakespeare enriches these speeches by marrying lofty thought to some of his most inspiring verbal music. Moreover Hamlet's death is followed by Horatio's benediction, in which he invokes the deepest religious emotions to add poignancy and elevation to the feelings aroused by the passing of his friend:

> Good night, sweet prince,
> And flights of angels sing thee to thy rest.
>   (v. ii. 370-71)

Coriolanus is treated in a completely different fashion. The very first comments made upon him are derogatory. The two citizens who discuss him in the opening scene are detractors. The first of them asserts that Coriolanus has served his country not from patriotic motives but only to please his mother and to flatter his own pride. The second feebly defends Coriolanus by saying, "What he cannot help in his nature, you account a vice in him." The first citizen, unimpressed by the notion that innate faults are not vices, replies, "He hath faults (with surplus) to tire in repetition." This very first expository scene presents Coriolanus' passion nakedly, stripped of all nobility. It is what Mark Van Doren calls "an animal pride—graceless, sodden, and hateful." This initial exposition is but the first of many conversations about Coriolanus, all contributing features to a disagreeable portrait.

The accumulation of derogatory comment does much to set the satiric tone of the play. "Groups of people," says Mark Van Doren, "tribunes, citizens, servants, officers laying cushions in the Capitol, travellers on the highway, the ladies of his household—are forever exchanging opinions on the subject of Coriolanus. And the individuals who share with him the bulk of our attention are here for no other purpose than to make leading remarks about him." [7] In other words the play is crowded with satiric commentators.

When two or three characters gather together, the subject of their conversation is always Coriolanus. And even his wife's friend Valeria and his mother Volumnia, in contriving what they think is praise of Coriolanus, reveal the savage results of his pride. Valeria's description of the little boy at play becomes a revelation of his father's heady violence. She says, "I saw him [the boy] run after a gilded butterfly; and when he caught it, he let it go again and after it again, and over and over he comes and up again; catch'd it again; or whether his fall enrag'd him or how 'twas, he so set his teeth and tear it! O, I warrant, how he mamock't it [tore it to shreds]" (I. iii. 66-71). Volumnia's comment on this incident —made with complete satisfaction—is "One on's father's moods." And she is right. Irascibility and anger are the emotions which Coriolanus most often displays—and properly, for they are the inevitable results of thwarted pride.

Of all the commentators Menenius is the least obvious in his hostility. That is because, being a buffoon, he inevitably draws the fire of some of the derision. Yet in his characterization of the tribunes, his unsavory metaphors arouse laughter, even while they furiously mock. Witness his vulgar description of the tribunes' attempt to act as judges: "When you are hearing a matter between party and party, if you chance to be pinch'd with the colic, you make faces like mummers, set up the bloody flag against all patience, and, in roaring for a chamber pot, dismiss, the controversy bleeding, the more entangled by your hearing . . . When you speak best unto the purpose, it is not worth the wagging of your beards; and your beards deserve not so honorable a grave as to stuff a botcher's cushion or to be entombed in an ass's packsaddle" (II. i. 81-7, 95-9). This is the buffoon at his expert best.

When this "perfect giber for the table" (and "giber" is an almost exact equivalent for our slang "wise-cracker") turns his wit upon Coriolanus, he realizes that it must combine exposition of the man's nature with his ridicule. Once while attempting to excuse his friend's violence, he says:

> His nature is too noble for the world.
> He would not flatter Neptune for his trident
> Or Jove for's power to thunder. His heart's his mouth;
> What his breast forges, that his tongue must vent,
> And being angry does forget that ever
> He heard the name of death.
>
> (III. i. 255-9)

The first line of his speech, torn from its context, has been used by many critics to prove that Coriolanus' pride is the tragic flaw in an otherwise noble nature.[8] But Menenius is speaking not of pride, but of headlong anger. Even if the old patrician had meant to say that the pride of Coriolanus was the infirmity of his noble mind, no one in an Elizabethan audience would have mistaken his opinion for Shakespeare's. By the third act even the slowest-minded spectator would have recognized Menenius as a sort of buffoon and his comments as food for laughter.

After this attempt to palliate his hero's anger, Menenius returns to his more characteristic vein of comment. Such is the tone of his description of his friend's appearance when rejecting the old man's appeal to save Rome: "He no more remembers his mother now than an eight-year-old horse. The tartness of his face sours ripe grapes. When he walks, he moves like an engine, and the ground shrinks before his treading. He is able to pierce a corslet with his eye, talk like knell and his hum a battery . . . He wants nothing of a god but eternity and a heaven to throne in" (v. iv. 14-26 *passim*). This is bitterly derisive comment, utterly inappropriate for a tragic hero on the verge of his catastrophe, but just the sort of talk best calculated to keep alert to the end of the play the satiric attitude of an unsympathetic audience.

VI

This purpose is accomplished throughout the drama in still more direct ways. Instead of revealing a rich inner nature in profound poetic soliloquies, Coriolanus exhibits over and over again his one ruling passion—the choler which Renaissance philosophers regarded as the inevitable result of wounded pride. At every one of his encounters with the people his rage boils at their impertinence. His contempt he displays through the insults which a "lonely dragon" or Caliban might pour upon "rank-scented" men. When his soldiers retreat before the attack of the Volscians, he shouts:

> All the contagion of the South light on you,
> You shames of Rome! you herd of—. Biles and plagues
> Plaster you o'er, that you may be abhorr'd
> Farther than seen, and one infect another
> Against the wind a mile! You souls of geese
> That bear the shapes of men, how have you run
> From slaves that apes would beat!
>
> (I. iv. 30-36)

For this voice we can feel only aversion. Yet its vigor and its lean thrust form an almost perfect expression of the spirit of Juvenalian satire. Indeed the bare poetic style of this play, lamented by most critics, is exquisitely adapted to the author's derisive intentions.

Understanding the easy inflammability of Coriolanus, the tribunes are able to teach the plebs just how to induce his paroxysms of anger. When thus beside himself, he becomes their easy victim: "Put him to choler straight," they advise,

> . . . Being once chaf'd, he cannot
> Be rein'd again to temperance; then he speaks
> What's in his heart; and that is there which looks
> With us to break his neck.
>
> (III. iii. 25-30)

By following these instructions the mob produces a rhythmical recurrence of Coriolanus' grotesque rage; and this stimulated repetition of a vice or a folly is of the very essence of satire of every sort. It turns Coriolanus into a jack-in-the-box. Every time his self-esteem is depressed, it springs back with the same choler-distorted face. This emotional automatism deprives his pride and his anger of all dignity. It makes him a natural object of derision.

Coriolanus is also his mother's puppet. Volumnia transforms him into a terrified little boy every time the two confront each other. Shakespeare may have intended her to represent an austere patrician woman of early Rome, a worthy mother of grim warriors. Yet she wins from her son not the respect of a man, but the frightened obedience of a whimpering urchin. His attitude toward her remains completely infantile.

It is Volumnia who has forced her son to become a soldier and to exult in the blood and sweat of war. Plutarch describes Coriolanus as driven to battle by an irresistible impulse of his own nature. But Shakespeare tells us that it was Volumnia, "poor hen, who clucked him to the wars and home." This barn-yard figure incidentally deprives the martial impulses of Coriolanus of every shred of dignity. As a soldier he was and remains his mother's creature. Her proud boast is the truth:

> Thy valiantness was mine, thou suck'st it from me.
> (III. ii. 129)

When he is at the front, she relieves her anxiety by imagining him wading in triumph through seas of carnage and blood.

Though Volumnia has also bred into her son his contempt for the people, she knows that he must placate them. She realizes that if he is ever to become consul, he must stand in the market place and humbly beg for their votes. So at first she entreats him to go through the distasteful ceremony merely to please her:

> I prithee now, sweet son, as thou hast said
> My praises made thee first a soldier, so,
> To have my praise for this, perform a part
> Thou hast not done before.
> (III. ii. 107-10)

But even for his mother's sake Coriolanus refuses to let his disposition be possessed by "some harlot's spirit," to turn his voice "into a pipe small as an eunuch," or to allow a "beggar's tongue make motion through his lips." His answer to her courteous pleading is a flat, "I will not do't."

Then Volumnia loses her temper and soundly scolds her son. Her burst of scorn and anger immediately brings him around, reducing him to the stature of a frightened child, ridiculously eager to pacify an irate parent:

> Pray be content [he almost whimpers];
> Mother, I am going to the market place.
> Chide me no more.
> . . . Look I am going.
>
> (III. ii. 130-32; 134)

The contrast between his arrogant attitude toward all other persons in the drama and his infantile cowering before his mother's severity is ridiculous, and is intended to be so.

His last scene with Volumnia, in which she finally dissuades him from leading the victorious Volscians into Rome, is a kind of incremental repetition of the interview just described. When neither her pathetic appeals, made as she kneels before him, nor his wife's tears divert him from his purpose, his mother again loses her temper. She rises from her knees, crying

> Come, let us go.
> This fellow had a Volscian to his mother;
> His wife is in Corioles, and his child
> Like him by chance. Yet give us our dispatch.
> I am hushed until our city be afire.
> And then I'll speak a little.
>
> (v. iii. 177-82)

The old woman's fierce indignation again cows her son. Terrified by her anger, he cries out, like a helpless little boy:

> O mother, mother!
> What have you done? . . .
>
> O my mother, mother! O!
> You have won a happy victory to Rome;
> But for your son—believe it, O, believe it!—
> Most dangerously you have with him prevail'd.
>
> (v. iii. 182-3; 185-8)

This repeated quailing before his mother deprives Coriolanus of the dignity every tragic hero must possess. He never submits to her will through conviction or a sense of duty. His surrender is

never evidence of filial respect. It is always a boy's frightened
submission to a domineering woman. His undeviating arrogance
toward the rest of humanity thus seems to be not exaggerated
self-esteem, but compensation for the fear of his mother. He
never attains the mean between these two unnatural extremes of
emotion, but careens wildly between them. This instability
renders him at once absurd and doomed. The forebodings which
seize him after his final yielding to his mother are fulfilled. They
set him in the path which leads straight to his downfall.

When Coriolanus returns to the Volscian army, he finds
Aufidius hostile. He has all along been jealous of the renegade
Roman and now sees a chance to destroy him. Knowing how easy
it is to drive Coriolanus into a fit of blind rage, he sets the stage
for the undoing of his enemy in a scene which constitutes the
finale of the drama. And a masterful scene it is—an admirable
catastrophe for a satirically conceived tragedy. It is an almost
exact replica of those in which Coriolanus has collided again and
again with the Roman mob. For Aufidius knows as well as the
Roman tribunes how to manipulate his foe for his sinister purpose. He stirs the commoners against his enemy by haranguing
them on the subject of Coriolanus' perfidy:

> He has betrayed your business, and given up
> For certain drops of salt your city—Rome,
> (I say "your city") to his wife and mother;
> Breaking his oath and resolution like
> A twist of rotten silk; never admitting
> Counsel o' the war; but at his nurse's tears
> He whin'd and roar'd away your victory.
>
> (v. v. 91-7)

In the course of this diatribe he taunts Coriolanus with epithets
like "traitor" and "boy of tears," words which drive the warrior
to an almost pathological seizure of rage. Then Coriolanus, shouting insults to the crowd, stirs the Volscian populace to fury.
Once aroused, they rush upon him with cries of "Tear him to
pieces!—Do it presently—He killed my son!—My daughter—He
killed my cousin Marcus! He killed my father." The lords of
Corioli, aghast at the blood-thirstiness of the mob, try in vain to
calm it. But Aufidius and his conspirators have aroused the

masses to the killing point. With cries of "Kill, kill, kill, kill, kill him" they fall upon Coriolanus and murder him.

This catastrophe gives final emphasis to the satiric view of Coriolanus. His automatic response to the artfully arranged provocation has at last entrapped him to his death. His end is the direct result of an over-stimulated reflex mechanism. The catastrophe of such an automaton is not tragic. It is so completely devoid of grandeur and dignity that it awakens amusement seasoned with contempt.

VII

This derision is much less absorbing than the pity and terror provoked by a genuinely tragic denouement. For that very reason a satiric play is better suited than a tragedy to present forcefully a political exemplum. In *Coriolanus* our interest is not held by the fall of a great man destroyed by forces beyond his control. It is rather caught by the picture of social and political chaos produced both by subversive forces of democracy and by a man who is temperamentally unable to be a successful ruler. The drama, then, is a satiric representation of a slave of passion designed to teach an important political lesson.

If this is true, why has *Coriolanus* never been a popular play? The principal reason is that critics and producers have invariably regarded it as a tragedy of an orthodox but greatly inferior sort. As a tragedy it lacks, as Stoll suggests, "constructive mechanism." Neither Fate nor a villain spins the plot. Coriolanus is destroyed by what is false within his nature. Yet we do not behold the inner emotional conflict that ends in disaster. We never see the dramatic struggle taking place within his mind and spirit. Therefore his nature inevitably seems poor and shallow. More than that, all the positive qualities which he displays are offensive. The remnants of a noble pride appear darkly through a cloud of childish impatience and uncontrolled rage. Finally, his catastrophe fixes ineradicably in the minds of all who expect a tragedy an impression of Shakespeare's artistic ineptitude. Coriolanus is manipulated into a fatal crisis and he meets his end in a riot which his mad fury has precipitated. No proper tragic hero moves thus toward his end in automatic response to artfully arranged stimuli. Nor can a death which comes to a man in a wild brawl signalize any triumph of the spirit.

These are defects only if Shakespeare intended *Coriolanus* to be a tragedy of the usual sort. If he meant the play to be more satire than tragedy, most of these qualities are virtues. Shakespeare naturally avoids arousing sympathy for a man whom he wishes to deride. For this reason he fills the early scenes with trenchant speech of hostile commentators, whose business is to draw a well-rounded satiric portrait of Coriolanus. Then the author traps his victim again and again so that we may see repeatedly the writhings of his anger. Finally he artfully designs a final scene which will make his satiric intention unmistakable. The murder of Coriolanus is not the moving death of a great hero; it is the deserved result of a supreme exhibition of his folly.

The bareness of the plot of *Coriolanus* also contributes to the satiric emphasis of the drama. True to the genius of satire it keeps the minds of the spectators riveted upon the ridicule of human faults. Derision, unless associated with moral indignation, does not easily awaken aesthetic pleasure. But in *Coriolanus* ridicule has been made to serve the teaching of sound political theory and only by a few can the descriptive forces in a healthy state be strongly enough felt to moderate the discomfort which most men feel at the persistent satire of a strong man.

NOTES

1. A. C. Bradley, "Coriolanus. Second Annual Shakespeare Lecture" (1 July, 1912), Proceedings of the British Academy 1911-12, pp. 457-73. Hazelton Spencer in *The Art and Life of William Shakespeare* (1940), 346-50, takes a similar view. "In *Coriolanus*," says the critic, "he [Shakespeare] frankly takes the line of least resistance." The idea is that he simply followed mechanically the facts laid down in his source—"that is all."

2. Bradley, op. cit. p. 461.

3. George Brandes, for example, in a chapter in *William Shakespeare, a Critical Study* (New York, 1902) emphasizes the absence in *Coriolanus* of "any humane consideration for the oppressed condition of the poor" and his "physical aversion for the atmosphere of the people." M. W. MacCallum expresses the more

measured view by admitting that "Shakespeare invariably treats crowds of citizens, whether in the ancient or modern world . . . as stupid, disunited, fickle" (*Shakespeare's Roman Plays and Their Background*, London, 1910, p. 470).

4. Serge Dinamov, *Works of Shakespeare*, 4 vols., I, xix.

5. These ideas have been thoroughly presented in James E. Phillips, Jr.'s *The State in Shakespeare's Greek and Roman Plays* (N. Y., 1940), *passim*.

6. William Fulbecke in his *Pandectes of the Law of Nations* (1602) cites the history of Coriolanus to confirm his contention that the people is the "beast with many heads." This example he offers as part of his evidence drawn from history to prove that democracy is contrary to natural law.

7. Mark Van Doren, *Shakespeare*, New York, 1939, p. 10.

8. John W. Draper in an article called "Shakespeare's *Coriolanus*: A Study in Renaissance Psychology," *West Virginia Bulletin* (Philological Studies III, Sept. 1939, pp. 22-36) develops these ideas. He believes that *Coriolanus* is a perfect illustration of the notions on this subject developed in Plutarch's *Morals*, La Primaudaye's *The French Academie*, and Thomas Adams' *Diseases of the Soul* (1616) first introduced into Shakespeare studies by Lily B. Campbell in her *Shakespeare's Tragic Heroes* (Cambridge, 1930).

G. Wilson Knight

"GREAT CREATING NATURE":
AN ESSAY ON *THE WINTER'S TALE*

The Winter's Tale presents a contrast of sinful maturity and
nature-guarded youth in close association with seasonal change.
But there is more to notice. Shakespeare's genius is labouring
to pit his own more positive intuitions, expressed hitherto mainly
through happy-ending romance and comedy, against tragedy:
they are to work as redeeming forces. The idyll of Florizel and
Perdita will fall naturally into place: but romance in Shakespeare
regularly enjoys the support, or at least the company, of humour.
In Leontes Shakespeare's tragic art has reached a new compact-
ness and intensity; and now in our next scenes, he gives us a
figure of absolute comedy, Autolycus.

Richest humour offers a recognition of some happy universal
resulting from the carefree stripping away of cherished values:
elsewhere [1] I have compared such "golden," or sympathetic,
humour, of which Falstaff is an obvious example, with humour
of the critical, moralistic, Jonsonian, sort, such as that Shakespeare touches in Malvolio. Falstaff, though utterly unmoral, yet
solicits our respect, and in that recognition consists the fun. The
fun itself is, moreover, in essence a lark-like thing; it will sing,
or dance, and may elsewhere house itself in spring-frolic and
lyrical verse, such as "It was a lover and his lass . . ." introduced by Touchstone in *As You Like It* (v. iii.). Autolycus is a
blend of burly comedian and lyrical jester.

From *The Crown of Life*, 1947, pp. 98-128. Reprinted by permission of Methuen & Co., Ltd.

He enters singing verses redolent of spring:

> When daffodils begin to peer,
>   With heigh! the doxy over the dale,
> Why, then comes in the sweet o' the year;
>   For the red blood reigns in the winter's pale.
>
> (IV. ii. 1)

He is spring incarnate; carefree, unmoral, happy, and sets the note for a spring-like turn in our drama, reversing the spring and winter conclusion of Shakespeare's first comedy, *Love's Labour's Lost*. His following stanzas continue with references to country linen on the hedge (cp. *Love's Labour's Lost*, v. ii. 914), song-birds, tooth-ache, ale, the lark and jay, "summer songs for me and my aunts," hay-merriment: it is a glorious medley of inconsequential realistic rusticity. Suddenly he comments in prose:

> I have served Prince Florizel and in my time wore
> three-pile; but now I am out of service.
>
> (IV. ii. 13)

He interrupts himself only to drop again into song—"But shall I go mourn for that, my dear?" Like Touchstone, and Poor Tom in *King Lear*, he has seen better days, but remains happy, his thoughts slipping naturally into song. He next explains his profession of minor thief, off the high road, as "a snapper up of unconsidered trifles" (IV. ii. 26).

His play with the Clown is supremely satisfying, and far more convincing than most stage trickery (e.g. Iago's of Cassio, Roderigo and Othello). The Clown is presented as a thorough gull, though not inhumanly so, as is Sir Andrew or Roderigo. Every phrase tells. As the supposedly injured man is carefully lifted—"O! good sir, tenderly, O!" (IV. ii. 76)—his purse is being delicately manœuvred within reach; the victim's attention is meanwhile firmly directed away from the danger-zone—"I fear, sir, my shoulder blade is out" (IV. ii. 78); and, when the business is successfully accomplished, there is the delightful *double entendre*. "You ha' done me a charitable office" (IV. ii. 82). Shakespeare's last work often recalls the New Testament, and here we have, in Autolycus' account of his beating, robbery and loss of clothes, a clear parody of the parable of the Good Samaritan, the pattern being completed by the Clown's continuation, "Dost lack any money? I have a little money for thee" (iv. ii. 83), and Autolycus' hurried and anxious disclaimer, "No, good sweet sir: no, I beseech you, sir . . . Offer me no money, I pray you! that kills my heart." (iv. iii. 85). There follows Autolycus' description of himself with some rather ordinary court-satire and finally the delightful conclusion, crying out for stage-realization:

Clown.	How do you now?
Autolycus.	Sweet sir, much better than I was: I can stand and walk. I will even take my leave of you, and pace softly towards my kinsman's.
Clown.	Shall I bring thee on the way?
Autolycus.	No, good-faced sir; no, sweet sir.
Clown.	Then fare thee well: I must go buy spices for our sheep-shearing.

(iv. iii. 119)

"Softly" is spoken with an upward lilt of the voice. Autolycus is a sweet, smooth-voiced rogue. The Clown says his last speech to the audience with a broad grin on his vacant face. When he is gone, Autolycus takes one agile skip, then:

> Jog on, jog on, the footpath way
> And merrily hent the stile-a:
> A merry heart goes all the day
> Your sad tires in a mile-a.

(iv. iii. 133)

The incident circles back to its start, enclosed in melody. It is all utterly unmoral, as unmoral as the scents of spring. This might well be called the most convincing, entertaining, and profound piece of comedy in Shakespeare. Such personal judgements are necessarily of doubtful interest, except to help point my argument that, so far from relaxing, Shakespeare's art is, on every front, advancing.

The sheep-shearing scene similarly sums up and surpasses all Shakespeare's earlier poetry of pastoral and romance. It is, however—and this is typical of our later plays—characterized by a sharp realism. The Clown's shopping list has already built a sense of simple cottage housekeeping and entertainment, with a suggestion of something out-of-the-ordinary in his supposed sister, Perdita:

> Three pound of sugar; five pound of currants; rice. What will this sister of mine do with rice? But my father hath made her mistress of the feast, and she lays it on.
>
> (IV. ii. 40)

His following reference to psalm-singing puritans sticks out awkwardly; more in place are the "nosegays" and "raisins o' the sun" (IV. iii. 43-53), especially the last. Autolycus has already sung of the "red blood" reigning after winter (IV. ii. 4), and soon our merry-makers are to be "red with mirth" (IV. iii. 54). We are to watch a heightening of English country festivity, touched with Mediterranean warmth, something, to quote Keats,

> Tasting of Flora and the country green,
> Dance, and Provençal song, and sun-burnt mirth.

So we move from spring to summer, under a burning sun.

The sun has not been so honoured before.[2] We have known the moon-silvered encounters of Romeo and Juliet and glimmering tangles of the "wood near Athens"; also the cypress shadows of *Twelfth Night* and chequered glades of Arden; but never before, not even in *Antony and Cleopatra*—a necessary step, where sun-warmth was, however, felt mainly through description, the action itself searching rather for "gaudy" (III. xi. 182) or moonlit nights—never before has the sun been so dramatically awakened, so close to us, as here; and there is a corresponding advance in love poetry, compassing, though with no loss of magic, strong fertility suggestion and a new, daylight assurance:

> These your unusual weeds to each part of you
> Do give a life: no shepherdess, but Flora
> Peering in April's front. This your sheep-shearing
> Is as a meeting of the petty gods,
> And you the queen on't.
>
> (IV. iii. 1)

So speaks Prince Florizel. But Perdita's answer witnesses both her country simplicity and feminine wisdom; she fears, as does Juliet, love's rashness and insecurity. Indeed, all Shakespeare's love-heroines, following the pattern laid down by Venus' prophecy in *Venus and Adonis* (1135-64), are given tragic undertones; they have an aura of tragedy about them. Florizel's love is more confident and showy (as usual in Shakespeare), but his use of mythology, as in "Flora" above, has a new, and finely convincing, impact. He catalogues the gods who have disguised themselves for love: Jupiter as a bellowing bull, Neptune a bleating lamb and, giving highest poetic emphasis to our play's supreme deity,

> the fire-rob'd god,
> Golden Apollo, a poor humble swain
> As I seem now.
>
> (IV. iii. 29)

"O Lady Fortune," prays Perdita in a phrase reminiscent of *Pericles*, "stand you auspicious" (IV. iii. 51). Though she remains doubtful, her doubts, a mixture of shyness and hard-headed feminine realism, only make the poetry more poignant. So, too, do the many homely reminders, as in the old shepherd's reminiscences of his dead wife's busy behaviour as hostess on such festival days as this, cooking, serving, and dancing in turn, bustling about, "her face o' fire" (IV. iii. 60) with both exertion and refreshment. Now Perdita, following Thaisa at the court of Simonides (the repetition is close, both fathers similarly reminding their apparently shy daughters of their duties), is "mistress of the feast" (IV. iii. 68; cp. "queen of the feast" at *Pericles* II. iii. 17), and has to conquer her shyness.

There follows Perdita's important dialogue with Polixenes. She, rather like Ophelia in a very different context, is presenting posies according to the recipient's age and offers the two older men (Polixenes and Camillo wear white beards, IV. iii. 417) rosemary and rue, which, she says, keep their savour "all the winter long" (IV. iii. 75): notice the recurring emphasis on age and seasons. Polixenes, however (forgetting his disguise?), appears to resent being given "flowers of winter" (IV. iii. 79) and

Perdita gracefully apologizes for not having an autumnal selection:

> *Perdita.*   Sir, the year growing ancient,
> Not yet on summer's death, nor on the birth
> Of trembling winter, the fairest flowers o' the
>   season
> Are our carnations, and streak'd gillyvors,
> Which some call nature's bastards: of that kind
> Our rustic garden's baren, and I care not
> To get slips of them.
> *Polixenes.*   Wherefore, gentle maiden,
> Do you neglect them?
> *Perdita.*   For I have heard it said
> There is an art which in their piedness shares
> With great creating nature.
> *Polixenes.*   Say there be;
> Yet nature is made better by no mean
> But nature makes that mean; so, over that art,
> Which you say adds to nature, is an art
> That nature makes. You see, sweet maid, we
>   marry
> A gentler scion to the wildest stock,
> And make conceive a bark of baser kind
> By bud of nobler race; this is an art
> Which does mend nature, change it rather, but
> The art itself is nature.
> *Perdita.*   So it is.
> *Polixenes.* Then make your garden rich in gillyvors
> And do not call them bastards.
> *Perdita.*   I'll not put
> The dibble in earth to set one slip of them;
> No more than, were I painted, I would wish
> This youth should say, 'twere well, and only
>   therefore
> Desire to breed by me. Here's flowers for you;
> Hot lavender, mints, savory, marjoram;
> The marigold, that goes to bed wi' the sun,
> And with him rises weeping: these are flowers

> Of middle summer, and I think they are given
> To men of middle age. You're very welcome.
> *Camillo.*   I should leave grazing, were I of your flock
> And only live by gazing.
> *Perdita.*   Out, alas!
> You'd be so lean, that blasts of January
> Would blow you through and through.
>
> (IV. iii. 79)

Of this one could say much. Notice first, the continued emphasis on seasons at the opening and concluding lines of my quotation; the strong physical realism (recalling Hermione's defence)
in Perdita's use of "breed"; and the phrase "great creating
nature" (to be compared with "great nature" earlier, at II. ii. 60).

The speakers are at cross purposes, since one is referring to art,
the other to artificiality, itself a difficult enough distinction. The
whole question of the naturalist and transcendental antinomy
is accordingly raised. The art concerned is called natural by
Polixenes in that either (i) human invention can never do more
than direct natural energy, or (ii) the human mind and therefore its inventions are nature-born: both meanings are probably
contained. Human civilization, art and religion are clearly in
one sense part of "great creating nature," and so is everything
else. But Perdita takes her stand on natural simplicity, growing
from the unforced integrity of her own country up-bringing, in
opposition to the artificialities of, we may suggest, the court: she
is horrified at dishonouring nature by human trickery. Observe
that both alike reverence "great creating nature," though differing in their conclusions. No logical deduction is to be drawn; or
rather, the logic is dramatic, made of opposing statements, which
serve to conjure up an awareness of nature as an all-powerful
presence, at once controller and exemplar. The dialogue forms
accordingly a microcosm of our whole drama.

There is a certain irony, too, in Polixenes' defence of exactly
the type of love-mating which Florizel and Perdita are planning
for themselves. Polixenes is, perhaps, setting a trap; or may be
quite unconsciously arguing against his own later behaviour.
Probably the latter.

Perdita next turns to Florizel:

Perdita.   Now, my fair'st friend,
I would I had some flowers o' the spring that
    might
Become your time of day; and yours, and yours,
That wear upon your virgin branches yet
Your maidenheads growing: O Proserpina!
For the flowers now that frighted thou let'st fall
From Dis's waggon! daffodils
That come before the swallow dares, and take
The winds of March with beauty; violets dim,
But sweeter than the lids of Juno's eyes
Or Cytherea's breath; pale prim-roses
That die unmarried ere they can behold
Bright Phoebus in his strength, a malady
Most incident to maids; bold oxlips and
The crown imperial; lilies of all kinds,
The flower-de-luce being one. O! these I lack
To make you garlands of, and my sweet friend,
To strew him o'er and o'er!

Florizel.   What! like a corse?
Perdita. No, like a bank for love to lie and play on;
Not like a corse; or if—not to be buried,
But quick and in mine arms. Come, take your
    flowers:
Methinks I play as I have seen them do
In Whitsun pastorals: sure this robe of mine
Does change my disposition.

                                    (IV. iii. 112)

Reference to the season-myth of Proserpine is natural enough;
indeed, almost an essential. You might call Perdita herself a seed
sowed in winter and flowering in summer. "Take" = "charm,"
or "enrapture." Though Autolycus' first entry suggested spring,
we are already, as the nature of our festival and these lines declare, in summer. Note the fine union, indeed identity, of myth
and contemporary experience, finer than in earlier Shakespearian
pastorals: Dis may be classical, but his "wagon" is as real as a
wagon in Hardy. See, too, how classical legend and folk-lore
coalesce in the primroses and "bright Phoebus in his strength," a

phrase pointing the natural poetic association of sun-fire and mature love (as in *Antony and Cleopatra*): the sun corresponding, as it were, to physical fruition (as the moon to the more operatic business of wooing) and accordingly raising in Perdita, whose poetry is strongly impregnated with fertility-suggestion (the magic here is throughout an earth-magic, a sun-magic), a wistful aside, meant presumably for herself. Perdita's flower-poetry reaches a royal impressionism in "crown imperial" and "garland" suiting the speaker's innate, and indeed actual, royalty. The contrasting suggestion of "corse" quickly merging into a love-embrace (reminiscent of the love and death associations in *Antony and Cleopatra* and Keats) finally serves to heighten the pressure of exuberant, buoyant, life. The "Whitsun pastorals," like our earlier puritans, though perhaps historically extraneous, may be forgiven for their lively impact, serving to render the speech vivid with the poet's, and hence, somehow, our own, personal experience.

Perdita's royalty is subtly presented: her robes as mistress of the feast have, as she said, made her act and speak strangely. Florizel details each of her graces (IV. iii. 135-43), wishing her in turn to speak, to sing, to dance—as "a wave o' the sea"—for ever. He would have her every action perpetuated, the thought recalling Polixenes' recollections of himself and Leontes as "boy eternal" (I. ii. 65). Florizel has expressed a delight in the given instant of youthful grace so sacred that it somehow deserves eternal status; when she moves he would have her, in a phrase itself patterning the blend of motion and stillness it describes, "move still, still so." Watching her, he sees the universe completed, crowned, at each moment of her existence:

> Each your doing,
> So singular in each particular,
> Crowns what you are doing in the present deed,
> That all your acts are queens
>
> (IV. iii. 143)

As once before, we are reminded, this time more sharply, of Blake's "minute particulars." The royalistic tonings here and in the "crown imperial" of her own speech (IV. iii. 126) not merely hint Perdita's royal blood, but also serve to stamp her actions with eternal validity; for the crown is always to be understood as a symbol piercing the eternity dimension. We are, it is true, being forced into distinctions that Shakespeare, writing from a royalistic age, need not actually have surveyed; but Florizel's lines certainly correspond closely to those in *Pericles* imaging Marina as a palace "for the crown'd Truth to dwell in" and again as monumental Patience sitting "above kings' graves" and "smiling extremity out of act" (*Pericles*, v. i. 123, 140). Perdita is more lively; time, creation, nature, earth, all have more rights here than in *Pericles;* but the correspondence remains close.

Perdita's acts are royal both in their own right and also because she is, in truth, of royal birth:

> This is the prettiest low-born lass that ever
> Ran on the green-sward. Nothing she does or seems
> But smacks of something greater than herself,
> Too noble for this place.
>
> (IV. iii. 156)

But this is not the whole truth. Later, after Polixenes' outburst, she herself makes a comment more easily appreciated in our age than in Shakespeare's:

> I was not much afeared; for once or twice
> I was about to speak and tell him plainly,
> The self-same sun that shines upon his court
> Hides not his visage from our cottage, but
> Looks on alike.
>
> (IV. iii. 455)

The lovely New Testament transposition (with "sun" for "rain") serves to underline the natural excellence and innate worth of this simple rustic community; and only from some such recognition can we make full sense of the phrase "queen of curds and cream" (IV. iii. 161). We may accordingly re-group our three royalties in terms of (i) Perdita's actual descent, (ii) her natural excellence and (iii) that more inclusive category from which both descend, or to which both aspire, in the eternity-dimension. A final conclusion would reach some concept of spiritual royalty corresponding to Wordsworth's (in his *Immortality Ode*); with further political implications concerning the expansion of sovereignty among a people.

The lovers are, very clearly, felt as creatures of "rare"—the expected word recurs (IV. iii. 32)—excellence, and their love, despite its strong fertility contacts, is correspondingly pure. Perdita, hearing Florizel's praises, fears he woos her "the false way" (IV. iii. 151); while Florizel is equally insistent that his "desires run not before his honour," nor his "lusts burn hotter" than his "faith" (IV. iii. 33). The statement, which appears, as in *The Tempest* later, a trifle laboured, is clearly central: Perdita, as mistress of the feast, insists that Autolycus "use no scurrilous words in's tunes" (IV. iii. 215). Our first tragedy was precipitated by suspicion of marital infidelity; and our young lovers express a corresponding purity.

The action grows more rollicking, with a dance of "shepherds and shepherdesses" (IV. iii. 165) in which Perdita and Florizel join. There follows Autolycus' spectacular entry as musical pedlar, preceded by a rich description (IV. iii. 191-201) of his rowdy-merry catches and tunes ("jump her and thump her," "whoop! do me no harm, good man"). He enters all a-flutter with ribbons and a tray of good things and describes his absurd ballads to the awe-struck Mopsa and Dorcas. Though the words may not be scurrilous, the songs are ribald enough, one telling of a usurer's wife "brought to bed of twenty money-bags at a burden"; and another sung originally by a fish representing a woman "who would not exchange flesh with one that loved her" and had been metamorphosed in punishment (IV. iii. 265, 282). They are little burlesques of our main fertility-myth, stuck in as gargoyles on a cathedral, and the two girls' anxious enquiries as to whether the stories are true, with Autolycus' firm reassurances, serve to complete the parody. Finally Autolycus conducts and joins in a catch, followed by another dance of "twelve rustics, habited like satyrs" (IV. iii. 354), given by carters, shepherds, neatherds, and swineherds. Here our rough country fun, heavily toned for fertility, reaches its climax.

But nature continues to provide poetry as refined as Florizel's image of winter purity (winter is also present in Autolycus' "lawn as white as driven snow" at IV. iii. 220):

> I take thy hand; this hand,
> As soft as dove's down, and as white as it,
> Or Ethiopian's tooth, or the fann'd snow that's bolted
> By the northern blasts twice o'er.
> (IV. iii. 374)

As in Keats' "Bright Star" sonnet, human love is compared to the steadfast gazing on earth, or sea, of heavenly light:

> He says he loves my daughter:
> I think so too; for never gazed the moon
> Upon the water as he'll stand and read
> As 'twere my daughter's eyes . . .
> (IV. iii. 171)

This (with which we should compare the similar love imagery of *Love's Labour's Lost*, IV. iii. 27-42) parallels Leontes' picture of Mamilius' "welkin eye" followed by fears for the "centre" (i.e. of the earth), forming an association of emotional and universal stability (I. ii. 137, 139); and also his later contrast and identification of "nothing" with "the world and all that's in it" and the "covering sky" (I. ii. 293-4). The universal majesty is continually imagined concretely as earth and sky facing each other, as in Leontes' "plainly as heaven sees earth or earth sees heaven" (I. ii. 315); it is the universe we actually know and see, without the cosmic, spheral, idealizing emphasis of *Antony and Cleopatra* and (once) *Pericles*. So Florizel, questioned by Polixenes, calls the universe as witness to his love:

> . . . and he, and more
> Than he, or men, the earth, the heavens, and all . . .
> (IV. iii. 383)

Should he prove false, then

> Let nature crush the sides o' the earth together
> And mar the seeds within!
> (IV. iii. 491)

Though reminiscent of nature's "germens" in *King Lear* (III. ii. 8), those "seeds" belong especially to this, as to no other, play. The emphasis on earth's creativeness is repeated:

> Not for Bohemia, nor the pomp that may
> Be thereat glean'd, for all the sun sees or
> The close earth wombs or the profound sea hides
> In unknown fathoms, will I break my oath
> To this my fair belov'd.
>
> (IV. iii. 501)

The sun, as the moon before, is thought as "seeing"; it is the "eye" of heaven of Sonnet XVIII. The sun is constantly reverenced throughout *The Winter's Tale*, either directly (as in "welkin eye" etc.) or "the fire-rob'd god, golden Apollo" (IV. iii. 29) and his oracle. Nature here is creative, majestic, something of illimitable mystery and depth ("profound sea," "unknown fathoms"); but it is never bookish. Nor is it dissolved into any system of elements. Earth, sea, sun and moon are felt rather as concrete realities of normal experience, nearer Renaissance commonsense than Dantesque or Ptolemaic harmonies, whilst housing strong classical-mythological powers.

As for Polixenes' brutal interruption, we recall Capulet, Egeus, York, Polonius, Lear: Shakespeare's fathers are normally tyrannical and Polixenes has, according to his lights, cause. His threats, excessive as Capulet's, drive home a contrast of social tyranny with rustic health, clinched by Perdita's admirable comment already noticed: there is court satire elsewhere (as at IV. ii. 94-101; IV. iii. 723-6). Of course, this contrast works within, without disrupting, the prevailing royalism: apart from the old shepherd, the country folk are mainly represented by three fools and a knave.

The pastoral interest slackens and significant passages become less dense as we become involved in the rather heavy machinery of getting everyone to Sicilia. Both Camillo's tortuous scheme and Autolycus' additions to it lack conviction, and we suffer rather as in *Hamlet* during Claudius' and Laertes' long discussion about the Norman, Lamond. There is, however, some purpose in the sagging action of *Hamlet*,[3] whereas here we seem to be confronted by plot-necessity alone. About Autolycus' lengthy fooling with the Shepherd and Clown there is, however, something to say.

The dialogue not only protracts the sagging action, but rouses discomfort, Autolycus' description of the punishments awaiting the rustics, though pictorially in tone here (involving "honey," "wasps," midday sun, flies: iv. iii. 16-25), being a trifle unpleasant. Resenting Autolycus' fall from his first entry, one is tempted to dismiss the incident as an error. Autolycus is, however, being used to elaborate the vein of court satire already suggested by Polixenes' behaviour; it is almost a parody of that behaviour. The pick-pocket pedlar, now himself disguised as "a great courtier" (iv. iii. 777), becomes absurdly superior and uses his new position to baffle the Clown precisely as Touchstone the courtier-fool baffles William. His elaborate description of torments is extremely cruel; but then the court—Polixenes' harshness fresh in our minds —is cruel.

But we can still disapprove the subordination of humour to satire; and yet this very subordination serves a further purpose concerned with the essence of humour itself. Autolycus is first a composite of spring music and delightful knavery; during the sheep-shearing festival he is a source of rather ribald entertainment and catchy song. Next, he goes off to sell his wares, and on his re-entry recounts his successful purse-picking, which now, however, wins less approval in view of our accumulated concern for the simple people on whom he battens as a dangerous parasite. He is later by chance forced to dress as a courtier and further looks like making a good thing out of the two rustics and their secret. He is advancing rapidly in the social scale; the fates assist him. As he says,

> If I had a mind to be honest, I see Fortune would
> not suffer me: she drops booties in my mouth.
> (iv. iii. 868)

He is now all out for "advancement" (iv. iii. 873). After donning courtier's clothes, his humour takes an unnecessarily cruel turn. Something similar happened with Falstaff, who, a creature of pure humour (and also robbery) in Part I of *Henry IV*, becomes less amusing in Part II where he has advanced socially, wears fine clothes, and is tainted by a courtier's ambition.[4] He is himself subscribing to the very values which we thought he scorned and our source of humour to that extent weakened. The humorous parasite cannot afford to be too successful, any more than the saint. So with Autolycus: the merry robber-tramp, as he makes his way, becomes less merry. His vices become less amusing as he indulges his lust for power; as his egotism expands, a cruel strain (compare Falstaff's attitude to his recruits and Justice Shallow) is revealed; and he is at once recognized as inferior to the society on which, as a happy-go-lucky ragamuffin, he formerly preyed for our amusement. More widely, we can say that the delicate balance of unmoral humour—and no finer examples exist than the early Falstaff and Autolycus—must be provisional only; it cannot maintain the pace, cannot survive as a challenge among the summery positives here enlisted against tragedy: Falstaff was, necessarily, rejected by Prince Hal. Moreover, just as the Falstaff of *Henry IV* becomes finally the buffoon of *The Merry Wives of Windsor,* so Autolycus' last entry, when they have all arrived in Sicilia, and the Shepherd and Clown are rich and he a recognized knave, is peculiarly revealing: we see him now bowing and scraping to his former gull.[5] Meanwhile, our humorous sympathies have passed over to the Clown, rather tipsy and talking of himself as having recently become a "gentleman born" (v. ii. 142-64), so providing a new and richly amusing variation in social comment.

The long scene (IV. iii.) accordingly has a falling movement; from exquisite pastoral and the accompanying flower-dialogue, through robust country merriment to an all but ugly humour. The romance is to survive; not so Autolycus, who is to lose dramatic dignity. No one will accuse Shakespeare of lacking humour, but it is too often forgotten that his humour works within the limits set by a prevailing "high seriousness."

Our final summing movement takes us back to Sicilia, where all the people foregather and the complications are resolved.

Leontes is a figure of accomplished repentance. From now on religious phraseology is insistent, with strong Christian tonings:

> Sir, you have done enough, and have perform'd
> A saint-like sorrow; no fault could you make
> Which you have not redeem'd; indeed, paid down
> More penitence than done trespass. At the last,

> Do as the heavens have done, forget your evil;
> With them forgive yourself.
>
> (v. i. 1)

His kingdom, as the oracle foretold, is, through his own sin, heirless (v. i. 10). The contrast in *Macbeth* between tyranny without issue and Banquo's descendants may assist our response to Leontes' punishment. Both heroes offend against creation and are accordingly themselves uncreative. Paulina stands beside him, a perpetual reminder, referring to Hermione as "she you kill'd" (v. i. 15):

> *Leontes.*   I think so. Kill'd!
> She I kill'd! I did so; but thou strik'st me
> Sorely to say I did; it is as bitter
> Upon thy tongue as in my thought. Now, good now
> Say so but seldom.
>
> (v. i. 16)

Paulina is here to personify Leontes' "thought." Cleomenes, who cannot be expected to consider her dramatic office, rebuffs her sharply; and Dion, in a speech (v. i. 24-34) loaded with regal and religious impressions ("sovereign name," "his highness," "royalty," "holy," "holier"), urges the King to marry to beget an heir. Paulina, however, demands respect to the gods' "secret purposes" and the oracle of "divine Apollo," which asserted that Leontes should remain heirless till his child was found (v. i. 35-40); and he, wishing he had always followed her counsel, agrees, while further imagining Hermione's return, in accusation. His remarriage, he says,

> Would make her sainted spirit
> Again possess her corpse and on this stage—
> Where we're offenders now—appear soul-vex'd,
> And begin, 'Why to me?'
>
> (v. i. 57)

The world of sinful men is widely conceived; but also, ever so delicately, Hermione's return is hinted. Paulina next suggests that had his dead queen "such power" (v. i. 60) of return, she would have full "cause" of anger. Were she, Paulina, the ghost, she would shriek, point to his second wife's eyes, calling out, like the ghost in *Hamlet*, "Remember mine" (v. i. 67):

> *Leontes.* Stars, stars!
> And all eyes else dead coals.
>
> (v. i. 67)

Leontes sits almost tranced, in a state of other-worldly remembrance, all but outside the temporal dimension. Paulina continues to play with the thought of Hermione's return. Leontes is not to marry

> Unless another
> As like Hermione as is her picture,
> Affront his eye.
>
> (v. i. 73)

His new wife shall be, she says, older than the first:

> She shall be such
> As, walk'd your first queen's ghost, it should take joy
> To see her in your arms.
>
> (v. i. 79)

Leontes enters into the grave game, willingly agreeing not to marry till Paulina bids him, and she clinches the compact, whilst further preparing for the resurrection:

> That
> Shall be when your first queen's again in breath;
> Never till then.
>
> (v. i. 82)

Observe how carefully we are being prepared for the conclusion, our thoughts whetted, our minds subtly habituated, if not to its possibility, at least to its conceivability.

On the entry of Florizel and Perdita our most important impressions concern Perdita herself, given the usual praise accorded these later heroines: she is "the rarest of all women" (v. i. 112), a "goddess" (v. i. 131), a "paragon" (v. i. 153), or —exactly suiting our recurring impressionism of earth and sun —"the most peerless piece of earth" "that e'er the sun shone bright on" (v. i. 94). She reminds the tactless but purposeful Paulina of that "jewel of children," Mamilius (v. i. 117). She is a creature

> Would she begin a sect, might quench the zeal
> Of all professors else, make proselytes
> Of who she did but follow.
>
> (v. i. 107)

Earthly and transcendental impressions intermix in her praise. Both recur together in Leontes':

> And you, fair princess—goddess! O, alas!
> I lost a couple, that 'twixt heaven and earth
> Might thus have stood begetting wonder as
> You, gracious couple, do.
>
> (v. i. 131)

Children, planted between heaven and earth, beget "wonder," a word to be used later on for miraculous events. Children are copies of their parents:

> Your mother was most true to wedlock, prince;
> For she did print your royal father off,
> Conceiving you.
>
> (v. i. 124)

We remember Mamilius' resemblance to Leontes and Paulina's description of Leontes' baby daughter. Children are nature's miracles, and these two as welcome "as is the spring to the earth" (v. i. 151). So Leontes prays that "the blessed gods" may "purge all infection from our air" whilst their stay lasts (v. i. 168), a phrase harking back to the description of Delphos, intimations of a transfigured nature matching our sense of a transfigured humanity. Man is, at his royal best, almost divine:

> You have a holy father,
> A graceful gentleman; against whose person,
> So sacred as it is, I have done sin.
> For which the heavens, taking angry note
> Have left me issueless . . .
>
> (v. i. 170)

The supreme punishment here, especially for a king, is to be left without natural issue; Florizel, however, lives, to render his father "bless'd" (v. i. 174). Through the royalistic convention the poetry touches some truth concerning man, his high worth in the creative chain, his ultimate stature, that outdistances political concepts.

This semi-divine essence is also dependent on the creative love-faith of the young pair. Disaster dogs them. After surviving "dreadful Neptune" (v. i. 154), they hear of Polixenes' pursuit. But, though "Heaven set spies" (v. i. 203) on them; though the "stars," in another typical image, will first "kiss the valleys" (v. i. 206) before they be united; indeed, though Fortune appear as a "visible enemy" (v. i. 216), their love is to remain firm. As Leontes gazes on Perdita, the stern Paulina remarks that his eye "hath too much youth in't" (v. i. 225), and reminds him of Hermione. "I thought of her," he answers, softly, "even in these looks I made" (v. i. 227).

Leontes' reunion with his daughter is presented indirectly by the gentlemen's conversation: it has already been dramatized in *Pericles* and our present dramatic emphasis is to fall on Hermione's resurrection. These gentlemen converse in a prose of courtly formality, leaving poetry to return in full contrast later. The scene is preparatory to the greater miracle and its style well-considered, introducing us lightly and at a distance to those deep emotions which we are soon to feel with so powerful a subjective sympathy. It strikes a realistic and contemporary note, using the well-known trick of laying solid foundations before an unbelievable event: we are being habituated to impossible reunions. Moreover, the slightly ornate decorum leads on to the formal, ritualistic, quality of the later climax. There is emphasis, as one expects, on Perdita's innate and actual royalty "above her breeding" (v. ii. 41) and a comparison of earlier events to "an old tale" (v. ii. 30, 67; cp. v. iii. 117). The description, plastic rather than dramatic, serves to create a *sub specie aeternitatis* effect, and so further prepare us for the statue-scene:

. . . They seemed almost, with staring on one another, to tear the cases of their eyes; *there was speech in their dumb-*

ness, language in their very gesture; they looked as they had heard of *a world ransomed, or one destroyed:* a notable passion of *wonder* appeared in them; but the wisest beholder, that knew no more but seeing, could not say if the importance were *joy or sorrow;* but in the extremity of the one it must needs be.   (v. ii. 12)

My italicized phrases are important. With the first compare the Poet's comment on a painting in *Timon of Athens:* "To the dumbness of the gesture one might interpret . . ." (I. i. 34): see also *Cymbeline,* II. iv. 83-5. The watchers are, to quote Milton, made "marble with too much conceiving"; made to share the frozen immobility of art. Leontes' reaction to Hermione's statue is to be similar. Next, notice the apocalyptic suggestion of "ransomed" and "destroyed": is the miracle a transfiguration of nature or wholly transcendental? Certainly it strikes "wonder." Last, observe the indecisive reference to "joy" and "sorrow," which recurs again in description of Paulina:

But O! the noble combat that 'twixt joy and sorrow was fought in Paulina. She had one eye declined for the loss of her husband, another elevated that the oracle was fulfilled.   (v. i. 80)

Exactly such a blend of joy and sorrow is to characterize our final scene. Though we are pointed to "the dignity of this act" performed by kings and princes (v. ii. 88), it is all carried lightly, the dialogue following on with courtly fluency:

One of the prettiest touches of all, and that which angled for mine eyes—caught the water though not the fish—was when at the relation of the queen's death, with the manner how she came to it . . .   (v. ii. 91)

And yet the easy, almost bantering, manner can, without losing its identity, handle the most solemn emotions justly, as in the account of Leontes' confession:

Who was most marble there changed colour; some swounded, all sorrowed; if all the world could have seen it, the woe had been universal.   (v. i. 100)

As in "ransom'd" and "redeem'd" earlier, the drama is, as it were, on the edge of something "universal": we watch more than a particular incident.

Now this dialogue has been leading us on very carefully to its own little climax, directly preparatory to the play's conclusion:

> No; the princess hearing of her mother's statue, which is in the keeping of Paulina—a piece many years in doing, and now newly performed by that rare Italian master, Julio Romano; who, had he himself *eternity* and could put *breath* into his work, would beguile *Nature* of her custom, so perfectly he is her ape: he so near to Hermione hath done Hermione that they say one would speak to her and stand in hope of answer: thither with all greediness of affection are they gone, and there they intend to sup.   (v. ii. 105)

For the general thought of art imitating nature's human handiwork, compare the "nature's journeymen" of Hamlet's address to the Players (*Hamlet*, III. ii. 38). Here the statue is already associated with "eternity," regarded as the creative origin; [6] "breath" is to be important again. The implications of "eternity" are semi-transcendental in attempt to define that unmotivated power behind the mystery of free generation in nature and in art; indeed, implicit in freedom itself. The Gentlemen next refer to the statue as "some great matter" already suspected from Paulina's continual visits to the "removed house" where it stands (v. ii. 117-20). We are made thoroughly expectant, attuned to a consciousness where "every wink of an eye some new grace will be born" (v. ii. 124); a queer phrase whose courtly ease points the miracle of creation in time—there was a mysticism within Renaissance courtliness, as Castiglione's book indicates—whilst recalling the apocalyptic phrase in the New Testament about men being changed "in the twinkling of an eye." Both through Paulina's dialogue with Leontes in v. i. and the Gentlemen's conversation we have been prepared for the resurrection. But there are earlier hints, not yet observed. At Hermione's death, Paulina asserted:

>   If you can bring
> Tincture or lustre in her lip, her eye,

> *Heat outwardly or breath within,* I'll serve you
> As I would do the gods.
>
> (III. ii. 205)

A warm physical realism is regularly here felt as essential to resurrection. Paulina is suggesting that it would need a Cerimon, in Christian thought Christ, to work the miracle: the possibility at least was thus early suggested. Later Florizel referred to just such superhuman power when, after calling vast nature and all men as witness, he swore:

> That, were I crown'd the most imperial monarch,
> Thereof most worthy, were I the fairest youth
> That ever made eye swerve, *had force and knowledge
> More than was ever man's,* I would not prize them
> Without her love.
>
> (IV. iii. 385)

This close association of royalty ("crowned," "imperial," "monarch") with superhuman strength and wisdom may assist our interpretations elsewhere of Shakespeare's later royalism, whose spirituality (to use a dangerously ambiguous word) was forecast in Romeo's and Cleopatra's dreams of immortal, and therefore *imperial,* love (*Romeo and Juliet,* v. i. 9; *Antony and Cleopatra,* v. ii. 76-100). The king is, at the limit, a concept of superman status. Florizel later addresses Camillo in similar style:

> How, Camillo,
> May this, almost a miracle, be done?
> That I may call thee something more than man,
> And after that trust to thee.
>
> (IV. iii. 546)

Another clear reminiscence of Cerimon, with suggestions of some greater than human magic; white magic.

Now, as the resurrection draws near, we are prepared for it by Perdita's restoration. St. Paul once seems, perhaps justly, to consider resurrection as no more remarkable than birth (see Romans, IV. 17 in Dr. Moffatt's translation).[7] Certainly here the safeguarding of Perdita is considered scarcely less wonder-

ful than the resurrection of the dead. That the child should be
found, says Paulina,

> Is all as monstrous to our *human reason*
> As my Antigonus to break his grave
> And come again to me.
>
> (v. i. 41)

Yet she is restored, as the Gentlemen recount, and human
reason accordingly negated. Scattered throughout are dim fore-
shadowings of the miraculous. Nevertheless, death looms large
enough still, in poetry's despite: Paulina sees to that. When a
gentleman praises Perdita she remarks:

> O Hermione!
> As every present time doth boast itself
> Above a better gone, so must thy grave
> Give way to what's seen now.
>
> (v. i. 95)

The temporal order demands that the past slip away, that it
lose reality; the more visible present always seems *superior*.
Paulina resents this; and her remark may be aligned with both
our early lines on boyhood never dreaming of any future other
than to be "boy eternal" (i. ii. 65) and Florizel's desire to have
Perdita's every act in turn—speaking, dancing, etc.—perpetuated. All these are strivings after eternity. Paulina, moreover,
here suggests that the gentleman concerned, who seems to be a
poet, is himself at fault: his verse, which "flow'd with her
[i.e. Hermione's] beauty once," is now "shrewdly ebb'd" (v. i.
102). The complaint is, not that Hermione has gone, but that
the gentleman has failed in some sense to keep level. Death is
accordingly less an objective reality than a failure of the subject to keep abreast of life. This may seem to turn an obvious
thought into meaningless metaphysics, but the lines, in their
context, can scarcely be ignored. Throughout *Troilus and
Cressida* (especially at iii. iii. 145-84, an expansion of Paulina's
comment) Shakespeare's thoughts on time are highly abstruse
(see my essay in *The Wheel of Fire*); so are they in the Sonnets.
Wrongly used time is as intrinsic to the structure of *Macbeth*
as is "eternity" to that of *Antony and Cleopatra* (see my essays on

both plays in *The Imperial Theme*). As so often in great poetry, the philosophical subtlety exists within or behind a speech, or plot, of surface realism and simplicity. Now *The Winter's Tale* is hammering on the threshold of some extraordinary truth related to both "nature" and "eternity." Hence its emphasis on the seasons, birth and childhood, the continual moulding of new miracles on the pattern of the old; hence, too, the desire expressed for youthful excellence perpetuated and eternal; the thought of Perdita's every action as a "crowned" thing, a "queen," in its own eternal right (IV. iii. 145-6); and also of art as improving or distorting nature, in the flower-dialogue, in Julio Romano's uncanny, eternity-imitating, skill. And yet no metaphysics, no natural philosophy or art, satisfy the demand that the lost thing, in all its nature-born warmth, be preserved; that it, not only its descendant, shall live; that death be revealed as a sin-born illusion; that eternity be flesh and blood.

The action moves to the house of the "grave and good Paulina" (V. iii. 1). The scene is her "chapel," recalling the chapel of death at III. ii. 240, where Leontes last saw Hermione's dead body. Paulina shows them the statue, which excels anything "the hand of man hath done" (V. iii. 17); and they are quickly struck with—again the word—"wonder" (V. iii. 22). Leontes gazes; recognizes Hermione's "natural posture" (V. iii. 23); asks her to chide him, yet remembers how she was tender "as infancy and grace" (V. iii. 27):

> O! thus she stood,
> Even with such life of majesty—warm life
> As now it coldly stands—when first I woo'd her.
> I am asham'd: does not the stone rebuke me
> For being more stone than it? O, royal piece!
> (v. iii. 34)

Sweet though it be, it remains cold and withdrawn, like Keats' Grecian Urn. Yet its "majesty" exerts a strangely potent "magic" (V. iii. 39) before which Perdita kneels almost in "superstition" (V. iii. 43). Leontes' grief is so great that Camillo reminds him how "sixteen winters" and "so many summers" should by now alternately have blown and dried his soul clean of "sorrow"; why should that prove more persistent than short-lived "joy"?

(v. iii. 49-53). Leontes remains still, his soul pierced (v. iii. 34) by remembrance. Paulina, however, speaks realistically of the statue as art, saying how its colour is not dry yet (v. iii. 47); half apologizing for the way it moves him, her phrase "for the stone is mine" (v. iii. 58) re-emphasizing her peculiar office. She offers to draw the curtain, fearing lest Leontes' "fancy may think anon it moves" (v. iii. 61). The excitement generated, already intense, reaches new impact and definition in Paulina's sharp ringing utterance on "moves."

But Leontes remains quiet, fixed, in an other-worldly consciousness, a living death not to be disturbed, yet trembling with expectance:

> Let be, let be!
> Would I were dead, but that, methinks, already—
> What was he that did make it?
>
> (v. iii. 61)

A universe of meaning is hinted by that one word "already" and the subsequent, tantalizing, break. Now the statue seems no longer cold:

> See, my lord,
> Would you not deem it breath'd, and that those veins
> Did verily bear blood?
>
> (v. iii. 63)

As the revelation slowly matures, it is as though Leontes' own grief and love were gradually infusing the thing before him with life. He, under Paulina, is labouring, even now, that it may live. The more visionary, paradisal, personal wonder of Pericles (who alone hears the spheral music) becomes here a crucial conflict, an *agon*, in which many persons share; dream is being forced into actuality. "Masterly done," answers Polixenes, taking us back to common-sense, and yet again noting that "the very life seems warm upon her lip" (v. iii. 65). We are poised between motion and stillness, life and art:

> The fixure of her eye has motion in't,
> As we are mock'd with art.
>
> (v. iii. 67)

The contrast drives deep, recalling the balancing of art and nature in Perdita's dialogue with Polixenes; and, too, the imaging of the living Marina as "crown'd Truth" or monumental Patience (*Pericles*, v. i, 124, 140). Paulina reiterates her offer to draw the curtain lest Leontes be so far "transported" (cp. III. ii. 159; a word strongly toned in Shakespeare with magical suggestion) that he actually think it "lives"—thus recharging the scene with an impossible expectation. To which Leontes replies:

> No settled senses of the world can match
> The pleasure of that madness. Let't alone.
>
> (v. iii. 72)

He would stand here, spell-bound, forever; forever gazing on this sphinx-like boundary between art and life.

Paulina, having functioned throughout as the Oracle's implement, becomes now its priestess. Her swift changes key the scene to an extraordinary pitch, as she hints at new marvels:

> I am sorry, sir, I have thus far stirr'd you: but
> I could afflict you further.
>
> (v. iii. 74)

She has long caused, and still causes, Leontes to suffer poignantly; and yet his suffering has undergone a subtle change, for now this very "affliction has a taste as sweet as any cordial comfort" (v. iii. 76). Already (at v. ii. 20 and 81, and v. iii. 51-3) we have found joy and sorrow in partnership, as, too, in the description of Cordelia's grief (*King Lear*, IV. iii. 17-26). So Leontes endures a pain of ineffable sweetness as the mystery unfolds:

> Still, methinks,
> There is an air comes from her: what fine chisel
> Could ever yet cut breath?
>
> (v. iii. 77)

However highly we value the eternity phrased by art (as in Yeats' "monuments of unaging intellect" in *Sailing to Byzantium* [8] and Keats' *Grecian Urn*), yet there is a frontier beyond which it and all corresponding philosophies fail: they lack one thing, breath. With a fine pungency of phrase, more humanly relevant than Othello's "I know not where is that Promethean heat . . ." (*Othello*, v. ii. 12), a whole world of human idealism is dismissed. The supreme moments of earlier tragedy—Othello before the "monumental alabaster" (v. ii. 5) of the sleeping Desdemona, Romeo in Capel's monument, Juliet and Cleopatra blending sleep and death—are implicit in Leontes' experience; more, their validity is at stake, as he murmurs, "Let no man mock me" (v. iii. 79), stepping forward for an embrace; as old Lear, reunited with Cordelia, "a spirit in bliss," says "Do not laugh at me" (*King Lear*, iv. vii. 68); as Pericles fears lest his reunion with Marina be merely such a dream as "mocks" man's grief (*Pericles*, v. i. 144, 164). Those, and other, supreme moments of pathos are here re-enacted to a stronger purpose. Leontes strides forward; is prevented by Paulina; we are brought up against a *cul-de-sac*. But Paulina herself immediately releases new impetus as she cries, her voice quivering with the Sibylline power she wields:

> Either forbear,
> Quit presently the chapel, or resolve you
> For more amazement. If you can behold it,
> I'll make the statue move indeed, descend,
> And take you by the hand; but then you'll think—
> Which I protest against—I am assisted
> By wicked powers.
>
> (v. iii. 85)

The "chapel" setting is necessary, for we attend the resurrection of a supposedly buried person; the solemnity is at least half funereal. Much is involved in the phrase "wicked powers": we watch no act of necromancy. The "magic" (v. ii. 39), if magic it be, is a white magic; shall we say, a natural magic; the living opposite of the Ghost in *Hamlet* hideously breaking his tomb's "ponderous and marble jaws" (i. iv. 50). The difference is that between Prospero's powers in *The Tempest* and those of Marlowe's Faustus or of the Weird Sisters in *Macbeth*. The distinction in Shakespeare's day was important and further driven home by Paulina's:

It is requir'd
You do awake your faith. Then, all stands still;
Or those that think it is unlawful business
I am about, let them depart.

(v. iii. 94)

The key-word "faith" enlists New Testament associations, but to it Paulina adds a potency more purely Shakespearian: music. Shakespeare's use of music, throughout his main antagonist to tempestuous tragedy, reaches a newly urgent precision at Cerimon's restoration of Thaisa and Pericles' reunion with Marina. Here it functions as the specifically releasing agent:

Paulina.   Music, awake her: strike! (*Music sounds*)
'Tis time; descend; be stone no more; approach;
Strike all that look upon with marvel. Come;
I'll fill your grave up: stir, nay, come away;
Bequeath to death your numbness, for from him
Dear life redeems you. You perceive she stirs:
                    (*Hermione comes down*)
Start not; her actions shall be holy as
You hear my spell is lawful: do not shun her
Until you see her die again, for then
You kill her double. Nay, present your hand:
When she was young you woo'd her; now in age
Is she become the suitor?
Leontes.   O! she's warm.
If this be magic, let it be an art
Lawful as eating.

(v. iii. 98)

"Redeems" (cp. "ransomed" at v. ii. 16), "holy" and "lawful" continue earlier emphases. The concreteness of "fill your grave up" has analogies in Shelley's *Witch of Atlas* (LXIX-LXXI) and the empty sepulchre of the New Testament. Such resurrections are imaged as a re-infusing of the dead body with life. Hermione's restoration not only has nothing to do with black magic; it is not even transcendental. It exists in warm human actuality (cp. *Pericles*, v. i. 154): hence our earlier emphases on warmth and breath; and now on "eating" too. It is, indeed, part after all of "great creating nature"; no more, and no less; merely another miracle from the great power, the master-artist of creation, call it what you will, nature or eternity, Apollo or—as in the New Testament—"the living God."

The poet carefully refuses to elucidate the mystery on the plane of plot-realism. When Polixenes wonders where Hermione "has liv'd" or "how stol'n from the dead," Paulina merely observes that she *is* living, and that this truth, if reported rather than experienced, would "be hooted at like an old tale" (v. iii. 114-17; cp. "like an old tale" at v. ii. 30, 67). Perdita's assistance is needed to unloose Hermione's speech; whereupon she speaks, invoking the gods' "sacred vials" of blessing on her daughter and referring to the Oracle (v. iii. 121-8). Leontes further drives home our enigma by remarking that Paulina has found his wife, though "how is to be question'd"; for, he says,

> I saw her
> As I thought, dead, and have in vain said many
> A prayer upon her grave.
>
> (v. iii. 139)

We are not, in fact, to search for answers on this plane at all: the poet himself does not know them.[9] Certainly our plot-realism is maintained: Paulina reminds us that her husband is gone; and we may remember Mamilius. It is the same in *Pericles*. The subsidiary persons are no longer, as persons, important: the perfunctory marrying of Paulina and Camillo to round off the ritual might otherwise be a serious blemish.

The truth shadowed, or revealed, is only to be known, if at all, within the subjective personality, the "I" not easily linked into an objective argument. It is precisely this mysterious "I" in the audience that the more important persons of drama, and in especial tragedy, regularly objectify. Now within the "I" rest all those indefinables and irrationalities of free-will and guilt, of unconditioned and therefore appallingly responsible action with which *The Winter's Tale* is throughout deeply concerned; as in Leontes' unmotivated sin for which he is nevertheless in some sense responsible; with his following loss of free-will, selling himself in bondage to dark powers, and a consequent

enduring and infliction of tyranny. The outward effects are suspicion, knowledge of evil and violent blame; with a final spreading and miserable knowledge of death ("There was a man
dwelt by a churchyard"—II. i. 28), leading on, with Paulina's
assistance, to repentance. Time is throughout present as a
backward-flowing thing, swallowing and engulfing; we are sunk
deep in the consciousness of dead facts, causes, death. Now
over against all this stands the creative consciousness, existing
not in present-past but present-future, and with a sense of causation not behind but ahead, the ever-flowing in of the new and
unconditioned, from future to present: this is the consciousness
of freedom, in which "every wink of an eye some new grace
will be born" (v. ii. 124). Hence our poetry plays queer tricks
with time, as in the "boy eternal" passage where consciousness is
confined to "to-day" and "to-morrow": in Florizel's dreams of
immediate perfection eternalized; in thought of "eternity"
(which includes the future, being over-dimensional to the time-
stream) as the creative origin; and in Paulina's annoyance at the
poet-gentleman's ready submission to time the destroyer. Freedom is creation, and therefore art; and hence our emphases on
art, in the flower-dialogue, in notice of Julio Romano's skill, in
the statue-scene; and here we approach a vital problem. It is
precisely the creative spirit in man, the unmotivated and forward
"I," that binds him to "great creating Nature," the "great nature"
by whose laws the child is "freed and enfranchised" from the
womb (II. ii. 60-61): he is one with that nature, in so far as he
is free. Our drama works therefore to show Leontes, under the
tutelage of the Oracle, as painfully working himself from the
bondage of sin and remorse into the freedom of nature, with
the aptly-named Paulina as conscience, guide, and priestess. The
resurrection is not performed until (i) Leontes' repentance is
complete and (ii) creation is satisfied by the return of Perdita,
who is needed for Hermione's full release. Religion, art, procreation, and nature (in "warmth," "breath" and "eating") are all
contributory to the conclusion, which is shown as no easy release,
but rather a gradual revelation, corresponding to Pericles' reunion with Marina, under terrific dramatic pressure and fraught
with an excitement with which the watcher's "I" is, by most
careful technique, forced into a close subjective identity, so that

the immortality revealed is less concept than experience. Nor is it just a reversal of tragedy; rather tragedy is contained, assimilated, transmuted; every phrase of the resurrection scene is soaked in tragic feeling, and the accompanying joy less an antithesis to sorrow than its final flowering. The depths of the "I," which are tragic, are being integrated with the objective delight which is nature's joy. The philosophy of Wordsworth is forecast; for he, too, knew Leontes' abysmal "nothing"; he too suffered some hideous disillusion, in part evil; he too laboured slowly for reintegration with nature; and, finally, he too saw man's true state in terms of creation and miracle. The response, in both Wordsworth and Shakespeare, is a reverential wonder at knowledge of Life where Death was throned.[10]

The Winter's Tale may seem a rambling, perhaps an untidy, play; its anachronisms are vivid, its geography disturbing. And yet Shakespeare offers nothing greater in tragic psychology, humour, pastoral, romance, and that which tops them all and is, except for *Pericles*, new. The unity of thought is more exact than appears: it was Sicily, at first sight ill-suited to the sombre scenes here staged, that gave us the myth of Proserpine or Persephone. The more profound passages are perhaps rather evidence of what is beating behind or within the creative genius at work than wholly successful ways of printing purpose on an average audience's, or an average reader's, mind; but the passages are there, and so is the purpose, though to Shakespeare it need not have been defined outside his drama. That drama, however, by its very enigma, its unsolved and yet uncompromising statement, throws up—as in small compass did the little flower-dialogue too —a vague, numinous, sense of mighty powers, working through both the natural order and man's religious consciousness, that preserve, in spite of all appearance, the good. Orthodox tradition is used, but it does not direct; a pagan naturalism is used too. The Bible has been an influence; so have classical myth and Renaissance pastoral;[11] but the greatest influence was Life itself, that creating and protecting deity whose superhuman presence and powers the drama labours to define.

NOTES

1. In writing of Byron in *The Burning Oracle*.
2. The heavy emphasis in *Love's Labour's Lost* remains throughout imagistic, in the manner of the Sonnets. This early play does much to define both the positive end of Shakespeare's work and the reasons for its postponement. See my remarks in *The Shakespearian Tempest*.
3. For a discussion of this "sagging action" see "Hamlet Reconsidered" in the enlarged (1949) edition of *The Wheel of Fire*.
4. This contrast has been well exposed by Professor J. Dover Wilson in *The Fortunes of Falstaff*. It is, however, there one strand only in a richer, satiric, design, with Falstaff becoming more forceful as he loses humour.
5. There is a deplorable stage tradition that Autolycus should again, in this late scene, start picking the purses of the Shepherd and Clown. The comedian will, of course, get his laughs; but for Shakespeare's opinion of such "pitiful ambition" see Hamlet's address to the Players (iii. ii. 50).
6. Compare the use of "eternity" as the home of divinity in close association with power at *Coriolanus*, v. iv. 26.
7. It must, however, be noted that the birth here concerned seems to be one of an abnormal, semi-miraculous, sort; but the Pauline doctrine of resurrection holds strong fertility suggestion elsewhere, as in the great passage on immortality at 1 *Corinthians*, xv, where the dead body is compared to a grain of wheat buried in earth.
8. A yet more relevant comparison with Yeats might adduce his drama *Resurrection*. Compare also the statue-interest of Ibsen's last play.
9. Note that Shakespeare here purposely drives the miraculous to a limit not touched in *Pericles*. For a full discussion of the metaphysical implications of the immortality dramatized in *The Winter's Tale* and other such works I must refer the reader to Chapter x of *The Christian Renaissance*.
10. We find a closely equivalent sense of the miraculous in the early scenes of *All's Well that Ends Well*, where Helena's mysterious art is clearly comparable with Cerimon's, and the style of speech continually takes on a rhymed formality similar to that in

Pericles. Lafeu's excellent comment might be read as a text for
The Winter's Tale:

> They say miracles are past; and we have our philosophical
> persons, to make modern and familiar things supernatural
> and causeless. Hence is it that we make trifles of terrors,
> ensconcing ourselves into seeming knowledge, when we
> should submit ourselves to an unknown fear. (II. iii. 1.)

Helena's success is "the rarest argument of wonder that hath
shot out in our latter times"; the "showing of a heavenly effect
in an earthly actor"; "in a most weak and debile minister, great
power, great transcendance" (II, iii. 8, 28, 40). See also the
many thoughts earlier on science, nature, death, "inspired merit,"
"skill infinite" and divine action at II. i. 102-89; with hint of a
medicine "able to breathe life into a stone" (II. i. 76). The relation of *All's Well That Ends Well* to the Final Plays deserves
more attention than can be accorded it here. See also *As You
Like It* (with Rosalind as magician), v. ii. 65-9.

11. And, it would seem, Greek drama too, especially Sophocles',
wherein a tyrant is punished like Leontes by the sudden loss of
his son (*Antigone*) and a child exposed like Perdita (*Oedipus*).

Theodore Spencer

SHAKESPEARE AND THE NATURE OF MAN: *THE TEMPEST*

The Tempest is a play with so many layers of meaning that no single interpretation can do it justice. Yet if, as our discussion of Shakespeare draws to a close, we come back to our starting point, and think of *The Tempest* not only in terms of the difference between appearance and reality, but also in terms of the three levels in Nature's hierarchy—the animal, the human and the intellectual—which were the bases of Shakespeare's view of man, we may have a central framework from which further and broader interpretations may radiate. For in this last of his complete plays, as in those he wrote at the beginning of his career, Shakespeare uses, however unconsciously, the common body of psychological assumption that was given him by his time.

And yet, like everything else in the last plays, that assumption is transfigured and transformed; it is presented in a different climate of reality from its presentation in the tragedies, and there is less need for either the background of kingship—the hierarchy of the state—or the background and hierarchy of the cosmos; the individual human life itself, in its finest manifestations, is enough. At the heart of *The Tempest* there is an incantation which accepts things as they are, a tone which has forgotten tragedy, an order melted at the edges into a new unity of acceptance and wonder.

The action of the play takes place on a deliberately unidenti-
fiable island, the kind of place where transfiguration is possible.

> The isle is full of noises,
> Sounds and sweet airs, that give delight, and hurt not.
> Sometimes a thousand twangling instruments
> Will hum about mine ears; and sometimes voices,
> Will make me sleep again.
>
> (iii, 2, 147)

In such a place, it is fitting that the animal level should be presented half-symbolically, through Caliban. We are no longer in
the climate of tragedy, where human beings themselves are seen
as animals, like the Spartan dog Iago or the wolfish daughters of
Lear. The "beast Caliban," as Prospero calls him, is a thing "not
honor'd with human shape (i, 2, 283)"; he is set apart—as it
were, abstracted, from human nature. Unlike human beings he is
unimprovable; he cannot be tamed by reason, he is

> A devil, a born devil, on whose nature
> Nurture can never stick; on whom my pains,
> Humanely taken, are all lost, quite lost.
>
> (iv, 1, 188)

And it is characteristic of him that he should take Stephano, the
lowest available specimen of human nature, for a god.

The human beings on the island are a various crew, perhaps
almost deliberately chosen to present as wide a range as possible.
Stephano and Trinculo are associated with Caliban; Alonzo and
Sebastian are selfish schemers, though royal; there is the good
Gonzalo, and there is Ferdinand, who, excellent young man as
he is, must still pass through some difficulties before he marries
Miranda, who is to him the "wonder" of the island, and like the
other heroines of the last plays, is a symbol of humanity at its
best. All these people, with the exception of Miranda, go through
some kind of punishment or purgation. The low characters are
merely punished, they get be-fouled and be-labored, as is appropriate—they are incapable of purgation. But the courtly figures,
Alonzo, Antonio and Sebastian, lose their human faculties for a
time, to emerge purified as rational beings. As we know, the

theme of purgation occurs earlier in Shakespeare, especially in *Lear*, but Lear loses his reason through a human agency, through filial ingratitude. Alonzo and Sebastian are purged through a superhuman agency, through magic. They enter the charmed circle made by Prospero (v, 1, 55) and once there, their reason, their specifically human faculty, is temporarily taken away, as —in such very different circumstances—Lear's reason was taken away. Their brains are useless, "boiled" within their skull; "ignorant fumes . . . mantle their clearer reason," until finally

> their understanding
> Begins to swell, and the approaching tide
> Will shortly fill the reasonable shores
> That now lie foul and muddy.
>
> (v, 1, 79)

As soon as he comes to himself, Alonzo resigns the dukedom, entreating Prospero to pardon his wrongs. Then Miranda and Ferdinand are discovered, and it is on a regenerated humanity that Miranda looks when she exclaims:

> How beauteous mankind is! O brave new world,
> That has such people in't!

Prospero—until he drowns his book—is clearly on a level above that of ordinary human nature. Yet though we may recognize him as a symbol of the third, the intellectual, level, Shakespeare's presentation of him is so shimmering with overtones and implications, that to think of him merely as a representative of pure intellect is an obvious falsification. Nevertheless we may say that his use of magic is a way of making his superiority dramatically effective, and the elves and demi-puppets that have been his agents were considered in certain contemporary circles of thought to be creatures above man in the hierarchy of Nature, between men and angels.[1] Prospero's command of them obviously involves a more than human power. Yet Prospero gives up this power, and returns to the human level again. I do not agree with those critics who say that Prospero, at the end of the play, "finds himself immeasurably nearer than before to the impassivity of the gods." "His theurgical operations," says Mr. Curry, "have accomplished their purpose. He wishes now to take the final step and to consummate the assimilation of his soul to the gods. And this step is to be accomplished through prayer." [2]

But this is clearly a misinterpretation of Shakespeare's meaning. Prospero adjures his magic not to become like the gods, but to return to humanity:

> I will discase me, and myself present,
> As I was sometime Milan.

He compares (v, 1, 170) Alonzo's "content" at his rediscovery of Ferdinand to his own content at being restored to his dukedom, and in fact much of the point of the play is lost if we do not see Prospero returning to worldly responsibility. He must be restored to his position in the state, as he must be restored to his position as a human being. In a sense his temporary control of the spirit world has also been a purgation; he has come to the conclusion that, though he can wreak supernatural havoc on his enemies,

> the rarer action is
> In virtue than in vengeance,

and, his domination of the spirits having been outside the limits of human nature, his wisdom makes him return to his rightful place as a governor of himself, and as a governor, through his dukedom, of other human beings as well. Prospero, on his enchanted island, has been like a god, controlling the world of nature and the elements:

> I have bedimm'd
> The noontide sun, call'd forth the mutinous winds,
> And 'twixt the green sea and the azur'd vault
> Set roaring war: to the dread-rattling thunder
> Have I given fire and rifted Jove's stout oak
> With his own bolt: the strong-bas'd promontory
> Have I made shake; and by the spurs pluck'd up
> The pine and cedar: graves at my command
> Have wak'd their sleepers, op'd, and let them forth
> By my so potent art.
>
> (v, 1, 41)

But he abjures his magic, and having "required Some heavenly music" so that the courtiers may be restored to their senses—in Shakespeare's theater the music would have come from above, from the musicians' gallery under the "heavens," which were painted with the stars—he breaks his staff and plans to drown his book of magic "deeper than did ever plummet sound." In the company of his fellow men, Prospero returns to Milan.

This is Shakespeare's conclusion, the conclusion of the dramatist, some of whose most normal and likeable characters—Berowne, Hotspur, Mercutio—had been, from the beginning, men with a strong sense of everyday reality. There is something of these men in Prospero, though Prospero is of course infinitely wiser than they are, since he has surveyed everything, and has risen to a control of the supernatural before returning to the normal human life which they exemplified so much more naïvely than he. But in one way they are closer to Prospero, to Shakespeare's final vision of man's nature, than the wracked and tortured heroes of the great tragedies. For those heroes were split by an internal conflict, a conflict that was expressed in terms of the conflict about man's nature that was so deeply embedded in the consciousness of the age: whereas in Prospero there is no conflict; in his control of his world, internal conflict has no place.

And yet the view of man's nature that is so profoundly and movingly illustrated in the great tragic heroes has, after all, a relation to the view of life that is illustrated by *The Tempest*. Evil does exist—in the plotting of the courtiers, in the untameable animal nature of Caliban. And it may not be too far-fetched to see, in the very different ways by which Hamlet, Othello, Lear and Macbeth become, at the end of the action, resigned to the situations in which they find themselves, some relation to the theme of acceptance and reconciliation which is dominant in *The Tempest*.

Theirs, however, was a tragic reconciliation, and though it ennobles our conception of their characters, it does not redeem the evil in man's nature which has brought about their downfall. In *The Tempest* the evil *is* redeemed. Here, as in all the last plays, there is a re-birth, a return to life, a heightened, almost symbolic, awareness of the beauty of normal humanity after it has been purged of evil—a blessed reality under the evil appearance. It is not merely a literal reality; the mountains and waters, the human beings, have changed since Shakespeare first looked at them in the early 1590's. The tragic period has intervened; the conflict has given the assurance a richer and deeper meaning. But the literal reality is there just the same, in a garland of flowers, in a harmony of music, as the basis for the acceptance and the vision.

NOTES

1. See W. C. Curry, *Shakespeare's Philosophical Patterns*, Baton Rouge, 1937, p. 194.
2. Op. cit., p. 196. In support of this view, Mr. Curry, like Mr. Middleton Murry, interprets Prospero's epilogue in religious terms:

> Now I want
> Spirits to enforce, art to enchant;
> And my ending is despair,
> Unless I be reliev'd by prayer,
> Which pierces so that it assaults
> Mercy itself and frees all faults.
> As you from crimes would pardon'd be,
> Let your indulgence set me free.

But the prayer is obviously merely a prayer to the audience. It is conventional for an actor to step half out of character in an epilogue, and that is what Prospero is doing here. His "prayer" consists of the last two lines, and has no metaphysical connotations.

Reuben Brower

THE TEMPEST

THE ISLAND is a world of fluid, merging states of being and forms of life. This lack of dependable boundaries between states is also expressed by the many instances of confusion between natural and divine. Miranda says that she might call Ferdinand

> A thing divine; for nothing natural
> I ever saw so noble.

Ferdinand cannot be sure whether she is a goddess or a maid, and Caliban takes Trinculo for a "brave god." There is a further comic variation on this theme in Trinculo's difficulty in deciding whether to classify Caliban as fish or man, monster or devil.

But "change" is most clearly and richly expressed through the sequence of tempest images (especially "cloud" and "sea-swallowed") and through the noise-music antithesis. All kinds of sounds, harmonious and ugly, like the manifestations of sea and storm, are expressive of magical transformation. "The fire and cracks / Of sulphurous roaring" (imagery in which both storm and sound analogies are blended) "infects" the courtiers' "reason," and *solemn music* induces the "clearing" of their understanding. The "music" and the "tempest" continuities, taken together as metaphors of "sea-change," are perhaps the most extensive of all the analogies in their organizing power. They recur often, they connect a wide diversity of experiences, and they express in symbolic form some of the main steps in the drama, in

From *The Fields of Light*, Oxford University Press, 1951, Galaxy Book, 1962, pp. 112-16, 120-21. Copyright 1951 by Oxford University Press, Inc. Reprinted by permission.

particular, the climactic moments of inner change: Ariel's revelation to the courtiers of their guilt, Alonso's first show of remorse, and the final purification.

The earth-air or Caliban-Ariel antithesis may seem to have very little to do with metamorphosis. But the relation of this theme to the key metaphor is clear and important. Air, Ariel, and his music are a blended symbol of change as against the unchanging Caliban, "the thing of darkness." He can be punished, but hardly humanized; he is, says Prospero,

> A devil, a born devil, on whose nature
> Nurture can never stick; on whom my pains,
> Humanely taken, are all lost, quite lost.

The other continuities parallel to earth-air, of slavery-freedom and conspiracy-sovereignty, are frequently expressive of major and minor changes of status among the inhabitants and temporary visitors on Prospero's island.

But the interconnection of Shakespeare's analogies through the key metaphor cannot be adequately described, since we are able to speak of only one point of relationship at a time. We can get a better sense of the felt union of various lines of analogy in *The Tempest* by looking at the two passages where Shakespeare expresses his key metaphor most completely, the "Full fathom five" song and Prospero's "cloud-capp'd towers" speech.

Rereading Ariel's song at this point we can see how many of the main continuities are alluded to and related in the description of "sea-change" and how the song anticipates the metaphorical design that emerges through the dialogue of the whole play. The total metaphorical pattern is to an amazing degree an efflorescence from this single crystal:

> Full fathom five thy father lies;
> Of his bones are coral made:
> Those are pearls that were his eyes:
> Nothing of him that doth fade,
> But doth suffer a sea-change
> Into something rich and strange.
> Sea-nymphs hourly ring his knell:
>   *Burthen:* 'Ding-dong!'
> Hark! now I hear them,—Ding-dong, bell.

In addition to the more obvious references to the deep sea and its powers and to the "strangeness" of this drowning, there are indirect anticipations of other analogies. "Fade" prefigures the "dissolving cloud" metaphor and the theme of tempest changes, outer and inner. "Rich," along with "coral" and "pearls," anticipates the opulent imagery of the dream-world passages and scenes, the "riches ready to drop" on Caliban and the expressions of wealth* and plenty in the masque. The song closes with the nymphs tolling the bell, the transformation and the "sea sorrow" are expressed through sea-music. Ferdinand's comment reminds us that the song has connections with two other lines of analogy:

> The ditty does remember my drown'd father.
> This is no mortal business, nor no sound
> That the earth owes:—I hear it now above me.

The song convinces Ferdinand that he is now King of Naples (the first of the interchanges of sovereignty), and it is a "ditty" belonging not to the "earth," but to the "air."

The sense of relationship between the many continuities is still more vividly felt in the lines of Prospero's most memorable speech:

> You do look, my son, in a mov'd sort,
> As if you were dismay'd: be cheerful, sir:
> Our revels now are ended. These our actors,
> As I foretold you, were all spirits and
> Are melted into air, into thin air:
> And, like the baseless fabric of this vision,
> The cloud-capp'd towers, the gorgeous palaces,
> The solemn temples, the great globe itself,
> Yea, all which it inherit, shall dissolve
> And, like this insubstantial pageant faded,
> Leave not a rack behind. We are such stuff
> As dreams are made on, and our little life
> Is rounded with a sleep.

In Prospero's words Shakespeare has gathered all the lights of

---

* "Rich" and "riches" occur no less than five times in the masque.

analogy into a single metaphor which sums up the metaphorical design and the essential meaning of *The Tempest*. The language evokes nearly every continuity that we have traced. "Melted into air," "dissolve," "cloud," and "rack" bring us immediately to Ariel and tempest changes, while "vision," "dream" and "sleep" recall other familiar continuities. "Revels," "gorgeous palaces," and "pageant" (for Elizabethans closely associated with royalty) are echoes of the kingly theme; and "solemn" is associated particularly with the soft music of change. The "stuff" of dreams is at once cloud-stuff (air) and cloth, both images being finely compressed in "baseless fabric." Taken with "faded" these images refer obliquely to the garments so miraculously "new-dyed . . . with salt water," one of the first signs of "sea-change" noted by Gonzalo. Within the metaphor of tempest-clearing and of cloud-like transformation, Shakespeare has included allusions to every important analogy of change in the play.

But it is through the twofold progress of the whole figure that the change metaphor is experienced and its most general meaning fully understood. We read first: that like the actors and scenery of the vision, earth's glories and man shall vanish into nothingness. Through a happy mistake we also read otherwise. By the time we have passed through "dissolve," "insubstantial," and "faded," and reached "leave not a rack behind," we are reading "cloud-capped towers" in reverse as a metaphor for tower-like clouds. "Towers," "palaces," "temples," "the great globe," "all which it inherit" are now taken for cloud forms. Through a sort of Proustian merging of icon and subject, we experience the blending of states of being, of substantial and unsubstantial, or real and unreal, which is the essence of *The Tempest* metamorphosis.

•　　•　　•

The larger meaning of Shakespeare's total design, which was anticipated in the cloud and dream metaphor of Prospero's visionary speech, is most clearly and fully expressed in these final transformations. In a world where everything may become something else, doubts naturally arise, and in the swift flow of change the confusion about what is and what is not becomes fairly acute.

When Prospero "discases" himself and appears as Duke of Milan, Gonzalo says with understandable caution:

> Whether this be,
> Or be not, I'll not swear.

And Prospero answers:

> You do yet taste
> Some subtilties o' the isle, that will not let you
> Believe things certain.

Whereas in the earlier acts the characters had often accepted the unreal as real (spirits, shipwrecks, drownings, visions), they now find it difficult to accept the real as truly real. The play concludes with their acceptance of the unexpected change to reality. But for the spectator there remains the heightened sense of the "thin partitions" that "do divide" these states. The world that common sense regards as real, of order in nature and society and of sanity in the individual, is a shimmering transformation of disorder. "We shall all be changed, in a moment, in the twinkling of an eye." (This or something like it is as near as we can come to describing the total attitude conveyed by *The Tempest*.)

Edward Hubler

THE ECONOMY OF THE CLOSED HEART

THERE IS no idea to which Shakespeare returns more often than
the doctrine taught by the parable of the talents. It is referred to
and expounded at length in the dialogue of the plays. It is often
a major dramatic theme. In the sonnets it is no less prominent
than in the plays. In both it is glanced at on innumerable occasions, when, most often, it is taken as correlative to an idea of
more immediate importance. None of Shakespeare's ideas is more
fixed or serves more often as a measure of character. The idea is,
of course, the concept of man's stewardship referred to in the
discussion of plenitude. Shakespeare's use of it in connection with
propagation will indicate to modern readers the pervasiveness of
his belief in it. In the very first sonnet the young man was told
that he consumed himself in not giving himself, and in the fourth
he was warned that "Nature's bequest gives nothing, but doth
lend." The point invariably made is that we hold our possessions
in trust, that we are the stewards and not the owners of our
excellence. It is our function to employ our excellence to the best
of our ability. Conversely, the man who simply preserves what
he is entrusted with is regarded as the "wicked and slothful
servant" of the parable, who said "I was afraid, and went, and
hid thy talent in the earth: lo, there thou hast that is thine."
Shakespeare states his view of the matter at the opening of
Measure for Measure:

From *The Sense of Shakespeare's Sonnets,* 1952, pp. 95-6, 100-
109. Copyright 1952 by Princeton University Press. Reprinted by permission of the publisher.

> Thyself and thy belongings
> Are not thine own so proper, as to waste
> Thyself upon thy virtues, they on thee.
> Heaven doth with us as we with torches do,
> Not light them for themselves; for if our virtues
> Did not go forth of us, 'twere all alike
> As if we had them not. Spirits are not finely touch'd
> But to fine issues, nor Nature never lends
> The smallest scruple of her excellence,
> But, like a thrifty goddess, she determines
> Herself the glory of a creditor,
> Both thanks and use.
>
> (I. i. 30-41)

In this instance the idea is allied to another of his most pervasive convictions—the belief that a virtue cannot finally be said to exist until it has expressed itself in action. Of that, more later. These ideas are among the *données* of Shakespeare's thought. When they are not made explicit, their values are always assumed . . .

In our time there was once a youth of one-and-twenty whose approach to emotion was simpler than Shakespeare's. He listened to his elders, and in due time he found that his experience squared with what he had been told. One day he had heard a wise man say that

> "The heart out of the bosom
> Was never given in vain;
> 'Tis paid with sighs a plenty
> And sold for endless rue."
> And I am two-and-twenty,
> And oh, 'tis true, 'tis true.[1]

In this poem the hurt of the open heart is observed in isolation and with a sentimentality nicely appropriate to twenty-two. Or perhaps the pain had not been isolated; it may be that it had subsumed all the other aspects of the experience. In either case it is what a well-lettered young man of melancholy spirit is supposed to feel, and it is what this particular young man had been taught to feel. It will serve as a contrast to Shakespeare's way of apprehending the same thing. In the Housman poem the view of the situation is simplicity itself: the heart gives itself in vain. It does not heed the wise men, and it learns that they were right. If we were to go beyond the poem we could only suppose that the young man should have listened to his elders in the first place. In Shakespeare's view the open heart must give itself away in order to maintain its existence. It is confronted with a perpetual dilemma: it can know of its being only through self-loss. The alternative is to conserve itself until it has withered away. Both courses of action are illustrated in the plays; both are observed in the sonnets with an acuteness Shakespeare was never to exceed.

Shakespeare noticed the obverse sides of things. Although the sonnets proclaim his affection for the young man and his indulgence of him, they also disclose the attitudes which Shakespeare takes to both the affection and the indulgence. He forgives a trespass, and then, in the thirty-fifth sonnet, he apologizes for the presumption of forgiveness, for, in his words, "excusing thy sins more than thy sins are." We should notice that the forgiveness also involves a certain debasement on the poet's part: "Myself corrupting, salving thy amiss." Nor does he view simply his desire to change himself. In the one hundred and eleventh sonnet he regrets the fate which has made him a man of the theatre, which

> . . . did not better for my life provide
> Than public means which public manners breeds.

And although he assures the friend that he will do anything to wipe away this stain, he realizes that the cleansing in itself is a kind of stain. There would be a need for a "double penance"—to remove the stain and "to correct correction." Protesting on another occasion (Sonnet 112) that he does not care what the opinion of critic or flatterer may be, provided he has the good opinion of his friend, he comments, "In so profound abysm I throw all care." It is the recognition of the obverse of one of his most firmly held tenets. The recognition does not destroy the belief; there is, as with Hamlet, the coexistent questioning of the value of the thing in which he believes. When the sonnets are aware that the friend's faults constitute a threat to the friendship, there is the recurrent accompaniment of ironic self-consciousness, arising, it appears, from a knowledge of the waywardness with which affection, in order to maintain its being in an imperfect world, bestows itself with imperfect cause. It must, at times, debase its currency in order to exist. The alternative to this dilemma is the economy of the closed heart.

The closed heart may be poor, but it is at ease. Those men are most content who, though they inspire affection in others, have no need of it themselves. They are the men "in hue, all hues in their controlling." They have the power to hurt, but they are not hurt. Their happiness is the ignorance of their incompleteness.

> They that have power to hurt and will do none,
> That do not do the thing they most do show,
> Who, moving others, are themselves as stone,
> Unmoved, cold, and to temptation slow;
> They rightly do inherit heaven's graces
> And husband nature's riches from expense;
> They are the lords and owners of their faces,
> Others but stewards of their excellence.
> The summer's flower is to the summer sweet,
> Though to itself it only live and die,
> But if that flower with base infection meet,
> The basest weed outbraves his dignity;
> For sweetest things turn sourest by their deeds;
> Lilies that fester smell far worse than weeds.
>
> (Sonnet 94)

Everything about the poem invites comment, from the private force of the opening phrases to the last line, which, one editor assures us, "is not true." The recorded conjectures about it are rich in everything that conjecture can lead to, and in recent years it has been the object of more critical analyses than any other sonnet. If we approach it in the light of Shakespeare's other works, we might find it less difficult than it appears.

A survey of Shakespeare's works will show that this sonnet employs his most familiar imagery and that the thought of the sonnet, bit by bit, is to be found everywhere. Primarily it is the articulation of the parts which puzzles. On first reading the sonnet, we shall, of course, notice the irony of the first eight lines; and everything that we find in the other works will confirm it. It is preposterous on the face of things to proclaim as the inheritors of heaven's graces those who are "as stone." It can be other than ironical only to the cynic, for even the hardhearted man thinks of himself as generous and cherishes an abstract admiration for warmth. In addition, it will be noticed that what Shakespeare says here contradicts everything that he has said elsewhere on the subject. The irony of the octave is Swiftian in both method and force. In specious terms the poet states as true that which he is well known to consider false: those men whose appearance does not square with reality, whose deeds do not fulfill their promise, who move others while remaining cold, are proclaimed the heirs to heaven's graces. They are the owners of themselves, whereas throughout Shakespeare's works self-possession in the sense of living without regard for others is intolerable.

After the stinging "Others but stewards of their excellence," there is a full stop, and the poet turns to one of his most familiar images, the flower which is still beautiful although it lives to itself alone. The analogy is obvious. In the opening sequence the flower had been the emblem of the young man "contracted to his own bright eyes." Throughout the sonnets the poet praises the flower for its beauty, which he insists is only one of its attributes, and, he also insists from time to time, not its supreme one. The beauty, he repeats, is made fairer by its odor, which in turn becomes the symbol of that which is usefully good, or of the essential nature of the flower, or of both. In some sonnets the odor, or essence, may be distilled into perfume, in which case its odor will live "pent in walls of glass" after the flower has died. In other instances the distillation of essence is a symbol of procreation. In still others the odor of the flower symbolizes moral good:

> By why thy odour matcheth not thy show,
> The soil is this, that thou dost common grow.
>
> (Sonnet 69)

And,

> O, how much more doth beauty beauteous seem
> By that sweet ornament which truth doth give!
> The rose looks fair, but fairer we it deem
> For that sweet odour which doth in it live . . . .
>
> (Sonnet 54)

In the sonnet under discussion, the flower living to itself, and having therefore failed to fulfill its function, is incomplete, though it still has physical beauty; but if it should meet with infection (that is, if the expression of its function should be perverted), its odor (that is, its essence, its soul, its human utility as expressed in the deeds of the young man and the perfume of the flower) becomes worse than that of weeds, worse, that is, than that from which nothing was expected.

"They that have power to hurt" is both a great poem and an imperfect one. There is neither weakness nor relaxation. It should be noticed that the failure is not, as is often the case, one of fitting the matter to the form. There is neither tacking on nor repetition of matter to fill out the prescribed length. It is rather that the unity is marred by a change in tone, though not in intensity, at the close of the octave, and that the cohesion of parts depends upon a context of ideas which are not sufficiently explicit in the poem, though they ought to be familiar to all readers of Shakespeare.

I do not want to appear to consider the poem clearer than it is. The first line is tauntingly obscure, and an understanding of the poem cannot proceed without an interpretation of it. However, it seems reasonable to resolve the enigma of "power to hurt" by reference to what follows and to other works of Shakespeare. This I have tried to do. The meaning of "do none" is apparent if we take it to be clarified by expansion in line two. It was sometimes Shakespeare's hasty way to say a thing obscurely and then to clarify it by repetition, as in *King Lear*:

> *Regan:*   I have hope
>   You less know how to value her desert
>   Than she to scant her duty.
> *Lear:*   Say, how is that?
> *Regan:* I cannot think my sister in the least would fail her
>   obligation.
>
>   (II.4.140-44.)

We may take it that the meaning of "do none" is restated in the line that follows: "That do not do the thing they most do show." This is quite clear, and its meaning is made specific in the next line: "Who, moving others, are themselves as stone." The "power to hurt" is, then, the power to move others by imposing on their unreciprocated loyalty, and "do none" is the condition of not doing what the loyal friend, because of his loyalty, had taken for granted. When Emilia discovers the murder of Desdemona and is threatened by Othello, she replies,

> Thou hast not half the power to do me harm
> As I have to be hurt.
>
> (v.2.162.)

Her power to be hurt resides, of course, in her loyalty to Desdemona. As for the "base infection," there is no knowing what it specifically was, or what it threatened to be, for it is referred to conditionally in the poem and may have been apprehended rather than actual. But it is clear from the importance attached to it that it refers to some offence of the spirit, a denial of something Shakespeare held essential to decent humanity. "Perhaps," Rebecca West speculates,[2] "the sin against the Holy Ghost is to deal with people as though they were things." In any case it is clear from many of the sonnets that the quality in the young man which most disturbed Shakespeare was the prudence of the closed heart.

What of the persons in the plays who were the lords and owners of their faces? Rosencranz and Guildenstern of course; they were the essence of prudent self-interest. Macbeth tried to be, and failed; he was too full of the milk of human kindness. That he failed was his misfortune on the prudential level; on the tragic level it is his glory. Lear and Gloucester were, at the beginning of the play; but their story is their growth in wisdom and warmth. We will look in vain for the type among the heroes, for they are heroes in proportion to their divergence from the type. What of the villains? Well, Edmund is almost a clear case, but he escapes the category by the pleasure he took in being loved. The only major character is Iago, and he, toward the end of the play, becomes the emblem of evil. The purest instance is Northumberland, Hotspur's father, who is motivated by "advised respects" throughout *Richard II* and remains unchanged throughout the two parts of *Henry IV*. He sends his son to death in a vain attempt to secure his own position and later, when still another rebellion is failing, he writes to his fellow rebels letters of "cold intent" announcing his retirement to Scotland. It is his whole character. As Shakespeare conceived the story of *Richard II*, it required an intermediary, a representative of Bolingbroke on whom the onus of usurpation would fall, allowing Bolingbroke a measure of integrity. And for this purpose, the creation of a despicable character, he found that the embodiment of the closed heart was what was needed. Later, when even the lesser characters are not so single, the villains are less purely villainous than Northumberland; but to the end a large measure of his soul is the hallmark of their villainy. Shakespeare had feared from the beginning of the sonnets that the young man was cold and self-contained, but it was not until the story was well advanced that the characteristic was clearly recognized, named, and condemned.

All this is far from a simple matter. It involves elements to which few readers will assign precisely the same values. It is further complicated by the young man's being something of a patron of literature in an age of fulsome deference to patrons. Doubtless this contributed to the poet's attitude, but criticism has already made too much of that. A mercenary motive will always be understood, and criticism may seize upon it without the appearance of naïveté. Though this is of great use in simplifying the critic's task, the critic who finds that the author of *King Lear* was primarily an opportunist will also find that his criticism discloses little but himself.

The finest poetry in the sonnets has for its subject the complicated friendship for the young man. It seems to me that this friendship had historical reality, and also that the historicity is not a primary matter. Whether it derives from real or imagined events, the poet's subject matter is his thoughts, emotions, and convictions; and they find expression in poetry through the poet's use of his tradition. Among the relevant aspects of the poet's personality at work here is Shakespeare's gregariousness. It seems that it was with him as with Socrates, who remarked in *Lysis* that while there were many things for which he had no violent desire, he had a passion for friends. This attitude is explicit in the sonnets and implicit in all of Shakespeare's works, as it is in Montaigne's. It would seem to have been in Shakespeare before he read Montaigne, but the priority doesn't matter. A poet adopts an idea because it awakens something in him, because he finds it true, or serviceably so in a germinal way.

Are there not times when even the mature poet is looking for his own thoughts and feelings in those of his fellow writers? And since the thoughts and feelings of an important writer are normally in a state of becoming—sometimes through conscious seeking, sometimes through assimilation, as a seed absorbs its nurture from the earth—we cannot often know what is his and what belongs to his tradition, or that, indeed, they are not the same thing. Granville-Barker has remarked that Shakespeare's writing doubtless taught him as much about people as living among them; that is, his writing required a doubling back on his own experience in order to understand it more fully. As a consequence the literary recreation of an experience may endow the poem with faculties which obscure the germinal experience even to the writer's fellow participants in it.

Like the other ideas common to the sonnets, Shakespeare's ideas of friendship recur throughout his works with a persistence which, for some, will indicate his belief and sketch an aspect of his character. Such readers will say, "Here Shakespeare speaks for himself." And even though they are right, they cannot always hope to convince others of a different persuasion of a matter so individually perceived. They would do better to observe that in by far the greatest number of recurrences the dramatist is setting forth an idea intended, as the dramatic context discloses, to arouse the admiration and sympathy of the audience, and that when the same idea is stated for the same purpose in varying contexts, it becomes apparent that the dramatist holds the idea to be one to which normal humanity will respond with warmth. The sensible man will conclude that it is only a small step from this to the belief that the dramatist responded to the idea in the same way, and that, in fact, he discloses his sympathies in the notions he takes for granted. But we shall do well to remember that the disclosure of such sympathies and thoughts sketches the dramatist's and poet's spiritual biography, or if we prefer a lesser phrase, his poetic personality. The reader cannot proceed from this to the facts of the poet's daily life; not, that is, without some external documentation. Yet what we can learn of Shakespeare from his works, stripped of particulars as it is, is not altogether a dusty answer. Of our friends and neighbors we want to know the facts, for association on the practical level of daily living requires judgments which had better have a factual basis. But of an acquaintance of long ago it is better to know that he had a capacity for loyalty and devotion, and a passion strong enough at times to deny the loyalty, than to know where and when he first encountered his mistress or what her name was. We may know Shakespeare essentially without a bill of particulars, and we may be excused for supposing that, granted the necessity of partial knowledge, we have the best.

It may be that the idea of friendship in the sonnets is an idealization, a purified recreation of the poet's experience, and that it has only a partial or intermittent coincidence with his daily life. Or it may be that Shakespeare came at last to find the idea embodied in a living presence, as Hamlet, knowing an ideal of friendship, found it embodied in Horatio, and henceforth bore them both in his heart's core. We cannot know. We know only that in the sonnets we have a sketch of a troubled friendship in which the poet believes at times that the friend conforms to the ideal, wants at other times to believe it, and fears sometimes that belief is vain.

NOTES

1. From *A Shropshire Lad* by A. E. Housman. Copyright, 1924, by Henry Holt & Company. By permission of the publishers.
2. Quoted by Donald Stauffer in *The New York Times Book Review,* December 14, 1947.